Discrimination and Employment Law

I0885327

Presenting the issues of discrimination in employment in a multifaceted manner, this book examines the standards on anti-discrimination law for employment at international and EU levels and those deriving from national jurisdictions. Bringing together top scholars in the field of anti-discrimination employment law, this book explains the conceptual and theoretical foundations of the principle of non-discrimination in employment and assesses the most significant changes to law and ongoing challenges in the Netherlands, Poland, Germany, the UK, Australia, New Zealand, Canada, India, Switzerland and Israel. Identifying emerging trends in anti-discrimination employment law, this book offers a comparative, problem-solving approach and an in-depth analysis of new developments in both anti-discrimination statutory law and case law. Addressing employment law with a focus on anti-discrimination law and human rights law, this book will be essential reading for students, academics and practitioners working in the fields of labour and employment law, anti-discrimination law and human rights law and offers an international comparative overview of the most up-to-date issues relating to discrimination.

Jo Carby-Hall is Professor of Law and Director of International Legal Research in the Centre for Legislative Studies at the University of Hull, UK.

Zbigniew Góral is Emeritus Professor of Law at the University of Lodz, Poland.

Aneta Tyc is Assistant Professor at the Department of European, International and Collective Labour Law at the Faculty of Law and Administration of the University of Lodz, Poland.

Discrimination and Employment Law

International Legal Perspectives

Edited by Jo Carby-Hall, Zbigniew Góral and Aneta Tyc

Routledge
Taylor & Francis Group
LONDON AND NEW YORK

First published 2023
by Routledge
4 Park Square, Milton Park, Abingdon, Oxon OX14 4RN

and by Routledge
605 Third Avenue, New York, NY 10158

Routledge is an imprint of the Taylor & Francis Group, an informa business

© 2023 selection and editorial matter, Jo Carby-Hall, Zbigniew Góral and Aneta Tyc; individual chapters, the contributors

The right of Jo Carby-Hall, Zbigniew Góral and Aneta Tyc to be identified as the authors of the editorial material, and of the authors for their individual chapters, has been asserted in accordance with sections 77 and 78 of the Copyright, Designs and Patents Act 1988.

All rights reserved. No part of this book may be reprinted or reproduced or utilised in any form or by any electronic, mechanical, or other means, now known or hereafter invented, including photocopying and recording, or in any information storage or retrieval system, without permission in writing from the publishers.

Trademark notice: Product or corporate names may be trademarks or registered trademarks, and are used only for identification and explanation without intent to infringe.

British Library Cataloguing-in-Publication Data
A catalogue record for this book is available from the British Library

Library of Congress Cataloging-in-Publication Data
A catalog record for this book has been requested

ISBN: 978-1-032-30846-3 (hbk)
ISBN: 978-1-032-30847-0 (pbk)
ISBN: 978-1-003-30696-2 (ebk)

DOI: 10.4324/9781003306962

Typeset in Times New Roman
by Apex CoVantage, LLC

Contents

Foreword

Discrimination is deviation from the principle of equality. It generally takes two forms, one of which is more common. In its widely practised and largely malign form, it involves treating equals unequally. When, for example, a job or an opportunity becomes available, those in charge are expected to lay down qualifications they can show to be objectively necessary for doing the job effectively. When some of those with the required qualifications are not considered while others similarly placed are, they are subjected to unequal treatment and are discriminated against. Discrimination also occurs when the qualification required has no objective basis and is capricious, irrelevant or largely designed to favour a particular individual or class of individuals. Those who are otherwise qualified for the job are rejected right at the beginning and are not even eligible to apply.

The second kind of discrimination has a very different motivation. It aims to assist long-oppressed groups by giving them some form of preferential treatment so that they can break out of the self-perpetuating cycle of disadvantage and compete with others on an equal basis over a period of time. The treatment may take the form of providing additional resources, giving additional weight to their distinguishing features or instituting a quota. This is generally called positive, preferential or compensatory discrimination, depending on what aspect of it is intended to be emphasised. Since the purposes and expected outcomes of this kind of discrimination are very different from those of the first kind, it might be better not to call it discrimination. However, since the term is too widely used to be dropped, and since it involves deviating from formal equality that is also the case with discrimination, we might retain it while continuing to emphasise its very different character.

Discrimination is unacceptable for several reasons, of which two are most important. First, it implies rejection, devaluation of one's membership of society, the belief that one has less worth and can be given less importance. Second, discrimination leads to disadvantage, denial of certain facilities and opportunities necessary for one's growth. One might be denied challenging jobs or admission in distinguished educational institutions, paid less than others and so on. The resulting disadvantages are carried over generations and get solidified into absence of drive and ambition, will to succeed, tenacity of purpose and a poor start in life. The individuals involved are unable to compete as equals with others and are even blamed for it themselves. The past discrimination which was partly the cause of their disadvantage is ignored and attention is focused almost entirely on their current inadequacies. Discrimination mutates into disadvantage and becomes invisible. Their disadvantages can be tackled by a sensitively defined and judiciously implemented policy of positive discrimination, but that is attacked as giving them an unfair advantage. It is therefore crucial that we should concentrate not only on discrimination but also on disadvantage, and integrate our struggle against malign discrimination with that for some form of positive discrimination.

In tackling discrimination the state has an important, though limited, role to play. Its intervention provides an unequivocal declaration of public policy, supports those who do not want to discriminate, gives protection to minority groups, discourages behavioural expressions of hatred and so on. The state also, however, has its limits. Laws through which it generally acts are too specific and precise to capture the nuances of discrimination. Many acts of discrimination are done by individuals unwittingly, casually, without much forethought or in the normal course of life. They might refuse to sit next to a member of the target group on a bus or a train, or to sell their property to them or make wounding passing remarks. So much of racism or sexism that hurts blacks or women results from these kinds of informal encounters. Serious literature and newspapers can also contribute to this and help create a discriminatory culture about which the state is unable to do much. A subtle and concerted effort to develop a culture based on mutual respect and civility in society at large is of vital importance.

Discrimination is rarely single and unidimensional. Its different forms – such as those based on race, sex, religion, ethnicity, disability and sexual orientation – intersect, sometimes reinforcing and on other occasions weakening each other. How to tackle them is a difficult question to decide. Since they are all often related, they might be best tackled by a single body. In practice this has not worked as well as one hopes. Forms of discrimination with wider constituencies, greater resources and greater visibility generally attract more attention and marginalise others. As the British experience shows, the best thing would be for a single body to be in charge of all forms of discrimination with its several specialised sections focusing on particular forms of discrimination.

Discrimination is a large subject, and I have touched upon only some aspects of it. All societies have to decide what constitutes discrimination, how it is related to disadvantage, who should bear the burden of proof, what protected characteristics to introduce and how to define and delimit them, when discrimination is inherent in certain kinds of relationship and claims a legitimate place in them and so on. Different societies answer these and related questions differently. None is absolutely right and none wholly misguided. A dialogue between them is invaluable as it alerts each to its own, and others', strengths and limitations. This volume is an indispensable aid to this process of mutual learning. Different chapters, all learned and reliable, concentrate on different countries and deal with their particular ways of defining, grounding and tackling different forms of discrimination. The editors' introduction contextualises the chapters well and guides the reader through their complex arguments. I found the volume most helpful and hope that other readers will do so too.

Bhikhu Parekh
University of Hull and House of Lords

Contributors

Gordon Anderson is Professor of Law at Victoria University of Wellington, New Zealand.

Susanne Burri was Associate Professor and is since she retired in 2020 a guest researcher at Utrecht University School of Law in the Netherlands.

Raphael Cohen-Almagor, DPhil, St. Catherine's College, University of Oxford, is Professor of Politics and Founding Director of the Middle East Study Centre, University of Hull.

Rachel Cox is a member of the Québec Bar and Full Professor at the Faculty of Law and Political Science at the Université du Québec à Montréal in Québec, Canada.

Dawn Duncan is Lecturer in Law, University of Otago, Dunedin, New Zealand.

Szilvia Halmos (PhD) is a Labour Court Judge at the Department of Labour Law of the Budapest-Metropolitan General Court, Hungary; European Law Advisor Judge; Visiting Lecturer at the Department of Labour Law, Faculty of Law, Pázmány Péter Catholic University, Budapest, Hungary.

Therese MacDermott is a professor at Macquarie Law School, Macquarie University, Australia.

Uki Maroshek-Klarman is Executive Director of the Adam Institute for Democracy and Peace and has a doctorate in political philosophy from Tel Aviv University.

Kurt Pärli is Full Professor for Social Private Law at the Faculty of Law at the University Basel, Switzerland.

Nimushakavi Vasanthi is Professor of Law at Nalsar University of Law, Telangana, India.

Manfred Weiss is Emeritus Professor of Law at the Goethe University Frankfurt/Germany.

Abbreviations

AC	Appeal Cases Law Reports
ADA	Age Discrimination Act
ADF	Anti-discrimination Facility
AllER	All England Law Reports
APRT	Act on Promotion of Remuneration Transparency between Men and Women
APTWFTC	Act on Part-Time and Fixed-Term Contracts
APUD	Act on Protection against Unfair Discrimination
Art.	Article
AWC	Act on Works Constitution
BHRC	Bar Human Rights Committee
CA	Court of Appeal
CC	Civil Code
CEDAW	Convention on the Elimination of All Forms of Discrimination Against Women
CERD	International Convention on the Elimination of All Forms of Racial Discrimination
CJEU	Court of Justice of the European Union
CLPR	Centre for Law and Policy Research
CRC	Convention on the Rights of the Child
CRPD	Convention on the Rights of Persons with Disabilities
CRvdM	College voor de Rechten van de Mens
DDA	Disability Discrimination Act
EAT	Employment Appeal Tribunal
ECHR	European Convention on Human Rights
EHRR	European Human Rights Reports
EOC	Equal Opportunity Commission
ET	Employment Tribunal
ETA m/w	Equal Treatment Act of men and women
ETC	Equal Treatment Commission
EU	European Union
EWCA	England and Wales Court of Appeal

FADO	Federal Anti-discrimination Office
FCC	Federal Constitutional Court
FLC	Federal Labour Court
GAET	General Act on Equal Treatment
GETA	General Equal Treatment Act
HL	House of Lords
ICCPR	International Covenant on Civil and Political Rights
ICESCR	International Covenant on Economic, Social and Cultural Rights
ICR	Industrial Cases Reports
IDEA	Indian Disability Evaluation and Assessment
IHR	Institute of Human Rights
ILO	International Labour Organization
IRLR	Industrial Relations Law Reports
J	Judge
JP	Justice of the Peace
LC	Labour Courts
LCA	Labour Court of Appeals
LGB	Lesbian, gay and bisexual
LJ	Lord Justice (Judge in the Court of Appeal)
MR	Master of the Rolls (Judge who in England and Wales presides over the Court of Appeal [Civil Division] and formerly was in charge of the Public Record Office)
NGO	Non-governmental organisation
OSNP	Orzecznictwo Sądu Najwyższego Izba Pracy, Ubezpieczeń Społecznych i Spraw Publicznych (Case law of the Supreme Court, Chamber of Labour, Social Security and Public Affairs)
P	President (of the Employment Tribunals)
PVV	Partij voor de Vrijheid
PwD Act 1995	Persons with Disabilities (Equal Opportunities, Protection of Rights and Full Participation) Act 1995
QB	Queen's Bench (Law Reports)
QC	Queen's Counsel
RPwD Act 2016	Rights of Persons with Disabilities Act 2016
SC	Supreme Court
SCC	Supreme Court Cases
SCP	Sociaal Cultureel Planbureau
S.I.	Statutory instrument
SUR Int'l J. on Hum Rts	Sur International Journal on Human Rights
TFEU	Treaty on the Functioning of the European Union
UK	United Kingdom
UN	United Nations

UNCRPD	United Nations Convention on Rights of Persons with Disabilities
U. Pa. J. Int'l L.	University of Pennsylvania Journal of International Law
USA	United States of America

1 International Legal Perspectives on Discrimination in Employment Law

An Overview

Jo Carby-Hall, Zbigniew Góral and Aneta Tyc

The principle of non-discrimination is one of the most current topics enjoying a worldwide impact. The aim of the book is to present the issues of employment discrimination law in a multifaceted manner by taking into account the standards at both international and EU levels, as well as those deriving from national jurisdictions. The selection of chapters includes the most recent and significant developments which have taken place in this field. Scholars representing different traditions of research and based in different countries contributed with their original chapters which have been divided in this monograph into three parts.

The volume opens with Part I, titled "Employment Discrimination Law in the European Union and its Member States". Chapter 2 is written by Szilvia Halmos, from Pázmány Péter Catholic University and Budapest-Metropolitan General Court. She presents cutting-edge research on the role of comparison in terms of equality in employment under EU law. She demonstrates that the classical, comparison-based approach of investigation on discrimination may prove to be too rigid to establish discrimination in more complex cases, where a comparator does not exist or is difficult to find. Drawing on the recent developments of equality theories – including those based on the idea that equality is an important element of human dignity – and analysing the CJEU case law, the author highlights the usefulness of the approach according to which scrutiny of discrimination should apply a wider range of methodologies and should go beyond the strict, comparator-based methodology. Thus, the existence of discrimination could be established where the comparator cannot be identified, just as in cases of pregnancy-based discrimination or those related to maternity or the fact of undergoing in vitro fertilisation treatment.

Chapter 3 is written by Susanne Burri, senior expert of the European Commission's European network of legal experts in gender equality and non-discrimination and guest researcher at Utrecht School of Law. Her chapter provides an insightful account of the Dutch equal treatment law applicable to employment. The principal object of analysis by which the author chooses to illustrate her argument that Dutch equal treatment law is a broad and sophisticated field of law, is a set of legal acts: namely, the General Equal Treatment Act, the Disability Discrimination Act, the Age Discrimination Act and the Equal Treatment Act of men and women, in addition to specific acts on flexible work and the Civil Code. The author assesses

DOI: 10.4324/9781003306962-1

positively the proposal to integrate these acts into one act. Moreover, in her chapter she highlights the significant role of the Dutch Equality Body, the IHR. The important function of this quasi-judicial and independent body is manifested in, *inter alia*, enforcing equal treatment legislation, combating specific forms of discrimination, combating stereotyping in employment and algorithmic discrimination in recruitment and selection.

Chapter 4, written by Manfred Weiss of the Goethe University of Frankfurt in Germany, combines academic rigour with a systematic and orderly approach thus allowing for a thorough discussion of the German law on discrimination in employment. The author acquaints the reader with German sources, in particular the Constitution; the GAET, which implements all the European directives on discrimination into German law; the APRT; and some interesting case law. He engages with studying in particular problematic cases related to exceptions to the prohibition of discrimination in employment (positive action and occupational requirements) and two discriminatory criteria, age and religion. As the contribution attests, the German legal system lacks the possibility for trade unions and anti-discrimination associations to file a lawsuit on behalf of individuals without involving them. Currently, employees refrain from bringing cases to court for fear of retaliatory measures taken by their employer. As a consequence, in most cases, the plaintiffs are either candidates seeking employment or former employees who bring court actions following the termination of their employment.

Aneta Tyc of the University of Lodz in Poland writes the concluding chapter in Part I. In Chapter 5 she points to the importance of the amendment of 16 May 2019 to the Labour Code. She highlights the fact that the intention of the legislature is to replace a semi-open catalogue of discriminatory criteria with an open one, namely, the one embracing both personal characteristics of the employee not related to the work performed and of social importance, as well as characteristics related to the work performed (which would go beyond the two already regulated in the Labour Code, i.e. employment for a definite or an indefinite term or on a full-time or part-time basis). Moreover, in her chapter the author mobilises a configuration of legal cases in order to reveal which criteria (out of the "other" discriminatory criteria than those regulated in the Labour Code) have been recognised by the Polish courts as discriminatory and which have not been so recognised. That research shows on the one hand that trainee attorney-at-law status, citizenship, appearance, worldview, motherhood, parenthood and HIV statuses have been included in the list of discriminatory criteria, even if they are not *expressis verbis* named in the Labour Code. On the other hand, the following criteria have not been recognised by the courts as discriminatory: the creation of one's image in a talk show TV programme; the way in which one becomes an employee and the amount of remuneration at the previous employer; the exercise by the employee of their right to appeal to the labour court against the termination of the employment contract; granting the right to additional severance pay, the acquisition of which depends on the conclusion of an agreement between the parties terminating the employment relationship; significant professional experience and achievements of the employee compared to other employees; and the employee's lack of acceptance for assigning their achievements towards third parties.

Part II, titled "Facets of Employment Discrimination in Common Law Jurisdictions", consists of three chapters. Chapter 6 is written by Jo Carby-Hall of the University of Hull. He explains that philosophical beliefs are a protected characteristic under the Equality Act 2010. However, given the fact that a legal definition of philosophical beliefs does not appear in the legislation, it falls on the case law to decide what exactly constitutes a philosophical belief and thus what qualifies as a protected characteristic. The words of Lord Nicholls' judgment heard by the Supreme Court in the *Williamson* case and of Burton J. in the Employment Appeal Tribunal case of *Nicholson* point to the five criteria which must be met for this purpose. Carby-Hall has provided an overview of case law answering the question of what does and does not qualify as a philosophical belief. The first group which qualifies as a philosophical belief embraces a belief in Scottish independence; a view that the United Kingdom should not be ruled by a hereditary monarch and that it should be a democratic and secular republic; a belief in humanism; a belief in democratic socialism; a view that the purpose of public service broadcasting is to foster a reasoning citizenry and to support the development of an inclusive, participatory and enlightened democracy; a belief in human-made climate change and the alleged resulting moral imperatives; a belief in the sanctity of life, namely, against fox hunting and hare culling; a belief that the public service is improperly wasteful of money; a Christian belief that a person should not tell lies under any circumstances and thus not deceive potential customers to obtain sales; a belief in commitment to public services for the common good; a distinction to be drawn between treatment on the grounds of a person's beliefs and on the grounds of the manifestation of those beliefs; and beliefs in spiritualism and the existence of psychic and paranormal phenomena. Ethical veganism belongs to this group as well. This latter court case, however, has been discussed in greater detail compared to the other cases by bringing readers closer to its background, its facts and the legal conditions to be met for ethical veganism to qualify as a protected characteristic.

There is, however, a rich landscape of case law according to which the concept of philosophical belief had been rejected. The following cases, *inter alia*, are cited and have been discussed by the author: the existence of only two sexes, male and female, and an opinion that therefore sex is biological and immutable; objection to, and lack of belief in, transgenderism, in other words refusal to identify patients by their chosen sex when carrying out medical assessments; wearing a silver cross round a claimant's neck against British Airways uniform rules; homosexuality being contrary to God's law and nature and that no Jewish people were killed by the use of poison gas in concentration camps during the Second World War; refusal to officiate in cases in which children were placed for adoption, care or fostering with same-sex partners; refusal to sign a copyright agreement because of the alleged interference with the claimant's own work as a writer and filmmaker; the importance of wearing a poppy from All Souls' Day on 2nd November to Remembrance Sunday, thus paying respects to those who have given their lives for us; vegetarianism not being a philosophical belief and thus a protected characteristic; a belief that challenges the tendency to favour what is palatable in social policy discussion over the truth (namely political correctness); and a belief on a government-led conspiracy theory surrounding the "New World Order" relating to the terrorist attacks of 7/7 and 9/11 in 2001 and 2005, respectively.

Finally, the author has investigated the influence of a growing and still developing corpus of case law on employers. They are advised to keep themselves informed of the legal evolution which is taking place to ensure that a given philosophical belief is respected at the workplace and at the time of recruiting prospective employees. Employers should adopt a zero-tolerance policy on offensive language, conduct and behaviour. Managers in companies should be offered training on the equal opportunities policy, bullying, intimidation and harassment. It would be also advisable to give employees guidance as to what extent they may express their views to colleagues and third parties. Moreover, effective grievance and disciplinary procedures should be established so as to deal with violations of discrimination laws. As regards the law itself, the author has concluded that the Equality Act 2010 does not state that the word "philosophical" includes "political". It is then problematic whether political beliefs are excluded from philosophical beliefs. Going further, it has been suggested that a vegan option would need to be taken into consideration by employers when organising events at the workplace where catering and drinks are offered. Employers are also advised to provide vegan workers with animal-free workwear and office equipment. As highlighted by the author, we should realise that the *Casamitjana Costa* case can have far-reaching consequences embracing not only the workplace but also other public spheres and areas (e.g. hospitals, prisons, supply of goods and services, transport, education). Remarkably, it will also exert influence on judicial thinking in future cases even though judicial precedent would not be applicable since most of the cases cited are Employment Tribunal cases.

Chapter 7 is written by Therese MacDermott, based at Macquarie University. She shows, first, that the principles of equality and non-discrimination have no roots in the Australian Constitution, and second, that anti-discrimination legislation in that country is characterised by parallel and overlapping federal, state and territory legislative schemes that make the system complicated and difficult to navigate. Besides, there is no uniform Equality Act in the federal area covering all protected characteristics. As the author states, there are many procedural differences regarding the way of dealing with cases; the practice of pursuing a case if it is not initially resolved by conciliation; types of remedies available; and the awarding of costs when the matter is resolved by a court or tribunal. The burden of proof has also been regarded as highly problematic for, as a matter of principle, it falls to the one who claims to have experienced discrimination to pursue a complaint against their employer. MacDermott has put forward a set of postulates in order to update and renew the Australian legislative framework and to trigger substantive change in workplaces. One of her constructive suggestions concerns the need to move away from reactive, complaints-based mechanisms and to enhance enforcement mechanisms. She believes that greater compliance could be attained by, for example, the possibility of proceedings being initiated by equality agencies, the regular audits of employment practices and compliance monitoring, the issuing of infringement notices and the use of enforceable undertaking. The author highlights the fact that the current legislative framework related to employment discrimination imposes very few positive rights or obligations, and it is structured in such a way that the prohibitions by statute of certain discriminatory conduct come to the fore. She has called for a change of the emphasis which should be placed upon a more positive, rights-based model and not upon negative prohibitions on discriminatory behaviour. Lastly, better mechanisms for providing information, advice and assistance (e.g. public funded legal representation) have been identified as needed from the point of view of victims of discrimination in order to empower them in finding appropriate and effective pathways to resolve their claims.

Chapter 8 is written by Gordon Anderson of Victoria University of Wellington and Dawn Duncan of the University of Otago. The authors point out that the current legislative framework concerning discrimination in employment in New Zealand embraces acts essentially enacted during the 1970s. These include the Race Relations Act of 1971 and the Human Rights Commission Act of 1977 that were consolidated into the Human Rights Act of 1993, the Equal Pay Act of 1972 and the Employment Relations Act of 2000. At the outset, the weighty impact of this legislation was noticeable and manifested itself, *inter alia*, in removing occupational barriers to women and eliminating separate male and female pay scales for the same work. However, the law has not changed much in the last 40 years and has remained adapted to economic, social and demographic problems of the 1970s. Thus, its further influence on achieving anti-discrimination goals was minimal. Like MacDermott, Anderson and Duncan have shown some shortcomings of the current system and have considered what reforms would lead to a more effective fight against discrimination. In New Zealand, the adjudicative stage of the process is accessible only after mediation which, first, does not lead to any formal admission that discrimination took place; second, is unlikely to fully satisfy a complainant, for it favours compromise; and third, has limited potential to discourage discrimination in broader terms because mediated resolutions are subject to a confidentiality agreement. Besides, the authors have noted that the solutions created are often apparent; for example, while it is admittedly true that the Office of Human Rights Proceedings is able to accept complaints for free legal representation, the fact remains that the number of successful applications is low. As regards pay equity, while the Equal Pay Amendment Act of 2020 somewhat addresses the original shortcomings of the 1972 Equal Pay Act, it does not oblige employers "to monitor, disclose or report on pay rates or on any actions taken by them to address issues identified". This means that due to the lack of pay transparency, bringing claims is more expensive and complicated for workers. Other than that, the Equal Pay Amendment Act has not created "a specialist pay equity agency to report on trends, provide specialist advice to parties, assist in the preparation, evaluation or resolution of pay equity claims, or monitor compliance". The authors have added that the amendments do not provide for any process for addressing pay equity related to historical racism in employment, the impacts of colonisation or the impacts of economic policies on Māori and Pacific workers. Moreover, people with diverse gender identities have not received any protection under the new Act. Finally, disabled people's right to non-discrimination should be strengthened through amendments to the Human Rights Act, for example, in terms of reasonable accommodation in employment.

Chapter 9, by Rachel Cox of the Université du Québec à Montréal, is the first in a cluster of chapters forming Part III, "Facets of Employment Discrimination in Other Parts of the World". With a view to clearing up much of the confusion about sexual harassment frameworks, the author sets about to elaborate the distinction between frameworks for psychological harassment and the employment injury and human rights regime based on the Québec Charter of Rights and Freedoms. This is due to the fact that in Québec, for the last couple of decades, the first two legislative backgrounds have been considered appropriate for violation of the right to a work environment free from sexual harassment. She poses the question of whether workers' interests are better protected through recourse via labour law institutions, through human rights institutions, or through the combination of both. A pragmatic approach indicates that labour law frameworks offer some advantages for complainants. These include more timely resolution of complaints and claims than in the case of the human rights regime, the simplicity of a single portal to file complaints, and the possibility of obtaining income replacement benefits without litigation if the claim is accepted. On the other hand, by examining a broad spectrum of case law, Cox proves that sexual harassment can be negated when it is framed as psychological harassment or an industrial accident. Thus, she acknowledges the need to strengthen interaction between the labour law framework and the human rights regime, believing that such a solution would allow all workers to exercise their right to a work environment free from sexual harassment. It would also be the best guarantor of ensuring access to effective and timely recourse in case of violation of this right.

Kurt Pärli, from the University of Basel, is the author of Chapter 10. He has succeeded in outlining a panorama of international conventions which bind Switzerland with regard to protection against discrimination. Unfortunately, there are problems with the country's approach to implementing international instruments. Shortcomings in this regard have been noted by the relevant supervisory bodies (e.g. the UN Committee on Economic, Social and Cultural Rights). Kurt Pärli explains the importance of implementation by the courts which can leverage concepts rooted in the EU anti-discrimination law, the judgments of the Court of Justice of the European Union and the rulings of the human rights treaty monitoring bodies. Indeed, Swiss courts offer protection against discrimination comparable to that resulting from Directive 2000/78/EC. In doing so, they apply the provisions on the protection of personality under employment law (Article 328 of the Swiss Code of Obligations) and data protection norms (Article 328b of the Swiss Code of Obligations), for in Switzerland there is no relevant legal norm for protection against discrimination in employment relationships. The author suggests that instead of adopting new legal regulation, Switzerland could also strengthen and supplement the existing civil law instruments.

We are also pleased to include a contribution from India in this collection. In Chapter 11, Nimushakavi Vasanthi, from NALSAR University of Law, presents an interesting case study on transformative equality and disability-based discrimination in employment. She explains that in 2007 India had ratified the United Nations Convention on the Rights of Persons with Disabilities, which provides for a transformative regime of rights consisting of a shift of understanding of disability from a welfare and medical model towards a rights-based model. Given this, it has been also highlighted that the Constitution of India of 1950 is endowed with a charter of rights guaranteeing, *inter alia*, the right to equality, prohibition of discrimination, and liberty and fundamental freedoms. In addition, India adopted the Persons with Disabilities Act of 1995 and the Rights of Persons with Disabilities Act of 2016, both of which introduce quotas in public employment in order to address discrimination. However, such a system has not led to a significant increase in participation in employment by people with disabilities. Vasanthi systematically discusses a 2019 decision of the Indian Supreme Court, *Surendra Mohan v State of Tamilnadu and Others*, and analyses the interwoven argumentation. According to that Court, it was fair, reasonable, just and logical to restrict eligibility to the position of a civil judge to a candidate with a specified degree of disability only, given the strenuous duties in such a post. In other words, the post of a civil judge could be held only by a person with partial blindness of 40%–50%; consequently Surendra Mohan, who had a 70% disability, was not even called for the oral test after successfully passing the written exam. Clearly, this decision confirms the inadequacy of a quota system to combat systemic discrimination. Fortunately, given the need to correct that injustice, the judgment was overruled. For this purpose the Court used a breadth of concepts of dignity, autonomy, participation, inclusive citizenship, accessibility, equality, non-discrimination and anti-stereotyping. As the author emphasises, such an approach makes it possible to move beyond specific acts of discrimination and concentrate on structural and systemic forms of discrimination. In contrast to the above-mentioned judgment, the author has also described another case, *Vikash Kumar v UPSC* of 2020, in which the Supreme Court immediately invoked the concepts of dignity, autonomy and inclusive citizenship and not only relied on the literal wording of the statute. Thanks to this fact, after the State refused the claim, the Court could decide that the support of a scribe was to be extended even if the required level of disability was not present. In her chapter the author has made the effort in explaining the role that judicial interpretation plays in integrating a rights-based approach to discrimination on the grounds of disability into constitutional and legislative frameworks.

Chapter 12 is written by Raphael Cohen-Almagor of the University of Hull and Uki Maroshek-Klarman from the Adam Institute for Democracy and Peace. The authors reveal to what unimaginably large extent women in Israel are discriminated against as compared to men. They demonstrate situations that are symptomatic of this gender discrimination, including the use of violence against women, including sexual harassment at the workplace; controlling power positions by men; the gender wage gap apparent in the fact that, for example, in 2018, women earned 69% of what their male counterparts earned; Jewish law (*Halacha*), which does not perceive men and women as equal; and Rabbinic Courts exercising jurisdiction over personal matters and favouring men. In conjunction with these manifestations of discrimination, women are disadvantaged due to some other factors, including the Israeli-Palestinian conflict that advances a militaristic agenda, the neoliberal economic structure and the education system. In the authors' view, a separation between state and religion would help fight against discrimination. The same beneficial effect would result from the empowerment of unorthodox Jewish denominations that are gender egalitarian. Also highlighted as advantageous is a legislative effort put forth by the Knesset, which passed several legal acts important from the point of view of women. Moreover, the authors clearly indicate that the National Labour Court and the Supreme Court for years have been advocating for women's equality. Lastly, the need for a comprehensive, written constitution – superseding *Halacha* – is a critical issue that the authors have raised in their conclusion. This most important instrument could undoubtedly help Israel safeguard democratic principles and human rights, including freedom from discrimination.

We had the privilege of working with a group of excellent employment and discrimination law researchers from around the world who contributed to the subject with highly enriching and diverse perspectives. We truly hope that the book manages to pass that interesting and scholarly experience on to its readers. A special thanks is addressed to our wonderful team of experts who made this project possible!

Part I

Employment Discrimination Law in the European Union and Its Member States

2 "It's All Relative?"

Role of Comparison in Terms of Equality in Employment Under EU Law

*Szilvia Halmos**

1 Introduction

Finding a comparator, that is, a person who is similarly situated as but enjoying a better treatment than a victim of discrimination, is a key investigative step in most discrimination cases. This comparative perspective reflects the relative nature of anti-discrimination law as a set of legal tools to achieve equality of, on the one hand, vulnerable, marginalised, biased groups and, on the other hand, dominant groups of society.

Nevertheless, the aforementioned classical methodology of investigation has proved to be too rigid to establish discrimination in more complex cases, where an actual comparator is difficult to find or, under the specific circumstances of the facts, the mere existence of a comparator is excluded.

This study is designed to describe the development of doctrinal approaches, as well as EU case law and secondary legislation addressing the aforementioned challenge of investigation of discrimination cases.

As is outlined below, the recent developments of equality theories support the approach that scrutiny of discrimination should apply a wider range of methodologies, which are appropriate to establish the occurrence of discrimination even where the comparator cannot be identified. Besides, this study tracks how the Court of Justice of the European Union (CJEU) has tackled practical difficulties in the application of the classic comparator-based model as well. As is demonstrated, the CJEU has implemented a sufficiently flexible framework of investigation, with respect to the effective enforcement of EU anti-discrimination law, including new approaches of identification of comparator(s). Further, the CJEU has set up the standards of determination of the comparator pool, requiring the national courts to carry out an in-depth analysis of the facts of the case. The most important constructs elaborated by the relevant jurisprudence of the CJEU, as also referred to below, have been included in the secondary anti-discrimination legislation of the EU, and by this have become minimum standards for national non-discrimination legislation of Member States. With respect to the particular importance and complexity of the criteria for the comparator pool in pay discrimination cases, a separate section discusses the abundant case law established concerning this question.

DOI: 10.4324/9781003306962-3

2 The Main Function of Non-discrimination Law and the Role of Relativity in the Light Thereof

The primary purpose of anti-discrimination law in employment is to provide legal tools to dismantle and disable harmful stereotypes deeply embedded in society, traditionally giving rise to the labour market segregation and marginalisation of vulnerable and disadvantaged groups of society. Freedom of contract, premised on the idea that parties possess equal bargaining power, which was obvious to market reality, could not provide equal allocation of goods and opportunities for everyone. Even though open exclusion and deprivation of rights of specific groups like women and racial and ethnic minorities have been outlawed throughout the centuries, eradication of marginalising stereotypes, unequal burdens of apparently neutral legislation, policies and practices to the detriment of vulnerable groups of society is a still ongoing and probably endless process.[1] These stereotypes create unjust hierarchic structures, dividing the society into dominant and minority groups according to certain characteristics (gender, race, age, physical and mental ability, religion, etc.). General tendencies may be observed, in that members of dominant groups employ hidden "scoring systems" deeming members of minorities as more risky, inferior in status and so forth, and underscoring them in societal interactions. This results in the outcast of persons bearing these characteristics from main resources and mainstream spheres of life.[2] Such scoring stereotypes may and often do drive the decision-making of employers, motivating them to treat persons with underscored characteristics in a more disadvantageous way than others. The main function of anti-discrimination laws penetrating the rules of private law is to neutralise these scoring mechanisms. This does not imply that all decisions based on irrational, intuitive and emotional reasons should be considered as invalid. However, provisions on non-discrimination rule out specific grounds of decisions that are "morally irrelevant", since they relate to certain personal characteristics ("protected characteristics")[3] which are

* Judge at the Budapest-Metropolitan General Court, Department of Labour Law; judge member of the European Law Advisors Network (ELAN); visiting lecturer at the Labour Law Department, Faculty of Law, Pázmány Péter Catholic University (Budapest, Hungary). Contact: halmos.szilvia@gmail.com.

1 See Sandra Fredman, *Discrimination Law* (Oxford: Oxford University Press, 2011 [2nd ed; reprint 2012]), p. 5; Botond Bitskey et al., Az antidiszkriminációs szabályozás reformja, 15 *Acta Humana: Hungarian Centre for Human Rights Publications*, 4, pp. 13–40 (2014); Botond Bitskey et al., Kell-e antidiszkriminációs törvény? 58 *Jogtudományi Közlöny*, 1, pp. 1–8 (2003); Tamás Gyulavári, Három évvel az antidiszkriminációs jog reformja után, 18 *Esély: Társadalom és Szociálpolitikai Folyóirat*, 3, pp. 3–35 (2007).

2 Vö. pl. Tal Z. Zarsky, Understanding Discrimination in the Scored Society, 89 *Washington Law Review*, 1375, pp. 1384–1385 (2014); Danielle K. Citron & Frank A. Pasquale, The Scored Society: Due Process for Automated Predictions, 89 *Washington Law Review*, 1 (2014); György Kiss, *Alapjogok kollíziója a munkajogban* (Pécs: Justis Tanácsadó Bt., 2010), p. 317.

3 The term "protected characteristic", as referred in anti-discrimination laws, covers important aspects of the identity of an individual or a group (e.g. gender, pregnancy, age, disability, colour, race or ethnicity, religion or belief, political views, sexual orientation), which often triggers negative bias

unchangeable (or at least are changeable at an unreasonably high cost), and therefore cannot be taken into consideration as objective justifications for a specific decision. Non-discrimination laws have, throughout the decades, acknowledged an increasing number of protected characteristics beyond the oldest ones (gender, race, colour), such as disability, age and sexual orientation, which, according to the general experience, often constitute the basis of underscoring of the persons concerned, making them particularly vulnerable in social interactions.[4]

Out of this perspective, we could conclude that, briefly speaking, there is no anti-discrimination law without comparison. Behind the principle of equality lies the Aristotelian idea according to which like should be treated alike, while unlike should be treated differently.[5] Provided that two persons or groups can be considered as similar in relation of a specific area of life, while they are different in terms of a protected characteristic, different treatment of them based on this protected characteristic is prohibited (this is the prohibition of direct discrimination). On the contrary, if the application of consistent treatment to persons or groups with and without a protected characteristic would have a much more adverse effect on the former, different treatment is appropriate respectively (this is the prohibition of indirect discrimination).[6]

Some decades ago, when most of the workplaces were of Tayloresque scale with easily comparable jobs with clearly identifiable group features,[7] individuals claiming discrimination could often point to counterparts with no protected characteristics who were treated better. Courts could then deduce that the protected trait was the reason for the adverse treatment at issue. In this sense, the comparison

---

and detrimental treatment of the individual concerned or group. Anti-discrimination laws prohibit certain types of discrimination (e.g. disadvantageous treatment, segregation, harassment) against persons on the grounds of such protected characteristics. For the definition of the concept of "protected characteristic", see especially European Union Agency for Fundamental Rights, *Handbook on European Non-Discrimination Law* (Luxembourg: Publications Office of the European Union, 2018), pp. 160–162, available at: https://fra.europa.eu/en/publication/2018/handbook-european-law-non-discrimination (accessed 5 May 2020).

4 David Feldman, *Civil Liberties and Human Rights in England and in Wales* (2nd ed., Oxford: Oxford University Press, 2002), pp. 135–139; Evelyn Ellis & Philippe Watson, *EU Anti-Discrimination Law* (2nd ed., Oxford: Oxford EU Law Library, 2013), pp. 2–3. See Diane Pothier, Connecting Grounds of Discrimination to Real People's Real Experiences, 13 *CJWL/RFD*, 37, 40, pp. 45–56 (2001).

5 Aristotle (translated by Miklós Szabó), *Nikomakhoszi Etika* (Budapest: Európa Kiadó, 1997), Vol. 6.

6 On the concepts of direct and indirect discrimination, see Justyna Maliszewska-Nienartowicz, Direct and Indirect Discrimination in European Union Law – How to Draw a Dividing Line? 3 *International Journal of Social Sciences*, 1, 41, p. 42 (2014); Dagmar Schiek, Lisa B. Waddington, & Mark Bell, *Cases, Materials and Text on National, Supranational and International Non-Discrimination Law* (Oxford and Portland, OR: Hart Publishing, 2007), pp. 353–359.

7 Friedrich Winslow Taylor laid down his theory on organisation of work and scientific management at the end of the 19th century. This theory had a great impact on the shaping of the organisation of work and management endeavouring to economic effectivity and increasing of production in the 20th century. His fundamental writings include Friedrich Winslow Taylor, Scientific Management, 7 *The Sociological Review*, 3, p. 266 (1914) and Friedrich Winslow Taylor, *Scientific Management* (New York: Harper & Brothers, 1947).

was used to show causation: that the challenged acts occurred because of the protected trait and would not have occurred in absence of it.[8] Thus, non-discrimination law could perform its function in the sense that it provided protection against underscoring on the basis of protected characteristics.

However, the application of the methodology described above of scrutiny brings increasing difficulties under the changed environment of employment. Structures of work tend to decline from the classic Tayloresque model. Atypical and flexible forms of labour relationships and in addition, the development of a wide range of growing legal relationships as the system of work becomes more widespread, demands the enactment of new laws. The determination of wages, working conditions and terms of contracts takes place in an individualised manner. It is increasingly difficult to find grouping schemes in order to identify workers in the same pool as the comparative pool of the individuals claiming discrimination.[9]

Besides, the development of theories of equality also supports a shift from the methodology of strict comparison. "Formal equality", as the original and most fundamental approach of equality, based on the idea of "likes should be treated alike", reflected by the prohibition of direct discrimination, exclusively requires the employer to be blind as regards protected characteristics. This means that it is forbidden to take into consideration any of these characteristics in any decisions of the employer (e.g. hiring and remuneration of workers, determining working conditions, terminating an employment relationship). Later on, anti-discrimination legislation has been enriched by the complementary, "substantial approach of equality" claiming that "alike should be treated differently". Accordingly, provided that an apparently neutral provision of an employer (i.e. which does not include an open distinction between persons/groups with and without a protected characteristic) imposes a considerably more adverse impact on the protected persons/group, the employer is precisely expected to be attentive to the existence of the protected characteristic and apply different treatment respectively, in order to enhance the actual equal opportunities of the vulnerable person/group. Otherwise, identical treatment would be considered as indirect discrimination.

However, the development of approaches of equality has not stopped at this stage. More recent theories are based on the idea that equality constitutes an important aspect of human dignity. It is, therefore, appropriate to rule out those employers' conducts which attach an adverse treatment to specific protected characteristics irrespective of the existence of a comparator person in an actual workplace having no such characteristics and suffering no adverse treatment.[10] This approach of equality is reflected in the constructs of harassment and sexual

8 Suzanne B. Goldberg, Discrimination by Comparison, 120 *Yale Law Journal*, 728, pp. 731–732 (2011).

9 Ibid.

10 In the academic literature there are a number of classifications of approaches of equality. A more detailed description of these classifications is presented by Kriszta Kovács (*Az egyenlőség felé. A hátrányos megkülönböztetés tilalma és a támogató intézkedések* [Budapest: L'Harmattan, 2012], pp. 30–56); Fredman, supra n. 1, at pp. 2–3, 20–21, 23–25; Ronald Dworkin & Sovereign Virtue,

harassment, the occurrence of which can be established even if, for instance, all the staff members are female and their supervisor has harassed all of them. Hence, there is no place for comparison.[11] We could conclude at first sight that this approach eliminates the relative nature of equality, and rather demonstrates its absolute fundamental rights' character. Nevertheless, this approach of equality also shows the relative character of equality, but the comparison should take place on a more general level, and not on the shop floor. Namely, if an individual is accorded an unfavourable treatment in causation of their protected characteristic, they are likely to have become the victim of the above described scoring mechanisms, which resulted in their detrimental treatment compared to the dominant groups of society. We can draw the same conclusion if we compare the concerned individual's actual situation on the one hand, and hypothetical situation on the other, in which they would be without their protected characteristic, putting the question, whether the employer had treated them in a less favourable way if they hadn't had a protected characteristic.[12] Since, as it has already been referred in this study, the primary function of anti-discrimination law is to combat these scoring schemes, it cannot be excluded that methodologies of scrutiny applied for discrimination cases could exceed the model of traditional comparison, implying two actual persons or groups existing in the work organisation in order to provide protection against employers maintaining the mentioned inequalities in the society.[13] In principle, it is, therefore, acceptable that the relativity of legal constructs related to equality in employment could be reflected on a more abstract level than in the comparison of the situations of actual workers of a company.[14]

3 Relativity in EU Law

The development of EU non-discrimination law[15] mirrors the stages of development of theories of equality as described above. At the beginning of the European integration, Article 119 of the Treaty on European Economic Communities, the

---

The Theory and Practice of Equality (Cambridge, MA: Harvard University Press, 2000), 113f., pp. 285–288.

11 See European Union Agency of Fundamental Rights, supra n. 3, at p. 66; Fredman, supra n. 1, at pp. 227–228.

12 See Goldberg, supra n. 8, at p. 806; Elisabeth Holzleithner, Mainstreaming Equality: Dis/Entangling Grounds of Discrimination, 14 *Transnational Law and Contemporary Problems*, pp. 927–957, p. 934 (2015).

13 Goldberg supra n. 8, 770.

14 In terms of necessity of exceeding the traditional comparison-based methodology: Aileen McColgan, Cracking the Comparator Problem: Discrimination, "Equal" Treatment and the Role of Comparisons, 6 *European Human Rights Law Review*, p. 650 (2006); Sophia Reibetanz Moreau, Equality Rights and the Relevance of Comparator Groups, 5 *Journal of Law and Equality*, p. 81 (2006); Belinda Smith, From Wardley to Purvis – How Far Has Australian Anti-Discrimination Law Come in 30 Years? 21 *Australian Journal of Labour Law*, pp. 3–30 (2008).

15 For reasons of space, this study cannot go into detail on the description of the development relevant to EC/EU law.

horizontal direct effect of which has been later acknowledged by the CJEU,[16] implemented the formal approach of equality in terms of prohibition of wage discrimination against women. Cases related to this Article drove the CJEU to conclude that the formal approach is not sufficient to provide effective protection for victims of pay discrimination; thus, the Court started to apply the notion of substantive approach of equality in discrimination cases. In the recent case law of the CJEU, the approach of "equality as an element of dignity" is given a greater degree of emphasis. We find the first emergence of this approach in a judgment of the CJEU as well.[17] Specific discriminatory conducts, such as sexual harassment and harassment, where no comparator is required to establish the discrimination, also reflect this approach.[18] The CJEU has developed novel tests, constructs and schemes of scrutiny (e.g. the shared burden of proof, indirect discrimination, the limits of positive actions), which were later on included in the EC/EU legislation, particularly in the directives on equal treatment in employment (hereinafter Directives).[19] Currently, as part of EU primary law, Article 21(1) of the Charter of Fundamental Rights of the EU (hereinafter Charter) sets out the right to equal

16 C-43/75. Gabrielle Defrenne v Société anonyme belge de navigation aérienne Sabena, ECLI:EU:C:1976:56 (Defrenne-II case); C-184/89. Helga Nimz v Freie und Hansestadt Hamburg, ECLI:EU:C:1991:50 (Nimz case); C-33/89. Maria Kowalska tegen Freie und Hansestadt Hamburg, ECLI:EU:C:1990:265; C-400/93. Specialarbejderforbundet i Danmark v Dansk Industri, formerly Industriens Arbejdsgivere, acting for Royal Copenhagen A/S., ECLI:EU:C:1995:155 (Royal Copenhagen judgment case); C-399/92. Stadt Lengerich v Angelika Helmig and Waltraud Schmidt v Deutsche Angestellten-Krankenkasse and Elke Herzog v Arbeiter-Samariter-Bund Landverband Hamburg eV and Dagmar Lange v Bundesknappschaft Bochum and Angelika Kussfeld v Firma Detlef Bogdol GmbH and Ursula Ludewig v Kreis Segeberg, ECLI:EU:C:1994:415 (Helmig case).

17 In the Coleman case (C-303/06. S. Coleman v Attridge Law and Steve Law, CLI:EU:C:2008:415 (Coleman judgment), AG Maduro proposed that "to protect the dignity and the autonomy of persons belonging to those suspect classifications . . . treating someone less well on the basis of reasons such as religious belief, age, disability and sexual orientation undermines this special and unique value that people have by virtue of being humans" (cited and commented by Fredman, supra n. 1, at p. 227).

18 Fredman, supra n. 1, at pp. 20–21.

19 Under "Directives" for the purpose of this study, the three most important directives are understood concerning combating discrimination in employment:

- Directive 2006/54/EC of the European Parliament and of the Council of 5 July 2006 on the implementation of the principle of equal opportunities and equal treatment of men and women in matters of employment and occupation (recast), OJ L 204, 26 July 2006, 23–36 ("Gender Directive"), (the gender directive repealed and recast a set of previous directives related to gender-based discrimination in the field of employment);
- Council Directive 2000/43/EC of 29 June 2000 implementing the principle of equal treatment between persons irrespective of racial or ethnic origin; OJ L 180, 19 July 2000, 22–26 ("Race Directive");
- Council Directive 2000/78/EC of 27 November 2000 establishing a general framework for equal treatment in employment and occupation, OJ L 303, 2.12.2000, 16–22 ("Framework Directive").

treatment in employment, in addition, with horizontal direct effect within the scope of application of the Charter.[20]

Corresponding to the subject matter of this study, the following legal constructs should be examined in more detail from the range of tools developed by the case law of the CJEU: (1) the rules on burden of proof, (2) the concept of hypothetical comparator and (3) the conduct of harassment.

3.1 The Role of Comparison at Application of Rules on Burden of Proof

The concept of shared or reversed burden of proof has been enabled in EU equality law through the case law of the CJEU. The biasing patterns motivating an employer to decide to underscore any person with a specific protected characteristic often remain undisclosed by the employee. Relevant data (e.g. concerning pay schemes applied by the employer) and documents (e.g. related to a hiring process) are often not available to the employee. Therefore, in many cases, the victim of discrimination would hardly be able to deliver any evidence to support their claim without a reduced burden of proof.[21] Beyond this practical argument, favourable rules on the burden of proof for the victims can be justified by doctrinal reasons as well. As already outlined above, anti-discrimination laws identify the marginalised groups of society

---

It is to be noted that other directives in the field of employment also set out rules on non-discrimination of workers under their scopes, such as:

- Council Directive 1999/70/EC of 28 June 1999 concerning the framework agreement on fixed-term work concluded by ETUC, UNICE and CEEP, OJ L 175, 10.7.1999, 43–48 ("Fixed-term Work Directive"), Annex, section 1;
- Directive 2008/104/EC of the European Parliament and of the Council of 19 November 2008 on temporary agency work, OJ L 327, 5.12.2008, 9–14 ("Temporary Agency Work Directive"), article 1, 2 and 5;
- Council Directive 97/81/EC of 15 December 1997 concerning the Framework Agreement on part-time work concluded by UNICE, CEEP and the ETUC – Annex: Framework agreement on part-time work, OJ L 14, 20.1.1998, 9–14 ("Part Time Work Directive"), Annex, section 1.

20 See Mark Bell, The Right to Equality and Non-Discrimination, in Tamara Hervey & Jeff Kenner (eds.), *Economic and Social Rights Under the EU Charter of Fundamental Rights: A Legal Perspective* (Oxford: Hart Publishing, 2003), pp. 91–110, p. 101; C-441/14. Dansk Industri (DI), agissant pour Ajos A/S v Sucession Karsten Eigil Rasmussen, ECLI:EU:C:2016:278 (Dansk Industri case); C-555/07. Seda Kücükdeveci v Swedex GmbH & Co. KG, ECLI:EU:C:2009:429 (Kücükdeveci case); C-414/16. Vera Egenberger v Evangelisches Werk für Diakonie und Entwicklung e.V, ECLI:EU:C:2018:257 (Egenberger case); C-176/12. Association de médiation sociale v Union locale des syndicats CGT and Others, ECLI:EU:C:2014:2.

21 See Kiss, supra n. 2, at p. 317, 22; Anne Beale, Proving Discrimination: The Shift of Burden of Proof and Access to Evidence, 2018, available at www.era-comm.eu/oldoku/Adiskri/03_Burden_of_proof/118DV18_Beale_Paper_EN.pdf (accessed 5 May 2020), p. 2; Monika Forejtova, The Effort to Achieve Equality with the Help of the Reversal of the Burden of Proof in Anti-Discrimination Litigation, 13 *International and Comparative Law Review*, 1, p. 135 (2013).

by defining protected characteristics. Relying on the general societal experience that persons with protected characteristics are commonly subject to detrimental treatment on the grounds of this characteristic, it is reasonable to set up the presumption that the precise reason for the detriment suffered was indeed this characteristic. Nevertheless, this presumption is rebuttable: the perpetrator (the employer) may establish that (1) there was no causal link between the protected characteristic and the disadvantage caused, or (2) even if there was causal link, it was justified by reason of a "weighty ground". This scheme legitimates that anti-discrimination laws use a higher standard of excuse against the perpetrators, on the one hand in procedural aspect (shared or reversed burden of proof) and on the other hand in the substantive aspect (narrowly formulated justification grounds and exemptions).[22]

Under EU law, rules on the shared burden of proof emerged first in the jurisprudence of the CJEU. In the reasonings of the first relevant cases, the CJEU relied on rather practical arguments in terms of justification of shared burden. The subject matter of the first landmark case (Danfoss)[23] related to the question of reversed burden of proof where wage (indirect) discrimination occurred. In this case, female workers received lower pay on average than male colleagues, and the system of pay that led to this result was completely lacking in transparency.[24] In the judgment, the CJEU indeed placed the burden of proof on the employer, arguing that otherwise female workers would be deprived of any effective means of enforcing the principle of equal pay before the national courts if the effect of adducing such evidence was not to impose upon the employer the burden of proving that its practice in the matter of wages is not in fact discriminatory. Apparently, the core of the argumentation of the CJEU was that the use of the ordinary scheme of the burden of proof would considerably hurdle the victim's effective assertion of their claim, in failure of sufficient information and evidences on the background of the employer's (allegedly discriminatory) provision.[25] This formula obviously left unanswered the question, to what extent it is expected from the victim of discrimination to support their claim to reverse

22 Szilvia Halmos, Az "egyéb helyzet" alapján történő diszkrimináció a foglalkoztatásban: A magyar gyakorlat elemzése az elmélet, a nemzetközi jog és az alkotmánybírósági gyakorlat tükrében, in Márta Ábrahám (ed.), *Mailáth György Tudományos Pályázat 2017: Díjazott dolgozatok* (Budapest: Országos Bírósági Hivatal, 2017), pp. 612–614.

23 C-109/88. Handels- og Kontorfunktionærernes Forbund I Danmark v Dansk Arbejdsgiverforening, acting on behalf of Danfoss, ECLI:EU:C:1989:383.

24 Summarised by Beale, supra n. 21, at p. 4.

25 As the subsequently developed case law clarified, no intention or subjective motivation of the employer is required to establish the discriminatory nature of a specific provision of the employer (See C-127/92. Dr. Pamela Mary Enderby kontra Frenchay Health Authority és Secretary of State for Health, ECLI:EU:C:1993:859 (Enderby judgment) and the attached Advocate General's opinion; C-177/88. Elisabeth Johanna Pacifica Dekker v Stichting Vormingscentrum voor Jong Volwassenen (VJV-Centrum) Plus, ECLI:EU:C:1990:383 (Dekker judgment), C-96/80. J.P. Jenkins v Kingsgate (Clothing Productions) Ltd., ECLI:EU:C:1981:80 (Jenkins judgment) (Ellis & Watson, supra n. 4, at pp. 163–169).

the burden of proof to the employer. The CJEU proceeded to a more general statement of principle in the *Enderby* case.[26] The CJEU stated that the existence of a prima facie case of discrimination casts the burden of proving objective justification onto the employer.[27] This line of case law was later continued and refined.[28]

The essence of the relevant judgments was ultimately consolidated and included in a directive on the burden of proof (covering only sex discrimination cases), which has been later repealed by the Gender Directive.[29] Currently, rules on shared burden of proof are included in all the three Directives. According to the current formulation of the main rule of the burden of proof in the Directives,

> Member States shall take such measures as are necessary, in accordance with their national judicial systems, to ensure that, when persons who consider themselves wronged because the principle of equal treatment has not been applied to them establish, before a court or other competent authority, facts from which it may be presumed that there has been direct or indirect discrimination, it shall be for the respondent to prove that there has been no breach of the principle of equal treatment.[30]

As it is apparent from the wording of the Directives, they do not set out a binding benchmark for the Member States' legislation in terms of the standard of proof which triggers the imposing the burden of proof to the employer. It is to a high extent upon the margin of discretion of the Member States' legislation to determine whether the identification of the comparator and supporting this should be imposed on the claimant's or the defendant's side in the course of taking of evidence.

The CJEU has considered in a number of discrimination cases which are the criteria of comparison.

In the *Glatzel* case, the claimant's application for a new driving licence for heavy goods vehicles was refused, since the medical examination revealed that he was suffering from unilateral amblyopia. He therefore failed to meet the requirements laid down in national law for the specific categories of licences. However, Mr Glatzel had a normal field of vision; his visual impairments affected, in particular, his central visual acuity, so he was capable of seeing objects appearing in his field of peripheral vision in essentially the same way as a person with normal vision and, was therefore, able to stop the power-driven vehicle he was driving

26 See supra n. 25.

27 See also C-381/99. Susanna Brunnhofer v Bank der österreichischen Postsparkasse AG, ECLI:EU:C:2001:358 (Brunnhofer judgment).

28 Royal Copenhagen- judgment; Helmig judgment; C-297/93. Rita Grau-Hupka v Stadtgemeinde Bremen, ECLI:EU:C:1994:406.

29 Council Directive 97/80/EC of 15 December 1997 on the burden of proof in cases of discrimination based on sex, OJ L 14, 20.1.1998, pp. 6–8.

30 Gender Directive, Article 19(2); Race Directive, Article 8; Framework Directive, Article 10.

even by using only his residual vision. Contrary to other categories of drivers, he was denied the opportunity to obtain a driving licence in "exceptional cases" after further examinations confirming his ability to drive. The CJEU had to decide whether the restriction concerning Mr Glatzel should be considered as discriminatory on the grounds of disability under Article 21(1) of the Charter, compared to persons with normal visual ability. The CJEU held that the EU legislature took care to create two categories of drivers on the basis of the size of the vehicle, the number of passengers carried and the responsibilities which accordingly result from driving such vehicles. The characteristics of the vehicles concerned, such as the size, weight or manoeuvrability of those vehicles, justify the existence of different conditions for the issue of a driving licence in light of the way in which they are driven. Consequently, the situations of those drivers of such vehicles are not comparable. In so far as those situations are not comparable, a difference in treatment was not considered to be discriminatory.[31]

In another case, the applicant P. used to work as a manager in an educational establishment operated by the county council. P. informed the employer of his intention to undergo a gender reassignment, including surgery to give P. physical attributes of a woman. In the course of the reassignment process, the employee was dismissed by the employer. The CJEU had to address, among other issues, the question of comparator. The CJEU held that where a person is dismissed on the ground that they intend to undergo, or have undergone, gender reassignment, they are treated unfavourably by comparison with persons of the sex to which they were deemed to belong before undergoing gender reassignment.[32]

In the two latter cases the CJEU highlighted that definition of comparator pools requires a more differentiated and individualised approach than comparing male and female, persons with and without disabilities and so forth. Instead, the criteria of the comparator pool to be formed in a certain case should reflect the individual circumstances of the facts. Comparators should encompass those ones who can be taken into account as the claimant's real counterparts, adjusted to the precise nature of the given characteristic. In disability discrimination, the claimant's ability for the functions of the job to be performed can be crucial as regards finding comparators. In gender discrimination cases, some specific aspect of one's sex or gender can be decisive in this regard.

The subject matter of the case of Frédéric Hay concerned equal treatment as regards granting marriage benefits for same-sex partners The claimant was employed by a bank which offered special marriage bonus and paid leave days to employees on the occasion of their marriage. The claimant applied for these benefits after he entered into a specific type of civil partnership open equally for opposite- and same-sex couples ("PACS"), but the bank refused to grant it.

31 C-356/12. Wolfgang Glatzel v Freistaat Bayern, ECLI:EU:C:2014:350.

32 C-13/94. P v S and Cornwall County Council, ECLI:EU:C:1996:170, referring to C-267/06. Tadao Maruko v Versorgungsanstalt der deutschen Bühnen, ECLI:EU:C:2008:179; C-144/08. Jürgen Römer v Freie und Hansestadt Hamburg, ECLI:EU:C:2011:286. Relevant cases are summarised in European Union Agency of Fundamental Rights, supra n. 3, at pp. 45–46.

The CJEU had to determine whether such a difference in treatment amounted to discrimination based on sexual orientation. The CJEU underlined that it is not required that the situations be identical, but only that they be comparable. The assessment of that comparability must be carried out not in a global and abstract manner but in a specific and concrete manner in the light of the benefit concerned. The CJEU recited its position outlined in another case in respect of registered life partnerships:[33] the comparison of the situations must be based on an analysis focusing on the rights and obligations of the spouses and registered life partners as they result from the applicable domestic provisions, which are relevant taking into account the purpose and the conditions for granting the benefit at issue in the main proceedings. It is not relevant in itself that national law generally treats registered life partnership as legally equivalent to marriage. Scrutinising and comparing the purposes and the formal requirements of same-sex relationships and marriages as laid down in current national law, the CJEU established that persons of the same sex may conclude a registered relationship in order to organise their life together by committing, in the context of that life together, to providing material aid and assistance to each other. PACS constitutes, like marriage, a form of civil union which places the couple within a specific legal framework entailing rights and obligations in respect of each other and against third parties. As a conclusion, persons of the same sex who could not marry and therefore could only conclude a civil partnership were in a situation comparable to that of married couples. The CJEU explained that although the difference in treatment is based on the employees' marital status and not expressly on their sexual orientation, it constitutes direct discrimination on the grounds of sexual orientation. The CJEU held it irrelevant that PACS was not only available for same-sex partners, and in this sense the legislation made no difference on the grounds of sexual orientation. It was crucial that homosexual employees were unable to marry and consequently meet the condition required for obtaining the benefits claimed.[34] Even though same-sex marriage has been introduced in France since this ruling,[35] which altered the legal context of this case on the national level, the CJEU's judgment is still to be observed as regards the aspects finding the appropriate comparator pool in a discrimination case. It emphasised that the precise nature of the detrimental treatment (i.e. the actual grounds for refusal to grant a specific employment-related benefit) can also be relevant in terms of defining comparator pools.[36]

33 Römer case, supra n. 32.

34 C-267/12. Frédéric Hay v Crédit agricole mutuel de Charente-Maritime et des Deux-Sèvres, ECLI:EU:C:2013:823. Discussion of the case at European Union Agency of Fundamental Rights 2018, supra n. 3, at p. 46.

35 The relevant national law (Loi no. 2013–404 du 17 mai 2013 ouvrant le mariage aux couples de personnes de même sexe) took effect in 18 May 2013. The text of the act is available at www.legifrance.gouv.fr/jorf/id/JORFTEXT000027414540?r=V660JkU8Td (accessed 21 January 2021).

36 See also Jule Mulder, Dignity or Discrimination: What Paves the Road Towards Equal Recognition of Same-Sex Couples in the European Union? 40 *Journal of Social Welfare and Family Law*, 1, 129, pp. 133–134, 136–138 (2018).

Finding the person or group in a comparable situation with the victims of discrimination may be particularly difficult in cases of multiple discrimination. Multiple discrimination is at present not addressed by the Directives, notwithstanding in certain recitals of the Race Directive and the Framework Directive.[37] Article 21(1) of the Charter contains an open list of possible protected characteristics, which could pave the way to references to multiple protected grounds, however, according to the practice of the CJEU extension of protected characteristics under EU secondary law is not possible.[38] It is to be noted that the CJEU has reaffirmed in an increasing number of cases that the equality directives do not themselves lay down the general principle of equality but simply give concrete expression and effect to that principle, which is enshrined in the Charter.[39] The consequent representation of this approach could in the future inspire the CJEU to deviate from a rigid reliance on the enumerative list of protected characteristics to an interpretation of EU law covering cases of intersectional discrimination. As some authors suggest, a dignity-based approach of equality could also justify a more flexible treatment of the list of protected characteristics (however, the CJEU does not seem to have adopted a purely dignity-focused approach so far).[40] So far, the CJEU has not allowed any reference to the Charter in order to create new or combined protected grounds.[41] As a result, the CJEU has not had to decide on the criteria of comparability in cases concerning multiple discrimination so far. Nevertheless, if the CJEU overturned its position related to multiple discrimination, it would probably induce a deviation from a comparator-based investigation of discrimination cases. Namely, defining an adequate comparator pool would be considerably more difficult where the victim possesses more protected characteristics.

3.2 Comparison – If There Is no Comparator or It Is Hypothetical

There are cases where the identification of a comparator is not possible. The CJEU reaffirmed in a series of cases that the actual existence of any comparator is not necessarily required. In the *Dekker* judgment, the CJEU held that only women can be refused employment on grounds of pregnancy, and such a refusal therefore constitutes direct discrimination on grounds of sex. This being the case,

37 Recital (3) of the Framework Directive; Recital (14) of the Race Directive.

38 Coleman case; C-13/05. Sonia Chacón Navas v Eurest Colectividades SA [GC], ECLI:EU:C:2006:456; C-310/10. Ministerul Justiţiei şi Libertăţilor Cetăţeneşti v Ştefan Agafiţei and Others, ECLI:EU:C:2011:467; C-406/15. Petya Milkova v Izpalnitelen direktor na Agentsiata za privatizatsia i sledprivatizatsionen kontrol, ECLI:EU:C:2017:198.

39 For instance in Kücükdeveci case, Dansk Industri case, Egenberger case.

40 Mulder supra n. 36, at p. 139; with reference to, *inter alia*, the following sources: Fredman, supra n. 1, at pp. 20, 22; Colm O'Cinneide, The Constitutionalization of Equality within the EU Legal Order: Sexual Orientation as Testing Ground, 22 *Maastricht Journal of European and Comparative Law*, 3, pp. 370–395 (2015).

41 C-443/15. David L. Parris v Trinity College Dublin and Others, ECLI:EU:C:2016:897; European Union Agency of Fundamental Rights, supra n. 3, at pp. 62–63.

the existence or the absence of a male comparator does not alter the assessment of the case.[42] Consequently, in cases of pregnancy-based discrimination, seeking of a comparator is not required. The same principles were applied in cases related to maternity leave[43] and undergoing in vitro fertilisation treatment.[44] In the *Mayr* case, the CJEU had to consider whether the dismissal of a female worker undergoing an in vitro fertilisation procedure was covered by the then-effective sex discrimination directive, even if she was not yet pregnant at the time of the dismissal. The CJEU established that workers of both sexes can be temporarily prevented from carrying out their work on account of the medical treatment they must receive. Nevertheless, the treatment in question in the main proceedings (in vitro fertilisation) directly affects only women. It follows that the dismissal of a female worker essentially because she is undergoing that important stage of in vitro fertilisation treatment constitutes direct discrimination on grounds of sex. In the reasoning of its judgment, the CJEU apparently did not address the question of comparator at all. As regards the inherent nature of the specific aspect of gender concerned by this case, no counterpart could ever be found from the opposite sex.

The concept of "hypothetical comparator", which has been elaborated in the case law of the CJEU, has already been included in the secondary EU law. Currently, all the three Directives allow to establish direct discrimination where the victim of discrimination is treated less favourably on grounds of sex than another is, was or would be treated in a comparable situation.[45] A reference to a hypothetical comparator means that a claimant could argue that they have been less favourably treated than another person without a specific protected trait would have been treated, even if the claimant cannot point at such an actual person.[46] In the *Feryn* case, the CJEU had to decide whether public statements by which an employer lets it be known that under its recruitment policy it will not recruit any employees of a certain ethnic or racial origin are sufficient to presume that the recruitment policy is directly discriminatory. The fact that an employer declares publicly that it will not recruit employees of a certain ethnic or racial origin constitutes direct discrimination under the Race Directive. Namely, such a declaration is clearly likely to strongly dissuade certain candidates from submitting their candidature, and accordingly, to hinder their access to the labour market. The existence of such direct discrimination is not dependant on the identification of a complainant who claims to have been the victim.

42 Dekker case, supra n. 25.

43 C-191/03. North Western Health Board v Margaret McKenna, ECLI:EU:C:2005:513 (McKenna case).

44 C-506/06. Sabine Mayr v Bäckerei und Konditorei Gerhard Flöckner, ECLI:EU:C:2008:119 (Mayr case). Summary of the CJEU case law related to the comparator: European Union Agency of Fundamental Rights, supra n. 3, at pp. 45–47.

45 Article 2(1a) of the Gender Directive; Article 2(2) of the Race Directive; Article 2(2a) of the Framework Directive.

46 Fredman, supra n. 1, at p. 161.

In further cases,[47] the CJEU outlined that the Directives cannot be interpreted in a way that a job applicant whose application was rejected should have access to information indicating whether the employer engaged another applicant. Nevertheless, it cannot be ruled out that a defendant's refusal to grant any access to information may be one of the factors to take into account in the context of establishing facts from which it may be presumed that there has been direct or indirect discrimination. It is for the referring court to determine whether that is the case in the main proceedings, taking into account all the circumstances of the case before it. This line of cases highlights that courts may, if appropriate, disregard the existence of the identification of an actual comparator, if the facts supporting the occurrence of discrimination can be established without this circumstance as well. This methodology is based upon the aforementioned idea that comparison is only a tool to establish causality between the protected ground and the unfavourable treatment, which can take place by means of other methodologies of scrutiny as well.

3.3 Discrimination Beyond Traditional Comparison

Inclusion of additional types of conducts among the possible forms of discrimination demonstrates that the development of EU law respects the idea that protection against discrimination should also cover cases where there is no place for a comparison-based approach. The conduct of harassment was introduced in the secondary law of the EC on the prohibition of discrimination on the grounds of gender in the 1990s.[48] Under currently effective EU law, harassment is prohibited under all the three Directives, furthermore the Gender Directive lays down the prohibition of sexual harassment as well (hereinafter together "harassment").[49] None of the relevant provisions stipulates that harassment can only be established if the victim can point at a person in a comparable situation, but without a protected characteristic, who has not been harassed by the perpetrator. This formulation of the relevant provisions is in line with the approach of equality as an element of human dignity.[50] However, this approach can also be discovered in connection with cases concerning other discriminatory conducts than harassment.[51]

Studying the development of EU law, we can conclude that both EU legislation and the case law of the CJEU tend to depart from the model of classic comparison in terms of scrutiny of discrimination cases. Rules on burden of proof as laid down in the Directives provide a sufficiently broad framework for the legislation

47 C-415/10. Galina Meister v Speech Design Carrier Systems GmbH, ECLI:EU:C:2012:217 (Meister case); C-104/10. Kelly v National University of Ireland (University College, Dublin), ECLI:EU:C:2011:506 (Kelly case).

48 Isabelle Chopin, Catharina Germaine, *A Comparative Analysis of Non-Discrimination Law in Europe 2017* (Luxembourg: European Commission, Directorate-General for Justice and Consumers, Publications Office of the European Union, 2018), p. 51.

49 Article 2(1c)(1d) of the Gender Directive; Article 2(3) of the Race Directive; Article 2(3) of the Framework Directive.

50 Fredman 2011, supra n. 1, at pp. 23–25.

51 Opinion of Maduro AG in the Coleman case as cited above.

and the courts of Member States to create the appropriate requirements of application of the comparison-based methodology, and, if it is reasonable with respect to the principle of effective enforcement of protection against discrimination, to decline from it, and to use another proper type methodology. It is not excluded under EU law to introduce tools of scrutiny completely disregarding the reference to a comparator or applying the concept of hypothetical comparator.

4 The Comparator in Cases of Pay Discrimination

With regards to the key significance of the issue, identification of a comparator in pay discrimination cases should be given particular attention. In cases concerning pay discrimination, it is of crucial importance to make a clear distinction between the circumstances that can be respected in terms of comparison and those ones which can be referred in terms of justification. First of all, the distinction between the criteria of comparison and justification is important. Identification of the comparator in cases of pay discrimination is, in general, in the interest of the employee in order to establish the facts to set up the presumption of discrimination. Conversely, if the shift of burden of proof has occurred, it is on the employer to demonstrate an objective justification of differential pay in order to prove that there has been no breach of the principle of equal treatment. Second, the scrutiny in terms of comparison requires a descriptive approach: criteria of comparison are used to set up the pool of workers who perform equal work or work of equal value. This establishes their entitlement for equal pay irrespective of their protected characteristics. By contrast, in assessing justification, it is to be examined whether a differential treatment between the members of this pool with and without protected characteristic took place on the grounds of any objective justification. This latter step of scrutiny obviously applies a normative perspective: the central question is, why the employer was not supposed to grant equal pay for the members of the pool.

Considering that the principle of equal pay for equal work or work of equal value is one of the oldest non-discrimination provisions, dating back to the start of the integration process, statutory law and the abundant case law of the CJEU provide sufficient indications for the identification of a comparator in these types of cases, as well as for the distinction between the criteria of comparison and justification.

The requirement to guarantee equal pay for equal work for men and women was already included in the EEC Treaty (Article 119 of this Treaty, replaced later by the Article 141 of the Treaty of the European Community). In the current framework of treaties, this requirement is laid down in Article 157 of the Treaty of the Functioning of the European Union. This provision (as well as the previously effective, corresponding provisions under previously effective primary law) has horizontal direct effect;[52] that is, even private persons and entities may rely upon it

52 See supra sec. 3.

before national courts against another private person or entity. Further, prohibition of discrimination in terms of pay is set out by all the three Directives.[53]

Contemplating the relevant case law of the CJEU, in essence, the comparator pool should be set up out of the employees who perform equal work or work of equal value. In any case, it is for the national court to decide whether, in the light of individual circumstances of the case, two types of work are of equal value.[54] The nature of the job to be performed by the compared workers is a decisive factor; however, other circumstances may also be of relevance, such as the training requirements and the working conditions.[55]

As the CJEU argued, in order to determine whether different groups of persons who perform seemingly identical tasks but who do not have the same training or professional qualifications for the practice of their profession do the same work, it is necessary to ascertain whether, taking into account the nature of the tasks that may be assigned to each group respectively, the training requirements for performance of those tasks and the working conditions under which they are performed, the different groups can be considered to be in a comparable situation. That is not the case for two groups of persons who have received different professional training and who, because of the different scope of the qualifications resulting from that training, on the basis of which they were recruited, are called on to perform different tasks or duties. Thus the term "the same work" does not apply where the same activities are performed over a considerable length of time by persons, the basis of whose qualification to exercise their profession is different.[56]

The CJEU stressed that the scope of the concept of "the same work", which is entirely qualitative in character in that it is exclusively concerned with the nature of the services in question, may not be confined to situations in which men and women are contemporaneously doing equal work for the same employer.[57]

The fact that the employees concerned are classified in the same job category under the collective agreement applicable to their employment is not in itself sufficient. Such a categorisation is only one of the factors that should be considered in order to decide whether the concerned employees do the same work or work of equal value.[58] In the course of any classification of workers, attention should be paid that any hidden application of gender-based stereotypes should be excluded. Such stereotypes may be manifested in pay schemes where jobs, the performance of which require greater physical effort, are granted higher pay. The CJEU emphasised that a job classification system for the purpose of determining

53 Article 4 of the Gender Directive; Article 3(1c) of the Race Directive; Article 3(1c) of the Framework Directive.

54 Royal Copenhagen case, supra n. 16.

55 Ibid.; McKenna case, supra n. 43; Brunnhofer case, supra n. 27; C-309/97. Angestelltenbetriebsrat der Wiener Gebietskrankenkasse v Wiener Gebietskrankenkasse (WGKK case) ECLI:EU:C:1999:241; C-129/79. Macarthys Ltd v Wendy Smith, ECLI:EU:C:1980:103 (Macarthys case).

56 WGKK case, supra n. 55.

57 Macarthys case, supra n. 55.

58 Brunnhofer case, supra n. 27.

rates of pay can use the criterion of muscle demand or muscular effort, or that of the heaviness of the work may not imply covert discrimination. It means that such classifications are only legitimate, if the nature of the tasks involved, the work to be performed does require the use of a certain degree of physical strength, so long as the system as a whole, by taking into account other criteria, precludes any discrimination on grounds of sex. For this purpose, it must, in so far as the nature of the tasks carried out in the undertaking permits, take into account criteria for which workers of each sex may show particular aptitude.[59]

Special care is to be taken with regard to the assessment of considering the comparability in piece-work systems. The CJEU highlighted that in these cases, work paid at time rate cannot usually as a matter of logic be applied.[60] In a piece-work pay scheme the principle of equal pay requires that the pay of two groups of workers, one consisting predominantly of men and the other predominantly of women, is to be calculated on the basis of the same unit of measurement. Where the unit of measurement is the same for two groups of workers carrying out the same work or work of equal value, the principle of equal pay does not prohibit workers belonging to one or the other group from receiving different total pay if that is due to their different individual output. It follows that in a piece-work pay scheme, the mere finding that there is a difference in the average pay of two groups of workers, calculated on the basis of the total individual pay of all the workers belonging to one or the other group, does not suffice to establish that there is discrimination with regard to pay. It is for the national court, which alone is competent to assess the facts, to decide whether the unit of measurement applicable to the work carried out by the two groups of workers is the same or, if the two groups carry out work which is different but considered to be of equal value, whether the unit of measurement is objectively capable of ensuring that their total pay is the same.[61]

The CJEU assessed the question whether employees involved in the comparison should be necessarily hired by the same employer. The Court concluded that there is nothing in the wording of the relevant Treaty provision to suggest that the applicability of that provision is limited to situations in which men and women work for the same employer. According to the "single source principle" established by the CJEU, those provisions may be invoked before national courts, in particular in cases of discrimination arising directly from legislative provisions or collective labour agreements, as well as in cases in which work is carried out in the same establishment or service, whether private or public.[62]

59 For the summary of relevant case law: EQUINET European Network of Equality Bodies, How to build a case on equal pay, Brussels 2016, available at http://equineteurope.org/2016/11/18/equinet-handbook-how-to-build-a-case-on-equal-pay/ (accessed 5 May 2020), pp. 33–34; Susane Burri: Equal pay issues in EU law and related CJEU case Law. Charts of presentation held at the European Academy of Law (ERA) December 2019, available at www.era-comm.eu/oldoku/SNLLaw/EqualPay.htm.

60 Royal Copenhagen case, supra n. 16; Ellis & Watson, supra n. 4, at p. 161.

61 For the summary of relevant case law, see EQUINET, supra n. 59, at pp. 33–34; Burri, supra n. 59.

62 C-320/00. A. G. Lawrence and Others v Regent Office Care Ltd, Commercial Catering Group and Mitie Secure Services Ltd., ECLI:EU:C:2002:498 (Lawrence case) and the AG Opinion

Consequences that could be drawn from the relevant judgments of the CJEU have already been summarised and included in the secondary EU law. Recitals (9) and (10) of the Gender Directive lay down the following guidance for the assessment criteria of comparison:

> In accordance with settled case-law of the Court of Justice, in order to assess whether workers are performing the same work or work of equal value, it should be determined whether, having regard to a range of factors including the nature of the work and training and working conditions, those workers may be considered to be in a comparable situation. The Court of Justice has established that, in certain circumstances, the principle of equal pay is not limited to situations in which men and women work for the same employer.

Article 4 of the same directive sets out that "[i]n particular, where a job classification system is used for determining pay, it shall be based on the same criteria for both men and women and so drawn up as to exclude any discrimination on grounds of sex".

It is useful to contemplate the criteria of possible justification grounds of granting different pay for the members of a comparator pool elaborated by the CJEU, in order to make a clear distinction between the criteria of comparison. It is, again, ultimately for the national court, which alone is competent to assess the facts, to establish whether, in the particular case before it, these justification criteria can be established.[63] The employer can justify the difference in remuneration paid to persons performing equal work or work of equal value with and without protected characteristics, provided that there are objective grounds unrelated to any discrimination based on this protected characteristic.[64]

Possible grounds of justification[65] may include, under certain circumstances, the length of service,[66] flexibility concerning various working times and locations,[67] education and vocational training,[68] and the strong individual bargaining position

attached; C-256/01. Debra Allonby v Accrington & Rossendale College, Education Lecturing Services, trading as Protocol Professional and Secretary of State for Education and Employment, ECLI:EU:C:2004:18 (Allonby case). Discussed by Gábor Kártyás, Csorba kiegyenlítés: a kölcsönzött munkavállalók egyenlő bánásmódhoz való joga az új munka törvénykönyve után, *Esély*, 3, 25, pp. 26–27 (2013) (the study discusses the pay discrimination of temporary agent workers as well).

63 Brunnhofer judgment, supra n. 27.

64 Ibid.; Macarthys judgment, supra n. 55; C-243/95. Kathleen Hill and Ann Stapleton v The Revenue Commissioners and Department of Finance, ECLI:EU:C:1998:298 (Hill and Stapleton case).

65 These criteria were examined related to cases of indirect discrimination, where the Directives allow that apparently neutral but prima facie discriminatory provisions, criterions or practices can be objectively justified by a legitimate aim, and the means of achieving that aim are appropriate and necessary (Article 2(1b) of all the three Directives); C-427/11. Margaret Kenny and Others v Minister for Justice, Equality and Law Reform and Others, ECLI:EU:C:2013:122 (Kenny judgment), C-17/05. B. F. Cadman v Health & Safety Executive, ECLI:EU:C:2006:633 (Cadman judgment).

66 Danfoss judgment, supra n. 23; Cadman judgment, supra n. 65; Nimz judgment, supra n. 16.

67 Danfoss judgment, supra n. 23; Enderby judgment, supra n. 25; C-170/84. Bilka–Kaufhaus GmbH v Karin Weber von Hartz, ECLI:EU:C:1986:204.

68 WGKK judgment, supra n. 55.

(market value) of the candidates in recruitment negotiations.[69] On the contrary, other, apparently neutral criteria did not prove to be sufficient grounds of justification, such as economic considerations of the employer[70] or performance of the employee.[71] This latter cannot be taken into account as a justification ground because it is not objectively known at the time when the employee is appointed; it can be assessed only subsequently.[72]

5 Conclusions

The main function of anti-discrimination law is combating structural detriments of vulnerable, marginalised minorities in society compared to dominant groups. Therefore, legal constructs on prohibition of discrimination necessarily contain a comparative perspective: they focus on the contrast between the situation of persons with protected characteristics and their counterparts. Methodologies originally applied to solve discrimination cases relied on the actual comparison of the situation or the treatment with persons with and without specific protected characteristics. As demonstrated by this study, the development of equality theories, the recent changes in the world of labour, and difficulties arising in case law in terms of identification of the comparator resulted in a departure from the classical, comparison-based approach of scrutiny. The relatively broad framework determined by the Directives on rules on the burden of proof provides the opportunity for national legislation and courts to use different methods of investigating discrimination: when it appears to be appropriate, disregarding the actual counterpart or even the hypothetical identification of a comparator is possible as well.

The CJEU case law provides a valuable contribution for national law enforcement bodies in terms of interpretation of national law concerning the question of comparator in compliance with EU law.

In the judgments analysed in this chapter, the CJEU outlines the criteria for the identification of the comparator(s). In these cases, the CJEU respectively points out that establishment of the comparator pool requires a careful consideration of the individual circumstances and the facts of the case, such as the nature of the detriment allegedly suffered by the claimant or specific aspects of the concerned protected characteristic. Scrutinising the grounds of these judgments can be especially useful for the solution of cases where the discrimination occurs on the grounds of a specific characteristic of the claimant, which is difficult to associate with any of the protected characteristics named in the EU anti-discrimination legislation (e.g. family status, adherence to the LGBTQ minority).

69 Enderby judgment, supra n. 25.
70 Hill and Stapleton judgment, supra n. 64.
71 Brunnhofer judgment, supra n. 27.
72 For the summary of CJEU case law on justification of discrimination: Sabine Wagner-Steinringl. Equal Pay: EU legal framework CJEU case law. Charts of presentation held at the European Academy of Law (ERA) April 2017, available at www.era-comm.eu/oldoku/SNLLaw/EqualPay.htm (accessed 5 May 2020).

Suffering a detriment on the grounds of a specific protected characteristic is at the heart of the definitions of discriminatory conduct under EU anti-discrimination law. Focusing on this central element of the definitions, the CJEU could elaborate the concept of hypothetical comparator, where, with regard to the circumstances of the case, the causal link between the detriment and the protected characteristic could be established without finding an actual comparator. While the reference to a hypothetical comparator has already been included in the definitions set out by the Directives, the case law enables an even more extensive interpretation of these definitions in terms of the comparator: in some cases of direct or indirect discrimination, it is not necessary at all to find a comparator.

In cases of pay discrimination, the identification criteria for identifying the comparator pool should be clearly distinguished from the criteria for justification of differential treatment. The CJEU case law also elucidates which facts of the cases should be assessed as factors determining wage categories, and which ones can be taken into account as grounds of justification of different pay. Distinction between the two groups of facts is of particular importance in terms of proper allocation of the burden of proof between the parties.

Acknowledgements

The author wishes to thank Gábor Kártyás (associate professor at the Labour Law Department, Faculty of Law, Pázmány Péter Catholic University and senior advisor of the Kúria [Supreme Court of Hungary]) for the peer review of the text and for his useful commentaries.

Bibliography

Articles

Bitskey, Botond et al., *Kell-e antidiszkriminációs törvény?* 58 Jogtudományi Közlöny, 1 (2003).

Bitskey, Botond et al., *Az antidiszkriminációs szabályozás reformja*, 15 Acta Humana: Hungarian Centre for Human Rights Publications, 4, 13–40 (2014).

Citron, Danielle K. & Frank A. Pasquale, *The Scored Society: Due Process for Automated Predictions*, 89 Washington Law Review, 1 (2014).

Forejtova, Monika, *The Effort to Achieve Equality with the Help of the Reversal of the Burden of Proof in Anti-Discrimination Litigation*, 13 International and Comparative Law Review, 1, 135 (2013).

Goldberg, Suzanne B, *Discrimination by Comparison*, 120 The Yale Law Journal, 728 (2011).

Gyulavári, Tamás, *Három évvel az antidiszkriminációs jog reformja után*, 18 Esély: Társadalom és Szociálpolitikai Folyóirat, 3 (2007).

Holzleithner, Elisabeth. *Mainstreaming Equality: Dis/Entangling Grounds of Discrimination*, 14 Transnational Law and Contemporary Problems, 927–957 (2015).

Kártyás, Gábor, *Csorba kiegyenlítés: a kölcsönzött munkavállalók egyenlő bánásmódhoz való joga az új munka törvénykönyve után*, 3 Esély, 25 (2013).

Maliszewska-Nienartowicz, Justyna, *Direct and Indirect Discrimination in European Union Law – How to Draw a Dividing Line?* 3 International Journal of Social Sciences, 1, 41 (2014).

McColgan, Aileen, *Cracking the Comparator Problem: Discrimination, "Equal" Treatment and the Role of Comparisons*, 6 European Human Rights Law Review, 650 (2006).

Moreau, Sophia Reibetanz, *Equality Rights and the Relevance of Comparator Groups*, 5 Journal of Law and Equality, 81 (2006).

Mulder, Jule, *Dignity or Discrimination: What Paves the Road Towards Equal Recognition of Same-Sex Couples in the European Union?* 40 Journal of Social Welfare and Family Law, 1, 129 (2018).

O'Cinneide, Colm, *The Constitutionalization of Equality within the EU Legal Order: Sexual Orientation as Testing Ground*, 22 Maastricht Journal of European and Comparative Law, 3, 370 (2015).

Pothier, Diane, *Connecting Grounds of Discrimination to Real People's Real Experiences*, 13 CJWL/RFD, 37 (2001).

Smith, Belinda, *From Wardley to Purvis – How Far Has Australian Anti-Discrimination Law Come in 30 Years?* 21 Australian Journal of Labour Law, 3–30 (2008).

Zarsky, Tal Z., *Understanding Discrimination in the Scored Society*, 89 Washington Law Review, 1375 (2014).

Books

Aristoteles (translated by Miklós Szabó), *Nikomakhoszi Etika* (Európa Kiadó, Budapest, 1997).

Dworkin, Ronald, *Sovereign Virtue. The Theory and Practice of Equality* (Harvard University Press, Cambridge, Mass, 2000).

Ellis, Evelyn & Philippe Watson, *EU Anti-Discrimination Law* (2nd ed. Oxford EU Law Library, Oxford, 2013).

Feldman, David, *Civil Liberties and Human Rights in England and in Wales* (2nd ed. Oxford University Press, Oxford, 2002).

Fredman, Sandra, *Discrimination Law* (OUP, Oxford, 2011 [2nd ed.; reprint 2012]).

Kiss, György, *Alapjogok kollíziója a munkajogban* (Justis Tanácsadó Bt., Pécs, 2010).

Kovács, Kriszta, *Az egyenlőség felé. A hátrányos megkülönböztetés tilalma és a támogató intézkedések* (L' Harmattan, Budapest, 2012).

Schiek, Dagmar, Lisa B. Waddington & Mark Bell, *Cases, Materials and Text on National, Supranational and International Non-Discrimination Law* (Hart Publishing, Oxford and Portland, Oregon, 2007).

Taylor, Friedrich Winslow, *Scientific Management*, 7 The Sociological Review 3, 266 (1914); Taylor, Friedrich Winslow, *Scientific Management* (Harper & Brothers, New York, 1947).

Studies in Handbooks

Bell, Mark, The Right to Equality and Non-Discrimination. In: Tamara Hervey, Jeff Kenner (eds.), *Economic and Social Rights Under the EU Charter of Fundamental Rights: A Legal Perspective* (Oxford, Hart Publishing), 91–110, 101 (2003).

Halmos, Szilvia, Az "egyéb helyzet" alapján történő diszkrimináció a foglalkoztatásban: A magyar gyakorlat elemzése az elmélet, a nemzetközi jog és az alkotmánybírósági gyakorlat tükrében. In: Márta Ábrahám (ed.), *Mailáth György Tudományos Pályázat 2017: Díjazott dolgozatok* (Országos Bírósági Hivatal, Budapest), 612–614 (2017).

Other Publications

Beale, Anne, *Proving Discrimination: The Shift of Burden of Proof and Access to Evidence*, 2018. www.era-comm.eu/oldoku/Adiskri/03_Burden_of_proof/118DV18_Beale_Paper_EN.pdf, accessed: 5 May 2020.

Burri, Susane, *Equal Pay Issues in EU Law and Related CJEU Case Law*. Charts of presentation held at the European Academy of Law (ERA) December 2019. www.era-comm.eu/oldoku/SNLLaw/EqualPay.htm.

Chopin, Isabelle & Catharina Germaine, *A Comparative Analysis of Non-Discrimination Law in Europe 2017* (European Commission, Directorate-General for Justice and Consumers, Publications Office of the European Union, Luxembourg), 51 (2018).

EQUINET European Network of Equality Bodies, *How to Build a Case on Equal Pay*, Brussels 2016. http://equineteurope.org/2016/11/18/equinet-handbook-how-to-build-a-case-on-equal-pay/, accessed: 5 May 2020.

European Union Agency for Fundamental Rights: Handbook on European Non-Discrimination Law; Publications Office of the European Union, Luxembourg, 2018, 160–162. https://fra.europa.eu/en/publication/2018/handbook-european-law-non-discrimination, accessed: 05 May 2020.

Wagner-Steinringl, Sabine. *Equal Pay: EU Legal Framework CJEU Case Law*. Charts of presentation held at the European Academy of Law (ERA) April 2017. www.era-comm.eu/oldoku/SNLLaw/EqualPay.htm, accessed: 5 May 2020.

CJEU Cases

C-43/75. Gabrielle Defrenne v Société anonyme belge de navigation aérienne Sabena, ECLI:EU:C:1976:56 (Defrenne-II case).

C-129/79. Macarthys Ltd v Wendy Smith, ECLI:EU:C:1980:103 (Macarthys case).

C-96/80. J.P. Jenkins v Kingsgate (Clothing Productions) Ltd., ECLI:EU:C:1981:80 (Jenkins judgment).

C-170/84. Bilka – Kaufhaus GmbH v Karin Weber von Hartz, ECLI:EU:C:1986:204.

C-109/88. Handels- og Kontorfunktionærernes Forbund I Danmark v Dansk Arbejdsgiverforening, acting on behalf of Danfoss, ECLI:EU:C:1989:383.

C-177/88. Elisabeth Johanna Pacifica Dekker v Stichting Vormingscentrum voor Jong Volwassenen (VJV-Centrum) Plus, ECLI:EU:C:1990:383 (Dekker judgment).

C-33/89. Maria Kowalska tegen Freie und Hansestadt Hamburg, ECLI:EU:C:1990:265.

C-184/89. Helga Nimz v Freie und Hansestadt Hamburg, ECLI:EU:C:1991:50 (Nimz case).

C-127/92. Dr. Pamela Mary Enderby kontra Frenchay Health Authority és Secretary of State for Health, ECLI:EU:C:1993:859 (Enderby judgment).

C-399/92. Stadt Lengerich v Angelika Helmig and Waltraud Schmidt v Deutsche Angestellten-Krankenkasse and Elke Herzog v Arbeiter-Samariter-Bund Landverband Hamburg eV and Dagmar Lange v Bundesknappschaft Bochum and Angelika Kussfeld v Firma Detlef Bogdol GmbH and Ursula Ludewig v Kreis Segeberg, ECLI:EU:C:1994:415 (Helmig case).

C-297/93. Rita Grau-Hupka v Stadtgemeinde Bremen, ECLI:EU:C:1994:406.

C-400/93. Specialarbejderforbundet i Danmark v Dansk Industri, formerly Industriens Arbejdsgivere, acting for Royal Copenhagen A/S., ECLI:EU:C:1995:155 (Royal Copenhagen case).

C-13/94. P v S and Cornwall County Council, ECLI:EU:C:1996:170.

C-243/95. Kathleen Hill and Ann Stapleton v The Revenue Commissioners and Department of Finance, ECLI:EU:C:1998:298. (Hill and Stapleton case).

C-309/97. Angestelltenbetriebsrat der Wiener Gebietskrankenkasse v Wiener Gebietskrankenkasse (WGKK case) ECLI:EU:C:1999:241.
C-381/99. Susanna Brunnhofer v Bank der österreichischen Postsparkasse AG, ECLI:EU:C:2001:358 (Brunnhofer judgment).
C-320/00. A. G. Lawrence and Others v Regent Office Care Ltd, Commercial Catering Group and Mitie Secure Services Ltd., ECLI:EU:C:2002:498 (Lawrence case).
C-256/01. Debra Allonby v Accrington & Rossendale College, Education Lecturing Services, trading as Protocol Professional and Secretary of State for Education and Employment, ECLI:EU:C:2004:18 (Allonby case).
C-191/03. North Western Health Board v Margaret McKenna, ECLI:EU:C:2005:513 (McKenna case).
C-13/05. Sonia Chacón Navas v Eurest Colectividades SA [GC], ECLI:EU:C:2006:456.
C-17/05. B. F. Cadman v Health & Safety Executive, ECLI:EU:C:2006:633 (Cadman judgment).
C-267/06. Tadao Maruko v Versorgungsanstalt der deutschen Bühnen, ECLI:EU:C:2008:179.
C-303/06. S. Coleman v Attridge Law and Steve Law, ECLI:EU:C:2008:415. (Coleman case).
C-506/06. Sabine Mayr v Bäckerei und Konditorei Gerhard Flöckner, ECLI:EU:C:2008:119 (Mayr case).
C-555/07. Seda Kücükdeveci v Swedex GmbH & Co. KG, ECLI:EU:C:2009:429 (Kücükdeveci case).
C-144/08. Jürgen Römer v Freie und Hansestadt Hamburg, ECLI:EU:C:2011:286.
C-104/10. Kelly v National University of Ireland (University College, Dublin), ECLI:EU:C:2011:506 (Kelly case).
C-310/10. Ministerul Justiţiei şi Libertăţilor Cetăţeneşti v Ştefan Agafiţei and Others, ECLI:EU:C:2011:467.
C-415/10. Galina Meister v Speech Design Carrier Systems GmbH, ECLI:EU:C:2012:217 (Meister case).
C-427/11. Margaret Kenny and Others v Minister for Justice, Equality and Law Reform and Others, ECLI:EU:C:2013:122 (Kenny judgment).
C-176/12. Association de médiation sociale v Union locale des syndicats CGT and Others, ECLI:EU:C:2014:2.
C-267/12. Frédéric Hay v Crédit agricole mutuel de Charente-Maritime et des Deux-Sèvres, ECLI:EU:C:2013:823.
C-356/12. Wolfgang Glatzel v Freistaat Bayern, ECLI:EU:C:2014:350.
C-441/14. Dansk Industri (DI), agissant pour Ajos A/S v Sucession Karsten Eigil Rasmussen, ECLI:EU:C:2016:278 (Dansk Industri case).
C-406/15. Petya Milkova v Izpalnitelen direktor na Agentsiata za privatizatsia i sledprivatizatsionen kontrol, ECLI:EU:C:2017:198.
C-443/15. David L. Parris v Trinity College Dublin and Others, ECLI:EU:C:2016:897.
C-414/16. Vera Egenberger v Evangelisches Werk für Diakonie und Entwicklung e.V, ECLI:EU:C:2018:257 (Egenberger case).

EU Legislation

Council Directive 97/80/EC of 15 December 1997 on the burden of proof in cases of discrimination based on sex, OJ L 14, 20.1.1998, p. 6–8.
Council Directive 97/81/EC of 15 December 1997 concerning the Framework Agreement on part-time work concluded by UNICE, CEEP and the ETUC – Annex: Framework

agreement on part-time work, OJ L 14, 20.1.1998, 9–14 (Part Time Work Directive), Annex, section 1.

Council Directive 1999/70/EC of 28 June 1999 concerning the framework agreement on fixed-term work concluded by ETUC, UNICE and CEEP, OJ L 175, 10.7.1999, 43–48 (Fixed-term Work Directive), Annex, section 1.

Council Directive 2000/43/EC of 29 June 2000 implementing the principle of equal treatment between persons irrespective of racial or ethnic origin; OJ L 180, 19.7.2000, 22–26 (Race Directive).

Council Directive 2000/78/EC of 27 November 2000 establishing a general framework for equal treatment in employment and occupation, OJ L 303, 2.12.2000, 16–22 (Framework Directive).

Directive 2006/54/EC of the European Parliament and of the Council of 5 July 2006 on the implementation of the principle of equal opportunities and equal treatment of men and women in matters of employment and occupation (recast), OJ L 204, 26.7.2006, 23–36 ("Gender Directive"), (the "Gender directive" repealed and recast a set of previous directives related to gender-based discrimination in the field of employment).

Directive 2008/104/EC of the European Parliament and of the Council of 19 November 2008 on temporary agency work, OJ L 327, 5.12.2008, 9–14 (Temporary Agency Work Directive), article 1, 2 and 5.

National Legislation of Member States

Loi n° 2013–404 du 17 mai 2013 ouvrant le mariage aux couples de personnes de même sexe) took effect in 18 May 2013. (The text of the act is available: www.legifrance.gouv.fr/jorf/id/JORFTEXT000027414540?r=V660JkU8Td; accessed: 21 January 2021.

3 Dutch Equal Treatment Law

A Sophisticated Field of Law

Susanne Burri

1 Introduction

Dutch legislation aimed at combatting discrimination has thoroughly evolved since 1975 and currently represents a broad and sophisticated field of law.[1] The application of the legal provisions to numerous situations – by the Dutch equality body in particular – offers rich insights into the potential of equal treatment law in practice. These specific aspects make Dutch equal treatment law particularly interesting for foreign scholars and practitioners.

This chapter provides an overview and assessment of the most relevant characteristics of Dutch equal treatment law applying to employment. The implementation of EU directives on equal treatment[2] has mainly shaped this field of law.[3] This shows, for example, in the legal definitions of forms of discrimination (e.g. direct and indirect discrimination, harassment and sexual harassment), allowed exceptions and justifications, the burden of proof, the protection against victimisation and enforcement and sanctions.

The most relevant statutory equal treatment legislation applicable to employment are the General Equal Treatment Act (GETA), the Disability Discrimination

1 The most recent and comprehensive handbook is Peter Vas Nunes, *Gelijke behandeling in de arbeid* (Den Haag: Boom juridisch, 2018), 870 pp.

2 See for an overview for example Evelyn Ellis & Philippa Watson, EU *Anti-Discrimination Law, Oxford EU Law Library* (2nd ed., Oxford: Oxford University Press, 2012); Susanne Burri, Equal Treatment: The EU Approach, in Frans Pennings & Gijsbert Vonk (eds.), *Research Handbook on European Social Security Law* (Cheltenham: Edward Elgar Publishing, 2015), pp. 231–256; Susanne Burri & Albertine Veldman, Gelijke behandeling als grondrecht (pp. 151–222) and Flexibele arbeid (pp. 223–248), in Frans Pennings & Saskia Peters (eds.), *Europees Arbeidsrecht* (Deventer: Wolters Kluwer, 2016).

3 The European network of legal experts in gender equality and non-discrimination publishes country reports on the implementation of the gender equality and non-discrimination directives, which are updated annually. See, for the Netherlands, Marlies Vegter, *European Network of Legal Experts in Gender Equality and Non-Discrimination, Country Report Gender Equality, Netherlands 2022* (Luxembourg: Publications Office of the European Union, 2022); Karin de Vries, *European Network of Legal Experts in Gender Equality and Non-discrimination, Country Report Non-discrimination, Netherlands 2021* (Luxembourg: Publications Office of the European Union, 2021), both available at www.equalitylaw.eu/country/netherlands.

DOI: 10.4324/9781003306962-4

Act (DDA), the Age Discrimination Act (ADA) and the Equal Treatment Act of men and women (ETA m/w) in addition to specific acts on flexible work (part-time and fixed-term employment contracts) and a few provisions in the Civil Code (CC). The assessment of this legislation forms the core of this chapter, while less relevant national and international standards applicable to employment issues are only addressed briefly. A few conclusions in the light of lessons to be learned from this complex field of law close this chapter.

2 Legislation

2.1 Constitution and International Equal Treatment Standards

Article 1 of the Dutch Constitution prohibits discrimination based on religion, belief, political opinion, race, sex or any other grounds. The list of discrimination grounds is thus non-exhaustive.[4] A proposal to mention explicitly the grounds of disability and sexual orientation in this article[5] was adopted not only in the Second but also in the First Chamber of Parliament in February 2021.[6] In order to amend the Constitution, a specific procedure has to be followed, requiring a majority of two-thirds of both Chambers of Parliament. This procedure has now been initiated.[7] Given the fact that statutory legislation includes the grounds of disability and sexual orientation, including these grounds explicitly in Article 1 of the Constitution would be welcome as this contributes to clarity.

Article 1 of the Constitution reflects a general principle that has to be taken into account by the legislature, the administration and the courts. According to Article 120 of the Constitution, formal statutory acts cannot be subject to a constitutional review by courts, and there is no constitutional court in the Netherlands. This limits the impact of Article 1 in practice, but as the fundamental principle of equality is enshrined in the first article of the Constitution, this article has certainly a great symbolic value. A legislative proposal published in 2001 to amend Article 120 of the Constitution in order to allow a partial constitutional review of statutory legislation was not adopted with the two-thirds majority required to amend the Constitution and was finally withdrawn.[8] The debate is ongoing, as a State Commission on the Parliamentary System in the Netherlands is in favour of a

4 The addition of 'any other grounds' was included by amendment with this aim: Kamerstukken II 1976–1977, 13872, 18.

5 The Minister of Internal Affairs decided to not include an explicit reference to the grounds 'age' and 'nationality' in Article 1 as these two grounds are not yet considered to be 'constitutionally mature': Kamerstukken I 2020–2021, 32411, G, pp. 1–2.

6 Kamerstukken I 2020–2021, 32411.

7 Stb. 2021, 87.

8 Kamerstukken II 2001–2002, 28331, 1. The proposal is withdrawn; Kamerstukken II 2018–2019, 32334, 13 Handelingen II 2018–2019, 10, 8.

constitutional court.[9] At the time of writing, April 2021, no legislative proposal on a constitutional court is (yet) pending.

In practice, specific statutory acts that elaborate Article 1 of the Constitution are the most important legal tools in Dutch law to combat discrimination in different areas, including employment. Statutory equal treatment legislation protects discrimination on the grounds of age. Given the non-exhaustive list of discrimination grounds in Article 1, it is accepted that Article 1 of the Constitution also applies to age discrimination. Article 1 requires equal treatment in equal circumstances of all persons in the Netherlands by the legislature, the administration and the courts in all fields of economic and social life. This article can be invoked in vertical relations (e.g. against an act adopted by a municipality), and the courts occasionally apply it in horizontal relations.[10] In practice the possibility to review statutory legislation in the light of European and international anti-discrimination provisions is also relevant.

The Netherlands is a State Party to the European Convention on Human Rights (ECHR), including Protocol 12, as well as the European Social Charter. Article 14 ECHR has a limited scope as it prohibits only discrimination in the enjoyment of rights of the ECHR. However, since April 2005, Protocol 12 (Article 1) prohibits discrimination in the enjoyment of any right set forth by law and ensures thus an independent right.

The Netherlands has ratified the major UN Conventions.[11] The Netherlands adheres to a monist system.[12] This entails that international standards of equal treatment and non-discrimination can be applied directly by Dutch courts even to review statutory legislation if a provision of an international treaty is sufficiently clear and precise.[13] This is, for example, the case of Article 26 of the International Covenant on Civil and Political Rights (ICCPR). In practice, Dutch statutory equal treatment legislation and provisions of the Civil Code are the most relevant in relation to employment and apply in horizontal relationships.

9 Staatscommissie Parlementair Stelsel. Its main assignment was to investigate whether the Dutch democracy is capable to continue functioning adequately in the context of societal changes. See for more information https://www.parlement.com/id/vkb8nqem2auu/staatscommissie_parlementair_stelsel, where a translation in English of the final report is available.

10 See D. E. Bunschoten, *Tekst en commentaar Grondwet & Statuut, Gelijkheidsbeginsel, verbod van discriminatie bij Grondwet*, Artikel 1 (5th ed., Deventer: Kluwer, 2018).

11 The International Covenant on Civil and Political Rights (ICCPR); the International Covenant on Economic, Social and Cultural Rights (ICESCR); the International Convention on the Elimination of All Forms of Racial Discrimination (CERD); the Convention on the Elimination of All Forms of Discrimination Against Women (CEDAW); the Convention on the Rights of the Child (CRC); the Convention on the Rights of Persons with Disabilities (CRPD); and Optional Protocols of the ICCPR, CERD and CEDAW.

12 In a monist system, national and international rules that a state has accepted form a unity. In a dualist system, national and international standards are two different systems and international rules have to be integrated into national law.

13 Arts 93 & 94 Constitution.

2.2 Equal Treatment Legislation

Several statutory equal treatment acts elaborate Article 1 of the Constitution, in particular for horizontal relations.[14] These acts apply to the private and the public sector and implement EU gender equality and non-discrimination directives.[15] In Dutch law, the more neutral term 'distinction' is used instead of 'discrimination', which has a pejorative connotation. The use of the term 'distinction' in Dutch law has been criticised both in academic literature and by the Council of State.[16] The Council of State considered that discrimination relates to specific grounds, such as race or sex, and that the Dutch implementing legislation should be in line with the EU terminology and therefore prohibit discrimination.[17] Some authors agreed and would reserve the term 'discrimination' for systematic forms of exclusion and disadvantage of certain less powerful groups in society on specific grounds.[18] The Equal Treatment Commission (ETC) preferred to use the term 'distinction', considering that defendants would be more ready to put their behaviour into question and amend it. In addition, the term 'discrimination' could suggest that intent to disadvantage would be required, which is not the case. The government decided not to change the terminology.[19] It is accepted that the term 'distinction' in Dutch equal treatment law is in conformity with the EU gender equality and non-discrimination law, in which the term 'discrimination' is used. It should be noted that not all forms of distinctions are prohibited, only unlawful distinctions. In the author's view, it would have been better for the sake of clarity and consistency to use the same terminology in Dutch legislation as in the EU directives. The term 'distinction' will be used here only when citing legal provisions.

The non-discrimination provisions are scattered over specific acts and different fields of law (civil law, working conditions law, criminal law). This makes the system very complex as there are differences in scope, who has to ensure the equal treatment norm and how to review the (un)lawfulness of a provision or practice, as well as the competent organ. However, a short overview of relevant

14 Dutch legislation is published in Dutch at https://wetten.nl.

15 In particular in the field of employment Directive 2006/54/EC of the European Parliament and of the Council of 5 July 2006 on the implementation of the principle of equal opportunities and equal treatment of men and women in matters of employment and occupation (recast) [2006] OJ L 204/23 (and repealed directives 75/117, 76/207, 86/378, 86/613, 97/80, 2002/73) as well as Council Directive 2000/43/EC of 29 June 2000 implementing the principle of equal treatment between persons irrespective of racial or ethnic origin [2000], OJ L 180/22 and Council Directive 2000/78/EC of 27 November 2000 establishing a legal framework for equal treatment in employment and occupation [2000] OJ L 303/16.

16 See for example Rikki Holtmaat, Marjolein van den Brink, Aart Hendriks et al., (eds.), *Gelijkheid en (andere) Grondrechten* (Deventer: Kluwer, 2004); Raad van State, Advies bij wetsvoorstel 'Implementatie Artikel 13-richtlijnen', Kamerstukken II 2001–2002, 28187 A.

17 Ibid., p. 4.

18 See for example Rikki Holtmaat, Gelijkheid en non-discriminatie als grondrecht. Een pleidooi voor het maken van onderscheid tussen discriminatie en ongelijke behandeling in: Holtmaat, van den Brink, Hendriks et al., supra n. 16, at pp. 67–96.

19 Kamerstukken II 2002–2003, 28770, 3, pp. 4–5.

acts and provisions is useful here as it highlights the broad scope of Dutch equal treatment law that is relevant in employment. The GETA, DDA and the ADA are the most important acts in practice, and the Institute for Human Rights (IHR)[20] – the Dutch Equality Body[21] – plays a fundamental role in the enforcement of these three acts.[22]

The GETA,[23] adopted in 1994 after lengthy parliamentary proceedings, prohibits discrimination on the grounds of religion, belief, political opinion, race, sex (which includes explicitly since 1 November 2019 sex characteristics, gender identity and gender expression),[24] nationality (citizenship), heterosexual or homosexual orientation, and civil status. The DDA, in force since 2003, covers disability or chronic illness.[25] The ADA, in force since 2004, applies to equal treatment on the grounds of age in employment.[26]

The ETA m/w of 1980[27] prohibits sex discrimination[28] in employment and specifies some aspects of equal treatment of men and women in access to employment, the principle of equal pay for work of equal value and equal treatment in pensions.[29]

Specific non-discrimination legislation on flexible work was adopted in 1996. The Act on working time prohibits discrimination based on working time, unless objectively justified.[30] Similarly, the Act on temporary or permanent employment contracts adopted in 2002 prohibits discrimination based on the temporary

20 And its predecessor, the Equal Treatment Commission (ETC). See www.mensenrechten.nl.

21 The obligation to appoint an equality body follows from EU directives, see for example Art. 20 of the Recast Directive 2006/54 and Art. 13 of the Race Directive 2000/43. See further Niall Cowley, European network of legal experts in gender equality and non-discrimination, Equality bodies making a difference (Luxembourg, Publications Office of the European Union, 2018), available at www.equalitylaw.eu/downloads/4763-equality-bodies-making-a-difference-pdf-707-kb.

22 As well as regards differences in working time and in permanent and fixed-term contracts.

23 Algemene wet gelijke behandeling, Stb. 1994, 230.

24 The aim of this inclusion is to protect transgender and intersex persons. Not all persons fit in the binary male/female model, and this addition is meant to include all sex-related aspects explicitly under the concept of sex. Sex characteristics of intersex persons prove that not all persons fit within the male/female binary. Gender identity and gender expression relate to transgender: Kamerstukken II 2016–2017, 34650, 3.

25 Wet gelijke behandeling op grond van handicap of chronische ziekte, Stb. 2003, 206.

26 Wet gelijke behandeling op grond van leeftijd bij de arbeid, Stb. 2004, 30.

27 Wet gelijke behandeling van mannen en vrouwen, Stb. 1980, 86 and Art. 7:646 CC.

28 The GETA is without prejudice to existing sex discrimination law: the ETA m/w and Arts. 7:646, 7:667 & 7:670 CC (Art. 4 GETA). Therefore, as regards sex discrimination, the GETA applies for example when there is no employer.

29 This act implements Council Directive 76/207/EEC of 9 February 1976 on the implementation of the principle of equal treatment for men and women as regards access to employment, vocational training and promotion, and working conditions [1976] OJ L 039/40, now repealed. In order to implement EU Directive 75/117 (Council Directive 75/117/EEC of 10 February 1975 on the approximation of the laws of the Member States relating to the application of the principle of equal pay for men and women [1975] OJ L 45/19) the 1975 Equal Pay Act between women and men was adopted, but now repealed: Wet gelijk loon voor mannen en vrouwen, Stb. 1975, 129.

30 Wet verbod van onderscheid naar arbeidsduur, Stb. 1996, 391 and Art. 7:648 CC. See also Council Directive 97/81/EC of 15 December 1997 concerning the Framework Agreement on part-time work concluded by UNICE, CEEP and the ETUC, [1998] OJ L 14/9.

or non-temporary character of the employment contract, unless objectively justified.[31] The Act on temporary agency work requires equal treatment in working conditions of temporary agency workers and workers fulfilling equal functions or functions of equal value in the undertaking where temporary agency workers are assigned.[32]

In the Civil Code, three articles require equal treatment in employment on the grounds of sex (Article 7:646 CC), working time (Article 7:648 CC) and temporary contracts (Article 7:649 CC).

The Act on working conditions imposes on employers the obligation to prevent (and if that is not possible, to reduce) psychosocial stress. Such stress can be due to direct or indirect discrimination and/or sexual harassment.[33] Similarly, employers in the public sector have such an obligation in accordance with the Act on civil servants.[34] Work councils have a specific obligation to ensure that discrimination does not occur in the undertaking and have to promote, in particular, equal treatment for men and women and the integration in the enterprise of persons with disabilities and minorities.[35]

Finally, a few provisions in the Criminal Code prohibit insulting and discriminatory (hate) speech, as well as incitation to hate speech and discrimination in the political, economic, social or cultural sphere.[36] However, these provisions do not often play a role in the field of employment.[37] Therefore, only the equal treatment provisions most relevant in employment are discussed in the next sections.

2.2.1 Scope

The scope of the Dutch equal treatment acts and provisions differs as to who has to ensure equal treatment, as well as who is protected against discrimination. The GETA, the DDA and the ADA encompass a general non-discrimination norm, without specifying who has to ensure that this norm is respected. Not only employers[38] but also other parties involved in employment issues are accountable

31 Uitvoeringswet EU-richtlijn 1999/70/EG (raamovereenkomst door het EVV, de UNICE en het CEEP inzake arbeidsovereenkomsten voor bepaalde tijd), Stb. 2002, 560 implements Council Directive 1999/70/EC of 28 June 1999 concerning the framework agreement on fixed-term work concluded by ETUC, UNICE and CEEP [1999] OJ L 175/43. See also Art.7:649 CC.

32 Art. 8 Wet allocatie arbeidskrachten door intermediairs, introduced by Stb. 2012, 173, which implements Directive 2008/104/EC of the European Parliament and of the Council of 19 November 2008 on temporary agency work [2008] OJ L 327/9.

33 Arts 1(3)(e) & 3(2) Arbeidsomstandighedenwet.

34 Art. 4(1) Ambtenarenwet 2017.

35 Art. 28 §3 Act on Work Councils (Wet op de ondernemingsraden).

36 Arts 137c–137g & 429quater Criminal Code (Wetboek van Strafrecht).

37 See however for an example about unlawful discrimination on the ground of race of a job applicant, District Court of Gelderland, 27 August 2014, ECLI:NL:RBGEL:2014:5457.

38 Discrimination by managers are attributed to the employer, see for example District Court The Hague, 21 March 2018, ECLI:NL:RBDHA:2018:3423.

for equal treatment, such as social partners in collective agreements,[39] pension funds, insurers and temporary work agencies.[40] Temporary work agencies have also the obligation to prevent discrimination by undertakings to which their clients are assigned.[41]

However, these norms do not apply to unilateral acts of the public authorities (*eenzijdig overheidshandelen*).[42] For example, decisions of civil servants when issuing passports based on the Act on Passports do not fall under the GETA, and therefore the IHR lacks competence.[43] This limit of the competence of the IHR – which offers a free and easily accessible procedure – is in the author's view a weak aspect of the statutory Dutch equal treatment legislation, as it restricts access to justice. During the evaluation of the GETA in 2008, many organisations pleaded for the extension of the scope of this Act in this respect. The government did not follow this recommendation, considering that there are enough possibilities to combat discrimination by the legislature, for example in the Constitution, in administrative law and in international treaties.[44] Courts are indeed competent to apply for example self-executing international equality norms, such as Article 26 ICCPR, when reviewing legislation. However, individuals might not want to start court proceedings which can be costly and lengthy compared to the IHR procedure when they feel discriminated against by a unilateral act of a public authority.

In three equal treatment provisions in the CC, the norm addressee is only the employer (Articles 7: 646 CC, 7: 648:CC & 7:649 CC).

Not only can job seekers and workers rely on the equal treatment provisions, but also the self-employed.[45] The protection of workers extends beyond the end of the employment relationship (e.g. in case of dismissal or victimisation). Who can complain follows also from CJEU (Court of Justice of the EU) case law. Non-discrimination law therefore applies to quasi-independent workers[46] or even in the absence of an identifiable victim.[47]

39 See for example opinion 2015–37 of the Institute for Human Rights (IHR). In this case, the IHR relied on the prohibition concerning working time in the Wet verbod van onderscheid naar arbeidsduur, which also provides a general norm: https://mensenrechten.nl/nl/oordeel/2015-37.

40 Sometimes both the temporary work agency and the hiring undertaking infringe the equal treatment legislation. See for example IHR opinions 2018–37: https://mensenrechten.nl/nl/oordeel/2018-37 and 2018–38: https://mensenrechten.nl/nl/oordeel/2018-38.

41 See for example IHR opinions 2020–86, https://mensenrechten.nl/nl/oordeel/2020-86 and 2020–87: https://mensenrechten.nl/nl/oordeel/2020-87.

42 Except for the ground race; see Art. 7a GETA.

43 IHR opinion 2016–91: https://mensenrechten.nl/nl/oordeel/2016-91.

44 Kamerstukken II, 28 481, 5, pp. 6–7.

45 See in particular Art. 6 GETA, Art. 5 DDA, Art. 4 ADA and Art. 3 ETA m/v.

46 Case C-256/01 Debra Allonby v Accrington & Rossendale College, Education Lecturing Services, trading as Protocol Professional and Secretary of State for Education and Employment ECLI:EU:C:2004:18.

47 Case C-54/07 Centrum voor gelijkheid van kansen en voor racismebestrijding v Firma Feryn NV ECLI:EU:C:2008:397.

The material scope of the GETA, the DDA, the ADA, the ETA m/w and the three provisions in the CC is broad and in conformity with EU law. Equal treatment legislation applies to all sectors of public and private employment. The GETA also applies to the supply of goods and services, and for race discrimination to social protection, including social security and social advantages (Article 7a GETA). The interpretation of the material scope in relation to employment of the GETA, the DDA and the ADA is generally extensive. In Article 5 §1 GETA, the prohibition of discrimination applies to:[48]

a. public advertising of a job opportunity and procedures leading to the filling of vacancies;
b. job placement;
c. the commencement or termination of an employment relationship;
d. the appointment and dismissal of civil servants;
e. terms and conditions of employment;
f. permitting staff to receive education or training during or prior to employment;
g. promotion;
h. working conditions.

The scope is similarly drafted in Article 4 DDA and Article 3 ADA. The description of material scope in the ETA m/w is roughly the same but adds specific obligations as regards recruitment. When a job opportunity is offered, it should be clear that the occupation can be fulfilled by a man or a woman, and this has also to be reflected in the job description. The material scope of the three CC provisions is more limited.[49]

The prohibition to discriminate in self-employment[50] covers the conditions for and access to self-employment and the possibilities to deploy self-employed activities.[51]

Dutch equal treatment law also covers vocational training and education. Article 7 GETA prohibits discrimination in the supply of or access to goods or services which embrace all forms of education;[52] the provision of career orientation and vocational guidance; and advice or information regarding the choice of

48 Please note that this translation is based on a translation provided by the IHR and is unofficial. The updated text is translated by the author, however not literally.

49 Art. 7:646 §1 CC (sex) and Art. 7:648 §1 CC (working time) not apply to recruitment and Art. 7:648 §1 (fixed-term) only applies to working conditions.

50 The term employed in Dutch law is *vrije beroep*, which translated means liberal professions. But this article applies broader to self-employment, see for example IHR opinion 2019–109: https://mensenrechten.nl/nl/oordeel/2019-109.

51 Art. 6 GETA, Art. 5 DDA, Art. 4 ADA and Art. 2 ETA m/w.

52 The scope of this article is much broader, as it also covers the supply of goods and services by for example by the public service and by institutions which are active in the field of housing, social services, health care, cultural affairs or education.

an educational institution or career. The scope of the prohibition of discrimination in the supply and access to services is similar in Article 5b DDA.[53] The scope of Article 5 ADA is more limited, as it prohibits discrimination in the provision of career orientation and vocational guidance, as well as in the access to, the supply, tests and ending of education aimed at entry to or functioning in the labour market.[54]

Discrimination in relation to the membership of or involvement in an employers' organisation or trade union, or a professional occupational organisation, as well as with regard to the benefits which arise from that membership or involvement, is prohibited as well.[55]

The GETA is not applicable to legal relations within churches and religious communities, as well as the office of minister of religion (Article 3 GETA). An employment relation with a private character falls also outside the scope of the GETA (Articles 5 §3a & 7 §3a GETA), for example, when a nurse is taking care of another person in the private household.

While the ADA is limited to labour issues (including pensions), the DDA covers the areas of housing and public transport in addition to the material scope of the GETA, as described above.

Finally, in 2019 an Act prohibiting face-covering clothing in education, public transport, public buildings and healthcare entered into force after a lot of public debate.[56] The adoption of this so-called burqa ban reflects the steady increase of Islamophobic feelings in the Netherlands and has been strongly criticised. The IHR considered the very broad and general scope of this Act not to be in line with the freedom of religion or the prohibition of discrimination on grounds of religion of the GETA and other non-discrimination provisions, such as Article 1 of the Constitution.[57] This Act is merely symbolic, as it is estimated that the number of Muslim women that would be affected by the ban is about 400. Mayors of several major cities including Amsterdam and Rotterdam have announced that they will not prioritise the enforcement of the ban.

2.2.2 Concepts

The grounds of discrimination such as race or disability are not defined in Dutch equal treatment legislation. The concept of 'race' has to be interpreted extensively

53 However, this provision does not apply to housing and public transport: Art. 5b §2 DDA.

54 Art. 4 ETA m/w is similar.

55 Art. 6a GETA, Arts 1 & 1a DDA, Arts 1 & 2 ADA and Art. 4a ETA m/w.

56 See Titia Loenen, European network of legal experts in gender equality and non-discrimination, Entry into force of Act prohibiting face covering clothing in education, public transport, public buildings and healthcare, available at www.equalitylaw.eu/downloads/4952-the-netherlands-entry-into-force-of-act-prohibiting-face-covering-clothin,g-in-education-public-transport-public-buildings-and-healthcare-pdf-85-kb.

57 CRvdM, Verbod gezichtsbedekkende kleding, available at https://mensenrechten.nl/nl/toegelicht/verbod-gezichtsbedekkende-kleding.

in accordance with the UN Convention on the elimination of race discrimination and also embraces colour, descent, and national or ethnic origin.[58] The concept of disability has now been defined by the CJEU taking into account the definition of the UN Convention on the Rights of Persons with Disabilities (which has been approved by the EU),[59] and this broad definition thus applies also in Dutch law. The GETA specifies since 2019 that sex includes sex characteristics, gender identity and gender expression.[60] The aim of this inclusion is to protect transgender and intersex persons.[61]

Dutch equal treatment legislation prohibits an unlawful 'distinction' (*onderscheid*). The drafting of the concepts of 'distinction' is similar in the GETA, the DDA, the ADA, the ETA m/w and Article 7:646 CC.[62] The concepts and system of the GETA are described here. The prohibition to discriminate includes an instruction to discriminate (Article 1 §1a GETA). The definitions of the concepts of 'distinction' in Dutch law follow closely the EU definitions of direct and indirect discrimination, harassment and sexual harassment. Just as in EU law, the approach is symmetric, meaning that, for example, the prohibition of sex discrimination can be relied on by either women or men.[63]

2.2.2.1 DEFINITIONS

The concepts are defined in Articles 1 & 1a GETA as follows:

> *Direct distinction*: '[I]f a person is treated differently from another person in a comparable situation is or would be treated on the grounds of religion, belief, political opinion, race, sex, nationality, hetero- or homosexual orientation or civil status' (Article 1 §1b GETA). Direct sex discrimination includes a distinction based on pregnancy, confinement and motherhood (Article 1 §3 GETA). Justifications (exceptions) to direct discrimination are only possible if specifically allowed in legislation. Which direct discrimination can be justified differs for each ground of discrimination (see section 2.2.3).

58 See for more information Karin de Vries, *Country Report Non-discrimination, Netherlands 2020* (Luxembourg: Publications Office of the European Union, 2020), pp. 16–18, available at www.equalitylaw.eu/country/netherlands.

59 This Convention applies to 'Persons with disabilities include those who have long-term physical, mental, intellectual or sensory impairments which in interaction with various barriers may hinder their full and effective participation in society on an equal basis with others' (Article 1). See Case C-335/11 HK Danmark, acting on behalf of Jette Ring v Dansk almennyttigt Boligselskab ECLI:EU:C:2013:222.

60 Art. 1(2) GETA: Wet verduidelijking rechtspositie transgender personen en intersekse personen, Stb. 2019, 302.

61 See supra n. 25.

62 See Arts 1 & 1a DDA, Arts 1 & 2 ADA and Art. 1 ETA m/w.

63 See for example IHR opinion 2019–93, in which the access to a party was denied to a man, an unlawful sex discrimination according to the IHR: https://mensenrechten.nl/nl/oordeel/2019-93.

Indirect distinction: '[I]f an apparently neutral provision, criterion or practice puts persons with a certain religion, belief, political opinion, race, sex, nationality, heterosexual or homosexual orientation or civil status at a particular disadvantage compared to other persons' (Article 1 §1b GETA). The prohibition on discrimination does not apply to indirect discrimination if the discrimination is objectively justified by a legitimate aim and the means used to achieve that aim are appropriate and necessary (Article 2 §1 GETA).

Both harassment and sexual harassment are forbidden (Article 1a GETA) and defined.

Harassment: '[A] conduct related to the race, sex . . .[64] occurs with the purpose or effect of violating the dignity of a person, and of creating an intimidating, hostile, degrading, humiliating or offensive environment'.
Sexual harassment: '[A]ny form of verbal, non-verbal or physical conduct of a sexual nature, with the purpose or effect of violating the dignity of a person, in particular when creating an intimidating, hostile, degrading, humiliating or offensive environment'.

There are no exceptions applicable to harassment and sexual harassment (Article 1a §4 GETA).[65] In the DDA and the ADA only harassment is prohibited, not sexual harassment.[66]

2.2.2.2 EFFECTIVE ACCOMMODATION

The DDA stipulates – in addition to the definitions of direct discrimination, indirect discrimination and harassment – that the prohibition to make a distinction comprises the obligation for who has to ensure that the norm is respected (e.g. employers or institutions for vocational training) to provide effective accommodation where needed, unless it would constitute a disproportionate burden.[67] The aim is to take into account differences (e.g. physical impairments) and provide unequal treatment by treating unalike cases unalike in proportion to their unlikeness. The effective accommodation has to be provided within a reasonable time and has to be appropriate and necessary in order to contribute to equal treatment of people with a disability or chronic illness.[68] For example, such effective accommodation can consist of stable working patterns[69] or providing access to

64 All the grounds mentioned in Article 1 §1b, thus all the grounds to which the GETA applies.
65 See also Art. 1a ETA m/w.
66 See Art. 1a DDA and Art. 2 ADA.
67 The aim of this provision is to implement the concept of reasonable accommodation in Art. 5 of Directive 2000/78/EC. According to the government, the term 'effective' reflects the need that the accommodation aims at the intended effect: Kamerstukken II, 2001–2002, 28 169, 3, p. 8, p. 25.
68 Kamerstukken II 2001–2002, 28 169, 3, p. 8, p. 25; 5, p. 13.
69 See for example IHR Opinion 2021–21. A man with a disability (chronic gastroenteritis) and caring responsibilities for his also disabled wife (who also falls under the scope of the DDA, see Case

transportation for a user of an electric wheelchair.[70] Not providing an effective accommodation can be justified if it would put a disproportionate burden on who has to ensure the norm (e.g. the employer). Whether a burden is disproportionate depends on the circumstances.

In 2016, in the framework of the implementation of the UN Convention on the Rights of Persons with Disabilities, a new general provision has been added to the DDA stipulating that every person has to be enabled to be autonomous in relation to its own possibilities (Article 1 DDA). In addition, a specific provision on access for persons with a visual impairment has been included in the DDA.[71]

2.2.2.3 MULTIPLE AND INTERSECTIONAL DISCRIMINATION

Dutch equal treatment legislation does not include the concepts of multiple or intersectional discrimination. In case of multiple discrimination, two or more grounds are at stake at the same time. Nevertheless, the omission in legislation does not preclude claims under multiple grounds.[72] The IHR tends to investigate all grounds mentioned in cases of multiple discrimination.[73]

Intersectional discrimination occurs when two or more grounds intersect: their respective roles cannot be disentangled and create specific forms of discrimination such as sexism and racism at the same time.[74] The concept of intersectionality

---

C-303/06 S. Coleman v Attridge Law and Steve Law [2008] ECLI:EU:C:2008:415) required the possibility to start his working day between 7:15 and 8:45 a.m. He was refused the job of team leader due to this demand of flexible working even if he fulfilled all the requirements for this function. The IHR considered this unjustified discrimination on the ground of disability or chronic illness and thus unlawful.

70 See for example IHR Opinion 2020–83. The specific electric system allowing the disabled man to enter the bus with his wheelchair did often not work or the drivers did not know how to manage the system and did not provide assistance. The man had in 9% of the cases to wait for another bus. The IHR considered that the transportation business infringed the law by not providing access which would allow the wheelchair user to make use of transport independently and unrestrictedly.

71 In addition to the general obligation to provide access, an effective accommodation includes anyhow providing access for assisting dogs (Art. 2 DDA), unless this would constitute a disproportionate burden (Art. 2a DDA); Stb. 2016, 215 & 216.

72 Sandy Fredman, European network of legal experts in gender equality and non-discrimination, Intersectional discrimination in EU gender equality and non-discrimination law (Luxembourg: Publications Office of the European Union, 2016), available at https://www.equalitylaw.eu/downloads/3850-intersectional-discrimination-in-eu-gender-equality-and-non-discrimination-law-pdf-731-kb, p. 53.

73 Sandy Fredman, European network of legal experts in gender equality and non-discrimination, Intersectional discrimination in EU gender equality and non-discrimination law (European Commission, 2016), available at www.equalitylaw.eu/downloads/3850-intersectional-discrimination-in-eu-gender-equality-and-non-discrimination-law-pdf-731-kb, p. 59. See for example IHR Opinion 2014–160; IHR Opinion 2019–21; IHR Opinion 2019–86; IHR Opinion 2020–45 and IHR Opinion 2021–28.

74 Kimberlé Crenshaw developed this concept, when a person is confronted with intersections of combined forms of discrimination. This is for example the case of minority women when subject to particular types of prejudices and stereotypes: Kimberlé Crenshaw, Demarginalizing the

and its potential is up to now mainly discussed within academics and civil society. It is not (yet) debated in relation to the Dutch equal treatment legislation. This might change in the future – at least in relation to gender – given the approach taken by the CEDAW Committee, which considers:

> The discrimination of women based on sex and gender is inextricably linked with other factors that affect women, such as race, ethnicity, religion or belief, health, status, age, class, caste and sexual orientation and gender identity. Discrimination on the basis of sex or gender may affect women belonging to such groups to a different degree or in different ways to men. States parties must legally recognise such intersecting forms of discrimination and their compounded negative impact on the women concerned and prohibit them.[75]

However, as long as intersectional discrimination is not explicitly acknowledged in CJEU case law[76] and/or in EU gender equality and non-discrimination legislation, it is not likely that the concept of intersectional discrimination will be integrated into Dutch equal treatment legislation. The specificities of the legal provisions (with regard to scope, justifications, obligations, for example) for each discrimination ground would add to complexity in deciding intersectional cases. This might explain why intersectionality is not specifically addressed in Dutch case law or opinions of the IHR (and its predecessor, the ETC).[77] For example, the IHR addresses headscarves issues – where religion and sex intersect – only under the scope of religion.[78]

In the author's view, recognising explicitly forms of intersectional discrimination when at hand in a case would contribute to more visibility of the problems at stake and might raise awareness of the complex and serious problems people face. This would be a welcome approach, as intersectional discrimination is also often a

---

intersection of race and sex: A black feminist critique of antidiscrimination doctrine, feminist theory and antiracial polities, University of Chicago Legal Forum, 139 (1989). See further for example Sandy Fredman, European network of legal experts in gender equality and non-discrimination, Intersectional discrimination in EU gender equality and non-discrimination law (European Commission, 2016), available at www.equalitylaw.eu/downloads/3850-intersectional-discrimination-in-eu-gender-equality-and-non-discrimination-law-pdf-731-kb.

75 CEDAW-Committee, General Recommendation on No. 28 on the Core Obligations of Parties under Article 2 of the Convention on the Elimination of All Discrimination Against women, p. 4.

76 See in particular Case C-443/15 David L. Parris v Trinity College Dublin and Others [2016] ECLI:EU:C:2016:897, on discrimination on the ground of age and sexual orientation.

77 See for a discussion Susanne Burri, Promises of an Intersectional Approach in Practice? The Dutch Equal Treatment Commission's Case Law, in Dagmar Schiek & Anna Lawson (eds.), *European Non-Discrimination Law and Intersectionality. Investigating the Triangle of Racial, Gender and Disability Discrimination* (Farnham: Ashgate, 2011), pp. 97–110. The keyword 'intersection' is listed on the website of the IHR See on intersection IHR opinion 2006-256, https://oordelen.mensenrechten.nl/oordeel/2006-256.

78 See Titia Loenen, The Impact of Anti-Discrimination Law in the Netherlands. A Case Study of Discrimination on the Grounds of Religion in Employment, in Barbara Havelková & Mathias Möschel (eds.), *Anti-discrimination Law in Civil Law Jurisdictions* (Oxford: Oxford University Press, 2019), pp. 233–243.

form of systemic and/or institutional discrimination and linked to relationships of power. Such approach is described by Sandra Fredman as follows:

> discrimination law should focus on relationships of power in order to determine who to protect and how. Since everyone has a range of identities, a relational view allows us to see that some characteristics signal privilege, while others are relationships of disadvantage. In addition, the ways in which detriment or disadvantage is experienced might be significantly shaped by circumstances and context.[79]

2.2.2.4 DISCRIMINATION BY ASSOCIATION

A concept that extends the scope of the protection against discrimination is the prohibition of discrimination by association. This is the case when a person is not discriminated against, but nevertheless suffers discrimination due to another person (e.g. being denied access to a facility or a service due to the disability of a child or a spouse). This concept was acknowledged by the CJEU for the first time in the *Coleman* case in relation to disability in the field of employment.[80] In this case, a mother who was the primary carer of her disabled son was treated less favourably than other employees. The CJEU considered that if such treatment is based on the disability of her child, even if the mother is not disabled, she is protected against direct discrimination on the ground of disability. Such protection also applies in case of harassment.

Opinions of the IHR offer diverse examples of discrimination by association; for example, discrimination due to the disability or nationality of a spouse.[81] In most of these cases, this concept allows the IHR to have competence to decide a case, which is certainly welcome as it broadens access to justice.

Not all unequal treatment in employment is unlawful. As we have seen, unequal treatment is sometimes even required; for example, when an effective accommodation has to be provided by an employer in order to enable a disabled person to access a building or service. Similarly, the aim of positive action measures is to eliminate or reduce disadvantages of some groups. Just as in EU law, the concept of positive action is framed as an exception to the prohibition of discrimination, in addition to diverse exceptions which depend on the ground. This makes the legal system even more complex.

79 Sandy Fredman, *European Network of Legal Experts in Gender Equality and Non-discrimination, Intersectional Discrimination in EU Gender Equality and Non-discrimination Law* (European Commission, 2016), p. 8, available at www.equalitylaw.eu/downloads/3850-intersectional-discrimination-in-eu-gender-equality-and-non-discrimination-law-pdf-731-kb.

80 Case C-303/06 S. Coleman v Attridge Law and Steve Law ECLI:EU:C:2008:415 and IHR opinion 2011–90. See also in the area of services the Case C-80/14 'CHEZ Razpredelenie Bulgaria' AD v Komisia za zashtita ot diskriminatsia ECLI:EU:C:2015:480.

81 See for example IHR Opinions 2012–204; 2012–197; 2013–11 and IHR Opinion 2021–21.

2.2.3 Exceptions

Positive action is allowed in relation to race, sex,[82] and disability or chronic illness.[83] Employment and labour market policies for certain age groups are possible as well.[84] Article 2 §3 GETA reads:

> The prohibition on discrimination contained in this Act shall not apply if the discrimination concerns a specific measure which has the aim of placing women or persons belonging to a particular ethnic or cultural minority group in a privileged position in order to eliminate or reduce de facto disadvantages in relation to the grounds of race or sex and the discrimination is reasonably proportionate to that aim.

Positive measures are therefore allowed only for some specific groups. Such measures are thus not required and have to meet the (rather strict) criteria developed by the CJEU. Giving absolute and unconditional priority to a woman for a post when a male and a female candidate are equally qualified is not allowed, for example.[85] The IHR has issued a few opinions on positive action measures taken by diverse Dutch universities in order to reach a better representation of female full and associate professors, in particular at faculties where the representation of women professors is very low.[86]

In some situations, specific exceptions to the principle of equal treatment are allowed, even if direct discrimination is at stake. Direct discrimination is then not prohibited when an exception applies. The list of these exceptions is exhaustive and these exceptions have to be interpreted strictly according to CJEU case law,[87] which approach is generally followed by Dutch courts and the IHR. The exceptions are specified per ground in the GETA,[88] the DDA and the ADA.

82 See also Art. 5§1 ETA m/v and Art. 7:646 §4 CC.

83 See Art. 3 §1c DDA.

84 Art. 7 §1a ADA.

85 See for a discussion in depth Christopher McCrudden, *European Network of Legal Experts in Gender Equality and Non-discrimination, Gender-Based Positive Action in Employment in Europe* (Luxembourg: Publications Office of the European Union, 2019), available at www.equalitylaw.eu/downloads/5008-gender-based-positive-action-in-employment-in-europe-pdf-1-9-mb.

86 See for example IHR 2011–198; IHR 2012–195 and IHR Opinions 2020–53 (see comment Marlies Vegter Netherlands Equality Body considers the positive action policy of the Technical University Eindhoven to be unlawful, available at www.equalitylaw.eu/downloads/5291-netherlands-equality-body-considers-the-positive-action-policy-of-the-technical-university-eindhoven-to-be-unlawful-73-kb) and IHR Opinion 2021–19 on a Irène Curie program of the Technical University Eindhoven, which was amended and then considered to be lawful by the IHR.

87 Case 222/84 Marguerite Johnston v Chief Constable of the Royal Ulster Constabulary ECLI:EU:C:1986:206, para 36.

88 As regards sex also in the ETA m/v and Art. 7:646 CC.

2.2.3.1 IN THE GETA

The prohibition of direct race discrimination does not apply (1) in cases where a person's racial appearance is a determining factor, provided that the aim is legitimate and the requirement is proportionate to that aim; and (2) if the discrimination relates to a person's racial appearance and constitutes, by reason of the nature of the concerned particular occupational activity or of the context in which it is carried out, a genuine and determining occupational requirement, provided that the aim is legitimate and the requirement is proportionate to that aim (Article 2 §4 GETA).

Discrimination on the grounds of sex is prohibited unless sex is a determining factor and in cases concerning the protection of women, notably in relation to pregnancy and motherhood (Article 2 §2 GETA).[89]

Examples of a determining factor relating to sex or race are roles for actors in a movie. The exception on occupational requirements applies not only to sex and race but to all the grounds mentioned in the GETA, in employment (Article 5 §3b & c GETA) and in services (Article 7 §3b & c GETA).

The prohibition on discrimination on the grounds of nationality does not apply if the discrimination is based on generally binding regulations or on written or unwritten rules of international law and in cases where nationality is a determining factor (Article 2 §5 GETA).

In addition, specific exceptions in relation to religion, belief or political opinion apply to employment, membership of organisations, and services. Article 5 §2 GETA on employment allows exceptions on the ground of religion, belief or political opinion for persons working in institutions based on religion, belief or political orientation, as well as for specific schools when there is an occupational requirement in the light of the foundation of the institution. Similar exceptions apply in relation to the membership of employers' organisations and unions (Article 6a §2 GETA) and services (Article 7 §2 GETA).

In addition, municipalities have the possibility to make a distinction on the ground of religion or belief for civil servants for civil marriages who do not want to marry same-sex couples due to their religion or belief (Article 5 §2a GETA).[90] However, this provision still offers the possibility to civil servants who are currently employed by the municipality to refuse to marry same-sex persons in civil weddings.[91]

2.2.3.2 IN THE DDA

The exceptions in the DDA are partially different. In addition to a provision on the possibility to provide specific facilities and take positive action measures in

89 See also Art. 5 ETA m/w and Art. 7:646 §2 & §3 CC.

90 Stb. 2015, 200.

91 See Kamerstukken II 2013–2014, 333 44, D, pp. 2–4. However, since 1 January 2020 civil servants responsible for civil marriages can only be appointed if they do not make a distinction as prohibited in art. 1 GETA, unless the distinction is based on a legal provision: Art. 16 CC; Stb. 2019, 173 and 385.

relation to disability or chronic illness, Article 3 DDA allows an exception when the distinction is necessary for the protection of safety and health.

2.2.3.3 IN THE ADA

There is a possibility to justify not only indirect but also objectively justified direct discrimination based on age in the ADA.[92] Objective justifications can be based on labour market policies based on law aimed at facilitating access to the labour market for certain age categories (Article 7 §1a ADA), as well as the ending of an employment or civil servant's relation due to pensionable age (Article 7 §1b ADA) or when otherwise objectively justified if the aim is legitimate and the means are appropriate and necessary (Article 7 §1c ADA).

2.2.4 Burden of Proof

The shift of the burden of proof from the complainant who has to establish facts for a presumed discrimination to the respondent in the equal treatment legislation applies to all grounds and all forms of discrimination, including harassment.[93] However, this burden of proof does not apply to all forms of victimisation.[94] The burden of proof is similar in the GETA, the DDA,[95] the ADA,[96] the ETA m/v[97] and Article 7:646 §12 CC and also applies to collective actions.[98] Article 10 §1 GETA on the burden of proof reads:

> If a person who considers that he has been wronged through a distinction as referred to in this Act establishes before a court facts from which it may be presumed that discrimination has taken place, it shall be for the respondent to prove that the action in question was not in breach of this Act.

If criteria applying to pay or recruitment for example lack transparency, it is for the employer to prove that their practice is not discriminatory.[99]

92 Harassment cannot be justified: Art. 7 §2 ADA.
93 As well as sexual harassment, as defined in Art. 1a §3 GETA, art. 1a §3 ETA m/w and Art. 7:646 §8 CC.
94 See sec. 2.2.5 below.
95 Art. 10 DDA, which also applies to the obligation to provide reasonable accommodation according to Art. 2 DDA.
96 Art.12 ADA.
97 Art. 6a ETA m/w.
98 Art. 3:305a CC and as regards civil servants: Article 1:2 §3 of the General Administrative Act (Algemene wet bestuursrecht).
99 See for example Case 318/86 Commission v France ECLI:EU:C:1988:352, §27 and Case 109/88 Handels- og Kontorfunktionærernes Forbund i Danmark (Union of Commercial and Clerical Employees, Denmark) and Dansk Arbejdsgiverforening (Danish Employers' Association), acting on behalf of Danfoss A/S ECLI:EU:C:1989:383, §11.

2.2.5 Victimisation

There are different forms of protection against victimisation in Dutch equal treatment legislation. Article 8a GETA and equivalent articles in statutory equal treatment legislation[100] stipulate that in case of a discriminatory ending of an employment relation or if a person has invoked an equal treatment provision or assisted in proceedings under the Equal Treatment Acts, the procedure of Article 7:681 CC applies. In this case the civil law procedure applies without the specific lighter burden of proof of the equal treatment legislation. The termination of the contract is then voidable.

In addition, Article 8a §1 GETA reads: 'It is unlawful to disadvantage persons because they have invoked this Act, either in or out of court, or have assisted others in this respect'.[101] 'Persons' is interpreted broadly and includes workers, temporary workers, colleagues and others. Assistance can be provided by means of testimony, for example. 'Disadvantage' is also interpreted broadly. In case unlawful disadvantage is established, no justification is possible.

Finally, specific protection against victimisation applies in relation to harassment and sexual harassment. Article 8a §2 stipulates that the fact that a person rejects or undergoes passively harassment or sexual harassment cannot be a ground for a decision concerning that person.[102] In such situations, the burden of proof of the equal treatment legislation applies, provided that a causal link between the adverse treatment and (sexual) harassment can be proved, which is not easy in practice.[103]

2.3 Enforcement and Sanctions

2.3.1 Enforcement

There are different ways to combat discrimination and enforce Dutch equal treatment legislation in employment. A person who considers having suffered discrimination and/or (sexual) harassment can start an internal complaint procedure of the undertaking or organisation which is responsible for the presumed unequal treatment and/or inform the work council (if available). Such procedures have to be meticulous.[104]

100 Art. 9 DDA, Art. 11 ADA and Art. 12f ETA m/w.

101 See also Art. 9a DDA, Art. 10 ADA, Art. 1b §4 ETA m/w and Art. 7:646 §14 CC. See on testimony Case C-404/18 Jamina Hakelbracht, Tine Vandenbon, Instituut voor de Gelijkheid van Vrouwen en Mannen v WTG Retail BVBA ECLI:EU:C:2019:523.

102 See also Art. 1a §4 ETA m/w and art. 7:646 §9. There is no equivalent provision in the DDA and the ADA.

103 See IHR opinion 2019–101 in which the IHR considered that such link was established.

104 See for example IHR opinion 2020–93, in which the HR manager investigate the complaint, heard both sides, and did not find the complaint justified. However, due to the fact that the result of the complaint procedure was not communicated to the person who started the procedure, she did not know why the employer did not take measures after her complaint. The IHR considered this an unlawful 'distinction'.

Diverse organisations, websites[105] and other entities provide information and advice on equal treatment in employment. The most specialised and important in practice are the Anti-discrimination Facilities (ADFs; *Anti-discriminatievoorzieningen* [ADV]) and the Institute for Human Rights (IHR; *College voor de Rechten van de Mens* [CRvdM]).[106]

The aim of the IHR is to protect human rights, including the right to equal treatment, to enhance awareness about these rights and promote their enforcement in the Netherlands.[107] The IHR is a quasi-judicial, independent body whose competences and tasks specifically include the enforcement of equal treatment legislation on all the grounds discussed above.[108] One of the current priorities of the IHR is combatting discrimination and stereotyping in employment, as well as algorithmic discrimination in recruitment and selection.[109] The IHR provides information and education, hears complaints about unequal treatment and issues (non-binding) opinions, investigates possible forms of structural discrimination[110] and gives advice to the government (on request or on its own accord). Employers and organisations can ask for an opinion of the IHR about their own (and/or future) policies, for example. The procedure of the IHR is free of charge, easily accessible, short and used much more often than court procedures. Each year the IHR issues more than 100 opinions, sometimes with specific recommendations. In about three out of four cases, when the IHR considered the law was breached, the responsible employer or party provided some redress (e.g. by amending the policy at stake).[111] The IHR has legal standing[112] but does not use it in practice, as

105 See for example the information the Ministry of Social Affairs and Employment provides on its website (www.rijksoverheid.nl/onderwerpen/gelijke-behandeling-op-het-werk) and the website Het juridisch loket (www.juridischloket.nl/).

106 See for an extensive discussion of the role and competences of both bodies: Karin de Vries, supra n. 58, at pp. 70–80.

107 Art. 1 §3 of the Act on the Institute for Human Rights (Wet College rechten van de mens, Stb. 2011, 573).

108 This applies to the GETA, DDA, ADA, ETA m/w, Arts 7: 646 & 7:648 CC (including the prohibition on the Act on Working Time and the Act on a Temporary Character of the employment contract). The same is true for its predecessor until October 2012, the Commission on Equal Treatment (Commissie gelijke behandeling).

109 IHR, When computers review your CV, who reviews the computers? Algorithms and discrimination in recruitment and selection, CRvdM (2020).

110 See for example on pregnancy discrimination: Susanne Burri, Combatting Pregnancy Discrimination in the Netherlands: The Role of the Equality Body, in Barbara Havelková & Mathias Möschel (eds.), *Anti-discrimination Law in Civil Law Jurisdictions* (Oxford: Oxford University Press, 2019), pp. 157–175; CRvdM, *Zwanger en werk: dat baart zorgen. Derde onderzoek naar discriminatie op de arbeidsmarkt van zwangere vrouwen en moeders met jonge kinderen* (CRvdM 2020), available at https://mensenrechten.nl/nl/publicatie/5fb7dfef1e0fec037359c640.

111 In 2020 the IHR issued 124 opinions: IHR annual report (Jaarverslag) 2020, p. 7. See on 'follow-up' the annual report 2019, p. 25, available at https://mensenrechten.nl/nl/publicatie/5ea1351a1e0fec037359c1f3.

112 Art. 13 of the Act Institute for Human Rights (Wet College voor de rechten van de mens).

this may conflict with the required objectivity and independence in the complaint procedure.

The main task of the local ADFs is assisting victims of discrimination on the same grounds as the IHR. The ADFs are independent and have legal standing, they also may assist victims in complaints handled by the IHR. The ADFs register complaints, thus alongside the complaints filed by the IHR, for example. In addition, the ADFs can take actions to combat discrimination forbidden under criminal law.[113] Each municipality has the obligation to establish and subsidise an ADF. Collective actions are possible in Dutch law according to Article 3:305a CC.[114]

The Dutch Institute for Human Rights, as well as the ADFs and diverse NGOs,[115] play very important roles in the enforcement of principle of equal treatment in practice in addition to unions.

Court civil procedures are also available, of course, but are still scarce as they are lengthy and costly.[116] The same is true for criminal procedures. Illustrative of this are the penal procedures against the Dutch Parliamentarian Geert Wilders, chair of the Dutch political party *PVV* (Party for Freedom) in relation to race and religious discrimination.[117]

Dutch courts can now ask prejudicial questions not only to the CJEU but also to the Dutch Supreme Court; for example, on the interpretation of EU case law at national level. Sometimes, this leads to a more satisfactory result for the plaintiffs, as for example when maternity leave lapses when it overlaps with school holidays.[118] This is contrary to EU law, as workers in such situation are entitled to each leave separately.[119] The Dutch Supreme Court took a different view in 2002 and has now applied the CJEU *Merino Goméz* judgment after a prejudicial question of the District Court in The Hague.[120] This example shows how crucial knowledge of the EU non-discrimination case law is at the national level and the impact collaboration between courts at national level can have in practice.

113 Art. 2 §1a Act on local antidiscrimination facilities (Wet gemeentelijke antidiscriminatievoor zieningen).

114 As regards civil servants: Art. 1:2 §3 of the General Administrative Act (Algemene wet bestuursrecht).

115 For example: 'Art. 1', see art1.nl; 'Radar', see radar.nl; 'atria', see atria.nl.

116 See for example on early retirement provisions in collective agreements of KLM pilots: Supreme Court 13 July 2012, ECLI:NL:HR:2012:BW3367.

117 See for example District Court The Hague 9 December 2016, ECLI:NL:RBDHA:2016:15014, discussed by Titia Loenen, European network of legal experts in gender equality and non-discrimination, Wilders found guilty of insulting a group and incitement to discrimination on grounds of race, available at www.equalitylaw.eu/downloads/3968-the-netherlands-wilders-found-guilty-of-insulting-a-group-and-incitement-to-discrimination-on-grounds-of-race-pdf-138-kb and Supreme Court 10 April 2018, ECLI:NL:HR:2018:539.

118 Supreme Court 6 November 2020, ECLI:NL:HR:2020:1748, discussed by Marlies Vegter available at https://www.equalitylaw.eu/downloads/5313-netherlands-supreme-court-rules-that-lapse-of-maternity-leave-of-teachers-in-secondary-education-in-case-it-overlaps-with-school-holidays-constitutes-discrimination-72-kb.

119 Case C-342/01 María Paz Merino Gómez v Continental Industrias del Caucho SA ECLI:EU:C:2004:160.

120 District Court the Hague 4 May 2020, ECLI:NL:RBDHA:2020:4429.

2.3.2 Sanctions

The IHR has no competence to apply sanctions such as rectification or financial compensation to the victim. However, the opinions are published on the website of the IHR with the name of the (presumed) discriminatory party (e.g. an undertaking).

The equal treatment legislation specifies two sanctions. According to Article 8 GETA, discriminatory dismissal or dismissal-related victimisation are voidable. The worker can ask the court to invalidate the termination of the employment relation and can claim wages.[121] Article 9 GETA stipulates that all contractual provisions which contradict with this Act shall be void.[122]

The courts can impose sanctions, which depend on the field of law (civil, criminal). Civil courts can grant pecuniary damages in civil procedures. For example, an employer has been fined for rejecting a student for an internship because of his sexual orientation.[123] The District Court of the Hague awarded a compensation of EUR 3000 for not extending a fixed-term contract due to pregnancy.[124]

3 Assessment and Conclusions

Dutch equal treatment legislation is scattered over specific acts, the civil code and criminal law provisions and sometimes lacks consistency.[125] Integration of the most relevant equal treatment acts into one act would be most welcome, as it would contribute to a better awareness, application and enforcement of Dutch equal treatment legislation. A proposal to integrate the GETA, DDA, ADA, ETA m/w and Article 7:646 CC into one act was subject to public consultation in 2010.[126] The ETC has published a positive advice on this proposal.[127] In 2013, the government informed the Second Chamber of Parliament that the drafting of a proposal was ongoing,[128] but a legislative proposal is still not published, and it is not clear whether it will ever be. In 2018, the IHR as well as the Dutch equal treatment law was evaluated positively, and the minister of internal affairs announced then only minor amendments.[129] A thorough review and integration of the legislation

121 According to Art. 7:681 CC. See the similar provisions in Art. 9 DDA, Art. 11 ADA and Arts 1b §5, 1c & 12f ETA m/w.

122 See the similar provisions in Art. 11 DDA, Art. 13 ADA, Arts 1b §6, 2 §3, 4 §3, 4a §3 & 12e ETA m/w, Art. 7:646 §11 CC, Art. 7:648 §2 CC & Art. 7:649 §2 CC.

123 See Rikki Holtmaat, Employer Fined for Discriminatory Rejection of an Internship Applicant, available at www.equalitylaw.eu/downloads/3812-the-netherlands-employer-fined-for-discriminatory-rejection-of-an-internship-applicant-pdf-43-kb.

124 District Court The Hague 21 March 2018, ECLI:NL:RBDHA:2018:3423, discussed by Marlies Vegter, available at https://www.equalitylaw.eu/downloads/5313-netherlands-supreme-court-rules-that-lapse-of-maternity-leave-of-teachers-in-secondary-education-in-case-it-overlaps-with-school-holidays-constitutes-discrimination-72-kb.

125 For example in relation to the prohibitions of harassment and sexual harassment, see supra 2.2.2.

126 See www.internetconsultatie.nl/integratiewetawgb/details.

127 IHR, Advies 2010/3 inzake concept-wetsvoorstel Integratiewet, available at https://mensenrechten.nl/nl/publicaties.

128 Kamerstukken II 2013–2014, 28 481, 22.

129 Kamerstukken II 2017–2018, 34 338, 3.

into one single act is therefore not likely in the near future. The ongoing process of amending the existing acts – even if the protection against discrimination is extended – is further increasing the complexity of the legislation.

As Dutch equal treatment legislation closely follows the EU system, this also means that the symmetric approach to the prohibition of discrimination – protecting not historically disadvantaged groups as well – also applies in the Dutch system. However, the provisions on positive action are drafted asymmetrically in Dutch law, as these aim at improving the position of women, persons belonging to a particular ethnic or cultural minority group and persons with a disability.[130] Still, positive action is framed as an exception to equal treatment and is interpreted strictly as required by the CJEU case law, even if the approach of the IHR is sometimes more lenient, for example on positive action measures for women at universities.[131] The IHR also provides guidelines on how to ensure that measures aimed at enhancing the representation of women are legally allowed.[132] This approach is therefore more in line with the asymmetrical approach in CEDAW and the recommendations of the CEDAW Committee.[133]

The IHR plays a very important role in enforcing equal treatment legislation, in particular due to the availability of the free, easily accessible and short complaint procedure. This procedure results in more than a hundred opinions published each year. The opinions of the IHR often receive quite some publicity. The IHR often refers in its opinions to relevant CJEU case law and thus contributes to a better knowledge and understanding of the binding judgments of the CJEU. EU law offers a broad and rich body of law and is fundamental in the field of equal treatment.

The follow-up policy of the IHR shows that in 2020, for example, in 78% of the cases (86% in 2019) an infringement of the equal treatment law is redressed by the defendant in some way (e.g. by amending the discriminatory policy, by providing information and/or compensation).[134]

The IHR combats also specific forms of discrimination including by commissioning research and launching public campaigns. This is the case of different aspects of pregnancy discrimination, for example, which have been specifically addressed by the IHR in research and public campaigns, as well as many opinions. The IHR has also commissioned research in relation to disability, age and algorithmic discrimination. It is crucial that the equality body has specialised staff and sufficient budget to be able to combat discrimination in practice. At the local level, the ADFs additionally provide advice and assist victims; the same is true

130 As well as employment and labour market policies for certain age groups: Art. 7 §1a ADA.

131 See for example IHR opinions 2011–198, 2012–195, 2020–53 and 2021–19.

132 See for example the guidelines of the IHR concerning the Irène Curie Fellowship Programme of the Eindhoven University of Technology, available at https://mensenrechten.nl/nl/nieuws/college-oordeelt-over-herziene-voorkeursbeleid-tu-eindhoven-en-geeft-praktische-handvatten.

133 In particular Arts 1, 2 and 4 and General recommendation No. 25, on article 4, paragraph 1, of CEDAW, on temporary special measures.

134 IHR, Jaarverslag 2020, p. 23, CRvdM 2020, available at https://mensenrechten.nl/nl/publicaties.

for diverse NGOs. Court cases are still quite scarce, however, and the proceedings are costly and lengthy.

Discrimination in Dutch society receives increasing attention.[135] Research shows that about one in four people living in the Netherlands (27%) reports having experienced discrimination.[136] The groups who report most incidents are Dutch Moroccans, Turkish and Muslims, people with disabilities, LGBT individuals, and women.

Diverse initiatives have recently been taken by the government to combat discrimination, such as an Action Plan 2018–2021 to combat discrimination in the labour market;[137] an investigation of the possibilities to appoint a national coordinator against discrimination and racism;[138] who is now appointed, and the appointment of a new national coordinator for anti-Semitism in 2021.[139] A legislative proposal is currently discussed in the Second Chamber of Parliament which aims at improving the monitoring of the application of the equal treatment norm in recruitment and selection.[140] The difference between law in the books and law in action and the lack of effectiveness of anti-discrimination legislation will probably lead to a parliamentary inquiry, as a Parliamentary Commission was installed by the Senate (the First Chamber of Parliament) to prepare such inquiry.[141] The final report is now published.[142]

Discrimination of ethnic minorities in the (access to the) labour market, as well as discrimination due to the use of algorithms, is widely debated. The same is true of sexism in relation to the #MeToo debate. Institutional discrimination by state organs in data systems related to social security and benefits is widespread,

135 See for example the letter of the government on tackling discrimination published on 15 June 2020, available at www.rijksoverheid.nl/ministeries/ministerie-van-binnenlandse-zaken-en-koninkrijksrelaties/documenten/kamerstukken/2020/06/15/kamerbrief-over-kabinetsaanpak-van-discriminatie.

136 The Netherlands Institute for Social Research (SCP), Ervaren discriminatie II, SCP (2020), (with summary in English), available at www.scp.nl/publicaties/publicaties/2020/04/02/ervaren-discriminatie-in-nederland-ii.

137 See Voortgangsrapportage Actieplan Arbeidsmarktdiscriminatie 2018–2021, available at www.rijksoverheid.nl/documenten/kamerstukken/2020/07/06/kamerbrief-voortgang-actieplan-arbeidsmarktdiscriminatie-2018-2021.

138 Nationaal Coördinator tegen discriminatie en racisme – een verkenning, available at https://www.rijksoverheid.nl/documenten/rapporten/2021/03/01/nationaal-coordinator-tegen-discriminatie-en-racisme—een-verkenning.

139 Nationaal Coördinator Antisemitismebestrijding, available at www.rijksoverheid.nl/onderwerpen/discriminatie/nieuws/2020/12/13/nationaal-coordinator-antisemitismebestrijding-in-2021-van-start.

140 Wetsvoorstel toezicht gelijke kansen bij werving en selectie, Kamerstukken II 2020–2021, 35673, 1–3.

141 See Kamerstukken I 2020–2021, 35 570, E and Tijdelijke commissie voorbereiding parlementair onderzoek effectiviteit anti-discriminatiewetgeving, available at www.eerstekamer.nl/commissies/tijdelijke_commissie_voorbereiding_3; discussed by Marlies Vegter at www.equalitylaw.eu/country/netherlands and www.eerstekamer.nl/nieuws/20201201/commissie_onderzoeksvoorstel_anti.

142 Gelijk recht doen. Een parlementair onderzoek naar de mogelijkheden van de wetgever om discriminatie tegen te gaan, Kamerstukken I 2012-2022 CXLVI, nr. X.

as nationality is used as one of the criteria to detect fraud which leads to ethnic profiling. Addressing such forms of discrimination presents huge challenges in an increasingly polarised society between minority and majority groups, which is also reflected in politics, in particular of right-wing parties. Combatting stereotyping and institutional and systemic discrimination, as well as instituting more effective anti-discrimination measures, are certainly needed in today's Dutch society.

Bibliography

Bunschoten, D.E., *Tekst en commentaar Grondwet & Statuut, Gelijkheidsbeginsel, verbod van discriminatie bij Grondwet, Artikel 1*, Deventer: Kluwer 5th ed. (2018).

Burri, Susanne, Promises of an intersectional approach in practice? The Dutch equal treatment commission's case law, in Dagmar Schiek & Anna Lawson (Eds.), *European non-discrimination law and intersectionality. Investigating the triangle of racial, gender and disability discrimination*, pp. 97–110, Farnham: Ashgate Publishing Limited (2011).

Burri, Susanne, Equal treatment: The EU approach, in Frans Pennings & Gijsbert Vonk (Eds.), *Research handbook on European social security law*, pp. 231–256, Cheltenham: Edward Elgar Publishing (2015).

Burri, Susanne, Combatting pregnancy discrimination in the Netherlands: the role of the equality body, in Barbara Havelková & Mathias Möschel (Eds.), *Anti-discrimination law in civil law jurisdictions*, pp. 157–175, Oxford: Oxford University Press (2019).

Burri, Susanne & Albertine Veldman, Gelijke behandeling als grondrecht (pp. 151–222) and Flexibele arbeid (pp. 223–248), in Frans Pennings & Saskia Peters (Eds.), *Europees Arbeidsrecht*, Deventer: Wolters Kluwer (2016).

Cowley, Niall, European network of legal experts in gender equality and non-discrimination, in *Equality bodies making a difference*, Luxembourg: Publications Office of the European Union (2018).

Crenshaw, Kimberlé, *Demarginalizing the intersection of race and sex: A black feminist critique of antidiscrimination doctrine, feminist theory and antiracial polities*, University of Chicago Legal Forum, 139 (1989).

de Vries, Karin, European network of legal experts in gender equality and non-discrimination, in *Country report non-discrimination, Netherlands 2021*, Luxembourg: Publications Office of the European Union (2021).

Ellis, Evelyn & Philippa Watson, *EU anti-discrimination law*, Oxford EU Law Library, Oxford: Oxford University Press, 2d ed. (2012).

Fredman, Sandy, European network of legal experts in gender equality and non-discrimination, in *Intersectional discrimination in EU gender equality and non-discrimination law*, Luxembourg: Publications Office of the European Union (2016).

Holtmaat, Rikki, Gelijkheid en non-discriminatie als grondrecht. Een pleidooi voor het maken van onderscheid tussen discriminatie en ongelijke behandeling, in Rikki Holtmaat, Marjolein van den Brink, Aart Hendriks et al. (Eds.), *Gelijkheid en (andere) Grondrechten*, Deventer: Kluwer (2004),

Holtmaat, Rikki, Marjolein van den Brink, Aart Hendriks et al. (Eds.), *Gelijkheid en (andere) Grondrechten*, Deventer: Kluwer (2004).

Loenen, Titia, The impact of anti-discrimination law in the Netherlands. A case study of discrimination on the grounds of religion in employment, in Barbara Havelková & Mathias Möschel (Eds.), *Anti-discrimination law in civil law jurisdictions*, pp. 233–243, Oxford: Oxford University Press (2019).

McCrudden, Christopher, European network of legal experts in gender equality and non-discrimination, in *Gender-based positive action in employment in Europe*, Luxembourg: Publications Office of the European Union (2019).

Netherlands Institute for Social Research, *Ervaren discriminatie II*, Den Haag: Sociaal en Cultureel Planbureau (2020).

Vas Nunes, Peter, *Gelijke behandeling in de arbeid*, Den Haag: Boom juridisch (2018).

Vegter, Marlies, European network of legal experts in gender equality and non-discrimination, in *Country report gender equality, Netherlands 2022*, Luxembourg: Publications Office of the European Union (2022).

Electronic Sources

College voor de Rechten van de Mens, *Zwanger en werk: dat baart zorgen. Derde onderzoek naar discriminatie op de arbeidsmarkt van zwangere vrouwen en moeders met jonge kinderen*, CRvdM 2020, available at: https://mensenrechten.nl/nl/publicatie/5fb7dfef1e0fec037359c640.

College voor de Rechten van de Mens, *Verbod gezichtsbedekkende kleding*, available at: https://mensenrechten.nl

Holtmaat, Rikki, European network of legal experts in gender equality and non-discrimination, *Employer fined for discriminatory rejection of an internship applicant*, available at: www.equalitylaw.eu/downloads/3812-the-netherlands-employer-fined-for-discriminatory-rejection-of-an-internship-applicant-pdf-43-kb

Institute for Human Rights, *When computers review your cv, who reviews the computers? Algorithms and discrimination in recruitment and selection*, CRvdM 2020, available at: https://mensenrechten.nl/nl/publicatie/5fbbba9f1e0fec037359c654

Loenen, Titia, European network of legal experts in gender equality and non-discrimination, *Entry into force of Act prohibiting face covering clothing in education, public transport, public buildings and healthcare*, available at: www.equalitylaw.eu/downloads/4952-the-netherlands-entry-into-force-of-act-prohibiting-face-covering-clothin,g-in-education-public-transport-public-buildings-and-healthcare-pdf-85-kb

Loenen, Titia, European network of legal experts in gender equality and non-discrimination, *Wilders found guilty of insulting a group and incitement to discrimination on grounds of race*, available at: www.equalitylaw.eu/downloads/3968-the-netherlands-wilders-found-guilty-of-insulting-a-group-and-incitement-to-discrimination-on-grounds-of-race-pdf-138-kb

Vegter, Marlies, European network of legal experts in gender equality and non-discrimination, *Netherlands equality body considers the positive action policy of the Technical University Eindhoven to be unlawful*, available at: https://www.equalitylaw.eu/downloads/5291-netherlands-equality-body-considers-the-positive-action-policy-of-the-technical-university-eindhoven-to-be-unlawful-73-kb

4 The German Law on Discrimination in Employment

Manfred Weiss

1 Introduction

In Germany the prohibition of discrimination is embedded in different legal sources, including the respective ILO Conventions, the Treaty on the Functioning of the European Union (TFEU), and Art. 14 on Prohibition of Discrimination of the European Convention on Human Rights. The focus of this short contribution, however, will be on German sources: the Constitution, legislation and case law. As far as case law is concerned, it is important to know that in Germany there is access to a specialised system of labour courts which is totally disconnected from the courts adjudicating civil law cases. The labour court system is organised on three levels: Labour Courts (LC), Labour Courts of Appeal (LCA) and the Federal Labour Court (FLC) on top.[1] If conflicts concerning civil servants are at stake, the administrative courts, also organised on three levels, are the competent bodies.

The German Constitution, the Basic Law of 1949, contains a general provision on equal treatment as a fundamental right (Art. 3).[2] Hierarchically, the Constitution supersedes ordinary legislation. The Constitution explicitly only refers to the vertical application in the relationship between citizens and the State. This reflects the traditional understanding of fundamental rights as a defence against State power, thereby guaranteeing the citizens an area of freedom in which the State cannot interfere. In the meantime, this traditional understanding only is considered a starting point. Fundamental rights nowadays in Germany are considered to be the expression of values on which the legal order as a whole is based. Therefore, they no longer can be ignored in the relationship between private actors. Inequality of power is not only a characteristic for the relationship between State and citizens but is a growing phenomenon also between private actors (e.g. as employers and employees). In Germany this insight has led to the concept of indirect

1 For details see M. Weiss, Labour Dispute Settlement by Labour Courts in Germany, 1 *Industrial Law Journal, Johannesburg* (1994).

2 Article 3 reads: "(1) All persons shall be equal before the law. (2) Men and women shall have equal rights. The state shall promote the actual implementation of equal rights for women and men and take steps to eliminate disadvantages that now exist. (3) No person shall be favoured or disfavoured because of sex, ancestry, race, language, homeland or origin, faith or religious or political opinions. No person shall be disfavoured because of disability."

DOI: 10.4324/9781003306962-5

horizontal application of fundamental rights.[3] This is a soft way of introducing the fundamental rights into relationships between private actors. The fundamental rights are not applied strictly the same way as in the relationship between State and citizens, but the general clauses of the law governing private relationships between private actors are to be interpreted in the light of values expressed by the fundamental rights. This, of course, gives the judiciary on all levels a broad leeway of interpretation in adapting the fundamental rights to the specific situation.

There is only one exception to this pattern of indirect horizontal application, a special aspect of prohibition of discrimination, namely, the prohibition of discrimination on grounds of trade union membership (Art. 9 para. 3 GG) which – as the text explicitly states – has direct horizontal effect.

The Federal Constitutional Court (FCC) acts as guardian of the Constitution, examining whether legislation, court decisions and acts of the executive are in line with the Constitution.

Nowadays, however, the recourse to the vague notions of Art. 3 of the Constitution is only very seldom needed, since there is special legislation. In 2006, after a long and very controversial debate, the General Act on Equal Treatment (GAET) transposed all the European Directives on discrimination into German law.[4] The GAET unites all the factors covered by the EC directives in the same statute and extends the coverage beyond the field of occupation to all factors.

Even if the principle of equal pay for equal work and work of equal value as contained in the TFEU has been reformulated in the GAET, it has turned out that there is still a significant gap between average wages of men and of women. In order to lower this gap, the legislature in 2017 passed the Act on Promotion of Remuneration Transparency between Men and Women (APRT). The idea is to lower or even overcome the gap by revealing the amount of remuneration. However, it turns out that the effect of this law is rather modest. One of the reasons is the fact that women are employed in low-paid branches to a greater extent than men.

This overview will not try to offer an empirical assessment on discrimination in Germany but somewhat focus on the GAET (section 2) and highlight some specific legal problems (section 3).

2 The Basic Structure of the General Act on Equal Treatment (GAET)

As far as the grounds for which discrimination is prohibited are concerned, the GAET simply has copied the Directives: race or ethnic origin, sex or sexual orientation, religion or belief, age or disability.

3 For a more specific explanation of this concept see M. Weiss, Fundamental Rights and German Labour Law, in J. Bellace & B. ter Haar (eds.), *Research Handbook on Labour, Business and Human Rights Law* (Cheltenham: Edward Elgar, 2020), p. 17(18).

4 For details see M. Weiss, Unfair Discrimination Law – Developments at European Level (with Specific Reference to the New German Act on Equal Treatment, in O. Dupper & C. Garbers (eds.), *Equality in the Workplace* (Cape Town: Juta, 2009), p. 63.

The GAET covers "employed persons". This term comprises employees, apprentices, job applicants and so-called employee-like persons. This latter category refers to persons who are self-employed but economically dependent. In short, the term "employed person" is much wider than the term "employee". Discrimination on any of the mentioned grounds is illegal in relation to conditions for access to employment, to self-employment or to occupation, including selection criteria and recruitment conditions, whatever the branch of activity and at all levels of the professional hierarchy, including promotion.

Discrimination comprises direct discrimination, indirect discrimination, harassment and instructions to discriminate. Again the legislature simply copied the definitions from the anti-discrimination Directives. Direct discrimination means less favourable treatment on any of the mentioned grounds. Indirect discrimination occurs where an apparently neutral provision, criterion or practice would put persons, due to any of the mentioned grounds, at a particular disadvantage compared with other persons, unless that provision, criterion or practice is objectively justified by a legitimate aim and the means of achieving that aim are appropriate and necessary. Furthermore, an instruction to discriminate against persons on any of the mentioned grounds shall be deemed to be discrimination. In the employment context, such an instruction will be deemed to be particularly clear if somebody persuades another person to act in a discriminatory manner or in a way that discriminates against an employed person. Multiple discrimination is also sanctioned. Discrimination on several of the mentioned grounds can only be justified if the justification covers all of these grounds.

With regard to the ground of disability prohibition of discrimination also requires reasonable accommodation. Reasonable accommodation means necessary and appropriate modification and adjustments not imposing a disproportionate or undue burden, where needed in a particular case, to ensure to persons with disabilities the enjoyment or exercise on an equal basis with others of all human rights and fundamental freedoms.

Under the GAET there are two general exceptions to the rule that unequal treatment on any of the mentioned grounds is illegal: (1) positive action[5] and (2) genuine and determining occupational requirements. Since indirect discrimination is already by definition excluded if there is a legitimate aim justifying the measure, these justifications mainly apply to direct discrimination. A difference of treatment is supposed to be lawful if the disadvantages linked to any of the mentioned grounds are prevented or compensated by appropriate and proportionate measures (so-called positive action). Differences of treatment based on a criterion related to any of the mentioned grounds shall not constitute discrimination where, by reason of the nature of the particular occupational activities concerned or of the context in which they are carried out, the criterion constitutes an essential and

5 As regards the European concepts of positive action see D. Schiek, Positive Action before the European Court of Justice: New Conceptions of Equality in Community Law? (2000) 16(3) *International Journal of Comparative Labour Law and Industrial Relations* (Wolters Kluwer) pp. 251–275.

decisive occupational requirement, provided that the objective is legitimate and that the requirement is proportionate.

Regardless of the general rules on justification, unequal treatment on grounds of religion or belief is also permissible if, in respect of employment by religious communities or by any institution assigned to them, a certain religion or belief constitutes a justified occupational requirement, taking into account either the self-perception of the respective religious community or the kind of activity to be performed. Furthermore, the ban of discrimination on grounds of religion and belief does not affect the right of any of those religious communities or of any institution assigned to them to ask of their employees loyal and honest conduct within the meaning of their respective self-perception.

In reference to age discrimination, the German legislature has used the options granted in Art. 6 of Directive 2000/78/EC to approve further specific exceptions from the ban of age discrimination.[6] According to the GAET, differences of treatment on grounds of age do not constitute discrimination if they are objectively and reasonably justified by a legitimate aim; the means of achieving that aim must be appropriate and necessary. This applies to individual employment contracts, as well as to collective agreements and to the employer's unilateral measures or instructions. Differences in treatment not constituting discrimination on the grounds of age may include the fixing of special conditions on access to employment and vocational training, employment and occupation, including dismissal and remuneration conditions, for young people, older workers and persons with caring responsibilities in order to promote their vocational integration or to ensure their protection. Further allowed is the fixing of minimum conditions of age, professional experience or seniority in service for access to employment or to certain advantages linked to employment. However, any such measure still has to be in pursuit of a legitimate aim and to comply with the principle of proportionality. Furthermore, differences in treatment not constituting discrimination on grounds of age may include the fixing of a maximum age for recruitment, which is based on the training requirements of the post in question or the need for a reasonable period of employment before retirement. What exactly constitutes a reasonable period of employment is, of course, open for interpretation.

The GAET also contains procedural rules. First of all, a vacancy may not be advertised contravening the ban for the mentioned grounds of discrimination. Even if the GAET does not explicitly provide for any sanction in case of non-compliance, the labour courts interpret any violation of this rule as an indication of discrimination in the course of hiring. Second, the GAET obliges the employer to take measures, including preventive measures, to protect employees against discrimination on any one of the mentioned grounds. The employer must, in a

6 As regards the German provisions implementing the ban on age discrimination see M. Schmidt, Germany, in M. Sargeant (ed.), *The Law on Age Discrimination in the EU* (Alphen aan den Rijn: Kluwer, 2008), p. 29; and M. Weiss, Active Ageing and Labour Law in Germany, in F. Hendrickx et al. (eds.), *Active Ageing and Labour Law* (Antwerpen: Intersentia, 2012), p. 215.

proper kind and manner, particularly in the framework of vocational training and advanced vocational training, clearly point out that discrimination is illegal and work towards ensuring that it does not happen. If the employer provides appropriate training of their employees in order to prevent discrimination, the employer will be deemed to have met their obligations under the Act. The text of the GAET and any information about the institution responsible for handling grievances in accordance with the Act have to be published within the establishment. Publication may take place by display at appropriate places or by use of the usual information and communication channels at the establishment concerned.

Any provisions in agreements contravening the ban on discrimination guaranteed in the Act are null and void. In case of access to employment, the main sanction for discrimination provided for by the GAET is compensation for material and immaterial damages. The applicant is entitled to compensation for any damages resulting from discrimination, unless the applicant infringed their duties neither negligently nor deliberately. A right to be hired or promoted, however, is explicitly excluded, unless this right should result from other legal grounds. For immaterial damages, the employee may claim adequate compensation. The right to compensation for immaterial damage is not dependent on the employer's fault. However, if discrimination results from the application of collective agreements, the employer is liable for compensation only if they have acted deliberately or been grossly negligent. In cases of discrimination in the course of the hiring process, compensation for immaterial damage may not exceed three months' remuneration if the applicant would not have been employed, even in the case of a non-discriminatory hiring procedure.

Compensation is to be claimed in writing within two months, unless the parties to a collective agreement applicable to the employment relationship have agreed otherwise. In cases of an application or a promotion, the period begins to run at the time when the person to be employed or to be promoted receives the negative answer; in all other cases, the period starts at the time when the employee notices the discrimination.

Germany does not know a class action. It is up to each individual to sue for compensation. Neither trade unions nor other associations have a process status which would allow them to litigate without the involvement of the respective individual. According to the GAET, the individuals can be supported by so-called anti-discrimination organisations, but they have to take the initiative.

A Federal Anti-discrimination Office (FADO) has been established which, according to the GAET, has many tasks. In particular, any persons who feel discriminated against may ask this institution for help. The FADO has to advise and support these persons and mediate conflicts if necessary. The FADO also has to take measures to prevent discrimination, to conduct and promote research on discrimination, and to present opinions on specific issues of discrimination.

3 Examples of Problematic Cases

Despite the legal ban, discrimination happens for all the different reasons listed in the law. However, there are of course many aspects which needed legal clarification up to now. For the sake of illustration, two exceptions (positive action and occupational requirement) and two grounds for which discrimination is forbidden (age and religion) are chosen here as examples. They have turned out to be particularly problematic.

3.1 Positive Action

Even before the passing of the GAET in Germany, it was very controversial whether and to what extent positive action might be possible. This was mainly clarified by two spectacular cases.

There was first a law for public servants in the State of Bremen, according to which in case of equal qualification the female should be recruited always as long as females are not yet represented by half in the respective unit. This provision was contested and brought to the CJEU.[7] There this provision was considered to be too rigid and not in line with the then-existing Directive on gender equality. The CJEU supported in principle a provision on positive action, but only with a hardship clause. This led to a respective amendment of the law of Bremen.

The test of this pattern came some years later when the State of North Rhine-–Westphalia passed a law for public servants, according to which again in case of equal qualification, females had to be recruited, as long as they were underrepresented in the respective unit. The difference to the law of Bremen was that the rule did not apply if "grounds in the personal situation of the competing applicant are more important". The CJEU[8] confirmed that this hardship clause meets the requirements established in the judgment on the law of Bremen.

This pattern no longer has been contested and is now understood to be in line with the new provision of the GAET on positive action.

In Germany, employees are represented by a so-called works council to be elected in each establishment of at least five employees. The works council is participating in management decision-making in different ways.[9] The details are contained in the Act on Works Constitution (AWC), which was amended in 2001. According to the amendment, there has to be gender balance in the works council. The underrepresented sex in the establishment has to be represented in the works council at least in the same proportion it has among the workforce of the respective establishment. This has far-reaching effects and exceeds the normal pattern of positive action.

3.2 Occupational Requirement

Different treatment for a ground for which, according to the GAET, discrimination is prohibited exceptionally is possible if this ground is an "essential and

7 CJEU of 17 October 1995 (Kalanke).

8 CJEU of 11 November 1997 (Marschall).

9 For a description of the system see M. Weiss, *Labour Law and Industrial Relations in Germany* (4th ed., The Hague: Kluwer 2008), pp. 222–246.

decisive occupational requirement". What this means in concrete cases has been an ongoing source of controversy. Well known are the classic examples whether males can be midwives or whether females can be pilots. In a recent case, the FLC[10] at least has made perfectly clear that this exception has to be interpreted in a very restrictive way. In a private high school in the State of Bavaria, sports education in higher grades takes place separately for girls and boys. The sports education for girls is conducted by female teachers and the sports education for boys by male teachers. The school advertised a vacancy for a female sports teacher for the girls' sports education. A male applicant who was refused employment because of his sex sued the school for damages. The question at stake was whether to be female was an "essential and decisive occupational requirement" for a sports teacher for girls. The separate sports education for the two sexes was not contested. The question was only whether only female or also male teachers can teach the girls. In a very profound analysis, taking recourse to scientific studies, the FLC took the position that a male teacher can do the job. The performance of the job is not dependent on the sex and, therefore, the female sex is not an essential and decisive occupational requirement. This very restrictive approach to the exception is not welcomed by everybody. Controversies on this issue will remain in the future.

3.3 Age

As already indicated, the GAET contains examples for justifying exemptions from age discrimination. This may refer to recruitment, to automatic termination of employment or to termination by way of dismissals, including terms of notice.

Litigation on the question whether advertisement of a job violates the prohibition of age discrimination has occupied the judiciary for nine years in a rather complex case. In 2009 an insurance company advertised trainee positions for graduates in different fields, among them law. The criteria set out in that advertisement were possession of a very good university degree in one of the specified fields, either completed within the last year or to be completed in the coming months. A presently unemployed applicant who had finished his legal studies years ago and who already had management experience was denied the job. He claimed damages for violation of age discrimination. The question had to be resolved whether the advertisement by requiring a recent termination of the studies was indirect age discrimination since statistically this favours younger persons compared to older ones. The employer held this requirement to be justified because in a trainee programme people are needed who still can be formed and adapted to the needs of the company. This according to the employer best can be achieved by persons soon after the end of their university education who not yet are spoiled by job routines which may limit their openness. After bitter fights which even went up

10 FLC of 19 December 2019.

to the CJEU,[11] the FLC[12] together with the LCA of the State of Hesse[13] ruled that this justification is not convincing, because time which passes since the end of education and job experience does not necessarily affect openness and adaptability. Therefore, the advertisement was considered to be indirect age discrimination. The case shows how difficult it can be in a specific case to make the assessment of indirect age discrimination.

This case, by the way, contained a further interesting aspect. Since the applicant applied also in many other companies where he was unsuccessful and, therefore, sued the companies for compensation, the question arose whether he might not be seriously interested in getting the job but only interested in getting the damages for discrimination by acquiring the formal status of an applicant. Such so-called court hopping might be an abuse of the available legal instruments and, therefore, not permitted. The CJEU stated that "it is for the national court to verify, in accordance with the rules of evidence of national law, . . . whether the factors constituting an abusive practice are present in the case before it". According to the FLC together with the LCA Hesse, the mere fact of multiple applications and claims for compensation is not yet an indication of abuse. Abusive practice needs further indications and can only be assumed exceptionally; the burden of proof is on the employer's side. This very restrictive interpretation, of course, means that abusive practice almost never can be verified.

As far as recruitment is concerned, it is particularly controversial whether it is possible to set a maximum age for recruitment in the respective job. This may be illustrated by a case which was brought to the CJEU. It referred to the maximum age to be employed by the fire brigade. The reason for this maximum age was the fact that only younger persons have the physical strength to meet the professional challenges in the fire brigade. According to the CJEU it is legitimate that the maximum age for recruitment is fixed in a way which makes sure that the employed person can perform the job for a longer period. It based its decision on the fact that by scientific research it was proved that normally people above age 45 no longer are able to meet these professional challenges. Therefore, the CJEU held this maximum age to be compatible with the Directive 2000/78/EC.[14]

Another very important aspect refers to the question whether and in what way it is possible to facilitate recruitment for elderly persons. This in Germany has become particularly controversial in reference to fixed-term contracts.

In Germany fixed-term contracts are regulated by the Act on Part-Time Work and Fixed-Term Contracts (APTWFTC) of 2000 implementing Directive 99/70/EC on Fixed-Term Contracts. A fixed-term contract for the newly hired can be concluded for a maximum of two years without any precondition. A contract for a shorter period may be renewed up to three times up to the same maximum

11 CJEU of 28 July 2016 (Kratzer).

12 FLC of 26 January 2017.

13 LCA Hesse of 18 June 2018.

14 CJEU of 12 January 2010 (Wolf).

duration. However, afterwards the conclusion of a fixed-term contract is only possible if there is a special justification by an objective reason.[15]

In order to facilitate employment of older employees, a significant exception of this scheme was made. Without any precondition, employees of at least 58 and later on 52 years of age could be employed by fixed-term contracts, even in an unlimited repetitive way. This pattern was destroyed by the famous *Mangold* judgment of the CJEU[16] even before the Directive 2000/78/EC was transposed into German law. The CJEU's judgment was based on age discrimination as a general principle of European law, merely specified by the Directive. As a consequence of this judgment, the law has been amended. Since 2007 the conclusion of employment contracts for a definite period of up to five years is lawful without any objective reason justifying the time limit, provided that at the beginning of the employment relationship the employee is at least 52 years old and provided that they have been without employment for at least four months. The employment contract may be prolonged repeatedly up to a maximum duration of five years. Even if the amended version of the law explicitly refers to prior unemployment, it is still debatable whether or not it is compatible with the ban on age discrimination in terms of Directive 2000/78/EC. Whether this measure has helped to significantly increase the employment of older employees is unknown. It may well be that employment would have happened anyway but perhaps for an indefinite period.

The real battleground for age discrimination has become termination of employment, be it by way of automatic expiry or by way of dismissal. Clauses providing for an automatic termination of the employment relationship at a certain age are very common in Germany. According to the GAET, an agreement providing for the automatic termination of the employment relationship, at the regular time when the employee may apply for the old-age pension, may not constitute age discrimination. Whether this is fully in line with Art. 6 of the Directive 2000/78/EC is an open question.

Since the GAET does not say anything about agreements on automatic termination at an earlier age, these are even more controversial. This has led to many court cases. A very good example in this context was the case of pilots of the Lufthansa airline.[17] According to the respective collective agreement, pilots were allowed to be employed only until the age of 60 for reasons of safety. This was challenged by a pilot. The CJEU accepted safety of air traffic as a legitimate goal. However, it was considered not to be a necessary precondition for the protection of public health and safety (Art. 2 para. 5 of the Directive 2000/78/EC) since the retirement age also for pilots nationally and internationally is fixed to 65. For the same reason, the termination at 60 was denied to be an occupational requirement in the sense of Art. 4 of the Directive 2000/78/EC. Finally, for the same reason it

15 For a detailed description see Weiss/Schmidt, supra n. 6, at pp. 52–58.

16 CJEU of 22 November 2005 (Mangold).

17 CJEU of 13 September 2011 (Prigge).

was considered not to be justified by Art. 6 of the Directive 2000/78/EC because traffic safety does not belong to the legitimate goals covered by this provision. The lesson for similar cases is simple: whether automatic termination below the normal retirement age can be lawfully fixed depends on the circumstances of each individual case.

The problems arising in context of automatic termination of employment, however, are minor compared to the problems which German law on age discrimination is facing in the context of dismissals. The first difficulty is posed by the fact that according to the GAET dismissals are governed exclusively by the rules on dismissal protection. Thereby, according to the text of the law the provisions of the GAET do not apply. This creates confusion. Protection against unfair dismissals is regulated by the Act on Protection against Unfair Dismissals (APUD), which covers employment relationships after six months of employment in establishments above a minimum size of ten employees[18] and by the Acts for special groups (persons in maternity, disabled persons, works council members, etc.). None of these laws contains any explicit ban on discrimination because of age. According to the APUD, dismissals are lawful only for incapacity, for misconduct or for urgent economic reasons.[19] In the latter case the selection of those to be dismissed is an important aspect. According to section 1 para. 3 APUD, the selection has to be based on four criteria: seniority, age, disability and obligation to pay maintenance. There is no hierarchy between the four items; however, this can be established by collective agreements or work agreements.[20] The problem in this context is the question whether it is compatible with the Directive 2000/78/EC to include seniority and age as criteria for selection. Both factors work in favour of employees who are employed for a longer period and for older employees. Prohibition of age discrimination, however, is not supposed to only protect the elderly but it means that age should not be a reason for different treatment of employees, thereby also protecting younger employees.

According to the FLC,[21] it is in line with the requirements of the GAET that age is included in the set of criteria for selection since in principle elderly people have worse chances at the labour market. The inclusion of age, however, only is justified in the context of the three other criteria and would not be justified if it would be the exclusive criterion. The FLC considers the regulation as embedded in the APUD to be a fair balance between the interests of younger employees and the necessary protection of elderly persons. This rather tricky approach is accepted up to now.

As indicated above, the controversy on age discrimination even refers to the term of notice for dismissals. According to the Civil Code (CC) the basic term of notice amounts to four weeks to the 15th or to the end of a month. However, the

18 For details see Weiss/Schmidt, supra n. 6, 1 at pp. 25–126.

19 Ibid., pp. 126–129.

20 Ibid., p. 129.

21 FLC of 15 December 2011.

old version of Section 622 CC provided for an extension of this term according to seniority. It ended at seven months after 20 years of employment. However, it only started to count at the age of 25. Those under this age remained on the basic term of four weeks no matter how long they were employed. The different treatment of those under 25 years was based on the assumption that the employer's interest in flexibility would be a legitimate aim for different treatment. Young people would be more flexible, more mobile and at least on average would have fewer constraints (family obligations, etc.). When this was contested in court, it was brought up to the CJEU. According to its judgment,[22] this reasoning is not a legitimate aim justifying different treatment because of age. The law was considered to be age discrimination and void. Now the counting for the prolongation of the term of notice starts from the first day of employment, irrespective of the employee's age.

3.4 Religion

Long before the GAET was passed, it was controversial whether there could be sanctions if a Muslim woman would wear a headscarf at work. This debate culminated in a case where in a warehouse in a small town a saleswoman converted to Muslim belief and from now on insisted on wearing a headscarf because her belief did not allow her to present her head in public without a headscarf. This was not accepted by the employer, who was afraid that clients might not like the new outfit of the saleswoman and therefore stay away, which would mean a financial loss for the warehouse. This impact was explained to the saleswoman. When she nevertheless refused to take off the headscarf at work, she was dismissed because – according to the employer – she no longer qualified for her job. When the woman brought the dismissal to court, she lost in the lower instances but won the lawsuit in the FLC.[23] The Court ruled that the employee's fundamental right of freedom of religion outweighs the employer's fundamental right of freedom to conduct a business, which both are contained in the Constitution. This was a strong signal for prohibition of discrimination because of religion, even if it is in conflict with legitimate economic considerations.

The controversy on the Muslim headscarf, however, turns out to be a minor problem compared to the highly complicated debate on the exceptions granted to the churches in reference to prohibition of discrimination because of religion. The Constitution contains an Article according to which "religious societies shall regulate and administer their affairs independently within the limits of the law that applies to all". This, of course, does not exempt the churches from the obligation to respect the prohibition of discrimination for religious belief. But as already mentioned, the GAET in line with the underlying EU Directive states that a

> difference of treatment on the grounds of religion or belief of employees of a religious community, of facilities affiliated to it . . . or organisations

22 CJEU of 19 January 2010 (Kücükdeveci).
23 FLC of 10 October 2002.

> which have undertaken conjointly to practice a religion or belief, shall not constitute discrimination where such grounds constitute a justified occupational requirement for a particular religion or belief, having regard to the ethos of the religious community or organisation in question and by reason of their right to self-determination or by the nature of the particular activity.

This very wide-ranging and at the same time rather unspecific wording has led to many uncertainties. To understand the dimension of the problem, it is important to know that the two big Christian churches (Roman Catholic and Protestant) together are Germany's largest private employer. Together they account for around 1.3 million employees. They predominantly run charitable facilities like hospitals, nursing homes and services, schools and preschools and provide developmental services and humanitarian aid. Even though these facilities are state funded to the utmost extent, the churches use them to promote their faith. The churches' right to do so is constitutionally protected. The question is how far-ranging is their autonomy in differentiation because of religion. A recent case as of 7 July 2020 at the FCC may be helpful to illustrate the problem.

A sub-organisation of the Protestant Church in Germany advertised a part-time position which was limited to a period of two years. The scope of work consisted in the preparation of a report on the German implementation of the UN Convention against racism, which was to be produced in consultation with human rights organisations and further stakeholders and was intended to show politicians, the administration and other organisations options for action based on human rights. The respective job holder was supposed to act independently, of course observing the church's ethos in writing the report. The job advertisement requested membership in a Protestant church or a Christian church belonging to the Association of Christian Churches in Germany and identification with the church's mission. A female applicant not belonging to any church who had graduated in social education disclosed her non-denomination in her application. She was not even invited for an interview. The position was filled by somebody of Protestant faith who had a similar formal qualification. The woman without Christian denomination claimed compensation for discrimination on grounds of religion. The church organisation was of the opinion that different treatment on the grounds of religion was justified because the religion of the job holder was an essential occupational requirement. To determine this requirement would be exclusively up to the church employer in accordance with its right of self-determination as guaranteed by the German constitution and the Directive 2000/78/EC. The LC approved the claim. The LCA dismissed the suit. The FLC referred the case to the CJEU[24] and subsequently granted the claim.[25] In the meantime, the church employer filed a constitutional complaint against the decision of the FLC with the FCC as of 7 July 2020.

24 CJEU of 17 April 2018 (Egenberger).
25 FLC of 25 October 2018.

For decades the FCC merely examined whether the requirement to be a member of a particular denomination is plausibly related to church doctrine and is not improper, thereby giving the autonomy of the churches a very wide range. In applying this rule the church employers could make a specific denomination to be an essential requirement even for jobs which had nothing to do with the spiritual mission of the church (e.g. medical doctors). The CJEU favours a much more restrictive interpretation, giving the Courts the power to examine whether the requirement imposed by a church employer was an essential, legitimate and justified professional requirement according to its ethos. Furthermore, according to the CJEU such an essential, legitimate and justified professional requirement must be both necessary and objectively required by the very nature of the respective job in question or by the circumstances in which it is carried out. The FLC followed the jurisdiction of the CJEU. In doing so, it has considerably restricted the broad autonomy of choice by church employers, as approved by the FCC, and subjected them to complete judicial control. Now it remains to be seen how the FCC will position itself in this matter, whether it will follow the CJEU or whether it will insist on its earlier line of reasoning and, thereby, accuse the CJEU to have transgressed its powers (ultra vires).

The involvement of so many courts in this case and the fact that the church employer even wants to bring the FCC in position against the CJEU gives an idea of the relevance and the impact of this conflict. It decides on prohibition of discrimination for grounds of religion in a multitude of jobs.

4 Conclusion

As this overview demonstrates, Germany's legal system, Constitution and legislation in combination with the case law of domestic courts and the CJEU protects comprehensively against discrimination in employment. This, however, does not mean that there are no victims of discrimination. The problem is not the substantial law; the problem is the procedural way to reach sanctions for discrimination. Employees in existing employment relationships might be discriminated against but still do not dare to sue the employer. They do not want to risk repression, which easily might happen. This explains why in most cases individuals only sue for compensation because of discrimination if they are denied recruitment or if they are dismissed. Therefore, it would be necessary that trade unions or anti-discrimination associations could start a lawsuit on behalf of individuals without involvement of these individuals. There were in the past quite a few attempts in this direction, but so far none of them was successful.

5 The "Other" Discriminatory Criteria

Unregulated in the Polish Labour Code but Clarified by Case Law

Aneta Tyc

1 Introduction

In Poland, there is a regulatory dualism relating to non-discrimination in employment. On the one hand, legislation is included in the Labour Code of 26 June 1974[1] and, on the other hand, in the Act of 3 December 2010 on the implementation of some regulations of the European Union regarding equal treatment.[2] It must be noted, however, that the scope of the latter Act is broad and not limited to the sphere of employment.[3] Besides, it introduces a closed catalogue of the following discriminatory grounds: gender, race, ethnicity, nationality, religion, belief, worldview,[4] disability, age and sexual orientation. This is crucial for the purpose of the chapter, which is to analyse the "other" discriminatory criteria in the case of the non-exhaustive statutory catalogue. Thus, the Act of 2010 is beyond the scope

1 Journal of Laws of 1974, No. 24, item 141, consolidated text of the Journal of Laws of 2020, item 1320.

2 Journal of Laws of 2010, No. 254, item 1700, consolidated text of the Journal of Laws of 2020, item 2156.

3 According to Article 4, the scope of the Act covers the following areas:

1. Participation in vocational training,
2. Conditions for taking up and pursuing economic or professional activity, including, in particular, in the framework of an employment relationship or civil law contracts,
3. Joining and working in trade unions, employers' organisations and professional associations,
4. Access to and conditions of using:

a. Labour market instruments and services,
b. Social security,
c. Health care,
d. Education and higher education,
e. Services, including housing services, goods and the acquisition of rights and energy, if they are offered to the public.

4 The term "worldview" is of German origin (Weltanschauung), and it was first used in Kant's "Critique of the Power of Judgment" (1790) (Jan Cieciuch, Czym jest światopogląd? Filozoficzny kontekst psychologicznego pojęcia, 10 *Psychologia Rozwojowa*, 2, p. 149 (2005)). A worldview is "a collection of attitudes, values, stories and expectations about the world around us, which inform our every thought and action" (Alison J. Gray, International Psychiatry, vol. 8, no. 3, available at www.ncbi.nlm.nih.gov/pmc/articles/PMC6735033/#r11; see the cited literature).

DOI: 10.4324/9781003306962-6

of this research. On the contrary, a non-exhaustive list of discriminatory criteria is included in the Labour Code. Hence, the objective of the chapter is to examine critically the "other" discriminatory criteria than those regulated in the Labour Code. To meet this purpose, the chapter has been divided into six parts, including the introduction. Section 2 focuses on the established line of case law related to the legal nature of the catalogue of discriminatory criteria. The amendment of 16 May 2019 to the Labour Code is also discussed in this section. Section 3 explores the discourse and debate in the doctrine as regards both the catalogue itself and the aforementioned amendment related to it. Section 4 introduces the reader to the case law on the criteria recognised as discriminatory and section 5 on the criteria which have not been found to be discriminatory. Section 6 provides some concluding remarks.

It should be stressed that in Poland the word "criterion" is used interchangeably with "feature", "characteristic", "ground", "cause" or "reason". These terms will therefore be used synonymously as well.

2 The Established Line of Case Law and the Amendment of 2019

The main problem arising from the content of the Polish Labour Code is whether an open catalogue concerns only "personal" characteristics or also those related to the work performed. The amendment of 16 May 2019 may be of key importance, but to understand this, it is first proposed to analyse the situation prior to that amendment.

The previous version of Article 18^{3a} § 1 of the Labour Code stated:

> Employees must be treated equally with regard to the establishment and termination of an employment relationship, terms of employment, promotion and access to training to raise professional qualifications, especially without distinction on the grounds of sex, age, disability, race, religion, nationality, political beliefs, trade union membership, ethnic origin, denomination, sexual orientation, as well as without distinction on the grounds of employment for a definite or an indefinite term or on a full-time or part-time basis.[5]

5 It should be noted that chapter II of the Labour Code titled "Fundamental Principles of Labour Law" includes two separate provisions, one of which refers to the principle of equality (Article 11^2), according to which "Employees have equal rights for equal performance of the same duties; this provision applies in particular to the equal treatment of men and women at work". The other refers to the principle of non-discrimination (Article 11^3), which is further regulated in Article 18^{3a} § 1 et seq. of the Labour Code. The previous version of Article 11^3 stated that: "No discrimination in employment, either direct or indirect, especially on the grounds of a person's sex, age, disability, race, religion, nationality, political beliefs, trade union membership, ethnic origin, denomination, sexual orientation, as well as employment for a definite or an indefinite term or on a full-time or part-time basis, shall be allowed".

Against the background of such a formulation, the courts developed a certain well-established pattern of proceedings. As indicated by the Supreme Court in a judgment of 6 April 2017[6] and in accordance with settled case law, the wording of the provision distinguished two groups of forbidden criteria. It required equal treatment of employees: first, irrespective of their personal characteristics or properties, and these were listed by way of example ("especially"); and second ("as well as"), without distinction on the grounds of employment for a definite or an indefinite term or on a full-time or part-time basis. The separation of these two groups of discrimination criteria with the phrase "as well as without distinction on the grounds of" allowed for the assumption that the exemplary listing of the reasons for discrimination ("especially") was only referring to the first of these groups. An illustrative list of the criteria was treated as referring to personal characteristics and qualities not related to the work performed, and of such great social importance that the legislature recognised them as prohibited criteria of differentiation in the field of employment. Thus, an open catalogue of these causes allowed for its supplementation only with other personal features of social importance, such as worldview, HIV status[7] and even appearance, if under certain circumstances it could be regarded as a cause of differentiation of employees which constituted discrimination.[8]

This meant that when a candidate for employment or an employee were treated less favourably on the "other" grounds related to the work performed, such behaviour was not regarded as discrimination (called by the courts "a qualified form of unequal treatment") but as "simple" unequal treatment. As a consequence, the claimant was deprived of the right to compensation.

The amendment of 16 May 2019 was aimed at changing this interpretation. According to the current version of Article 18^{3a} § 1 of the Labour Code:

> Employees must be treated equally in regard to the establishment and termination of an employment relationship, terms of employment, promotion and access to training to raise professional qualifications, especially without distinction on the grounds of sex, age, disability, race, religion, nationality, political beliefs, trade union membership, ethnic origin, denomination, sexual orientation, employment for definite or an indefinite term, employment on a full-time or part-time basis.[9]

6 III PK 100/16, LEX no. 2331696.

7 According to the statistics relating to discrimination against HIV-infected persons in selected countries from 2008 to 2013, 11 percent of HIV-infected persons in Poland were refused employment during that period (values based on the People Living with HIV Stigma Index). See www.statista.com/statistics/282982/discrimination-of-hiv-infected-persons-in-selected-countries/.

8 See also the Supreme Court judgment of 2 October 2012, II PK 82/12, OSNP 2013, no. 17–18, item 202, LEX no. 1365774; the Supreme Court judgment of 13 February 2018, II PK 345/16, LEX no. 2488644. Similarly, see Marzena Szabłowska-Juckiewicz, *Odpowiedzialność odszkodowawcza podmiotu zatrudniającego za naruszenie zasady równego traktowania* (Warsaw: Wolters Kluwer, 2019), pp. 97–98.

9 An open catalogue of forbidden criteria is also included in Article 11^3 of the Labour Code in the light of which "No discrimination in employment, either direct or indirect, especially on the

As pointed out in the justification of the project of the Act of 16 May 2019,[10] the change consisting of removing the formulation "as well as without distinction on the grounds of" from the provision was intended to mean that any unequal treatment of employees, unjustified by objective reasons, will be considered to be discrimination. In the opinion of the project initiator, there are no rational premises differentiating discrimination and unequal treatment. In other words, the project initiator wanted to change the interpretation, according to which only the worse treatment of an employee due to some personal characteristics or properties not related to the work performed or due to employment for a definite or an indefinite term or on a full-time or part-time basis constituted discrimination. The project initiator criticised the view that inequality resulting from reasons other than those deemed to be discriminatory was not regarded as discrimination, even if the employer violated the principle of equal treatment of employees. It was contested that, as a consequence, an employee was not entitled to compensation.

3 Uncertainty as to the Direction of the Case Law After the Amendment of 2019

The position adopted, *inter alia*, by the aforementioned judgment of 6 April 2017 has been positively assessed by a large part of academic legal writing. For example, Monika Tomaszewska pointed out that it was

> an attempt to separate the principle of non-discrimination from the principle of equality, finding a compromise solution for an already poorly formulated provision. The amendment ruined what has been achieved through the interpretation of Article 18^{3a} of the Labour Code.

She highlighted the fact that discrimination should be treated as a qualified form of unequal treatment, which has a cause related to personal characteristics.[11]

According to that author, the legislature has not achieved its purpose by amending the wording of Article 18^{3a} of the Labour Code.[12] She mentions two important

grounds of a person's sex, age, disability, race, religion, nationality, political beliefs, trade union membership, ethnic origin, denomination, sexual orientation, employment for a definite or an indefinite term, employment on a full-time or part-time basis, shall be allowed".

10 www.sejm.gov.pl/sejm8.nsf/druk.xsp?nr=1653.

11 Monika Tomaszewska, Art. 18(3(a)) Zakaz dyskryminacji – definicje [in:] Krzysztof Wojciech Baran (ed.), *Kodeks pracy. Komentarz*. Vol. I. Art. 1–113 (Warsaw: Wolters Kluwer, 2020), LEX. Similarly, e.g., judgment of the Court of Appeal in Wrocław of 10 May 2018, III APa 8/18, LEX no. 2940121; order of the Supreme Court of 7 January 2014, I PK 174/13, LEX no. 1646039; judgment of the Court of Appeal in Poznań of 18 April 2013, III APa 21/12, LEX no. 1327589; the Supreme Court judgment of 10 May 2018, I PK 54/17, LEX no. 2486202; Anna Błaszczak, Efektywność środków ochrony przed dyskryminacją w Polsce, Przegląd Prawa Publicznego 2015, n. 6, p. 37 et seq.; Grzegorz Jędrejek, *Dochodzenie roszczeń związanych z mobbingiem, dyskryminacją i molestowaniem* (Warsaw: Wolters Kluwer, 2017), LEX.

12 Monika Tomaszewska, Art. 18(3(a)) Zakaz dyskryminacji – definicje, supra n. 11.

factors that lead to such a conclusion. One of them is related to the fact that there are still two separate provisions on the principle of equality (Article 11^2 of the Labour Code) and the principle of non-discrimination (Article 11^3 of the Labour Code). Therefore, both principles should be assigned a specific but different normative content. She claims that otherwise one of these provisions should be considered redundant. The second factor is connected with the necessity to provide a pro-EU interpretation of national provisions implementing EU directives and the Charter of Fundamental Rights of the European Union.

The question is begged as to what a pro-EU interpretation means. After all, someone may say that there is an exhaustive catalogue of discrimination grounds at the level of EU law.[13] Article 19 of the Treaty on the Functioning of the European Union (Article 13 of the Treaty Establishing the European Community[14]) authorises the Council to take "appropriate action to combat discrimination based on sex, racial or ethnic origin, religion or belief, disability, age or sexual orientation". Similarly, the EU directives – issued within the competencies conferred on the EU – create an exhaustive list of the grounds of discrimination.[15] However, Article 21 of the Charter of Fundamental Rights of the European Union[16] provides for an open catalogue of discriminatory grounds.[17] Polish authors focus on the fact that discriminatory grounds included in the Charter refer only to human personal characteristics innate or acquired as a result of the development of their activity. Thus, they do not refer to characteristics related to the work performed. Such an interpretation is perceived as being in line with the spirit of EU law.

13 At the margin, in Poland any ideas for defending an exhaustive catalogue of discriminatory grounds modelled on EU directives would be contrary to Article 32 of the Constitution of the Republic of Poland of 2 April 1997 (Journal of Laws No. 78, item 483, available at: www.sejm.gov.pl/prawo/konst/angielski/konse.htm), which adopts a broad approach:

1. All persons shall be equal before the law. All persons shall have the right to equal treatment by public authorities.
2. No one shall be discriminated against in political, social or economic life for any reason whatsoever.

14 Furthermore, see Mark Bell, Anti-Discrimination Law and the European Union, in Paul Craig and Gráinne de Búrca (eds.), *Oxford Studies in European Law, General* (Oxford: Oxford University Press, 2002), p. 121 et seq.

15 For a detailed discussion, see Marcin Wujczyk, Zasady równego traktowania i zakazu dyskryminacji, Krzysztof Wojciech Baran (ed.), *System Prawa Pracy. Vol. X. Międzynarodowe publiczne prawo pracy. Standardy europejskie* (Warsaw: Wolters Kluwer Polska, 2020), Lex; Marzena Szabłowska-Juckiewicz, Odpowiedzialność, supra n. 8, at p. 52 et seq.

16 Official Journal of the European Union, 26 October 2012, C 326, p. 391.

17 It states that: "1. Any discrimination based on any ground such as sex, race, colour, ethnic or social origin, genetic features, language, religion or belief, political or any other opinion, membership of a national minority, property, birth, disability, age or sexual orientation shall be prohibited. 2. Within the scope of application of the Treaties and without prejudice to any of their specific provisions, any discrimination on grounds of nationality shall be prohibited". See more: Zbigniew Góral, *O kodeksowym katalogu zasad indywidualnego prawa pracy* (Warsaw: Wolters Kluwer, 2011), p. 157.

Importantly, not all authors looked favourably at the Polish case law distinguishing two groups of forbidden criteria. Helena Szewczyk has always maintained that the enumeration of the discriminatory criteria in the Labour Code was exemplary, regardless of whether these criteria related to the employee's personal characteristics or their life choices unrelated to the work performed, or whether they related to the work performed, the legal status of the employer and so forth.[18] She pointed out that most often direct discrimination will occur due to reasons related to personal characteristics of the employee or their life choices unrelated to the work performed. The "other" criteria that are relevant in practice may embrace in particular family status, financial or property status, marital status, clean criminal record, health, appearance, social origin and social activity. Among the discriminatory criteria related to the work performed and the status of the employer, that author listed type of work, professional qualifications, quantity and quality of work, workload, working conditions and so forth.[19]

Ewa Podgórska-Rakiel seems to hold the same opinion. She claims that the amendment of 16 May 2019 of the national anti-discrimination law is aimed at protecting an employee as the weaker party to the employment relationship. The current wording of Article 18^{3a} § 1 (and Article 11^{3}) of the Labour Code will make it easier for employees and employment candidates to pursue claims for discrimination on the basis of a discriminatory criterion, when it is not explicitly mentioned in this provision.[20]

It is not certain in which direction the case law will go after the 2019 amendment. However, the author of this chapter does not believe that the courts will change their method of operation which has been developed over the years simply because of eliminating the formulation "as well as" from Article 18^{3a} § 1 of the Labour Code. In fact, according to the opinion expressed by the Supreme Court on the 2019 amendment, "the proposed changes . . . are redundant as they do not bring any new normative content".[21]

In the light of the above, one should look at the judgments passed in recent years which relate to the "other" discriminatory criteria, that is, other than those mentioned in Article 18^{3a} § 1 of the Labour Code.

18 Similarly, the Supreme Court judgment of 12 September 2006, I PK 87/06, Orzecznictwo Sądu Najwyższego Izba Pracy, Ubezpieczeń Społecznych I Spraw Publicznych 2007, no. 17–18, item 246; the Supreme Court judgment of 12 September 2006, I PK 89/06, Monitor Prawa Pracy 2007, no. 2, p. 88; the Supreme Court judgment of 22 February 2007, I PK 242/06, Monitor Prawa Pracy 2007, no. 7, p. 336.

19 Helena Szewczyk, *Glosa do wyroku SN z dnia 2 października 2012 r., II PK 82/12* (Warszawa: Wolters Kluwer, Orzecznictwo Sądów Polskich, 2014), no. 11, p. 1508.

20 Ewa Podgórska-Rakiel, *Zmiany dotyczące równego traktowania w zatrudnieniu oraz mobbingu* (LEX, 2019), online access.

21 The Supreme Court's opinion is available at the Polish Sejm website: www.sejm.gov.pl/sejm8.nsf/druk.xsp?documentId=F69FFA3A32FD99C0C1258154005CD665.

4 Criteria Recognised as Discriminatory by the Polish Case Law

4.1 Trainee Attorney-at-Law Status

One of the most interesting and controversial cases dealt with by the Polish courts concerned a trainee attorney-at-law status as a discriminatory criterion. The dispute arose against the background of the following facts. In 1996, the claimant was employed in the Tax Office where she gained professional experience. In 2004, she was transferred to the Tax Control Office where she held a post of a "senior referendary" (*starszy referendarz*), which is a post in which people are employed immediately after graduation. A few months later, she asked her employer for consent to undergo the attorney-at-law training, which he agreed to do. At the same time, the claimant's superiors assured her that after passing the attorney-at-law examination, she would be employed as a legal adviser. However, her employer failed to fulfil his promise and the claimant – until the end of her employment with the defendants, which was October 2008 – continued in the post of senior referendary, despite having successfully passed the qualification exam for a fiscal control inspector and the attorney-at-law examination. Her superiors did not submit any promotion applications concerning the claimant in order to promote her to a higher position, which carried a higher salary. Her superiors believed that she was in a privileged position compared to other employees because she exercised her (statutory) right to be released from work in order to participate in compulsory attorney-at-law classes two days a week. In the years 2003–2009, two persons employed in the defendant's office in a position of referendary and three persons employed in a position of senior referendary (including the claimant) passed the examination for the position of fiscal control inspector. As of 31 October 2008, there was no one (except the claimant) employed in a position of senior referendary at the defendants' office who would have passed the qualification exam for a fiscal control inspector in 2004–2008 and had a university degree in law or administration. In addition, the claimant maintained that during her employment at the defendant's office, she was not qualified – just like the other employees – to participate in training courses to raise professional qualifications. She only attended classes preparing for the qualification exam for a fiscal control inspector and the attorney-at-law examination while other employees attended many other courses. The courts therefore had to decide whether a trainee attorney-at-law status was an objective reason justifying that the claimant was not referred for professional training.

The court of first instance found that there was direct discrimination against the claimant because she was not treated on an equal footing with other comparable employees as regards promotion to a higher position which attracted higher remuneration. As established by the court, the scope of her activities in the position of senior referendary was identical to the activities performed by senior tax commissioners working together with the claimant. This means that the claimant, as a person with the same qualifications as other comparable employees performing the same job, was employed in a lower, less-paid position. It is worth noting that in the light of witness statements, she was a diligent and conscientious employee dedicated to expanding her qualifications. However, the claimant's lack of promotion resulted from the erroneous assumption presented by her superiors that being a trainee attorney-at-law, she was privileged over other employees. Such reasoning was assessed by the court as unjustified and discriminatory against the claimant.

According to the judgment of the court of second instance, the reason indicated by the claimant (that of being a trainee attorney-at-law) could not be considered a criterion of discrimination, because it was not her personal quality but a circumstance related to the employment relationship between the parties. Moreover, the court of second instance held that a trainee attorney-at-law status constituted an objective reason justifying that the claimant was not referred for professional training. Having considered the fact of the case, this court held:

> The contract concluded between the claimant and the defendant's office in August 2004, concerning the attorney-at-law training, became an element of the employment relationship between the parties. By implementing this contract, the employer fulfilled its obligation . . . to facilitate the improvement of professional qualifications by an employee, including granting a leave from work in order to participate in compulsory classes.

The court concluded that there was no breach of the principle of non-discrimination. Besides, it was pointed out that the claimant's situation was special and individual. No other employee of the respondent's office was in the same situation at the same time.

The Supreme Court did not share this view and ruled in favour of the claimant. It was held that some assumptions of the court of second instance were incorrect, namely:

1. That a trainee attorney-at-law status cannot constitute a protected characteristic;
2. That the claimant was not discriminated against in terms of promotion, remuneration and referral to training;
3. That a trainee attorney-at-law status was an objective reason justifying that the claimant was not referred for professional training;
4. That the work performed by the claimant while employed as a senior referendary and the work performed by persons employed as senior tax commissioners is not work of equal value, despite the requirement of comparable professional qualifications, scope of duties, responsibility and effort;
5. That the claimant was to be refused compensation for unequal treatment in employment.

The Supreme Court ruled that conducting a specific test shall help determine whether there is a justified presumption of direct discrimination in a particular case. This test consists in analysing whether there would be discrimination if the claimant did not have the feature indicated by them as the cause of unequal treatment. In the case under discussion, the court of second instance should have asked the following question: would the claimant been promoted to a higher position and would she have received a higher salary after having passed the qualification examination for a fiscal control inspector if she had not undergone the attorney-at-law training at that time and had not taken advantage of exemptions from work to which she had been entitled in order to participate in compulsory attorney-at-law classes? As the Supreme Court pointed out, such an analysis was not carried out by the court of second instance.

The Supreme Court did not share the view of the court of second instance, that being a trainee attorney-at-law cannot constitute a protected characteristic due to the fact that it is not her personal quality but a circumstance related to the employment relationship between the parties. The Supreme Court argued that completing the attorney-at-law training was closely related to the claimant, and it was neither related to employment with the defendant employer nor to the performance of employee duties.

This case shows large discrepancies in interpretation which may arise in practice in respect to what is "closely related to the claimant" or "related to the work performed". It is worth noting that the judgment was issued long before the amendment was made to the Labour Code.

4.2 Motherhood/Parenthood

In another judgment, dated 9 May 2019, the Supreme Court[22] referred to motherhood as a discriminatory criterion. The claimant was employed as a medical representative in an international pharmaceutical company. After returning from maternity leave, she applied for a reduction in working time and submitted a medical certificate on breastfeeding. The claimant thus wanted to exercise her statutory rights related to motherhood. The employer should therefore have reduced her working time and should have granted her breaks from work for breastfeeding. Moreover, the employer should have allowed his employee to return to work in her previous position with a guarantee of the previous remuneration in all its components. However, this did not happen. In addition, the employer did not apply to the claimant the rule adopted by him according to which the area where employees performed their activities was assigned according to the place of their residence. The claimant was also assigned to work with employees of an external company, which resulted in a reduction in quarterly bonuses. Another manifestation of discrimination was related to the fact that the claimant was allowed to work without compulsory product training. Moreover, immediately upon the return of the claimant from maternity leave, the employer was delaying the claimant's admission to work and prompted her to take annual leave. He also delayed

22 III PK 50/18, LEX no. 2692145.

the allocation of a company car and computer equipment. Subsequently, when he referred her for training, he did not provide her with accommodation, even if other employees were granted such an opportunity. The above had additional negative consequences for the claimant, as she had to leave the house during the night in order to be on time for the training. At the same time, she had no opportunity to rest after a long and exhausting business trip. Then, the employer accused the claimant of not being sufficiently concentrated and active during her training. The claimant's superior who was supervising her work also behaved in a discriminatory and improper way. He abused his superior position and humiliated the claimant, pointing out that she was not doing her job well. He was criticising the way she was working, was refusing to accept her arguments, was constantly controlling her, even going so far as to follow her. She was stressed and had the impression that the employer was looking for a reason to dismiss her. The stress made her sick. Sending the claimant on a delegation immediately after the maternity leave resulted in the fact that she – being on business trips for many hours – had two breast infections with high fever. Ultimately, also due to the nature of her job and health problems, she stopped feeding.

The actions and omissions of the defendant should be considered, in the opinion of the court of first instance, as discrimination of the claimant due to the fact that she exercised her rights related to motherhood as guaranteed by the Labour Code. The employer's behaviour had a negative impact on the claimant's private and professional life, as well as on her mental health. The claimant undertook psychiatric treatment, which she continued for about a year. She took sedatives and psychotropic drugs and limited her role as mother and wife in the family.

The court of second instance and the Supreme Court rightly confirmed that motherhood as a personal trait was the reason for the claimant's discrimination, although it is not mentioned in the Labour Code. As highlighted by the Supreme Court, the discriminatory practices of the defendant employer violated the claimant's dignity in all respects, that is as a human person, a social being as a member of the Polish civil society, and as an individual belonging to a group of female employees returning to work after maternity leave.

The courts adopted a similar line of reasoning as regards parenthood as a discriminatory criterion. According to the judgment of the Court of Appeal in Warsaw of 31 May 2019,[23] unequal treatment of an employee due to the fact that they have taken parental leave, and consisting in setting a significantly lower basic remuneration after returning from this leave as compared to employees working in the same positions, constitutes discrimination on the grounds of parenthood.[24]

Under Polish law, after returning from parental leave, the employee is entitled to remuneration not lower than the remuneration they were entitled to on the day of starting work in the position held before the leave. Therefore, if, during the

23 III APa 4/14, LEX no. 2767461.

24 See also the Supreme Court judgment of 25 February 2016, II PK 357/14, OSNP 2017, no. 10, item 122 or LEX no. 2007791.

employee's leave, there were changes in remuneration regarding this position, these changes also apply to the employee's remuneration. In short, the basis of reference for determining the amount of remuneration is not the remuneration received by the employee before the leave, but the remuneration currently applicable to their position.[25]

On the facts of the case of 31 May 2019, after returning from parental leave, the claimant was not admitted to the position she held before the leave. Besides, at some point, she realised, by accidentally listening to the conversation of her female colleagues, that her remuneration was underpaid in relation to the remuneration received by other comparable employees. In this situation, she took steps towards the employer aimed at determining whether her remuneration was significantly underpaid and by what amount. The claimant addressed several letters to the employer clearly formulating her allegations about the amount of remuneration. The employer avoided providing information in this regard. The fact of entrusting the claimant with duties other than those performed before the parental leave, which she did not feel competent to perform; the lack of agreement with the employer on clarifying the amount of her remuneration in comparison to the remuneration of other employees; and the feeling of harm resulted in the claimant's stress. She felt aggrieved, cheated and treated worse than other employees. This situation increased her sense of injustice, induced a feeling of helplessness and violated her dignity as an employee who is entitled to remuneration adequate to the work performed, comparable to the remuneration of other qualified employees holding positions, and performing duties analogous to the position and duties of the claimant. According to the Court of Appeal's legal justification to the judgment:

> Discrimination was manifested in the refusal to provide working conditions from before the leave and, above all, in the payment of lower remuneration in relation to comparable employees. It resulted in a breach of the claimant's . . . dignity as an employee entitled to rights related to motherhood . . . and to a fair, not understated as a result of discrimination remuneration for work and a sense of normal psychological comfort.

It is gratifying in both cases to know that the courts issued fair judgments, even if motherhood and parenthood are not included in the Polish Labour Code.

4.3 Citizenship

In its judgment of 7 May 2019,[26] the Supreme Court had the opportunity to rule also on the issue of citizenship as a discriminatory criterion.

The facts of the case indicated that the defendant employer made the amount of the security staff's remuneration dependent on whether the employee had German

25 See the Supreme Court judgment of 29 January 2008, II PK 143/07, OSNP 2009, no. 3–4, item 67.
26 II PK 31/18, LEX no. 2654306.

citizenship. Employees with German citizenship employed before 2000 were remunerated in accordance with the rules of the collective agreement of 1973, and employees with Polish citizenship were remunerated in accordance with less favourable provisions of labour law in force in Poland. For persons who had only Polish citizenship, the amount of remuneration was set in zlotys; for those employed before 2000 having German or dual citizenship, the amount of remuneration was set in marks (and later in euros). The differences between the remuneration rates after their conversion were significant. Moreover, the employees with German or dual citizenship had a weekly working time of less than 40 hours – namely, 38.5 hours – and they were also entitled to 30 days' vacation every year, which was more than that provided for by the Polish Labour Code. Such differences persisted throughout the claimant's employment.

These different rules applied mainly to employees who were employed before 1 April 2000. On 1 April 2000, a new collective agreement came into force, as a result of which uniform rules of remuneration for employees with and without German citizenship were introduced among newly employed persons. However, the difference in remuneration compared to employees with German citizenship employed before 1 April 2000 had not been closed. The court of first instance made a detailed analysis of the remuneration of security guards. It compared the remuneration of the claimant and other employees with German and dual citizenship. This procedure showed that the citizenship factor had a clear impact on the amount of remuneration received. The court referred to the Labour Code and noted that the activities undertaken by the employer consisting in different shaping of the remuneration rules in relation to employees with only Polish citizenship and employees with (also) German citizenship were discriminatory, which should result in a sanction in the form of an award for compensation. It concluded that citizenship is the discriminating factor in terms of remuneration for work. The court stressed that there was no discrimination with regard to remuneration of employees in the same grades as the claimant, that is in the security and passport departments, but only those employed after 2000. However, discrimination was found in relation to employees employed before 2000. The court judged that wage discrimination on the basis of citizenship, which occurred in a different context many years ago, cannot be explained by the principle of acquired rights, as pleaded by the employer. Also, further increases in the remuneration of employees treated more favourably contradicts the assertion that the employer made every possible effort to eliminate discrimination.

The court of second instance allowed the defendant's appeal. It did not dispute the fact that the defendant, until 1 April 2000, differentiated the amount of remuneration of security workers and those employed in other positions considered to be comparable, depending on whether the worker in question had German citizenship. However, the appellate court emphasised that the differentiation of the situation of persons employed before 2000 was maintained by applying a legally permissible criterion, that is, the principle of protection of acquired rights. This principle was also applied when implementing the new collective agreement of 2000.

In the case under examination the Supreme Court identified "partial" discrimination, which is discrimination which consists in maintaining the impact of the prohibited criterion, even if it does not apply to all employees. As pointed out by the Supreme Court, failure to take any action to equalise the level of remuneration, and on the contrary maintaining it by raising the salaries of the favoured employees, may constitute discrimination, especially if such a state persists over a period of many years. The Supreme Court also emphasised that

> the facts of the case may be classified as indirect discrimination . . . where the date of employment constitutes the "apparently neutral criterion", which means that the fact of having German citizenship by those employed before April 1, 2000 causes "unfavorable disproportions" in terms of the amount of remuneration for the same work.

As regards the concept of acquired rights invoked by the court of second instance, it remains problematic whether the category of acquired rights applies to contractual provisions. The employment contract may be amended with the use of available legal solutions. This means that the principle of respect for acquired rights does not apply in this case. At most, there are contractual provisions which are binding on the parties until they are changed. In conclusion, the maintenance by the employer of the differences in remuneration rates originating from the employee's citizenship constitutes discrimination.

4.4 Appearance

Another judgment of the Supreme Court extending the catalogue of discriminatory grounds dates back to 4 October 2007[27] and relates to personal appearance.

The claimant had been employed by the defendant employer since 1997 and her supervisor had no objection to her work. In 2003, there was a change in the position of the claimant's superior. The court of first instance found that the new superior did not treat all employees equally. She showed a particularly negative attitude towards employees younger than her, including the claimant having a well-groomed and attractive appearance. The new superior repeatedly used invectives against the claimant, such as "idiot" or "moron". She did so in the presence of other employees and clients. She falsely accused the claimant of not properly performing her duties. She was constantly looking for an excuse to punish the claimant, was interested in her private life, and requested her to work overtime. It happened that the superior changed the previously established working time schedule, did not inform the claimant about it, and then accused her of being late.

One day, at the request of the superior, the claimant was issued a reprimand for non-compliance with internal procedures. Despite the fact that the claimant informed the director "about the whole situation", no investigative steps were

27 I PK 24/07, LEX no. 406847.

taken. From the beginning of 2004, the claimant was treated for inflammation of the respiratory tract, anaemia, depression and anxiety disorders. Finally, the claimant was served with the statement of the defendant on the termination of the employment contract with a three-month notice period due to the abolition of her job.

The court of first instance found that the above-mentioned treatment of the claimant was due to her age and attractive appearance. The court highlighted that although overtime work is the employee's duty, it must result from the specific needs of the employer and be ordered rationally, taking into account the employee's right to rest. With regard to the claimant, this work was maliciously imposed and was primarily aimed at humiliating her. According to the court of first instance, the employer, by tolerating the behaviour of the claimant's superior, breached the obligation to provide employees with safe and hygienic working conditions.

The court of second instance shared the factual findings and the legal basis of the judgment under appeal. It also emphasised the importance of the prohibition of discrimination as one of the fundamental principles of labour law based on the Polish Constitution.

The Supreme Court confirmed that the claimant had been subjected to harassment by behaviour, the purpose or effect of which, according to its definition, was to violate the dignity of, or to humiliate the employee, because of her young age and "distinctive appearance". For these reasons the claimant encountered different and unequal treatment than other employees. In particular, she was forced to perform work under different conditions than other employees, namely, to work overtime.

There is no doubt that the extension of the catalogue of prohibited discriminatory criteria to personal appearance was perfectly justified in circumstances such as those described in the aforementioned judgment.

5 Criteria Not Recognised by the Courts as Discriminatory

5.1 Creation of One's Image in a Talk Show TV Programme

In Poland, some cases were also examined to determine that in a specific factual situation, the catalogue of discriminatory criteria could not be expanded. A vivid example was provided by the Supreme Court judgment of 29 November 2017.[28] As the facts of the case indicate, the employer was looking for a person for the position of manager with a strong personality and with a natural predisposition to build authority in a masculine environment of drivers. He informed the claimant that she would be employed and referred her for a medical examination. However, on the same day, he announced to her the need to stop the recruitment process due to her participation in a TV talk show programme. After reviewing the

28 I PK 367/16, LEX no. 2433082.

recording of this programme, the employer decided that the claimant, due to her attitude and views presented on TV, did not meet the requirements for a candidate for the position of manager. He also expressed concerns that the claimant's potential subordinates watched the programme. According to the employer, the claimant's participation in the programme made her appear as a person with no opinion of her own, completely subordinated to her husband's will, and giving the impression of a person not predisposed to manage a team of employees composed mostly of male drivers. Incidentally, the employer did not employ another person as a result of external recruitment, but the duties of the manager were taken over by his deputy.

The claim was based on the employer's failure to comply with the prohibition of discrimination in employment, the manifestation of which was a refusal to recruit the claimant because of "gender and cultivating traditional values and traditional division of roles in the family". The court of first instance ruled that the decision taken by the defendant had a logical justification, not constituting a breach of the prohibition of discrimination in employment. It resulted from the assessment that the claimant presented herself in the programme as a person giving the impression of not having the capacity to manage a team of male employees. In this situation, the employer's concerns about the cooperation of the claimant with future subordinates who watched the programme and commented on it to the employer could be right. The court submitted that the views presented by the claimant in a TV programme diverge from the view generally accepted in society about the division of roles in the family and that they could hardly be considered traditional. Bearing in mind the above, and that the defendant did not employ another person as a result of external recruitment, the court assumed that the claimant was wrong to allege that an employment contract was not signed with her due to her "gender and cultivating traditional values and traditional division of roles in the family".

The court of second instance upheld the judgment of the first instance court and pointed out that after the recruitment process the defendant had not confirmed the conclusion of an employment contract with the claimant in any form and – after watching the programme and consulting the opinions of the employees – did not admit her to work.

The court of second instance highlighted the fact that the employer had reasons for assessing that the self-presentation of the claimant on the TV revealed a different image of her than that presented during recruitment. At the interview the claimant presented herself unreliable, namely in the light as expected by the employer looking for a suitable person for the position of manager. He drew a conclusion that in reality she is the person who was featured on the TV show. Thus, the defendant could doubt the real and actual personality of the recruited candidate and, caring for the interests of the employing establishment, lose the will to employ a person who does not possess the qualities required for a managerial position. In this situation, there was no discrimination, which would allow a claim for damages.

The claimant lodged an appeal against this judgment to the Supreme Court. She stated that an important legal issue in the case boils down to a question whether publicly manifested attitudes presented by a potential employee with respect to marital relations, which may not necessarily be true and may be a form of creation for a popular TV programme such as a talk show, may constitute an allowed criterion of employment discrimination.

The Supreme Court dismissed the appeal. It pointed out that – according to an established line of case law – the prohibited criteria for differentiating the situation of employees include those explicitly mentioned in the Labour Code and, in addition, personal qualities of the employee which are socially relevant and are not related to the work performed.[29] The prohibited criteria embrace circumstances that are not based on the employee's obligations, the manner of their performance or their qualifications.[30] The Supreme Court ruled that some caution should be exercised in expanding the catalogue of prohibited discriminatory criteria, because they should be relevant from the social point of view, and it is difficult to consider the quite controversial "creation of one's image in a talk show TV programme" as such a criterion. This Court also highlighted that

> the creation of her own image by the claimant by "a kind of subordination of one spouse to the other" resulted in the defendant having reasonable grounds to believe that the claimant did not have the necessary qualities required of an employee in a managerial position.

5.2 The Way in Which One Becomes an Employee and the Amount of Remuneration at the Previous Employer

Another judgment rendered in favour of the employer was issued by the Supreme Court judgment on 2 October 2012[31] in a situation where two court instances ruled otherwise. The facts of the case are as set out below. The claimant was employed in the hospital as an electrician. The defendant who won the tender for the technical service of the hospital took over the employees of the technical department, including the claimant, and concluded new employment contracts with them. The claimant's hourly rate at the time of concluding the employment contract with the defendant was lower than that of his colleague who was employed in the same position with the same scope of duties and powers. Moreover, the claimant – unlike his colleague – did not receive a pay increase after one year.

The court of first instance shared the claimant's opinion that he had been discriminated against throughout his employment, and discrimination consisted of a lower hourly rate and no pay increases. It was established that the work of the claimant and his colleague was the same and of equal value. Importantly, the

29 See the Supreme Court judgment of 20 July 2017, I PK 216/16, LEX no. 2389574.

30 See the Supreme Court judgment of 5 October 2007, II PK 14/07, OSNP 2008, no. 21–22, item 311.

31 II PK 82/12, OSNP 2013 no. 17–18, item 202, LEX no. 1365774 (already cited in sec. 2 above).

defendant failed to demonstrate that she followed objective criteria when differentiating the remuneration of both employees.

The court of second instance shared the arguments of the court of first instance and pointed out that the prohibited grounds of discrimination listed in Article 18^{3a} § 1 of the Labour Code constitute an exemplary catalogue. Moreover, the court identified a criterion differentiating the remuneration of individual employees employed in the same position as the claimant. That was the way in which they became employees of the defendant, namely whether they were taken over from the hospital or were independently employed by the defendant. The second criterion, referring only to employees transferred from the hospital, was the amount of remuneration received by them while employed by the previous employer. However, the defendant failed to demonstrate that any of these criteria justified the different treatment of the claimant in terms of the amount of remuneration in relation to other electricians. In the opinion of the court of second instance, there are situations in which in the circumstances of a given case it is impossible or very difficult to indicate a prohibited criterion of differentiating employees. For example, the employer may differentiate employees in a discriminatory manner, guided by a personal aversion to some of them, or by the fact that an employee does not claim equal treatment in the course of employment, as in the case of the claimant. For this reason, the employer bears the burden of proving that he was guided by objectively justified criteria differentiating the situation of individual employees (e.g. in terms of the amount of remuneration). The employee should only prove that unequal treatment in employment took place. The claimant demonstrated this circumstance, while the defendant failed to cope with her procedural burden.

The Supreme Court pointed out that the court of second instance wrongly equated the principle of non-discrimination with the principle of equal treatment of employees who fulfil the same duties in the same way. The principle of non-discrimination means that certain persons or groups are not to be treated less favourably on discriminatory grounds. The Supreme Court highlighted that such criteria as the way in which the claimant and his colleagues became employees of the defendant and the amount of remuneration received by them while employed by the previous employer cannot be considered as discriminatory criteria of differentiation. They do not refer either to socially significant personal characteristics or personal characteristics of the claimant, or to the prohibited criterion of differentiation based on employment for a definite or indefinite term, employment on a full-time or part-time basis.

Similar reasoning of the court was expressed in the Supreme Court judgment of 4 November 2015[32] and the judgment of the Court of Appeal in Gliwice of 29 June 2017.[33] According to the courts, transfer of undertaking to another employer does not constitute a discriminatory criterion. In the first of the aforementioned cases, the claimant referred to the fact that the employees who had been taken

32 II PK 36/15, LEX no. 1936723.

33 VIII Pa 60/17, LEX no. 2363729.

over by the defendant (Polish State Railways) received lower remuneration than that paid by the employer to their own employees. However, the claimant did not receive compensation because – in the light of an established line of case law – the breach of the principle of equal rights does not constitute discrimination. Both court instances and the Supreme Court agreed that transfer of undertaking to another employer cannot be considered as a criterion relating to the personal characteristics of the claimant.

In the second case, the failure to pay the claimant an additional annual bonus (the 14th salary) and the related difference in remuneration compared to other employees of the defendant resulted from the fact that the claimant was "a transferred employee", and at the new employer her remuneration terms were set out in the same way as at the previous employer. Therefore, there was no unequal treatment in the case of the claimant. As is apparent from the Labour Code, the new employer is bound by the content of the employment relationship existing on the date of transfer. This means that the employment relationship with the new employer, especially in terms of the type of employment contract and remuneration conditions, is under the same conditions as with the previous employer.

5.3 The Exercise by the Employee of Their Right to Appeal to the Labour Court Against the Termination of the Employment Contract

In the judgment of 14 December 2017,[34] the Supreme Court referred to the exercise of employee rights as a discriminatory criterion.

The claimant, employed in the Youth Educational Centre (hereinafter "Centre") as an educator, appealed against the competent *poviat*[35] for compensation for breach of the principle of equal treatment in employment. It took place against the background of the following facts. By a resolution, the Poviat Council closed down the Centre and the employer terminated the employment relationship with the claimant by respecting the notice period. Importantly, the claimant was a member of the trade union (NSZZ Solidarność) and acted as the union's representative in the Centre. She took steps to safeguard jobs, applying to the Voivode[36] for annulment of the resolution on the closing down of the Centre. She also appealed to the labour court against the termination of the employment relationship.

The court of first instance adjudicated compensation for unequal treatment in employment from the defendant district. According to the findings of that court, the director of the Centre did not present the employees with any selection criteria for re-employment (after annulment of the resolution on the closing down of the Centre). Ultimately, the Centre re-employed people with a lower degree of professional qualifications than the claimant. Besides, no employee who appealed

34 I PK 340/16, LEX no. 2439132.

35 Poviat – a unit of local government and administrative division in Poland. The higher-level unit is the voivodeship, and the lower-level unit is the commune.

36 Voivode – state administration body in Poland; a representative of the government in the voivodship.

against the termination of the employment contract to the labour court or signed the aforementioned application to the Voivode was re-employed. The court of first instance stated that not being in a legal dispute with the employer was the only criterion determining the re-employment of employees. In other words, the claimant was refused re-employment solely because she had taken steps to safeguard her job and because she was in a dispute with her employer.

The defendant appealed against the above judgment. The court of second instance stated that the claimant saw discrimination in the refusal to withdraw the notice previously submitted to her due to the closing down of the Centre and in the refusal to re-employ her. As the reasons for such a state of affairs, she indicated the fact that she exercised her employee rights.

According to the court of second instance, the exercise by the employee of their right to appeal to the labour court against the termination of the employment contract does not constitute a ground of discrimination within the meaning of Article 18^{3a} § 1 of the Labour Code. This is due to the fact that it does not refer to the personal characteristics of the employee and does not fit into the closed catalogue of grounds related to the work performed, that is, employment for a definite or an indefinite term and employment on a full-time or part-time basis.

The Supreme Court considered that the claimant's appeal should be upheld. Admittedly, the Supreme Court shared the opinion of the court of second instance that the exercise of employee rights cannot be considered as a discriminatory ground, but it also pointed out that trade union membership, by contrast, falls within the statutory catalogue of grounds for discrimination. This criterion of discrimination was indicated by the claimant in the course of the trial. She was arguing that, as a trade union activist, she opposed the closing down of the Centre, challenging the decision to do away with the Centre, and arguing that although she had higher professional qualifications than other educators and a longer period of work than other employees of the Centre, she was omitted when recruiting the teaching staff precisely because of her union activities. However, this circumstance was not considered in its entirety by the court of second instance. Therefore, the Supreme Court quashed the judgment under appeal and remitted the case to the court of second instance for reconsideration.

5.4 Other Criteria

The Supreme Court determined which criteria are not of a discriminatory nature also on the other two occasions.

First, it stated that granting the right to additional severance payment, the acquisition of which depends on the conclusion of an agreement between the parties terminating the employment relationship, does not constitute a discriminatory criterion.[37] In the claimant's opinion, he should receive an additional severance payment under the collective agreement even if his employment was terminated

37 The Supreme Court judgment of 26 July 2011, I PK 27/11, LEX no. 1001277.

by notice. The court of first instance dismissed the claim. The justification emphasised that

> in line with the defendant's practice and established custom, the defendant did not pay additional severance payments to employees with whom the contract was terminated by notice. The intention of the defendant and the trade unions was that additional severance payments would be provided only in the event of termination of contracts with employees by mutual agreement.

According to the Supreme Court, "the fact that the defendant had never paid a severance payment to an employee whose employment contract was terminated by notice, was also not without significance".

Second, in the light of the judgment of the Supreme Court of 6 April 2017[38] cited above, related to the action brought by an academic teacher against the university, it follows that significant professional experience and achievements of the claimant compared to other employees of the defendant, or the claimant's lack of acceptance for assigning his achievements to third parties, certainly do not constitute discriminatory grounds. While the above-mentioned qualities may be regarded as the claimant's personal qualities, which are desirable for every employee, it should be assumed that they are closely related to the work performed by the claimant. Consequently, they cannot be considered as discriminatory criteria.

6 Conclusion

The aim of this chapter is to present the "other" discriminatory criteria in the case of the non-exhaustive statutory catalogue included in the Polish Labour Code. The research omits the Act of 3 December 2010 on the implementation of some regulations of the European Union regarding equal treatment. As suggested by its name, it was to implement certain EU directives. Thus, the legislature – unreflectively copying the content of directives – established a closed catalogue of discriminatory criteria. It is thought that such an approach raises doubts as to its compliance with Article 32 of the Constitution, which suggests a prohibition of discrimination on any grounds.

The chapter recapitulates a crucial portion of the debate related to the legal nature of the catalogue of discriminatory criteria included in the Labour Code. The Polish courts and a significant part of the doctrine have treated for years this catalogue as a semi-open one. This means that the idea of an open catalogue has been applied to personal characteristics of the employee not related to the work performed and of social importance, while the closed catalogue has only embraced employment for a definite or an indefinite term or on a full-time or part-time basis.

38 III PK 100/16, LEX no. 2331696.

Against that background, the purpose of this chapter was to explore the case law on the "other" criteria recognised as discriminatory and those which have not been found to be discriminatory. The first of these groups included the following criteria: worldview, HIV status, a trainee attorney-at-law status, motherhood, parenthood, citizenship and appearance. By contrast, the second group embraced creation of one's image in a talk show TV programme; the way in which one becomes an employee and the amount of remuneration at the previous employer; the exercise by the employee of their right to appeal to the labour court against the termination of the employment contract; granting the right to additional severance pay, the acquisition of which depends on the conclusion of an agreement between the parties terminating the employment relationship; significant professional experience and achievements of the employee compared to other employees, or the employee's lack of acceptance for assigning their achievements to third parties.

The amendment of 2019 to the Labour Code resulted in deleting the phrase "as well as without distinction on the grounds of", which separated both groups of criteria – those related and not related to the work performed. According to the justification of the project of the Act of 16 May 2019, the intention of the legislature was to award the victim compensation not only in the case of discrimination but also when "simple" unequal treatment has been diagnosed. Thus, a semi-open catalogue should turn into an open one.

Such an approach would undoubtedly be advantageous from the point of view of the employees. For example, it would probably lead to an award of compensation to the electrician employed in the hospital in circumstances such as those described in the judgment of the Supreme Court of 2 October 2012. In fact, one can say, even intuitively, that that judgment was not entirely fair.

On the other hand, this chapter has outlined problems related to the amendment made in 2019. One of them is connected with the fact that national law must be interpreted in conformity with European Union law. The second concern identified is linked to the need to give a different meaning to the two principles existing in the Labour Code, that is, the principle of equality and the principle of non-discrimination. The latter problem, however, does not appear to be very serious. As pointed out by Zbigniew Góral well before the amendment, unequal treatment does not always mean discrimination.[39] For example, additional rights for pregnant and breastfeeding women or additional breaks for rest and rehabilitation for people with disabilities mean that these groups of people are not treated equally with other employees, but it is definitely not discrimination. Moreover, the principle of equality of law is addressed to the legislature and means an order to create law which gives employees equal rights due to the performance of the same obligations. On the other hand, the principle of non-discrimination is addressed to entities applying the law, in particular to employers, and it results in the prohibition of differentiating the legal situation of employees on the basis of legally prohibited criteria.

39 Zbigniew Góral, O kodeksowym, supra n. 17, at pp. 155–156.

Soon we shall see if the courts will change their position on the catalogue of forbidden criteria and will treat it as an open one instead of one which is semi-open. However, taking into account the position of the Supreme Court which called the amendment "redundant", one may doubt that case law in Poland will change.

Bibliography

Law Cases (Chronological)

The Supreme Court judgment of 12 September 2006, I PK 87/06, OSNP 2007, no 17–18, item 246.

The Supreme Court judgment of 12 September 2006, I PK 89/06, Monitor Prawa Pracy 2007, no. 2.

The Supreme Court judgment of 22 February 2007, I PK 242/06, Monitor Prawa Pracy 2007, no. 7.

The Supreme Court judgment of 4 October 2007, I PK 24/07, LEX no. 406847.

The Supreme Court judgment of 5 October 2007, II PK 14/07, OSNP 2008, no. 21–22, item 311.

The Supreme Court judgment of 29 January 2008, II PK 143/07, OSNP 2009, no. 3–4, item 67.

The Supreme Court judgment of 26 July 2011, I PK 27/11, LEX no. 1001277.

The Supreme Court judgment of 2 October 2012, II PK 82/12, OSNP 2013, no. 17–18, item 202, LEX no. 1365774.

Judgment of the Court of Appeal in Poznań of 18 April 2013, III APa 21/12, LEX no. 1327589.

Order of the Supreme Court of 7 January 2014, I PK 174/13, LEX no. 1646039.

The Supreme Court judgment of 4 November 2015, II PK 36/15, LEX no. 1936723.

The Supreme Court judgment of 25 February 2016, II PK 357/14, OSNP 2017, no. 10, item 122 or LEX no. 2007791.

The Supreme Court judgment of 6 April 2017, III PK 100/16, LEX no. 2331696.

Judgment of the Court of Appeal in Gliwice of 29 June 2017, VIII Pa 60/17, LEX no. 2363729.

The Supreme Court judgment of 20 July 2017, I PK 216/16, LEX no. 2389574.

The Supreme Court judgment of 29 November 2017, I PK 367/16, LEX no. 2433082.

The Supreme Court judgment of 14 December 2017, I PK 340/16, LEX no. 2439132.

The Supreme Court judgment of 13 February 2018, II PK 345/16, LEX no. 2488644.

Judgment of the Court of Appeal in Wrocław of 10 May 2018, III APa 8/18, LEX no. 2940121.

The Supreme Court judgment of 10 May 2018, I PK 54/17, LEX no. 2486202.

The Supreme Court judgment of 7 May 2019, II PK 31/18, LEX no. 2654306.

The Supreme Court judgment of 9 May 2019, III PK 50/18, LEX no. 2692145.

Judgment of the Court of Appeal in Warsaw of 31 May 2019, III APa 4/14, LEX no. 2767461.

Sources of Law (Alphabetical)

Act on the implementation of some regulations of European Union regarding equal treatment of 3 December 2010, Journal of Laws of 2010, No. 254, item 1700, consolidated text of the Journal of Laws of 2020, item 2156.

Charter of Fundamental Rights of the European Union, Official Journal of the European Union, 26 October 2012, C 326, p. 391.

Constitution of the Republic of Poland of 2 April 1997, Journal of Laws No. 78, item 483, www.sejm.gov.pl/prawo/konst/angielski/konse.htm.

Labour Code of 26 June 1974, Journal of Laws of 1974, No. 24, item 141, consolidated text of the Journal of Laws of 2020, item 1320.

Books

Bell, Mark, Anti-discrimination law and the European Union. In: *Oxford studies in European law, general*, eds: Paul Craig and Gráinne de Búrca, Oxford: Oxford University Press, 2002.

Góral, Zbigniew, *O kodeksowym katalogu zasad indywidualnego prawa pracy*, Warsaw: Wolters Kluwer, 2011.

Jędrejek, Grzegorz, *Dochodzenie roszczeń związanych z mobbingiem, dyskryminacją i molestowaniem*, Warszawa: Wolters Kluwer, LEX, 2017.

Podgórska-Rakiel, Ewa, *Zmiany dotyczące równego traktowania w zatrudnieniu oraz mobbingu*, LEX 2019 (online).

Szabłowska-Juckiewicz, Marzena, *Odpowiedzialność odszkodowawcza podmiotu zatrudniającego za naruszenie zasady równego traktowania*, Warsaw: Wolters Kluwer, 2019.

Tomaszewska, Monika, Art. 18(3(a)) Zakaz dyskryminacji – definicje. In: *Kodeks pracy*, Komentarz. Vol. I. Art. 1–113, ed: Krzysztof Wojciech Baran, Warszawa: Wolters Kluwer, LEX, 2020.

Wujczyk, Marcin, Zasady równego traktowania i zakazu dyskryminacji. In: *System prawa pracy*, Vol. X, ed: Krzysztof Wojciech Baran, Międzynarodowe publiczne prawo pracy. Standardy europejskie, Warszawa: Wolters Kluwer Polska, Lex 2020.

Journals

Błaszczak, Anna, Efektywność środków ochrony przed dyskryminacją w Polsce, *Przegląd Prawa Publicznego* 2015, no. 6.

Cieciuch, Jan, Czym jest światopogląd? Filozoficzny kontekst psychologicznego pojęcia, *Psychologia Rozwojowa* 2005, vol. 10, no. 2.

Gray, Alison J., *International Psychiatry*, vol. 8, no. 3. www.ncbi.nlm.nih.gov/pmc/articles/PMC6735033/#r11.

Szewczyk, Helena, Glosa do wyroku SN z dnia 2 października 2012 r., II PK 82/12, *Orzecznictwo Sądów Polskich* 2014, no. 11.

Websites

www.sejm.gov.pl/sejm8.nsf/druk.xsp?documentId=F69FFA3A32FD99C0C1258154005CD665

www.sejm.gov.pl/sejm8.nsf/druk.xsp?nr=1653

www.statista.com/statistics/282982/discrimination-of-hiv-infected-persons-in-selected-countries/

Part II

Facets of Employment Discrimination in Common Law Jurisdictions

6 Philosophical Beliefs as Protected Characteristics in British Discrimination Law

An Evolutionary Tract and Its Consequences[1]

Jo Carby-Hall

Prologue

Under British law, it is unlawful to discriminate against people because of their age; gender reassignment; being married or in a civil partnership; being pregnant or on maternity leave; disability; race, including colour, nationality, ethnic or national origin; sexual orientation; sex; and religion or belief. These are known as "protected characteristics" and offer protection against discrimination. It is the Equality Act 2010[2] which consolidates previous discrimination laws[3] and which protects people from discrimination in the workplace and in wider society.[4] The aims of this Act are threefold; namely, to eliminate discrimination, harassment and intimidation; to advance equality of opportunity between people who share a protected characteristic and people who do not share it; and to advance equality of opportunity between people who share a protected characteristic and people who do not share it.

This chapter is modest in that it proposes to narrow down the aforementioned protected characteristics and focus only on the protected characteristic of religion or belief by analysing the legal and consequential evolution of the concept of

1 This chapter illustrates the relatively recent case law evolution on the concept of philosophical belief as a protected characteristic in one of the most interesting developing areas of discrimination law.

2 Equality Act 2010 c. 15. Discrimination can be direct or indirect and amount to harassment and victimisation.

3 The Equal Pay Act 1970; Sex Discrimination Act 1975; Race Relations Act 1976; Disability Discrimination Act 1995; and three Statutory Instruments: Employment Equality (Religion or Belief) Regulations 2003; Employment Equality (Sexual Orientation) Regulations 2003; Employment Equality (Age) Regulations 2009. The Act has similar provisions to those of the EU Equal Treatment Directives 200/78/EC, 2000/43/EC and 2006/54/EC. The Act provides protection beyond those Directives based on citizenship and nationality as well as extending individuals' rights beyond the workplace in religion or belief, disability, age, sex, sexual orientation and gender reassignment.

4 See S. Deakin and G. Morris "Labour Law" (2012) Hart. chap. 6 and Ewan McGaughey "A Casebook on Labour Law." Hart. (2018) chaps 12–14.

DOI: 10.4324/9781003306962-8

philosophical belief as a protected characteristic. Religion will also be featured on the periphery.

Divided into three parts, the chapter aims to analyse the concept of philosophical belief as a protected characteristic under the discrimination law. The first part attempts an in-depth analysis of the *Casamitjana Costa* case heard in 2020 which serves to introduce the reader to a typical case heard on this topic and its denouement. The content of this part will consist of (a) the backcloth to and (b) the facts of the case with (c) the legal conditions to be met for "ethical veganism" to constitute a "philosophical belief" to qualify as a "protected characteristic." This case will provide the springboard and link for the discussion which will take place in the second part, namely the legal evolution which will comprise of (a) cases where the tribunals and courts considered the philosophical belief to be non-existent and (b) cases where the tribunals and courts have upheld the concept of philosophical belief. These will lead to the third part, which consists of an epitome divided into (a) the summing up of the case law forming an eclectic list of beliefs and (b) the impact of this case law on employers and submissions on how employers should act in relation to this legal evolutionary tract.

PART 1. The *Casamitjana Costa* Case

A United Kingdom Employment Tribunal in *J. Casamitjana Costa v The League Against Cruel Sports*[5] had to determine at a preliminary hearing whether ethical veganism could amount to a "philosophical belief" and thus qualify as a "protected characteristic" within the meaning of the Equality Act 2010. In order to analyse this case, it is proposed to divide part 1 of this chapter into eleven morsels; namely, (1) the background to the case, (2), the facts of the case, (3) the legal conditions to be met for a philosophical belief to qualify as a protected characteristic, which will include (i) the philosophy behind ethical veganism being based on the concept of Ahimsa; (ii) whether the Claimant qualified on the facts of the case as an ethical vegan; (iii) the legal principles for a philosophical belief to qualify as a protected characteristic under the Equality Act 2010; and (iv) the decision reached by the Employment Tribunal in the *Casamitjana Costa* case. This case will provide the springboard for a discussion in part 2 on the wider effects and consequences of this and other judgments in an evolving society through case law evolution and societal evolution. An epilogue will follow in part 3.

1.1 The Backcloth to the Case

The Claimant, Mr Jordi Casamitjana, was an ethical vegan who was not only on a vegan diet but also was against the use and abuse of animals for any purpose. Ethical veganism thus controlled every aspect of his life. The Respondent, the

5 Case Number: 3331129/2018 heard at the Norwich Employment Tribunal on 2 January 2020 (Reading Day) and 3 January 2020 (Oral Evidence) before Employment Judge Robin Postle.

League Against Cruel Sports, was a welfare animal charity which campaigned against blood recreational sports which hunt animals, such as fox hunting, the shooting down of birds, stag and roe hunting, bull and cock fighting, and so on. The Claimant was employed by the Respondents from 2004 to 2007 and again from 29 August 2016 to 6 April 2018 when he was summarily dismissed by the Respondents on grounds of gross misconduct. Having made enquiries in connection with the Respondents' pension funds, the Claimant noticed that such funds were invested unethically by companies which harmed animals. This being against his ethical principles, he took steps to ensure that his pension contributions were invested in ethical funds. He also took steps to inform his fellow employees by e-mail who were not aware of their contributions going into unethical companies' funds. He informed them of the measures he took to change his own funds, expressed his own personal opinions and provided ten alternative fund choices. The Respondents sent a letter dismissing him summarily stating: "Based on your understanding and belief, if given the opportunity, you will act in the same way. . . . I consider your e-mail biased because of your ethical principles and could influence them to change their pension arrangement." The claimant brought an action against the Respondent on the grounds of direct or indirect discrimination, victimisation or harassment by reason of his ethical veganism beliefs.

Initially, two issues needed to be decided by the Employment Tribunal in this case: the ethical belief aspect and the summary dismissal aspect. This chapter is concerned solely with an analysis of the first aspect,[6] as the summary dismissal aspect falls outside its scope.[7]

1.2 The Facts of the Case

The Claimant, a zoologist and a vegan,[8] dedicated his life to helping and protecting animals in need. As a vegan, he stopped, as from the year 2000, to eat meat, fish and animal products, whether they be milk, honey, eggs and so on, and got rid of all his clothing and household furniture and furnishings containing animal products. The same could be said about any personal care products he used to

6 Unusually in this preliminary hearing, the Respondents conceded that ethical veganism could amount to a philosophical belief (ibid., p. 1, para. 1).

7 It is pointed out that terms of settlement relating to the dismissal were agreed between the parties with the payment of compensation by the Respondents and an agreed statement by them that the Claimant "showed a great deal of professionalism, expertise and commitment to the protection of animals. The only reason for [his] . . . dismissal . . . was his communications to his colleagues in relation to our pension arrangements . . . we now accept that . . . [he] did nothing wrong with such communications, which were motivated by his belief in ethical veganism." The case was thus dismissed upon withdrawal by the Claimant. (Consent judgment J. Casamitjana Costa v League Against Cruel Sports Watford Employment Tribunal 24–28 February and 1 March 2020 before Employment Judge Hyams).

8 Prior to 2000, when he became a vegan without first becoming a vegetarian, he would eat meat, fish and animal products such as butter, cheese, eggs and honey and drink cow's milk, sheep's milk, etc.; he wore clothes which contained animal products such as woollen and leather goods and had animal products in his house.

ensure that they did not contain animal products and/or were not tested on animals during their manufacture.

He took reasonable steps to ascertain whether a product or service he used complied with ethical veganism. Where he was unable to ascertain the animal involvement in an essential product or service or was misled regarding such involvement or if no alternatives could be identified for the product or service, the Claimant would not consider that he had transgressed his ethical beliefs,[9] for he would have exhausted all reasonable steps to ensure that his consumption was such as to cause as little as possible to the suffering or exploitation of sentient beings no matter how remote that be.

With regard to the food he consumed, the Claimant would carefully examine the labels which showed the ingredients and thus ascertain that he enjoyed a 100% vegan diet, and if the labels were unclear he would have gone so far as to contact the manufacturer to ascertain that the food was genuinely vegan and contained no animal additives. Were there to have been any doubt, he would avoid purchasing that food product. Additionally, he would not have entertained storing such products at his home. Furthermore, he would not have allowed another person to bring non-vegan food to his home.

His breakfasts invariably consisted of tea served with oat milk, organic porridge, dried berries, walnuts and ground flax seeds.

Were the Claimant to attend a social or work function where food is prepared or spend the night or nights in an hotel, he would inform the appropriate person(s) of his vegan diet. Regarding his attendance to social gatherings, he would try to avoid them if non-vegan food were to be served. Also, when travelling over lengthy periods of time, he would take an additional dietary supplement. Were he to travel to remote places, he would rather go hungry than consume animal products, thus adhering to his vegan principles. Nor, as a vegan, would he consume foodstuffs which are known to contain animals during their ripening, such as figs which, when ripe, may contain worms or be "grown with a symbiotic relationship to a microscopic wasp," where one "cannot be sure whether any of the wasp larva is still inside the ripened fig."[10] The same may be said of apples and pears, where wasps or their larva may be found, or bananas, which spiders have been known to inhabit. Although he would drink alcoholic beverages, he would not do so if they contained animal products.[11]

9 The Vegan Society rules accept that sometimes it is unavoidable to use animal by-products where no alternative exists.

10 Op. cit. Case number 3331128/2018, p. 5 para 20.8.

11 "Bison" is a renowned Polish Vodka. It is not believed that it contains animal products in its manufacture. Would the name per se be sufficient to deter a vegan from consuming such an alcoholic drink? It is thought not! However, common animal products hidden in alcoholic drinks include carmine which consist of crushed scales of cochineal insects; chilin derived from the shells of lobsters and crabs; casein obtained from milk; albumin derived from dried blood or eggs; pepsin, a foaming agent in beer derived sometimes from pigs; cider incorporates gelatine in its manufacture; white,

Because of deficiencies in his diet, the Claimant was supplied by the Vegan Society with selenium, a B12 supplement, vitamin D and iodine.[12]

The above treats the vegan diet alone, but the Claimant went well beyond that aspect. He would refuse to purchase products tested on animals if alternatives exist unless it is impossible to avoid them, such as testing for medicines.[13] He did not wear clothing which contained animal products and sought vegan shops for his suits, shoes and hosiery. He thus avoided leather, ivory, wool, fur, silk, horn, teeth or tortoiseshell goods. His jackets and shoes thus consisted of no animal products and all his clothes consisted of synthetic fibres.[14] He avoided sitting on leather seats and holding leather straps.

He used vegan-friendly shampoo and soap to wash himself and used an electric shaver to shave using Ecotricity, which is the only British power supplier that does not use biofuels from the animal agricultural industry to generate green electricity and green gas.

Were he to travel to within an hour's walking distance, he would avoid using a bus, train or other form of public transport to avoid injuring, maiming or killing insects, birds or other animals.

Since his becoming a vegan, the Claimant has always worked in animal protection organisations, had no companion animals living with him, never attended or visited zoological gardens, animal fights or races, circuses or spectacles where live animals perform.[15] He would invariably take part in animal protection marches, protests and demonstrations and deliver speeches in support of ethical veganism at such events.

Since becoming a vegan, he has not dated anyone who was not a vegan, nor had he cohabited with such a person.

The Claimant would take stern steps to ensure that financial products – as occurred in this case with his and others' pensions – which invested in pharmaceutical companies which tested on animals are avoided.

When paying for goods, the Claimant would use coins or credit/debit cards in order to avoid as far as possible, the use of paper money, some of which contains animal products.[16]

---

rosé and sparkling wines contain isinglass, which derives from fish swim bladders; cream-based liqueurs like Advocaat and Bailey's contain milk products; and some soft drinks like Red Beverage use crushed insect scales known as cochineal extracts. The full extent of the amount of animal products in drinks is difficult to quantify in the United Kingdom because there exist no laws to list ingredients of alcoholic content higher than 1.2%.

12 Which is a chewable pill.

13 For example, for coronavirus vaccines. Animal testing could be cruel because animals are tortured, maimed, blinded and killed. Animal testing also takes place in beauty products such as L'Oreal, Estée Lauder, Johnson & Johnson, Reckitt Benckiser, Church & Dwight, Unilever and Palmolive. There are also many non–cruelty testing brands such as Always, Hugo Boss, Pantene, Burberry, Bulgari, Vichy, Davidoff, Garnier, Giorgio Armani, Gucci, Dior, Calvin Klein and many more.

14 Plants, cotton, hemp and linen.

15 Examples include killer whales (orcas) and dolphins in marine parks in Malta, China, Russia, Canada, Tenerife, Antibes (France), Japan, Argentina, the USA, etc.

16 A five-pound note for example, contains animal products.

1.3 The Legal Conditions to Be Met for "Ethical Veganism" to Constitute a "Philosophical Belief" to Qualify as a "Protected Characteristic"

Can ethical veganism constitute a philosophical belief and thus qualify as a protected characteristic under the provisions of the Equality Act 2010?[17] In answering, it is intended to analyse in the first instance what ethical veganism consists of. In the second instance, an evaluation will be made if, on the facts of the case, the Claimant qualified as such. There will then follow in the third instance an analysis on the legal principles which have been set out for a philosophical belief to qualify as a protected characteristic under s. 10 of the Equality Act 2010.

1.3.1 The Philosophy Behind Ethical Veganism is Based on the Concept of Ahimsa

Ethical veganism is based on the concept of Ahimsa (doing no harm), which is one of the ideals of Hinduism, Buddhism and Jainism. It means that one should avoid harming any living (sentient) being and not to desire to harm such being. Ahimsa does not only apply to non-violence but also to avoid any harm whether physical, mental or emotional. The definition of Ahimsa consists of a religious philosophy that all life, including that of animals, is sacred. An example is being a vegetarian because of the importance of animals' lives. It means non-injury and non-killing. It implies total avoidance of harming any living creatures not only by deeds but also by words and thoughts.[18]

Ethical veganism is not only about choices of diet but choices on what a person wears, what personal care products they use, what hobbies they enjoy and what work they do. Ethical vegans are persons who live, as far as possible, without using animal products. The Vegan Society defines veganism as follows:

> A philosophy and way of life which seeks to exclude, as far as possible and practical, all forms of exploitation and cruelty to animals for food, clothing, or any other purpose and by extension promotes the development and use of animal free alternatives for the benefit of humans/animals and the

17 The Equality Act 2010 consolidates, updates and supplements the numerous prior Acts and Regulations which formed the basis of anti-discrimination laws in Great Britain. These consisted primarily of the Equal Pay Act 1970, the Sex Discrimination Acts 1975 and 1986, the Race Relations Act 1976, and the Disability Act 1995, and three major Statutory Instruments protecting discrimination in employment on grounds of religion and belief (Religion and Belief Regulations 2003 S.I. 1660), sexual orientation and age. All these were repealed or revoked by the Equality Act 2010 Schedule 27, Part 1 (Repeals and Revocations).

18 Mahatma Gandhi took the religious principle of Ahimsa and turned it into a non-violent tool for mass action. He used it to fight not only colonial rule but also social evils such as racial discrimination and untouchability. According to Gandhi, "Ahimsa, non-violence, comes from the strength, and the strength is from God, not man. Ahimsa always comes from within."

> environment, in dietary terms it denotes the practice of dispensing with all products derived wholly or partly from animals.[19]

Ethical vegans are

> moralistically orientated and opposed to all forms of exploitation of . . . animals and to embody genuine philosophical concern for all sentient life . . . veganism is living according to a belief or condition that it is wrong to exploit and kill living beings unnecessarily and that moral conviction is cogent, serious and important.[20]

1.3.2 On the Facts of the Case, Did the Claimant Qualify as an Ethical Vegan?

The philosophy as defined by the Vegan Society and Ahimsa was one to which the Claimant adhered slavishly and religiously. The lengthy catalogue on the proven facts of the case[21] showed ample evidence that the Claimant's philosophical belief acted as his moral and life framework. Notwithstanding that the Respondents readily conceded that the Claimant's belief was genuinely held, based on the vast amount of evidence produced regarding the manner in which the Claimant conducted his life and the basis of his philosophy, Employment Judge Postle decided, independently from the Respondents' concession, that "the Claimant genuinely and sincerely" held "his beliefs in ethical veganism."[22]

1.3.3 The Legal Principles for a Philosophical Belief to Qualify as a Protected Characteristic Under the Equality Act 2010

The Employment Judge based his judgment on s. 10 of the Equality Act 2010 provisions, which mirror the European Convention on Human Rights (hereinafter referred to as ECHR) and the Human Rights Act, 1998, which constitutes the British legislation which puts into effect the ECHR provisions.[23]

Section 10 of the Equality Act 2010 provides:[24]

> Belief means any religious or philosophical belief and a reference to the belief is a reference to a lack of belief. In relation to the protected characteristic of religion and belief (a) a reference to a person who has a protected

19 Definition of veganism. The Vegan Society. One world. Many lives. Our choice.

20 Employment Judge Postle in Case Number 3331129/2018, op. cit. p. 4. paras 14 and 15.

21 See pp. 100 to 103 above.

22 Employment Judge Postle in Case Number 3331129/2018 op. cit., p. 10 para. 33.

23 Unless a construction would run contrary to a fundamental feature of the legislation. See the judgment of Lord Nicholls of Birkenhead in *Ghaidan v Godin-Mendoza (FC)* [2004] 2 AC 557 (HL), particularly at paras. 29 and 30.

24 Equality Act 2010 s. 10 (2) (3) (a) (b).

> characteristic is a reference to a person of a particular religion or belief; (b) a reference to persons who share a protected characteristic is a reference to persons who are of the same religion and belief.

It appears that s. 10 of the 2010 legislation mirrors consciously Articles 9 and 14 of the ECHR. Article 9 provides that

> 1. Everyone has a right to freedom of thought, conscience and religion, this includes freedom to change his religion or belief and freedom, either alone or in community with others and in public or in private to manifest his religion or belief, in worship, teaching, practice and observance. 2. Freedom to manifest one's religion or belief shall be subject only to such limitations as are prescribed by law and are necessary in a democratic society in the interests of public safety for the protection of public order, health or morals, or for the protection of rights and freedoms of others.

Article 14 of the ECHR talks of the enjoyment of the rights and freedoms set forth under Article 9(1) and (2), which "shall be secured without discrimination on any ground such as religion, political or other opinion."

Section 3 of the Human Rights Act 1998 provides: "So far as is possible to do so, primary legislation and subordinate legislation must be read and given effect in a way which is compatible with the Convention rights."[25]

Employment Judge Postle proposed:

> Where the inclusionary language of section 10 mirrors that in Article 9, it would be both bizarre and by reason of section 3 of the Human Rights Act 1998 unlawful if a belief were recognised under the Convention but not under the Equality Act 2010.[26]

Be that as it may, the legislation mentioned above was not the only factor which determined the *Casamitjana Costa* case, for there was important case law which was taken into consideration by the Employment Tribunal judge. Lord Nicholls' judgment in *R (Williamson) et al. v Secretary of State for Education and Employment*[27] gives guidance on the court's role in identifying whether a religious belief is genuinely held under Article 9 of the ECHR. He said:[28]

> It is necessary first to clarify the court's role in identifying a religious belief calling for protection under Article 9. Where the genuineness of a Claimant's

25 Accordingly, a tribunal or court must read any statute passed by Parliament so as to uphold Convention rights, where this is possible.
26 Case Number 3331129/2018 p. 8 para. 26.
27 [2005] AC 248; [2005] UK HL 15.
28 Ibid. at para. 22 of the judgment.

> professed belief is an issue in the proceedings the court will inquire into and decide this issue as a question of fact. This is a limited inquiry. The court is concerned to ensure an assertion of religious belief is made in good faith: "neither fictitious, nor capricious and it is not an artifice" . . . emphatically, it is not for the court to embark on an inquiry into the asserted belief and judge its "validity" by some objective standard such as the source material upon which the claimant founds his belief or the orthodox teaching of the religion in question or the extent to which the claimant's belief conforms to or differs from the views of others professing the same religion. Freedom of religion protects the subjective belief of an individual . . . religious belief is intensely personal and can vary from one individual to another. Each individual is at liberty to hold his own religious beliefs however irrational or inconsistent they may seem to some, however surprising.

Article 9 of the ECHR is not confined solely to the freedom to hold a belief. It also[29] "includes the right to express and practice one's belief," for without this freedom the right would become ineffective.

Lord Nicholls talked of the necessity an evaluative filter in the context of manifestation and expression. He said:[30]

> Everyone . . . is entitled to hold whatever belief he wishes. But when questions of "manifestation" arise, as they do in this type of case, a belief must satisfy some modest, objective minimum requirements. These threshold requirements are implicit in Article 9 of the European Convention and comparable guarantees in other human rights instruments. The belief must be consistent with basic standards of human dignity or integrity. Manifestation of a religious belief, for instance, which involved subjecting others to torture or inhuman punishment would not qualify for protection. The belief must relate to matters more than merely trivial. It must possess an adequate degree of seriousness and importance. As has been said it must be a belief on a fundamental problem. With religious belief this requisite is easily satisfied. The belief must also be coherent in the sense of being intelligible and capable of being understood. But again, too much must not be demanded in this regard. Typically, religion involves belief in the supernatural. It is not always susceptible to lucid exposition or, still less, rational justification. The language used is often the language of allegory, symbol or metaphor. Depending on the subject matter, individuals cannot always be expected to express themselves with cogency or precision. Nor are the individual's beliefs fixed and static. The beliefs of every individual are prone to change over his lifetime. Overall, these threshold requirements should not be set at a level which would deprive minority beliefs of the protection they are intended to have under the Convention.

29 Ibid. at para. 16 of the judgment.

30 Ibid. at para. 23 of the judgment.

The learned judge Nicholls then goes on to say:[31]

> This leaves on one side the difficult question of the criteria to be applied in deciding whether a belief is to be characterised as religious. The question will seldom, if ever, arise under the European Convention. It does not arise in the present case. In the present case it does not matter whether the claimant's beliefs regarding the corporal punishment of children are categorised as religious. Article 9 embraces freedom of thought, conscience and religion. The atheist, the agnostic and the sceptic are as much entitled to freedom to hold and manifest their beliefs as the theist. These beliefs are placed on an equal footing for the purposes of this guaranteed freedom. Thus, if its manifestation is to attract protection under Article 9 a non-religious belief, as much as a religious belief, must satisfy the modest threshold requirements implicit in this article. In particular, for its manifestation to be protected by Article 9 a non-religious belief must relate to an aspect of human life or behaviour of comparable importance to that normally found to religious beliefs. Article 9 is apt, therefore, to include a belief such as pacificism: *Arrowsmith v United Kingdom* [1978] 3 EHRR 218. The position is much the same with regard to the respect guaranteed to a parent's "religious and philosophical convictions under Article 2 of the First Protocol: See *Campbell and Cosans v United Kingdom* 4 EHRR 293."

Resulting from the Employment Tribunal case of *Granger Plc v Nicholson*,[32] the criteria provided by Lord Nicholls in the *Williamson* case above came within the auspices of s. 10 of the Equality Act 2010.

In addition, there exists the Equality Act 2010 Statutory Code of Practice drawn up by the Equality and Human Rights Commission.[33] Mr Trevor Phillips, who chairs this Commission, explains in his foreword that this Code

> is authoritative, comprehensive and a technical guide to the detail of law. It will be invaluable to lawyers, advocates, human resources personnel, courts and tribunals, anyone who needs to understand the law in depth, or to apply it in practice. . . . The Code draws on case law and precedent where and how different provisions to bear in real-life situations.

The Statutory Code per se does not impose any obligations.

> Nor is it an authoritative statement of the law; only the courts and tribunals can provide such authority. However, the Code can be used in evidence in legal proceedings brought under the Act. Tribunals and the courts must take into account any part of the Code that appears to them relevant to any questions arising in proceedings.[34]

31 Ibid. at para. 24 of the judgment.
32 [2010] ICR 360 (ET).
33 www.equalityhumanrights.com.
34 Equality Act 2010 Statutory Code of Practice, para. 1.13.

That Code provides for the "Protected Characteristics," one of which includes religion and belief.[35] The words of Lord Nicholls' judgment in the *Williamson* case and of Burton J. in the EAT case of *Nicholson* will readily be recalled therein.

> For a philosophical belief to be protected under the Act, (a) it must be genuinely held; (b) it must be a belief and not an opinion or viewpoint based on the present state of information available; (c) it must be a belief as to a weighty and substantial aspect of human life and behaviour; (d) it must attain a certain level of cogency, seriousness, cohesion and importance; (e) it must be worthy of respect in a democratic society, not incompatible with human dignity not in conflict with fundamental rights of others.[36]

1.3.4 The Decision Reached by the Employment Tribunal in the Casamitjana Costa Case

In finding for the Claimant, Employment Judge Postle considered that each one of the criteria mentioned above for a philosophical belief to qualify as a protected characteristic under the 2010 legislation had been met. With regard to *a genuinely held belief* and having read and heard the evidence, he had no doubt whatsoever that "the claimant genuinely and sincerely holds his belief in ethical veganism."[37] As for *a belief and not a viewpoint* criterion,[38] Employment Judge Postle considered that ethical veganism carries with it

> an important moral essential . . . founded upon longstanding tradition recognising the moral consequences of non-human animal sentience . . . upheld by both religious and atheist alike . . . the Claimant personally holds ethical veganism as a belief. He has . . . dedicated himself to that belief throughout what he eats, where he works, what he wears, the products he uses, where he shops and with whom he associates. It clearly is not simply a viewpoint but a real and genuine belief and not an irrational opinion.

On the criterion of a *weighty and substantial aspect of human life* he considered that

> The relationship between humans and other fellow creatures is plainly a substantial aspect of human life, it has sweeping consequences on human behaviour and . . . is capable of constituting a belief which seeks to avoid the exploitation of fellow species.[39]

35 Other "Protected Characteristics" include age, disability, gender reassignment, marriage and civil partnerships, pregnancy and maternity, race and sexual orientation. Code of Practice, para. 2.2.

36 Equality Act 2010 Code of Practice, para. 2.59. (a) to (e) inserted by the author.

37 Case Number 3331129/2018, para. 33. Somewhat unusually and interestingly in such cases, the Respondents conceded ab initio that the Claimant's belief was genuinely held.

38 Ibid. para. 34 of the judgment.

39 Ibid. para. 35 of the judgment.

Regarding *the attaining of a certain level of cogency, cohesion and importance criterion*, ethical veganism is a belief which fulfils each of these three requirements.

> the definition of the Vegan Society, namely a philosophy and a way of life which seeks to exclude as far as possible and practical all forms of exploitation and cruelty to animals for food, clothing or any other purpose and . . . promotes the development and use of animal free alternatives for the use of humans, animals and the environment. In dietary terms it denotes the practice of dispensing of all products derived wholly or partly from animals.[40]

Furthermore, there is a community within businesses and restaurants which adheres to this ethical principle. "The belief concerns the relationship between individuals and other living things in diet, clothing, consumption, travel and relationships and indeed many other aspects of daily life."[41] Finally, the criterion on *worthy of respect in a democratic society and compatible with human dignity* was also referred to in this case in that in modern day thinking "ethical veganism does not in any way offend society, . . . is increasingly recognised nationally, particularly by the environmental benefits of vegan observance."[42]

Employment Judge Postle was thus satisfied that there was in this case "overwhelming evidence . . . that ethical veganism [was] capable of being a philosophical belief and thus a protected characteristic under the Equality Act 2010."[43]

PART 2. Legal Evolution

The decision reached in the *Casamitjana Costa* case came as no surprise, for it followed the decisions in previous cases relating to a philosophical belief as a protected characteristic under the British equality laws. The legal right to manifest one's belief must not be discriminated against. The *Casamitjana Costa* case is, at the time of writing, the latest in a series of cases heard by the courts and tribunals on claimants' philosophical beliefs and adds to the evolution in society not only in the United Kingdom where the vegan society is growing,[44] but also could influence other European countries[45] where similar developments are taking place.

The British courts and tribunals examine if a belief – whether religious or philosophical – qualifies as a protected characteristic under the discrimination laws. It

40 Ibid. para. 36 of the judgment.
41 Ibid. para. 37 of the judgment.
42 Ibid. para. 38 of the judgment.
43 Ibid. para. 39 of the judgment.
44 Statistics show that the number of vegans in Great Britain has quadrupled between 2014 and 2019, when there were 600,000 vegans, or 1.16% of the population (Ipsos Mon. Survey commissioned by the Vegan Society).
45 It is noted that in Portugal there exists a law since 2017 making it illegal not to provide vegan food in certain establishments. https://metro.co.uk/2017/03/10/it-is-now-illegal-not-to-offer-vegan-food-at-prisons-hospitals-and-schools-in-Portugal6501872/. It is believed to be the only country in Europe to have enacted such a law.

is proposed to analyse briefly how this evolution has taken place by examining a limited selection of cases which has proved to be both unsuccessful and successful, for both form part of that legal evolution. By "unsuccessful" is meant that the court or tribunal has found the belief to be unjustified, whereas by "successful" the court or tribunal held the philosophical belief to be justified.

2.1 Cases Where the Court or Tribunal Has Found the Belief to Be Unjustified

Starting with the latter – namely the belief was held to be unjustified – nine cases have been selected for brief analysis. In *McClintock v Department of Constitutional Affairs*,[46] the EAT upheld the decision of an Employment Tribunal which concluded that a Justice of the Peace (JP)[47] – who was a member of the Family Panel and resigned from the Panel's membership because the Department of Constitutional Affairs[48] refused to exempt him of his duty to officiate in cases in which he might have to place children for adoption, care or fostering with same-sex partners – had not been directly or indirectly discriminated upon. The UK law had been changed to prevent discrimination against same-sex couples and that the sex of the couple would not be the only justifiable reason for refusing placement. Mr McClintock cited bullying at school as an example of evidence to show that children placed with same-sex couples would be disadvantaged when compared to children placed with a heterosexual family. He also pleaded that children were being treated as part of an unacceptable social experiment as guinea pigs and that by placing a child with a same-sex family, he would be neglecting his statutory duty to do what is in the child's best interests. Furthermore, he pleaded that his religious beliefs as a Christian forbad him to sit on such cases. This case was decided under the now revoked[49] Religion and Belief Regulations 2003 by reference to whether the claimant had a relevant belief. On the facts of this case, the Employment Tribunal held that the claimant's objection was not founded on any philosophical or religious belief. On appeal Elias P., in the EAT, upholding the Employment Tribunal's judgment posited:[50]

> As the tribunal . . . correctly observed, to constitute a belief there must be a religious or philosophical viewpoint in which one actually believes. It is not

46 [2008] IRLR 29 (EAT). See too Jonathan Petre, "Magistrate appeals in gay adoption row." www.telegraph.co.uk/news/uknews1567011/Magistrate-appeals-in-gay-adoption-row.html.

47 Justices of the Peace, also known as magistrates, are ordinary people not trained in the law who hear cases in the Magistrates' Courts in their communities. They sit in benches of three, which include two "wingers" and one who sits in the centre who receives special training and who acts as chairperson known as the Presiding Justice. JPs deal with less serious criminal cases as, for example, minor thefts, motoring offences, public disorder and criminal damage.

48 Now renamed the Ministry of Justice.

49 Revoked by the Equality Act 2010 Schedule 27 Part 1 (Repeals and Revocations). See too n. 14 above.

50 [2008] IRLR 29 (EAT), para. 45 of Elias P's judgment.

> enough to have an opinion based on some real or perceived logic or based on information or lack of information available. Mr. McClintock had not as a matter of principle rejected the possibility that single sex parents could ever be in a child's best interests; he felt that the evidence to support this view was unconvincing, but did not discount the possibility that further research might reconcile the conflict which he perceived to exist.

Talking of the test for determining whether views can properly to be considered to fall into the category of philosophical belief Elias P. said,[51] it "is whether they have sufficient cogency, seriousness, cohesion, and importance and are worthy of respect in a democratic society."

Referring to the McClintock case, to quote Burton J.'s apt words in the EAT case of *Grainger PLC & Others v T. Nicholson*:[52] "He did not . . . have . . . a fixed homophobic belief."

Another case in which the belief was held to be unjustified was *Eweida v British Airways plc.*,[53] which was a religious belief case of a British Airways (BA) ground hostess wearing a silver cross round her neck in contravention of the then BA's uniform rules initially heard in the Employment Tribunal. The case went on appeal to the Employment Appeal Tribunal, to the Court of Appeal, having been refused an appeal by the Supreme Court and had gone to the European Court of Human Rights in Strasbourg. Having been offered an out-of-court settlement which she refused, she lost her case in the Employment Tribunal when that tribunal found that she was in breach of BA's rules. Her appeal to the EAT failed. Her appeal to the Court of Appeal for a costs capping order and substantive grounds also failed, with Sedley L.J. agreeing with the EAT decision. Her appeal to the Supreme Court was refused. She then appealed to the ECHR on the grounds that the British government failed to provide domestic law to protect her rights under Article 9 of the European Convention on Human Rights. That court found some inadequacies in the UK equality laws and awarded her damages and costs.

Elias P. cross-referenced to the ECHR jurisprudence, which by then included both the *Campbell* and *Williamson* cases[54] in construing the Employment and Equality (Religion and Belief) Regulations 2003 and said "[t]he protection afforded to those holding a religious or philosophical belief is a broad one. The belief can be intentionally personal and subjective." Referring to Article 9 of the ECHR, which protected the right to freedom of religion in the *Williamson* case, Elias P. noted that

> by s. 3 of the Human Rights Act 1998, it is incumbent on domestic courts to construe domestic laws compatibly with Convention rights, and therefore the

51 Ibid. para. 41.
52 [2010] 2 All ER 253, para. 16.
53 [2009] ICR 303.
54 See above at pp. 105 et seq.

> same (or at least no less favourable) approach must be adopted in the concept of religion and belief in the 2003 Regulations.[55]

Similarly, the philosophical belief was held to be unjustified in the Court of Appeal case of *Gray v Mulberry Company (Design) Ltd.*[56] The claimant was working for the respondent, which produces luxury goods. The contract of employment contained a confidentiality clause which the claimant signed, and in addition she had to sign a copyright agreement which she refused to sign because it interfered with her own work as a writer and film-maker. It was very important to her "to own all rights, including copyright to my own writing, film making and creative output."[57] She believed that the copyright agreement could extend to her artistic activities away from work. The respondent amended the agreement, but the claimant considered the amendments to be "general and open to interpretation." The claimant was consequently dismissed with notice. Not having met the qualifying period for her to bring unfair dismissal proceedings, she was given permission by the Employment Judge to amend her claim to one of discrimination on grounds of belief.

She stated in the Employment Tribunal and on appeal to the Employment Appeal Tribunal that she was

> passionate about my belief, to the right of an individual, not only to own, but to profit from and receive credit for their own work if wished. In order to explore these ideas further, I wrote a feature film . . . which explained issues of ownership of intellectual property.[58]

Having examined the facts of the case and applied these to the law, both tribunals held that the claimant's belief did not qualify for protection under the Equality Act 2010. The term "philosophical belief" is not defined by the Act, but case law has established criteria for the belief to be protected. These include first that the belief be genuinely held. The Employment Tribunal "accepted that the belief was genuinely held in the sense that the Claimant honestly believed it." In the second instance, it must not be an opinion or viewpoint. The tribunal considered that the "Claimant's opinion was a viewpoint held by her as a belief. It was not just an opinion based on logic which, if the foundations changed, was capable of causing her to have altered her view." Third, it must relate to "a weighty and substantial aspect of human life and behaviour. The fact that copyright law existed to reflect the Claimant's belief perhaps indicated that it was sufficiently weighty and serious to warrant protection at law." Fourth, the belief has to attain a certain level of cogency, seriousness, cohesion and importance. The tribunal thought that

55 [2008] IRLR 29 (EAT), para. 27 of Elias P's judgment.
56 [2019] EWCA Civ. 1720.
57 Ibid. para. 5 of the judgment.
58 Ibid. para. 8 of the judgment.

there was a "considerable range of levels of cogency and seriousness in which these beliefs might have been held." However, "the claimant's own expression of her beliefs . . . concentrated upon an individual's right to create, produce and write and the benefit that she had from those activities which was something entirely different." Her case therefore failed on that criterion. Finally, whether the belief should be worthy of respect in a democratic society, not be incompetent with human dignity or conflict with others' fundamental rights, the tribunal "accepted that that element of the test was met."[59] The Employment Tribunal found that the Claimant did not hold a philosophical belief which was capable of protection under the 2010 Act.

Bean L.J. commented:

> The dispute was as to how narrowly or broadly the copyright assignment should be defined, a question on which equal and opposite views about reasonableness or legitimacy of the clause could be held. The Claimant's crisis of conscience . . . about signing and/or refusal to sign was not the result of her belief . . . but the result of her wish to achieve greater protection for her own creative works. . . . The Claimant's case failed on that basis and we can detect no error in law in the ET's approach.[60]

A belief on a conspiracy theory surrounding the "New World Order" relating to the terrorist attacks of 7/7 and 9/11 in 2001 and 2005, respectively, was held not to qualify as a philosophical belief to attract protection under the Employment Equality (Religion and Belief) Regulations, 2003. In *Farrell v South Yorkshire Police Authority*,[61] Mr Farrell, a principal intelligence analyst employed by the police authority, held a belief in a "New World Order" whereby the global financial institutions and rich countries of the world conspired to introduce a "secret satanic ideology to enslave the masses and claim control of the global resources." He further believed that the United States orchestrated the terrorist attack of 7 July 2005, as did the British government on 11 September 2001. Mr Farrell was asked to prepare a report on the level of threats in that police area, and therein he presented his views on the New World Order, accusing the US and the UK of orchestrating those attacks "to divert attention from their own secret scheming and evil ways of the elite." Disciplinary proceedings were taken against him which resulted in his dismissal by reason of his views being incompatible with his employment. The Claimant brought an action against his employers claiming unfair dismissal and unlawful discrimination because of his beliefs.

59 Ibid. para. 19 of the Court of Appeal and paras 5.7.1 to 5.7.5 of the Employment Tribunal judgment quoted by Bean L.J., with whom Simler L.J. and Arnold L.J. contributed. These criteria are discussed more fully at pp. 105–109 above.

60 Ibid. paras. 38 and 39.

61 Unreported case No. ET/2083085/10.

In examining Mr Farrell's case, the Employment Tribunal considered the five criteria established by case law.[62] Four of the criteria were satisfied; namely a genuine belief, must be a belief and not an opinion, a belief on a weighty and substantial aspect of human life and behaviour and worthy of respect in a democratic society. However, upon scrutiny, the tribunal held that Mr Farrell's beliefs on the New World Order conspiracy failed to satisfy the requirement under the 2003 Regulations that the belief must attain a certain level of cogency, seriousness, cohesion and importance because such beliefs did not meet even[63] the minimum standards of cogency and coherence. Furthermore, the tribunal in applying an objective test[64] considered that his beliefs were "absurd." Failure to meet *all* the requirements of the 2003 Regulations meant that Mr Farrell's claim for discrimination could not proceed.

In the case of *Lisk v Shield Guardian Co. Ltd. & others*,[65] the Claimant alleged direct discrimination, harassment and victimisation under the Equality Act 2010 for his belief that "we should pay our respects to those who have given their lives for us by wearing a poppy from All Souls Day on 2nd November to Remembrance Sunday" or "that it is necessary to pay respect to those who gave their lives by wearing a poppy." The tribunal had to decide whether this was a philosophical belief. Having considered the criteria. Employment Judge George held that[66]

> the belief that one should wear a poppy to show respect to servicemen; however admirable cannot . . . be characterised as a philosophical belief. It seems to me to lack the characteristics of cogency, cohesion and importance that were required in the case of *Grainger plc v Nicholson*. In my view it cannot fairly be described as being a belief as to a weighty and substantial aspect of human life and behaviour. I would rather characterise it as a belief that we should express support for the sacrifice of others and not as a belief in itself. That seems to me to be too narrow to be characterised as a philosophical belief. As a consequence . . . the complaints of direct discrimination and harassment on the protected ground of philosophical belief are dismissed.

62 For those five criteria, see p. 109 above and pp. 105–109 for a fuller discussion.

63 It should be noticed that in its scrutiny, the tribunal took into consideration two important factors, namely (a) the level of cogency and cohesion required which was not mentioned in the EAT *Grainger PLC v Nicholson* case where Burton J. talked of "a certain level" (at para. 24 (iv) of his judgment) without specifying that level; (b) the standard required to demonstrate cogency and coherence of a claimant's beliefs should not be placed too high. Lord Nicholls in the *Williamson* case (at para. 23) said: "The belief must also be coherent in the sense of being intelligible and capable of being understood. But again, too much should not be demanded in that regard. . . . Depending on the subject matter, individuals cannot always be expected to express themselves with cogency or precision. . . . Overall those threshold requirements should not be set at a level which deprive minority beliefs of the protection they are intended to have under the Convention."

64 The objective test used in this case is a welcome new feature for judges to consider when deciding cases.

65 Unreported case No.ET/3300873/2011.

66 Ibid. at para. 10 p. 4.

In *Maya Forstater v CDG Europe, Centre for Global Development and Masood Ahmed*,[67] the Claimant argued that there are two sexes, male and female, and that therefore sex is biological and immutable. There therefore cannot be intersex conditions holding the transgendered status of trans women or trans men, even if a Gender Recognition Certificate is obtained under the Gender Recognition Act 2004.[68]

The Employment Tribunal held that the specific belief (or lack of belief) of the Claimant is not a philosophical belief protected under the Equality Act 2010. Employment Judge J. Taylor said:[69]

> I accept that the Claimant genuinely holds the view that sex is biological and immutable. For her it is more that [*sic*] an opinion or viewpoint based on the present state of information available. Even though she has come to this belief recently she is fixed on it and appears to be more so. She is not prepared to consider the possibility that her belief may not be correct. I accept that the belief . . . goes to substantial aspects of human life and behaviour.

He then considered whether the belief that sex is immutable lacks a level of cogency and cohesion and came to the conclusion that[70] "[o]n balance, I do not consider that the Claimant's belief fails the test of being able to 'attain a certain level of cogency, seriousness, cohesion and importance.'" However, the judge considered that the Claimant's view, in its absolutist nature[71]

> is incompatible with human dignity and fundamental rights of others. She goes so far as to deny the right of a person with a Gender Recognition Certificate to, I try to buy local produce be the sex to which they [*sic*] have transitioned. I do not accept the Claimant's contention that the Gender Recognition Act produces a mere legal fiction. It provides a right, based on the assessment of the various interrelated convention rights, for a person to transition, in certain circumstances and thereafter to be treated for all purposes as the being of the sex to which they have transitioned . . . a fundamental aspect of the reasoning of the ECHR was that a person who has transitioned should not be forced to identify their [*sic*] gender assigned at birth. Such a person should be entitled to live as a person of the sex to which they [*sic*] transitioned. That was recognised in the Gender Recognition Act which states that the change of sex applies "for all purposes." Therefore, if a person has transitioned from male to female and has a Gender Recognition Certificate

67 Case No. ET/2200909/2019.

68 The Legal Gender Recognition in Europe is based on case law of the European Court of Human Rights interpreting the European Human Rights Convention on, among others, gender recognition procedures. The defined standards are thus binding on all Council of Europe Member States. See Marjolein van den Brink "Trans and intersex equality rights in Europe. A comparative analysis" (2018) European Commission.

69 Case No. ET/2200909/2019 at para. 82 of the judgment.

70 Ibid. at para. 83 of the judgment.

71 Ibid. at para. 84 of the judgment.

> that person is legally a woman. That is not something that the Claimant is entitled to ignore.

He concluded by saying that[72]

> the Claimant is absolutist in her view of sex and it is a core component of her belief that she will refer to a person by the sex she considered appropriate even if it violates their dignity and/or creates an intimidating, hostile, degrading, humiliating or offensive environment. The approach is not worthy of respect in a democratic society.

In *Conisbee v Crossley Farms Ltd et al.*,[73] the Employment Tribunal held that the claim that vegetarianism is a protected characteristic under the 2010 Act was not well founded and was thus dismissed. In applying the five tests, Employment Judge Postle considered that the Claimant had a genuine opinion and viewpoint that the world would be a better place if animals were not killed for food, hence his being a vegetarian. Nevertheless, that opinion was not strong enough to qualify as a belief for protection under the 2010 Act. Nor could the "weighty and substantial aspect of human life and behaviour" test apply, as it was a lifestyle choice of the Claimant. Regarding the belief attaining a certain level of cogency, seriousness, cohesion and importance, Employment Judge Postle said:

> Here the tribunal reminds itself that it must guard against applying too stringent standards, that is to say, set the bat too high. The tribunal do [*sic*] accept there are many vegetarians across the world, however the reason for being a vegetarian differs greatly among themselves, unlike veganism where the reasons for being a vegan appear to be largely the same. Vegetarians adopt the practice for many different reasons; lifestyle, health, diet, concern about the way animals are reared for food and personal taste. Vegans simply do not accept the practice under any circumstances of eating meat, fish, dairy products and have distinct concerns about the way in which animals are reared, the clear belief that killing and eating animals is contrary to a civilised society and also against climate control. There you can see the clear cogency and cohesion in vegan belief which appears contrary to vegetarianism. i.e. having numerous, differing and wide varying reasons for adopting vegetarianism.

72 Ibid. at para. 90 of the judgment.

> Since writing this chapter. this case has been reversed on appeal to the EAT. Mr. Justice Choudhury P. considered that the ET erred in law in reaching its decision and that the claimant's philosophical belief does fall under s. 10 of the Equality Act 2010. Choudhury P. said "Where a belief . . . appears to be in accordance with the law of the land, then it is all the more jarring that it should be declared as one not worthy of respect in a democratic society."
>
> (at para 115 of the judgment, p. 55)

73 Case No. ET/3335357/2018.

However, the practice of vegetarianism was found to be worthy of respect in a democratic society and was not incompatible with human dignity. The tribunal thus concluded that it was not persuaded that vegetarianism amounted to a philosophical belief capable of protection under the Equality Act 2010.

The issue of what is known as "misgendering" featured in the case of *Dr. David Mackereth v Department of Work and Pensions et al.*,[74] where the Claimant, a Christian medical practitioner employed by the Department of Work and Pensions (DWP) as a disability assessor, was dismissed for refusing to identify patients by their chosen sex when carrying out medical assessments. His refusal was based on his religious or philosophical beliefs, namely, Genesis 1:27:[75] conscientious objection to, and lack of belief in, transgenderism. Prior to his dismissal he was warned that he could not continue to work for the DWP if he refused to identify patients by their chosen sex. The contract provided "The Department of Work and Pensions requires all Health and Disability Assessors to use such pronouns as may be preferred by the particular client, regardless of that client's biological sex. The penalty for non-compliance is suspension and/or dismissal."[76]

The medical practitioner brought a claim against the DWP before the Employment Tribunal on the grounds that by dismissing him, his employers had breached his rights to freedom of thought, conscience and religion contrary to the Equality Act 2010 provisions. He argued that he was "not attacking the transgender movement" but "being compelled to use a specific pronoun constituted an attack on his 'freedom of speech and freedom of belief.'" Dr Mackereth believed that "gender is defined by biology" and therefore "if upsetting someone can lead to doctors being sacked then, as a society, we have to examine where we are going." He would "not refer to a six foot bearded man as madam." The tribunal found otherwise and held that terminating the Claimant's contract, the DWP had not been in breach of the Equality Act.

In considering the five tests, Employment Judge Perry concluded that[77] "all these heads, belief in Genesis 1:27, a lack of belief in transgenderism and conscientious objection to transgenderism . . . are incompatible with human dignity and conflict with the fundamental rights of others specifically here with transgender individuals."[78]

74 Case No. ET/1304602/2018.

75 Ibid. at para. 6(a): "So God created man in His own image; in the image of God He created him; male and female. He created them. It follows that every person is by God as either male or female. a person cannot change their [*sic*] sex/gender at will. Any attempt or pretence of doing so is pointless, destructive and sinful" (Genesis 1:27).

76 Ibid. at para. 23(a) (c) of the judgment.

77 Ibid. at para. 197 of the judgment.

78 Dr Mackereth said, "I believe that I have to appeal in order to fight for the freedom of Christians to speak the truth. If they cannot, then freedom of speech has died in this country, with serious ramifications for the practise of medicine in the United Kingdom" (BBC West Midlands). This case went on appeal to the EAT Case No EA-2019-001051-LA. Neutral citation [2022] EAT. 99. Mrs Justice Eady P. in dismissing the appeal did not agree entirely on how the ET interpreted some of the five *Grainger* criteria. The ET, therefore, erred in law in some of its decisions relating to those criteria.

Another case which has failed to meet the criteria is *Ellis v Parmagon Ltd.*,[79] where the claimant's beliefs were twofold: first, that homosexuality was contrary to God's law and nature; and second, that no Jewish people were killed by the use of poison gas in concentration camps during the Second World War.

In connection to the first belief, which he demonstrated by a letter which he wrote in his local newspaper in which he concluded that the Bible infers that death is the appropriate penalty for those who approve of homosexuality, the Employment Tribunal held that the belief relied upon failed the test by reason of it not being worthy of respect in a democratic society and being in conflict with the fundamental rights of others. As for the Holocaust denial, where he held the belief that there is no reliable witness testimony that Jews were gassed in gas chambers during the Second World War and that the testimonies of Nazis convicted at the Nuremberg trials were forced through brutality and therefore were unreliable, the Employment Tribunal was of the opinion, first, that the Claimant's belief was not worthy of respect in a democratic society which relied on offensive and bigoted material consistent with anti-Semitism, and second, did not qualify as being sufficiently cogent for protection because it was based on a "knowingly partial and distorted approach to the evidence available to a lay person who shares his degree of interest in the subject." Thus homophobic and anti-Semitic views were not held to be philosophical beliefs under the Equality Act 2010.[80]

It will be recalled that both unsuccessful and successful cases are being analysed in order to illustrate the legal evolution which is currently taking place in this field. Having dealt with a selection of unsuccessful cases, it is now proposed to analyse a selection of successful cases, by which is meant that the tribunals and courts have held that the philosophical belief qualified as a protected characteristic under the provisions of the Equality Act 2010. To have done so and justified their existence meant that the cases met all five criteria which developed through the case law. Nine cases falling in the successful category have been selected for analysis.

79 [2014] EqLR 343. (Discrimination Law Association Briefings 922–934 – March 2020.)

80 See too *Dr. A. Dunn v University of Lincoln* Case No. 2601819/17 (Unreported), a claim on dismissal and direct discrimination regarding the protected characteristic of religion or belief, that latter being "A belief that challenges the tendency to favour what is palatable in social policy discussion over the truth, in colloquial terms this policy is known as 'political correctness.'" Although Employment Judge Blackwell and the two members found the Claimant's belief to be "unfamiliar territory," the tribunal decided that the Claimant's belief was "more of an opinion than a belief" and was "not a weighty and substantial aspect of human life and behaviour" and "lacked cogency and cohesion." (para. 23 (a) (b) (c)). In *Kelly and Others v UNISON* 28th January (2010) (Unreported) the claimants were socialist party activists who were banned from office for 3 to 5 years for writing a leaflet criticising the trade union's Standing Orders Committee. The claimants brought an action in the Employment Tribunal under the 2003 Regulations on the grounds that they were discriminated against as racists, renowned socialist party members, Trotskyists and Marxists. Employment Judge Weiniger held that even if Trotskyism and Marxism qualify as philosophical beliefs they are unworthy of respect in a democratic society and are thus not protected from discrimination under the 2003 Regulations.

2.2 Cases Where the Court or Tribunal Has Found the Belief to Be Justified

In *J. Casamitjana Costa v The League Against Cruel Sports*, the Employment Tribunal held, on the facts of the case, that the Claimant's belief relating to veganism, having met the five criteria developed by the case law which define the term "philosophical belief," fell within the category of a "protected characteristic." This case, having been fully analysed,[81] is not discussed here.

The House of Lords case of *R (Williamson and Others) v Secretary of State for Education and Employment*[82] resulted in an unsuccessful challenge to the prohibition of corporal punishment in all schools under the provisions of the Education Act 1996.[83] Head teachers in several Christian private schools in England and Wales and parents whose children attended those schools which were founded especially to provide a Christian education based on biblical observance which included therein the use of corporal punishment on a limited scale as forming part of their beliefs. They claimed that the prohibition of corporal punishment under s. 548 of the Education Act 1996 was a breach of their religious freedom under Article 9 of the European Convention on Human Rights and the Human Rights Act 1998 and therefore incompatible with the legislation.

The House of Lords was unanimous that there was a big difference between freedom of religious beliefs and freedom to *manifest* those beliefs. Any interference was deemed justified and

> necessary in a democratic society . . . for the protection of rights and freedoms for others. The statutory ban pursues a legitimate aim: Children are vulnerable, and the aim of the legislation is to protect them and promote their wellbeing. Corporal punishment involves deliberately inflicting physical violence. The legislation is intended to protect children against the distress, pain and other harmful effects this infliction of physical violence may cause. That corporal violence may have those harmful effects is evident.[84]

He continued by stating that

> Parliament was entitled to decide that manifestation of those beliefs in practice was not in the best interests of children. Parliament was entitled to decide that, contrary to the claimants' submissions, a universal ban is preferable to a selective ban which exempts schools where parents or teachers have an ideological belief in the efficacy and desirability of a mild degree of carefully controlled corporal punishment. Parliament was entitled, if it saw fit, to lead

81 See pp. 100–110 above.
82 [2005] 2 A.C. 246 and UKHL 15.
83 The claimants' case failed in the Administrative Court (Elias J.) and the Court of Appeal.
84 [2005] 2 A.C. 246 at para. 49 of the judgment.

> and guide public opinion. Parliament was further entitled to take the view that a universal bar was the appropriate way to achieve the desired end.[85]

It is submitted that the prohibition of corporal punishment is a protected characteristic but not of the same kind as the ones mentioned in this chapter, each of which has been created by case law. The protected characteristic on the prohibition of corporal punishment has been created by statute, namely by the Education Act 1996. The philosophical belief may be said to have emanated from the legislature "to lead and guide public opinion," thus showing the evolution which has taken place in both law and society.[86] It is also important to note that it is Lord Nicholls in this very case who sowed the seeds of the five criteria[87] used by Burton J. in the EAT case of *Grainger Plc & Others v Nicholson* and in all subsequent cases on the topic.

The summary of the Employment Appeal Tribunal epitomises the case of *Grainger Plc & Others v Nicholson*[88] as follows:

> A belief in manmade climate change, and the alleged resulting moral imperatives, is capable, if genuinely held, of being a *philosophical belief* for the purpose of the 2003 Religion and Belief Regulations. The belief must be of a similar cogency or status of a religious belief, the ECHR jurisprudence is directly material and the limitations on the concept and extent of the *philosophical belief* can be derived from that, without the need to place any additional limitation on the nature or source of the belief.

This summary gives the reader a taste on what this complicated case is about.

The brief facts were that Mr Nicholson, who was employed as head of sustainability by Grainger, a property investment company, was made redundant. Mr Nicholson claimed that his beliefs on climate change had contributed to his dismissal, which was therefore unfair, and that he was discriminated against contrary to the 2003 Regulations because of his asserted philosophical beliefs about climate change and the environment. He also said that he had not agreed with senior management's views and the company's carbon emissions policy. He claimed that senior directors had obstructed him from performing his duties to make the company more environmentally and socially responsible. He also claimed that he was denied access to enable him to calculate the company's carbon footprint. He claimed that in spite of having good written policies on the environment, the

85 Ibid. at para. 50 of the judgment.

86 See Dr. Anja Hellman, Professor Yvonne Kelly, and Professor Richard G. Wall, "Equally Protected? A review of the evidence on the physical punishment of children" with a foreword by Professor Sir Michael Marmot, who stressed that "physical punishment has the potential to damage children and carries the risk of physical abuse." November 2015. UCL.

87 See pp. 105–109 above.

88 [2010] ICR 360.

company was not managed in accordance with those policies. Furthermore, the executives travelled in some of the most highly polluting cars on the road, and when the chief executive of the company left his BlackBerry in London while in Ireland on a business trip to Ireland, "he ordered one of his staff to get on a plane and deliver the device to him."[89]

An Employment Tribunal held a pre-hearing review in March 2009 to consider whether Mr Nicholson's views of climate change were capable of constituting a philosophical belief for the purposes of the Employment Equality (Religion or Belief) Regulations, 2003.[90] The Employment Tribunal expressed the view that Mr Nicholson's views on climate change were capable of constituting a philosophical belief. Messrs Grainger appealed against the tribunal's decision arguing that Mr Nicholson's views on climate change were based on fact, politics and science and therefore did not constitute a philosophical belief within the meaning of the 2003 Regulations. Burton J. in the Employment Appeal Tribunal upholding the Employment Tribunal decision that Mr Nicholson's beliefs could constitute a philosophical belief, sent the case back for re-hearing to the Employment Tribunal subject to certain important amendments on applying the correct test having been made by the EAT.

Mr Nicholson's witness statement read as follows.[91]

> 2. I have a strongly held philosophical belief about climate change and the environment. I believe we must urgently cut carbon emissions to avoid catastrophic climate change. 3. It is not merely an opinion but a philosophical belief which affects how I live my life including my choice of home, how I travel, what I buy, what I eat and drink, what I do with my waste and my hopes and my fears. For example, I no longer travel by airplane, I have eco-renovated my home, I have reduced my consumption of meat, I compost my food waste, I encourage others to reduce their carbon emissions and I fear very much for the future of the human race, given the failure to reduce carbon emissions on a global scale.

The Employment Judge reached no conclusion regarding the above statement made by the Claimant and said:[92]

> The Claimant has not been cross-examined on that evidence, but it is doubtful if whether such cross-examination would be permitted, since this is not the function of the Tribunal to examine the beliefs of Claimants appearing before it. Instead it is the function of the Tribunal to analyse those beliefs to see whether they engage relevant legislation.

89 *Guardian*, 3 November 2009.
90 It will be recalled that the wording of those Regulations was retained in the Equality Act 2010.
91 *Grainger Plc and Others v T. Nicholson* [2009] ICT 360 at para. 3 of Burton J.'s judgment.
92 In para. 6 of the Employment Judge's judgment.

This statement was found by Burton J. not to be correct and referred to paragraph 22 of Lord Nicholls' judgment in the *Williamson* case,[93] where in the case of a philosophical belief cross-examination is likely to be needed, especially since the Employment Judge considered that[94]

> because the Claimant has settled views about climate change, and acts upon these views in the way in which he leads his life. In my judgment, his belief goes beyond mere opinion, such as might be held on some aspects of climate change, such as whether it is environmentally desirable to travel by air.

It was therefore plainly not open to the Employment Judge to do so without cross-examination or inquiry. Thus, the asserted belief held by the Claimant on which he bases his claim of discrimination is capable of being a belief for the purposes of the 2003 Regulations.

Burton J. in the Employment Appeal Tribunal upheld the decision of the Employment Tribunal Judge subject:[95] first, to the Judge's judgment as amended by Burton J. to include the following "the asserted belief held by the Claimant upon which he bases his claim of discrimination is *capable* of being a belief for the purposes of the 2003 Regulations"; second, at any full hearing there will need to be evidence and cross-examination relating to (1) how far the belief said to qualify for protection under the Regulations is required to be similar to a religious belief; (2) what limits should be placed on the expression "philosophical belief" (i.e. settled belief? philosophical belief? not a scientific belief?); (3) cross-examination as to how genuine the belief is, as per Lord Nicholls in para. 23 of the *Williamson* case; and (4) references to the criteria set out in para. 24 by Lord Nicholls in the *Williamson* case.

The case of *D. Maistry v British Broadcasting Corporation*[96] treats numerous issues but we shall only concentrate on one of these, namely, that of philosophical belief. The Claimant referred to statements made by Lord Reith and Mark Thompson, the director general of the BBC, who stated that the purpose of public service broadcasting is to foster a reasoning citizenry and to support the development of an inclusive, participatory and enlightened democracy. He relied on Mr Thompson's statement that public service broadcasting is founded on the idea of "public space" – a place which is neither government, nor the state, nor purely governed by commercial transactions. A person can thus encounter culture, education and debate and where they can share experiences. The Claimant's view of public space has been given the cohesion, seriousness, cogency and importance by philosophers such as Jurgen Habermas and Dewey.[97] Regarding the strength of

93 The reader is referred to n. 25 at p. 106 above, where Lord Nicholls' judgment will be found.

94 In para. 13 of the Employment Judge's judgment.

95 *Grainger Plc and Others v T Nicholson* [2010] ICR 360 at para. 32.

96 Case No. ET/1313142/2010.

97 Ibid. para. 5 of the judgment.

his belief, his record included the following. He was a student leader, trade unionist and journalist in South Africa during the apartheid struggle and was banned in studying in a South African university because he supported Stephen Biko[98] in the black student boycotts in 1972. He was a founding member of the Media Workers' Association in South Africa and represented South Africa internationally. He was forced to flee South Africa in 1987 after his reports for international news outlets led to security police raids on the Press Trust of South Africa News Agency. The lessons on apartheid strengthened his belief that committed and concerned journalism is an essential component of democracy and that the public service broadcasting provides an effective space for enhancing citizenship. The Claimant also referred to the fact that the BBC is funded by a licence fee and has a mission to inform, educate and entertain. Its Royal Charter and Agreement sets out six public purposes: sustaining citizenship and civil society, promoting education and learning and stimulating creativity and cultural excellence. He quoted Professor Georgina Born (Oxford Professor of Music and Anthropology), who said of the BBC that "in the face of international conflicts and domestic tensions, it offers precisely that independent arena for staging a politics of complex cultural dialogue that is required in order to cultivate commonality, reciprocity and toleration." Such were the Claimant's beliefs.[99]

Employment Judge Hughes had no doubt in finding that the five criteria in the leading case of *Nicholson* (see above) were fulfilled. He found that the claimant's beliefs were genuinely held, the Claimant's asserted belief was worthy of respect in a democratic society and not incompatible with human dignity, it was a weighty and substantial aspect of human life and behaviour, his was a belief and not an opinion or viewpoint, and that belief also attained a certain level of cogency, seriousness, cohesion and importance.[100]

Although the case of *Hasham v Milton Park (Dorset) Limited t/a Orchard Park*[101] features other matters, we shall concentrate solely on the Claimant's belief of the sanctity of life, namely, his beliefs against fox hunting and hare culling, both of which constitute a philosophical belief for the purposes of the Employment Equality (Religion and Belief) Regulations 2003. The Claimant lived and

98 Stephen Biko was a charismatic, prominent South African anti-apartheid activist in the Black Consciousness Movement (BCM) in the 1960s and 1970s. The BCM, led by Biko, was an anti-apartheid movement which emerged out of the political vacuum created by the jailing and banning of the African National Congress and the Pan African Congress leadership after the Sharpeville massacre in 1960. The BCM empowered and mobilised the black population. It expressed group pride and helped instil a new cultural and philosophical outlook among the black population. The BCM became one of the most influential anti-apartheid movements in South Africa, when many countries on the African continent gained independence and South Africa increased its repression of black liberation movements. In 1997, two decades after the assassination of Biko, four former police officers including Colonel Gideon Nieuwoudt admitted killing Biko on 12 September 1977.

99 Ibid. paras. 6–8 of the judgment.

100 Ibid. paras. 16–19 of the judgment.

101 Case No. ET/3105555/2009.

worked to prevent cruelty to animals, his beliefs affected every aspect of his life on a daily basis, and he made conscious decisions based on what he believed was right and wrong. Apart from the clothes he wore, his philosophical belief affected all the work he did, the places he visited and how he spent his time and resources. He believed that hunting was morally unacceptable and it was wrong to take pleasure in killing animals either for sport or for pest control. "My belief is perhaps the largest and most prominent part of my identity as well as being the guiding force in the way I live my life and the work I do," he pleaded and proved. He was also a vegan.[102] The Claimant was cross-examined on his beliefs by the Respondent for some two hours.[103]

Having had regard to the way the Claimant gave his evidence both in chief and at cross-examination, Employment Judge Guyer found the Claimant a credible witness whose evidence he accepted. Having applied the five limitation criteria established by case law and citing such case law as *Williamson* and *Nicholson* (above), he concluded that the Claimant's beliefs qualified for protection as a philosophical belief under the 2003 Regulations on the grounds that his beliefs derived from a philosophical commitment to the sanctity of life and animal welfare; his beliefs affecting every area of his life; his beliefs were cogent, serious, coherent and important; and his views formed an established part of debate in most democracies. There was no fundamental right to engage in blood sport. His beliefs and conduct in opposing hunting and so forth were always peaceful.[104]

In *A. Gibbins v British Council*,[105] it was held that the Respondent did not discriminate directly or indirectly because of her philosophical belief. This case included unfair dismissal and wrongful dismissal issues. We shall only deal with the philosophical belief issue. That issue was republicanism. The Claimant believed that the United Kingdom should not be ruled by a hereditary monarch and that it should be a democratic and secular republic. She developed this belief over time from involvement in antiracism demonstrations in Southwell; the death of Blair Peach; and the influence of Tony Benn, a republican whose works she read, and later through personal contact while working on environmental campaigns for Friends of the Earth. She was a labour party and trade union member and also worked for Amnesty International. She became concerned of the monarch being commander-in-chief of the British armed forces and the role played by the Judicial Committee of the Privy Council in deciding appeals against the death penalty in Commonwealth jurisdictions. Her travels to countries which had human rights violations "further confirmed my belief in the need for strong democratic republican government systems founded in international law."[106] She had atheist and socialist beliefs and she was sometimes known as "the reds under the beds" and "the

102 Ibid. paras. 9–24 of the judgment.
103 Ibid. paras. 25–35 of the judgment.
104 Ibid. paras. 41–59 of the judgment.
105 Case No. ET/2200088/2017.
106 Ibid. para. 16 of the judgment.

quiet Corbynista."[107] A discussion took place on Facebook on "white privilege,"[108] which used insulting and foul language against the two-year-old Prince George, the Queen's grandson. It appears that someone commented on the burdens the young prince would experience when he grows up. To that the Claimant retorted,[109]

> but are you happy that he will grow up to inherit the burden/privilege? I understand that a 3year old will grow no different than his circumstances. All I wish to suggest is that most children in the world don't have as many reasons to smile. That's sad for kids in UK, just as it is elsewhere. Not everyone has a good life and opportunity.

All this discussion came into the public domain.[110] It was also published in the *Sun* newspaper.[111]

Employment Judge Goodman, following the Employment Appeal Tribunal case of *Nicholson* (above), by which he was bound by judicial precedent, had to assess, as a matter of fact, whether Ms Gibbins' belief was genuine and thus qualified as a philosophical belief under the provisions of s. 10(2) of the Equality Act 2010. The tribunal accepted that her belief was genuine, as indeed did the Respondent's witnesses. It was therefore not an opinion or a viewpoint. The tribunal found the Claimant's articulation of her belief "not easy to follow," for republican leaders are also commanders-in-chief of their armed forces, for example, the United States; and the death penalty features in democratic and sometimes socialist republics, for example, in some US states and Cuba, respectively. "But the lack of logic cannot be fatal otherwise much religious belief might fail the test," said Employment Judge Goodman, no doubt taking cognisance of what Lord Nicholls said in the *Williamson* case, namely[112] "too much must not be regarded in this regard . . . Overall, these threshold requirements should not be set at a level which would deprive minority beliefs of the protection they are intended to have." The Employment Judge continued:[113]

> We understand the claimant's belief as an identification with opposition to inherited wealth and privilege, in which the monarchy is what now remains in

107 Ibid. para. 17 of the judgment.

108 Ibid. para. 21 of the judgment which means "That cheeky grin is the (already locked-in) innate knowledge that he is Royal, rich, advantaged and will never know 'any' difficulties and hardships in life. Let's find photographs of 3yo Syrian refugee children and see if they look alike, eh?" The Claimant also stated at paragraph 24 that "I am sound in my socialist, atheist and Republican opinions. I do not believe the Royal family have any place in a modern democracy, least of all when they live on public money. That's privilege, and it needs to end."

109 Ibid. para. 25 of the judgment.

110 Ibid. para. 28 of the judgment.

111 Ibid. para. 38 of the judgment, which reads "George and the Dragon: 3-year old Prince George hit by vile rant from British Council boss paid hundreds by taxpayers to promote UK . . . Irate Giddens [*sic*] attacked future monarch saying he was "privileged, rich and looks like . . ."

112 See p. 107 above.

113 Case No. ET/2200088/2017 paras. 97–99 of the judgment.

> Britain of an earlier and wider system of rule by an aristocratic elite. This sits with left-leaning views on other matters of social organisation, even though others on the left may take more pragmatic views on the role of the monarch in the UK constitution. The extent to which that view of the monarchy is symbolic of a wider evil in social organisation is characteristic of belief rather than fact-based opinion. . . . The belief is also a belief about how we should be governed, weighty and substantial. . . . We concluded that it was a philosophical belief, such that its holders are to be protected from discrimination.

C. *McEleny v Ministry of Defence*[114] has proved a complicated case, in that the Respondent sought a reconsideration[115] of the original judgment made by Employment Judge Frances Eccles and thereafter sought a further judgment treating another matter by Employment Judge Lucy Wiseman, who dismissed the case after a fifty-page judgment. It is proposed to discuss the *McEleny* case upon its reconsideration which confirmed, with no amendments, the original decision. Employment Judge Frances Eccles stated:

> By judgment dated 25th July 2018, the Employment Tribunal found that the claimant's belief in Scottish independence amounts to a philosophical belief within the meaning of Section 10(2) of the Equality Act 2010 and be relied upon by the claimant as a protected characteristic for the purposes of claiming direct discrimination under Section 13 of the Equality Act 2010.

The tribunal had to consider first whether it was necessary in the interests of justice to reconsider the original judgment and if so, whether confirmation of the original judgment, variation or revocation should take place. The Respondent sought reconsideration of this case on the grounds that the tribunal failed correctly to identify the Claimant's belief when considering whether it met the five tests in the *Nicholson* case. In dismissing each of the Respondent's allegations the Employment Judge confirmed that[116]

> based on the evidence before me I found that the claimant believes that Scotland should be an independent country. . . . From the evidence before me I found that the claimant supports the SNP because achieving independence is its principal policy. . .. From the evidence before me I found that the claimant has believed in the right of the Scottish people to self-determination since childhood. I was satisfied that self-determination . . . is an integral part of the claimant's belief in Scottish independence being concerned with how people living in Scotland are governed, where sovereignty lies and whether decisions taken regarding the future of Scotland are to be taken in Scotland or

114 Case No. ET/4105347/2017 with a judgment date of 9 February 2019.

115 Under Rule 71 of the Employment Tribunals (Constitution and Rules of Procedure) Regulations 2013 for reconsideration of the Judgment.

116 Case No. ET/4105347/2017 paras. 4–6 of the judgment.

> elsewhere . . . I was persuaded from the evidence before me that the claimant's belief that Scotland . . . should be independent was of significant weight and importance to human life and behaviour to be philosophical in nature . . . I was persuaded that it is a belief of material relevance and application to human life and behaviour generally. . . . The fact that there was a referendum in which 1.5 million of the Scottish electorate voted in favour of independence supported the claimant's position that his belief was a sufficient level of cogency, seriousness, cohesion and importance to satisfy the fourth test in [*Nicholson*].

She concluded:[117]

> Having considered the respondent's submissions, I am not persuaded that it would be in the interests of justice to reconsider my judgment . . . I have not been asked to consider new evidence. There is no suggestion of a procedural or administrative error by either the tribunal or the party. The application for reconsideration of the judgment on the grounds advanced by the respondent is therefore refused.

C. Oliver v Department of Work and Pensions[118] is another multifaceted case where only the discrimination on grounds of philosophical belief on democratic socialism will be discussed. The claimant stated that the Labour Party is not simply an organisation, for it encapsulates and enshrines a set of core beliefs recognised by the general public. He described those beliefs as "democratic socialism." He stated that those beliefs are summarised at the back of the membership card of that party as follows:[119]

> The Labour Party is a democratic socialist party. It believes that by the strength of our social endeavour we enshrine more than we achieve alone so as to create for each of us a community in which power, wealth and opportunity are in the hands of the many and not the few, where the rights we enjoy reflect the duties we owe and where we live together, freely in the spirit of tolerance and respect.

Furthermore, the claimant agreed that labour values, namely democratic socialism, a strong welfare state, fiscal controls and nationalisation of key services were among his strong philosophical beliefs and showed how he conducted his life. The claimant gave evidence that he earned only £1,000 a month as a county councillor, has no savings and does not own his house. These being the facts, Employment Judge N. J. Roper had to apply the law.

117 Ibid. para. 7 of the judgment.
118 Case No. ET/1701407/2013.
119 Ibid. para. 13 of the judgment.

He considered the five criteria setting out the limits placed on the definition of philosophical belief made by Burton J. in *Nicholson,* in which there was some debate on whether the claimant had been properly cross-examined. In the *Oliver* case the claimant gave evidence and was cross-examined in some detail. Both parties agreed that the belief was genuinely held and that the belief was worthy of respect in a democratic society, was not incompatible with human dignity and did not conflict with the fundamental rights of others. The difference between the parties was to the extent to which limitations (ii), (iii) and (iv) were met.[120] Employment Judge Roper said:[121]

> I find on the balance of probabilities that the claimant has more than a passing interest in, and is more than merely a repeat voter for, the Labour Party. I accept his assertion that he has a strong support for, interest in, and connection with the history and moral tenets of the Socialist Labour Party. This strong belief affects how he conducts his life. He lives for the Labour Party and for supporting its aims and beliefs, and other causes which [he] . . . espouses and supports. I find that he personally has a philosophical belief in democratic socialism, beyond being (as the respondent has argued) merely "a political animal" who chooses to support a particular political party. I find . . . that this amounts to a belief and is not just an opinion and viewpoint based on the present state of information available; is a belief as to a weighty and substantial aspect of human life and behaviour; and which has attached a certain level of cogency, seriousness, cohesion and importance. . . . It follows that the constituent elements of a philosophical belief are met in the claimant's case. I find that the claimant's belief in "democratic socialism" is within the definition of philosophical belief and is sufficient to be potentially protected by section 10 of the Equality Act 2010.

The interesting case of *A. Power v Greater Manchester Police Authority*[122] which was heard in the Employment Tribunal, the Employment Appeal Tribunal and the Court of Appeal brings a novel aspect in the field of religious or philosophical beliefs. This case concerns both the issues of philosophical beliefs as well as dismissal. Unlike other cases in this chapter, where issues arising therein other than philosophical beliefs have been ignored, in this case the analysis demands that the issue of dismissal which arose be treated. This case is of interest not only because it expands protection to employees who hold the protected belief in spiritualism but also because it demarcates religious or philosophical beliefs and religious or philosophical proselytising in the place of work.

120 Ibid. para. 32 of the judgment.
121 Ibid. paras. 33 and 34 of the judgment.
122 Employment Appeal Tribunal [2010] UKEAT 0087/10 and [2011] EWCA Civ. 534 before Stanley Burnton L.J.

Mr Alan Power was a "committed spiritualist" who held genuine and *bona fide* beliefs on the existence of psychic and paranormal phenomena. He also took courses on and experimented in spiritualism. He was employed by the Manchester Police for a relatively short while before he was dismissed. Mr Power brought a claim in the Employment Tribunal of direct discrimination on the grounds of his religious and/or philosophical beliefs. Not having been employed for the qualifying period of two years, he could not bring a claim for unfair dismissal. Discrimination on grounds of religious or philosophical belief in the context of employment is not subject to any minimum qualifying period of employment and therefore if the claimant were able to establish that he was discriminated against by being dismissed for his religious or philosophical beliefs he would be enabled to have a good claim. The tribunal members were unanimous in the view that the respondent believed that based on information received it would be wholly inappropriate to allow the claimant to continue in his employment. This view was held by reason of the claimant's conduct which was totally unconnected with his religious/philosophical beliefs, namely the claimant's disruptive attitude during role play where he was playing the role of a shoplifter at Bruche police training college near Warrington he became visibly aroused during the frisking process. Other police forces refused to employ him because of his inappropriate behaviour. There were also other concerns such as the delivery of a CD-ROM and posters to the respondent's premises which, in the quoted words of Burnton L.J.[123]

> were related to the claimant's beliefs. It was not because the claimant held those beliefs but because of the unacceptable way in which he was perceived of expressing those beliefs that the respondent decided to dispense with the claimant's services. Based on Chondol such a conclusion does not constitute unlawful discrimination contrary to the Regulations.

Prior to analysing the case of *Chondol* and other relevant cases, it is important to give the Employment Tribunal judgment, approved by both the Employment Appeal Tribunal and the Court of Appeal, on the issue of religious or philosophical belief. The Employment Tribunal held that – in line with the *Nicholson* case – the claimant's spiritualist beliefs in psychics, God and eternal life were capable of constituting religious and philosophical beliefs for purposes of the Employment Equality (Religion and Belief) Regulations 2003.[124] In doing so, the Employment Judge traced the history of the Spiritualist church, which enjoys being the eighth-largest British faith group in the UK, and the fact that the claimant's belief in afterlife and communicating with spirits was worthy of respect in a democratic society and had the necessary cogency, seriousness, cohesion and importance such as to amount to a philosophical belief.

123 [2011] EWCA Civ. 534 para. 5 (quoted from the Employment Tribunal judgment).
124 S.I 2003 1660.

Thus, the Employment Tribunal (whose decision was endorsed by the EAT and by the Court of Appeal) added belief in the psychic field as a category of religious or philosophical belief which is protected by law. What is particularly important in this case is that the tribunal drew a distinction between treatment on the grounds of a person's *beliefs* on the one hand and on the grounds of the *manifestation* of those beliefs on the other. McMullen J. Q.C.[125] in the EAT said in his conclusion:[126]

> We are quite satisfied, on the authorities referred to (see especially MR in Ladele at para. 35) that a distinction falls to be drawn between treatment on the grounds of a person's beliefs and on the grounds of the manifestation of those beliefs. That was the point in Ladele, Chondol and McFarlane. Having correctly directed themselves as to that distinction in law the tribunal majority, in our collective judgment, found that the reason for the Respondent's dismissal of the Claimant was, in part, the manifestation of his spiritual beliefs in the materials which he had earlier distributed, not the fact of his beliefs. Accordingly, there is no error in law disclosed in this appeal and it must be dismissed.

A brief analysis of the relevant parts of each of the three cases mentioned is important to authoritatively support the aforementioned significant distinction drawn in the *Power* case. In *Islington London Borough Council v Ladele*,[127] the Master of the Rolls said

> she did not want a registrar "who does not wish to participate in civil partnership duties." It seems clear to me that this statement was directed not to Ms Ladele's belief to civil partnership, but to the manifestation of that partnership, namely her refusal to conduct such partnership duties.

In *Chondol v Liverpool City Council*,[128] the EAT held that a social worker who was dismissed for promoting his religious beliefs did not suffer religion or philosophical belief discrimination. The Employment Tribunal was right to hold that Mr Chondol was not dismissed on the grounds of his religion but rather on the grounds that he was "improperly foisting" his religion on service users.

125 A Queen's Counsel (QC) is an advocate appointed by a female monarch to be one of "Her Majesty's Counsel learned in the law" or a King's Counsel (KC) when a monarch is a male. Only barristers-at-law could be appointed as QC or KC before 1995. Since 1995 solicitors can also be appointed as such.

126 [2010] UKEAT 0087/10 at para. 17 of his judgment.

127 [2009] EWCA Civ. 1357; Case No. A2/2009/0518 para. 35.

128 Case No. EAT/0298/08.

Similarly, in *McFarlane v Relate Avon Ltd*,[129] it was argued by the appellant's counsel "that for a religious belief to be effectively protected it is necessary to prevent discrimination on the ground not only that a belief is held but that it is manifested."[130] It was thus submitted that the two issues are inseparable. The EAT was unable to accept that argument. Underhill J. said that[131]

> It is of course correct that persons with a religious belief are likely to manifest their belief in their conduct. We further accept that in some cases where the employer objects to such manifestation it may be impossible to see any basis for the objection other than an objection to the belief it manifests; and in such a case a claim by the employer to be acting on grounds of the former but not the latter may be regarded as a distinction without a difference. But in other cases there will be a clear and evidently genuine basis for differentiation between the two and in such a case the fact that the employee's motivation for the conduct in question may be found in his wish to manifest this religious belief does not mean that that belief is the ground of the employer's action. Take the case of an employee who wears an item of jewellery or clothing of a religious significance. In the absence of any other context, it may be permissible to infer that the employer who dismisses the employee for wearing an item in question does so because of an objection to the belief so manifested: the protestation "I don't mind you being a Christian/Muslim, but I object to you wearing a cross/veil" might, without more, be rejected as spurious. If however it appeared from the context that there was some other ground for the objection – such as a general policy about the wearing of jewellery or practical reasons why the wearing of a veil was regarded as inappropriate – the position would be entirely different. In such a case any claim would have to be on a basis of indirect discrimination. We note that in *Eweida v British Airways* . . . although a direct discrimination case was advanced before the employment tribunal, it was not pursued in this Tribunal. See also the decision in this Tribunal in *Chondol v Liverpool City Council* . . . which recognises (at para. 23) the legitimacy of this distinction between objecting to a religious belief and objecting to inappropriate proselytisation.

Nor is there any inconsistency between that conclusion and the requirements of Article 9 of the Convention on Human Rights. The appellant's counsel referred to the judgment of the European Court of Human Rights case of *Kokkinasis v Greece* (04307/88 [1993] EHRR 397 where the court emphasised the importance of Article 9 and observed that without the right to manifest one's religion the rights enshrined therein "would be likely to remain a dead letter."

129 UKEAT/0106/09/DA and [2010] EWCA Civ. 771 which refused the application made to the Court of Appeal.

130 Ibid. para. 17 of the EAT judgment delivered by Underhill J.

131 Ibid. para. 18 of the judgment.

Underhill J. considered that[132]

> subsequent case law makes clear that it does not follow that an employee has an unqualified right to manifest his religion. In *Kalac v Turkey* [1997] EHRR 552 *27* the court stated plainly (see para. 27 at p. 564) that "*Art. 9 does not protect every act motivated or inspired by a religion or belief. Moreover in exercising his freedom to manifest his religion, an application may need to take his specific situation into account.*" The same observation was repeated in *Sahin v Turkey* [2005] 19 BHRC at para 66. In *R (Williamson) v Secretary of State for Education and Employment* [2005] 2 AC 246 Lord Nicholls described this as representing the consistent position of the Strasbourg jurisdiction – see para. 30 at p. 261A. Likewise in *K(SB) v Governors of Denbigh High School* [2007] 1 AC 100, Lord Bingham referred at para. 22 of his speech, to both *Kolac* and *Sahin* together with the earlier decision in *Ahman v United Kingdom* [1981] 4 EHRR 126 and continued at para 23 (p. 112 G–H). "*The Strasbourg institutions have not been at all ready to find an inference with the right to manifest religious belief and practice or observance where a person has voluntarily accepted an employment or role which does not accommodate that practice or observance and there are other means open to the person to observe his or her religion without undue hardship or inconvenience.*"

There is thus strong legal evidence resulting from both the United Kingdom case law and the case law of the Court of Human Rights in Strasbourg that manifestation of one's religious or philosophical beliefs is not protected under British discrimination laws.

The case of *Hawkins v Universal Utilities Ltd. t/a Unicom*[133] is unlike the other cases in that it was decided on supposition. The claimant, a telesales agent, was dismissed for failing to meet his targets. He claimed that the real cause for his dismissal was because of his Christian beliefs not to tell lies. He alleged that while training he was told to "be creative" and while talking to "gatekeepers" such as personal assistants, secretaries and so forth he was advised "to lie" to them. Furthermore, he claimed to have heard some of his colleagues lying to potential customers on the telephone, thus deceiving them. The claimant lost his case because he was unable to produce sufficient evidence to support his claim that the employer required him and his other colleagues to lie and thus deceive potential customers or those unwilling to be involved in deceitful activity would be placed at a disadvantage compared to those who believe that it is good to lie and be deceitful. The tribunal also found that belief to be a manifestation of a religious belief.

132 Ibid. para. 20 of the judgment.
133 Case No. ET/2501234/2012.

The Employment Tribunal did however state that a well-founded belief that a person should not tell lies under any circumstances and thus not deceive potential customers to obtain sales would qualify as a philosophical belief under s. 10 of the Equality Act 2010. Based on judicial precedent in the EAT case of *Nicholson*, Burton J.'s five criteria would need to be met to qualify as a philosophical belief: namely, the belief needs to be genuine; it needs to be weighty and substantial aspects of human life and behaviour; it has a certain level of cogency, seriousness and cohesion and importance; and is worthy of respect in a democratic society.

Commitment to public services can qualify as a philosophical belief under the Equality Act 2010. An Employment Tribunal in *J. Anderson v Chesterfield High School*[134] held that the claimant did indeed have a philosophical belief. Inspired by his parents and a local community activist, the claimant maintained a deep-seated belief and conviction to serve the community for the common good. He was an active Labour Party member employed as a community development worker in Liverpool, he obtained a diploma in social work from John Moores University while given a placement at Sefton in the Education Welfare Department, and upon receipt of his diploma he was given a permanent post at Sefton. He was promoted to senior education officer. His belief in public service made him participate in local government, and he became a Liverpool city councillor and elected as leader of the labour group on Liverpool City Council. In addition, he set up a charity called Sefton Welfare for Pupils to raise money to assist parents to buy school uniforms and encourage school attendance. He supported the release of a Liverpool Football Club member wrongfully convicted in Bulgaria. He took part in developing events for Liverpool European City of Culture. He served on the Board of Liverpool Vision which is dedicated to the economic development of the City of Liverpool. Other goals which he achieved while Leader or Mayor which contributed to the common good of the city included the return of cruise liners to the port, the Oliver King Foundation, opposition to the "bedroom tax" and his work with Tesco to raise money for local food banks. In his campaign manifesto to be elected Mayor he said "I am Liverpool through and through. I have lived and worked here all my life. I raised my children here and I have dedicated my life to working hard for the city and its residents."

Humanism[135] has been held to constitute a philosophical belief. In *Streatfield v London Philharmonic Orchestra Ltd*[136] the claimant, Ms Streatfield, was a violinist with the London Philharmonic Orchestra (LPO) whose name was included in a letter, followed by LPO and published by a national newspaper, which protested against an invitation to the Israeli Philharmonic Orchestra which gave a performance during the proms in 2011. Following a disciplinary hearing on the grounds

134 Case No. UKEAT/2006/14/MC based on the dictum of Serota J. Q.C. paras. 5 and 6 (paras. 15, 16, and 18 of the Employment Tribunal judgment).

135 Humanism is described as a rational outlook or system of thought attaching prime importance to human rather than divine or supernatural matters.

136 Case No. ET/2390772/2011.

that the Claimant was bringing the LPO into disrepute, she was suspended on full pay for six months. She brought an action against the LPO for discrimination, victimisation and harassment on the ground of her philosophical belief, namely her humanistic belief. The Employment Tribunal, applying the five criteria set out in *Nicholson*, held that humanism is capable of being a philosophical belief under the Equality Act 2010 for it was a belief and not an opinion or viewpoint; a belief capable of fulfilling the substantial and weighty aspects of human life and behaviour; a belief worthy of respect in a democratic society; and a belief was not incompatible with human dignity or in conflict with the fundamental rights of others. The tribunal heard that the claimant genuinely held the philosophical belief of humanism throughout her life by way of her education, by the way in which she educated her own children and by the choice of her partner.

M. Harron v Chief Constable of Dorset Police[137] was a case relating to both disability and philosophical belief under the Equality Act 2010. We shall only deal with the latter claim. The Claimant had a belief (which the Employment Tribunal thought to be genuine) that the public service was improperly wasteful of money. He stated that he felt compelled to express those beliefs even if he suffered discrimination on grounds of his philosophical beliefs. The Employment Tribunal judge considered whether his belief met the necessary criteria to merit the protection of the Equality Act 2010 and considered that it did not because it failed in three of the five *Nicholson* criteria.[138] The EAT allowed the appeal on the grounds that it was unclear whether the Employment Judge had in mind the proper approach to the criteria as expressed by Lord Nicholls in *Williamson* and what his reasons were for holding that there had been a failure to meet those criteria. Langstaff J. sitting alone in the EAT referred the case back to the same Employment Tribunal for it to re-consider the case.

Langstaff J. referred extensively to Lord Nicholls' dictum at paragraph 23 of the *Williamson* case,[139] highlighting key phrases such as the belief satisfying "some modest, objective minimum requirements," "consistent with basic standards of human dignity and integrity," "relating to matters more than merely trivial," "it must possess an adequate degree of seriousness and importance." "a fundamental problem," "coherence in the sense of being intelligible and capable of being understood," "the fact that too much should not be demanded in this regard," and "overall, these threshold requirements should not be set at a level which would deprive minority beliefs of the protection they are intended to have." He also

137 Case No. UKEAT/0234/15/DA. See too in the Employment Tribunal Case No. 3101466/2013 and Case No. 3100607/2014.

138 See para. 39 of the Employment Judge's reasons. He agreed with the first and last criteria, namely genuine belief and worthy of respect in a democratic society, etc., but rejected the other three criteria, namely the fact that it must be a belief and not a viewpoint, it must be a weighty and substantial aspect of human life and behaviour and it must have a level of cogency, seriousness, cohesion and importance.

139 *M. Harron v Chief Constable of Dorset Police* UKEAT/0234/15/DA para. 32. See p. 107 in particular and generally pp. 108–109 above.

referred to Burton J.'s five criteria in *Nicholson*[140] and the Code of Practice.[141] In addition, Langstaff J. commented that "the bar should not be set too high although . . . for a belief to qualify as one which is philosophical it must at least reach a certain measure of seriousness and cogency as" the *Nicholson* case requires.[142] Furthermore, Langstaff J. considered that the Employment Tribunal did not err in law in finding that the belief which operated solely in the workplace, namely Dorset Police, would constitute too narrow a focus to qualify for protection. "That might be thought to exclude beliefs that had so narrow a focus as to be parochial rather than fundamental."[143] The EAT said that the right approach was to apply the case law and the Code of Practice to see if the belief qualifies for protection under the provisions of the Equality Act 2010. The Claimant also appealed on the grounds that "the word 'philosophical' does not appear in European case law and Article 9 in respect of a qualifying belief."[144] To this the EAT said that the *Nicholson* criteria "do encompass the meaning of belief as it is applied in domestic law in a manner which is consistent with the European authorities."

PART 3. Epilogue

Picking up the threads of what has been said calls for some concluding remarks. These will feature under two headings. First, a summing up of the case law which forms an eclectic list of cases which failed to meet the test to qualify as philosophical beliefs and those cases which fulfilled Burton J.'s five criteria in the *Nicholson* case. There will then be a discussion on other relevant issues pertaining to philosophical beliefs and related matters. In the second instance a discussion will take place on the impact of this legal evolution on the employer.

3.1 Summing Up the Case Law – Forming an Eclectic List of Beliefs

A philosophical belief is usually[145] a non-religious belief which includes secularism, atheism, humanism, democratic socialism and so on. In order that such a belief qualifies under the provisions of the Equality Act 2010 as a protected characteristic, the claimant must prove that they have genuine, strong and sincere beliefs which satisfy each of the five criteria mentioned by Burton J. in the EAT case of *Nicholson*. Those beliefs must form part of the claimant's daily life at home, at play and at work, of their diet, behaviour, travel arrangements, habits, policies, upbringing, education, and so on. In other words, the claimant needs to *live* their belief in their daily life.

140 See p. 109 above.
141 See pp. 135–136 above.
142 *M. Harron v Chief Constable of Dorset Police* UKEAT/0234/15/DA at para. 40.
143 Ibid. para. 37 of the judgment.
144 Ibid. para. 32 of the judgment.
145 Although religion may feature in some cases which relate to philosophical beliefs, as for example in *Chondol* or *Ladele*.

Thus, the following cases, amongst others, have been ascribed by tribunals not to constitute a philosophical belief within the meaning of the Equality Act 2010 or prior to that Act, the Equality (Religion and Belief) Regulations of 2003: the importance of wearing a poppy in November (*Lisk*); homosexuality being against God's law and the Holocaust having never happened (*Ellis*); the 9/11 and 7/7 terrorist attacks being government-led conspiracies (*Farrell*); refusal to place children for adoption care or fostering with same-sex partners (*McClintock*); refusal to sign a copyright agreement (*Gray*); wearing a silver cross round a Claimant's neck against British Airways rules (*Eweida*); there are only two sexes and therefore sex is biological and immutable (*Forstater*); vegetarianism not a philosophical belief (*Conisbee*); political correctness (*Dunn*); and refusal to identify patients by their chosen sex when carrying out medical assessments (*Mackereth*).

Philosophical beliefs which have proved successful include, amongst others, veganism (*Casamitjana Costa*); climate change and environment (*Grainger*); public service broadcasting (*Maistry*); sanctity of life (*Hasham*); United Kingdom to be a democratic and secular republic (*Gibbins*); Scottish independence (*McEleny*); democratic socialism (*Oliver*); spiritualism and psychics (*Power*); Christian belief not to tell lies (*Hawkins*); serving the community for the common good (*Anderson*); humanism (*Streathfield*); distinction between religion, belief and manifestation of religious and philosophical beliefs (*Chondol, Ladele, McFarlane*); and public sector money being wasted (*Harron*).

Philosophical beliefs are a protected characteristic under the provisions of the Equality Act 2010.[146] A person must not be discriminated against because of their (or an associate person's) philosophical belief. However, the 2010 Act does not give a precise definition of what a philosophical belief consists of, so it befalls upon the case law to establish this fact. So as to qualify for such protection under the 2010 Act, the philosophical belief must comply with the five criteria pronounced by Burton J. in *Nicholson*. Such belief can be a single issue and therefore not shared by others, and it does not matter if no one else has the belief in question.

It is important to note that each case is decided in accordance with its own facts. The facts are then applied to the law, taking into account especially the five criteria, also known as limitations, set out by Burton J. in the EAT case of *Nicholson* before a decision is taken by the tribunal. A detailed judgment is given by the judge to explain why, and how, the judge came to their conclusion.

In deciding a philosophical belief case, the threshold requirements should not be set too high by the tribunal. They should be set at a level which would not deprive minority beliefs of the protection they are intended to have. This was stressed by Lord Nicholls in the *Williamson* case and again by Burton J. in *Nicholson.*[147] As seen above, the concept of "philosophical belief" is a wide term covering a vast range of views so long as they meet the relatively low level test mentioned above.

146 As well as the predecessor of that Act, namely the Employment Equality (Religion or Belief) Regulations 2003 whose provisions have been incorporated in the 2010 Act.

147 Op. cit. at para. 23 of his judgment in *Williamson* and para. 22 of *Nicholson*, respectively.

This is of significant importance because, if the Claimant is successful in proving that they have been discriminated against on grounds of philosophical belief, there are no limits on the damages to which the employer would be subjected.

The reader would have noticed that the cases which come before the tribunals and courts often deal with matters which are additional to deciding whether a claimant's belief qualifies as a philosophical belief. Such additional matters may include dismissals, redundancies and other issues. Where a belief has been found by an Employment Tribunal to qualify as a philosophical belief which falls within the protection of the Equality Act 2010, it does not automatically or necessarily mean that the Claimant has been discriminated against. The issue of philosophical belief needs to be decided first before the tribunal can decide if the employee has been discriminated against by reason of dismissal because of the claimant's conduct, or redundancy, disability, age, sex and so on. The actual discrimination judgment is therefore a two-stage process. The tribunal will thus decide first whether the Complainant's belief qualifies as a philosophical belief, and second it will decide upon the appropriate claim, whether it be dismissal or some other issue. The case of *Power* (above) epitomises this situation. Power's belief, it will be recalled, was held by the tribunal to constitute a philosophical belief, but his dismissal for gross misconduct was held to be fair, as the tribunal's decision was based on Power's conduct surrounding his philosophical belief rather than the belief itself. Tribunals thus distinguish between discrimination per se and situations where the employee has been dismissed for a good reason during their employment, thus not allowing individuals to abuse the philosophical belief criteria.

It is noticeable that most cases decided are heard by Employment Tribunals. These constitute rulings "at first instance." As such, and under the British doctrine of judicial precedent,[148] those rulings are not binding on either, other Employment Tribunals or the EAT and the higher courts although they may have a persuasive effect upon them. Although it is unlikely that this will occur, any of those Employment Tribunal decisions may be reversed by the EAT, the Court of Appeal or the Supreme Court.

Since the beginning of this millennium, the number of philosophical beliefs has increased considerably. They have increased so as to take into account a faster and broader spectrum of modern trends which are evolving in society.

148 The British doctrine of judicial precedent is founded on the principle of stare decisis, which means to stand by the decision. Essentially, it refers to the idea that once a court has made a decision, both they and other courts beneath them are bound by that decision except in certain limited circumstances, as for example if the court can differentiate the facts of the case before it from the other case which binds it. Thus courts which are lower in the hierarchy are bound by the courts which are above it. The Supreme Court is not bound by its own precedent. Although this doctrine has many disadvantages, it has the advantage of creating certainty and consistency within the judicial system and enables a speedier judicial process to be effectuated. There are three types of precedents: original precedents, binding precedents and persuasive precedents.

A good example of this is the case of *Casamitjana Costa*[149] in which ethical veganism – as opposed to veganism – a significant lifestyle change that took place in the Claimant, was held to constitute a philosophical belief. Vegetarians[150] attempted unsuccessfully to transform their beliefs into philosophical beliefs as did Scientologists[151] into religious beliefs. There is no reason why vegetarianism could not qualify as a philosophical belief if the five criteria in *Nicholson* were to be met. Similarly, there is no reason why Scientologists may not succeed to enjoy at least the status of philosophical belief and thus have the protection of the Equality Act 2010 now that they can conduct marriage ceremonies and their church is a place of worship. Philosophical beliefs are changing rapidly and employers need to have the right policies to enable them to adapt to modern ongoing developments.

Political party beliefs and ideology have proved to be a thorn in the philosophical belief arena. Some cases of a purely political nature, such as *Oliver*[152] (democratic socialism) or *Gibbins*[153] (republicanism) or again *McEleny*[154] (Scottish independence), have each succeeded in qualifying as well-founded philosophical beliefs. Furthermore, it is suggested that beliefs in a political theory or system such as Trotskyism, Leninism, Stalinism or Marxism could well qualify as a philosophical belief, but the issue of whether a belief in a political party qualifies as a philosophical belief remains problematic. In *Redfearn v United Kingdom*,[155] the British tribunals and courts and on appeal the ECHR had to decide whether dismissal of an employee on grounds of his allegiance to the British National Party (BNP) constituted discrimination on grounds of belief in contravention of the Equality Act 2010. The brief facts were that Mr Redfearn was a bus driver employed by Serco who provided transport services to local authorities. The majority (some 78%) of Redfearn's passengers were Asians. Redfearn was a BNP member, and a newspaper wrote an article on Redfearn's role as a candidate for the BNP local elections. As a result of that article, the Unison trade union wrote to Serco stating that many of Serco's employees and customers found Redfearn's continued employment an embarrassment, pointing out the BNP's racist agenda, and asked Serco to take the necessary action to ensure that its employees were not subjected to racial hatred promoted by the BNP. Unison's request was supported

149 For a fuller analysis of this case see pp. 100–110 above.

150 See *Conisbee v Crossley Farms Ltd* Case No, ET/3335357/2018 at pp. 117–118 above.

151 See *Regina v Registrar General ex parte Segerdal* [1970] 2 QB 697, where Lord Denning, MR Winn and Buckley LJJ concurring, held that the Church of Scientology chapel was not "a place of meeting of religious worship" within the meaning of s.2 of the 1855 Act which would require reverence to a deity. Their services did not meet that test and valid marriage ceremonies could not be conducted there. Scientology could not therefore be regarded as a religion.

152 The case of *Oliver* is discussed at pp. 128–129 above.

153 *Gibbins'* case is evaluated at pp. 125–127 above.

154 See the analysis on the *McEleny* case at pp. 127–128 above.

155 [2012] ECHR 1878, ECtHR.

by the GMB trade union as well as Serco's employees. Upon having been elected a BNP councillor, Redfearn was summarily dismissed by Serco on grounds that he would "present a risk to the health and safety of its employees and customers" and damage the reputation of Serco and risk the termination of Serco's contracts with local authorities. There were no complaints whatsoever about Redfearn's work or conduct.

Redfearn brought an action in the Employment Tribunal claiming direct race discrimination. It is important to note that Redfearn had only one year's service with his employer so he could not bring an action for unfair dismissal, which required at least two years' service. Instead he claimed that Serco had treated him less favourably by dismissing him on grounds of ethnicity of the employees and customers he transported. The Employment Tribunal dismissed the racial discrimination complaint as it was satisfied that if any discrimination existed against Redfearn, it was not on racial grounds but on health and safety grounds.

Redfearn appealed to the Employment Appeal Tribunal which found, *inter alia*, that the treatment he received was capable of qualifying as racial discrimination because of the broad construction given by the statutory words "on racial grounds."

Serco appealed to the Court of Appeal which found that Redfearn had not been treated less favourably on the ground that he was white, but on the ground of a particular non-racial characteristic, notably membership of and becoming a councillor of BNP, a political party. Serco did not adopt a policy of discrimination. The dividing line of colour and race was made by BNP. As such, the discrimination was on political grounds which fell outside the anti-discrimination laws. The Court of Appeal thus held that a political party falls outwith the sphere of British discrimination laws, therefore philosophical beliefs cannot apply to political parties.

An appeal was made by Redfearn to the European Court of Human Rights (ECHR)[156] on the grounds that his dismissal interfered with his right to freedom of assembly and associations as well as freedom of expression under article 11 of the European Convention of Human Rights. The ECHR agreed with Redfearn that there was a violation of his rights and held that the United Kingdom has to take reasonable and appropriate measures to protect employees, including those with two years' service from dismissal on political opinion and affiliation, either through the creation of a further exception to the two-year qualifying period or through a freestanding claim for unlawful discrimination on grounds of political opinion or affiliation.[157]

156 *Redfearn v the United Kingdom* [2012] ECHR 1878 ECtHR.

157 The Enterprise and Regulatory Reform Act 2013 s. 13 makes it automatically an unfair reason for dismissal in the Employment Relations Act 1996 and does not require compliance with the unfair dismissal two year qualification period to be asserted. The affected employee may thus bring a claim for unfair dismissal from the first day of employment if they are dismissed by reason of their political beliefs.

Be it as it may, the ECHR decision in *Redfearn* and the fact that there has been a removal by the Equality Act 2010 of the requirement that a philosophical belief be "similar"[158] to a religious belief has raised questions on whether or not political parties' members may hold philosophical beliefs.[159]

There has been an interesting case on left-wing democratic socialism qualifying as a protected philosophical belief. In *Henderson v General Municipal and Boilermakers Union*,[160] Mr Henderson professed to be a left-wing democratic socialist.[161] He was employed by the GMB and dismissed for gross misconduct. He brought an action in the Employment Tribunal for unfair dismissal, unlawful direct discrimination and harassment by reason of his political beliefs. That tribunal held that his dismissal was fair but that he was subjected to unfair direct discrimination and harassment for which the GMB had to pay a solatium.[162] On appeal to the EAT. Simler J. reversed the ET's decision on unlawful direct discrimination and harassment because of Henderson's left-wing democratic socialist beliefs but upheld the ET's finding that left-wing democratic socialism qualified as a philosophical belief because it was not challenged in the appeal.

Prior to giving her judgment, Simler J. made two important remarks, both of which are worth noting. First, during the proceedings, counsel for GMB appeared

158 There was an amendment to the original definition inserted from 30 April 2007 by the Employment Act 2006, s. 77 (1). Prior to that amendment, the word "similar" appeared before the words "philosophical beliefs." The reason for that amendment was not contentious. In Lucy Vickers' book titled *Religious Freedom, Religious Discrimination and the Workplace* (2008) (at n. 21, p. 17) she stated "to be defined as 'similar' to religion was viewed as offensive to some humanists and atheists, and the definition was amended by the Equality Act 2006 to remove the term 'similar.'" Baroness Scotland, the then Attorney General, was quoted in Hansard at the Equality Bill stage (on 13 July 2005 at col. 1109) in connection to the deletion of the word "similar" that "it was felt that the word 'similar' added nothing and was, therefore, redundant. This is because the term 'philosophical belief' will take its meaning from the context in which it appears; that is as part of the legislation relating to discrimination on the grounds of religion or belief. Given that context, philosophical beliefs must therefore always be of a similar nature to religious beliefs. It will be for the courts to decide what constitutes a belief . . . but case law suggests that any philosophical belief" must contain the aforementioned five criteria. She goes on to say that "an example of a belief that might meet this description is humanism, and examples of something that might not . . . would be a political party or a belief in the supreme nature of the Jedi Knights" (of Star Wars). The lady may well be right in the latter case but may be proved wrong in the former!

159 See Leto Coriolu, The Right to be Offended by Members of the British National Party; An Analysis of Serco Ltd v Redfearn in the Light of the European Convention of Human Rights, 35 *Industrial Law Journal*, 4, pp. 415–430 (December 2006).

160 [2015] UKEAT 0073/14/130DM.

161 By "left-wing democratic socialist" is meant (a) beliefs in creating "socialism through democratic processes" and spreading "its ideals within the context of a democratic political system through a working class industrial and political movement" and (b) a belief in "participation in the management of factories and other commercial enterprises by the people who work" therein. "Crossing workers' the picket lines contradicts its aims because it undermines workers' ability to control their workplaces."

162 That is, compensation for a disappointment, inconvenience or wounded feelings.

to argue that "less protection for a philosophical [belief] as opposed to a religious belief is to be accorded by the legislation." To this argument Simler J. retorted:[163]

> This proposition is not accepted. The law does not accord special protection to one category of belief and less protection for another. All qualifying beliefs are equally protected. Philosophical beliefs may be just as fundamental or integral to a person's individuality and daily life as religious beliefs . . . the tribunal identified precisely what the claimant's belief is . . . specifying the central tenets of his belief . . . it concluded that he is a left-wing democratic socialist.

Second, she confirmed that the ET concluded that "left-wing democratic socialism is a protected belief for the purposes of the Equality Act 2010 and this conclusion is not challenged on this appeal." The last five words seem to indicate that since that philosophical belief finding of the ET was not challenged on appeal, Simler J. did not wish to deal with it by bringing that aspect up. It is arguable that had it been challenged would she have held a different opinion to that held by the Employment Judge bearing in mind what Baroness Scotland said in the House of Lords when the Equality Bill was being debated in Parliament? The Baroness clearly stated that "support of a political party" was excluded.[164] Thus such "support of a political party" was never intended by Parliament to be included as a philosophical belief! For the present, however, left-wing democratic socialism remains on the list of accepted philosophical beliefs for the purpose of the Equality Act 2010. It should be noted that *Oliver*[165] (2013), where democratic socialism was held to constitute a philosophical belief, was similar to that in the *Henderson* case. It is thought that that case would certainly have been discussed had it "been challenged on this appeal." Furthermore, *Gibbins*[166] (2017) whose philosophical belief was republicanism and *McEleny*[167] (2019) whose philosophical belief was Scottish independence which, though not directly relevant to "supporting a political party," were very political in nature. Had both these cases been heard before 2015 when *Henderson* was heard, Simler J. may well have considered them too. Lady Scotland did however qualify her statement by saying that "it will be for the courts to decide what constitutes a belief."[168]

Deep divisions and a rich variety of views exist and will carry on existing after "Brexit is done"[169] in British society and at the workplace as a result of the June 2016 referendum on whether the United Kingdom should remain in the European Union. The referendum returned a small majority vote in favour of

163 [2015] UKEAT 0073 14 1303 at para. 62 of the judgment.
164 See n. 158 at p. 141 above and Hansard 13 July 2005 col. 1109.
165 See pp. 128–129 above.
166 See pp. 125–127 above.
167 See p. 142 above.
168 See n. 158 above.
169 To quote the frequently used words of former Prime Minister Boris Johnson.

leaving, known since as Brexit. Given the strength of feelings and emotions which exist between the remain and exit protagonists, it is surprising that there have been no discrimination cases brought on philosophical beliefs at the workplace by reason of intimidation and harassment by employers and colleagues alike. Political opinions at the workplace are not covered by any specific British law. However, the Equality Act 2010 provisions would apply where discrimination on political beliefs relating to Brexit were to qualify as a philosophical belief. To do so, the Burton J. five characteristics in the EAT case of *Nicholson* will need to be met. Such philosophical belief does not need to be one which affects all or numerous aspects of a claimant's life. A philosophical belief on a single issue which affects an important aspect of a claimant's life suffices to qualify for protection from discrimination. Granted that cases on discrimination on political grounds have succeeded, there is no reason why a strongly held belief for or against Brexit which meets the *Nicholson* five criteria should not succeed in becoming a philosophical belief capable of protection from discrimination at the workplace.

The case of *Allison Bailey v Stonewell Equity Ltd. and Garden Court Chambers Ltd et al*[170] needs a brief mention. It is a lengthy and complicated case in which a variety of topics feature on transgender, gay, lesbian and other related issues. What is of direct relevance to philosophical beliefs is that some of the cases mentioned in this chapter which deal with philosophical beliefs feature in *Bailey's* case. These include, *inter alia*, the *McClintock, Mackereth, Williamson, Grainger* and *Forstater* cases, The decision in *Bailey* goes beyond the *Forstater* decision regarding the nature of the gender critical views which the Equality Act protects. In *Forstater*, the claimant expressed views on gender which constituted a philosophical belief which is protected under the Equality Act. What is significant in the *Bailey* case is that Stonewell Equity's campaigning on gender self-identity could constitute a protected belief. The EAT made reference to the five criteria to be considered which qualify as a philosophical belief with reference to case law in *Grainger*, *Williamson*, *McClintock* and *Mackereth.*

3.2 The Legal Evolution and Its Impact on Employers

There is little doubt that the legal and societal evolution which is taking place has had a significant influence on the decisions of tribunals and courts in the field of philosophical belief. Were the *Casamitjana Costa* case to have been heard at the time when the Equality Act 2010 was enacted, it would have been doubtful if ethical veganism would have qualified as a protected belief. This case, decided in 2020, held that the claimant's belief qualified as a protected philosophical belief under the Equality Act 2010 and has led to strong opinions from the public, the press and practicing lawyers as to its significance for employers and employee rights. The *Casamitjana Costa* case and the scores of other cases

170 Case Number 2202172/2020-ET.

which have recently qualified as protected philosophical beliefs[171] are no different from employers having previously to deal with race, sex, age, sexual orientation, disability, gender reassignment, pregnancy, marriage and partnership, and religious discrimination, all of which constitute protected characteristics. Those more recent cases reflect the evolution which is taking place in society, such as climate change, Scottish independence, republican thinking and so on. Discrimination law must also change to take into account the changes which are taking place in societal values.

The evolution on philosophical beliefs is an area of discrimination law which will continue to expand as different beliefs are being tested by the tribunals and the courts. Did not Burton J. in *Nicholson* say that beliefs in such concepts as pacifism, communism and free market capitalism might in future also qualify for protected characteristic status?[172] These beliefs impose on employers additional responsibilities and a need for them to implement the provision of strong equal opportunities, guidance and diversity policies in the workplace so as to prevent conduct which could contravene the provisions of the Equality Act 2010. Such policies need to be flexible to enable them to adapt to changes in culture and practices within their workforce without employers having to fear being sued for discrimination.

Before discussing briefly those employers' responsibilities, two matters need a mention. First, it is stressed that the tribunals and courts have not opened the floodgates in finding philosophical beliefs which constitute protected characteristics. The tribunals and courts are acting in a responsible and serious manner by observing slavishly – and thus applying to the facts of each of the cases before them – the five criteria established in *Nicholson*. Each belief of an individual claimant is assessed on its own merits and must meet the same set of rigorous criteria before their belief qualifies as a philosophical belief and thus protected under the law of discrimination. Each of the five criteria needs to be met otherwise the belief will not qualify as a philosophical belief. In Mrs Gray's[173] case it will be recalled that her belief in the sanctity of copyright law did not qualify because one of the five criteria disqualified her, namely that the tribunal did not consider that she held the belief with "sufficient cogency, seriousness, cohesion and importance." In the second instance, it cannot be emphasised enough that a significant majority of those cases have been heard by Employment Tribunals and that their verdicts do not create any binding judicial precedent. Each case is carefully considered on its own merits and based on its facts. It should be pointed out that even though a philosophical belief has been found to exist in a previous case, the claimant will still have to prove that she or he holds the belief which they claim and furthermore, that that belief was the cause of the dismissal, redundancy, harassment and so on which the claimant is complaining of.

171 See pp. 120–136 above.
172 See *Grainger v Nicholson* [2010] ICR 360 at pp. 121–123.
173 See pp. 113–114 above.

It is therefore not a foregone conclusion that even a strong and genuinely held belief will receive the protection under the Equality Act 2010, and it is irrelevant how passionately the claimant believes in their cause if that cause is incoherent to the tribunal. Tribunals will analyse the nature of the belief itself rather the extent to which the claimant believes in it.

In the knowledge that there is every likelihood that there will be numerous future cases in the field of philosophical beliefs as protected characteristics in discrimination laws, the employer would be strongly advised to keep abreast with the legal evolution which is, and will continue be, taking place. In this manner the employer will be able to ensure that a given philosophical belief is respected at the workplace and that the employees are not disadvantaged because of their belief. There will be cases where the employer would have a legitimate reason for treating employees who hold protected philosophical beliefs in the same manner as other employees even though the employee perceives that as putting them at a disadvantage. In such circumstances caution should be taken by the employer.

Employers should consider the potential risk of belief discrimination at the time of recruiting prospective employees, for the Equality Act 2010 applies to every stage of the employment process, including that of applying for jobs. In implementing their respective policies they should take into account their workforce needs such a time off, annual leave and dress codes, particularly where such workforce consists of diverse nationalities and religions.

The current political climate – for example, Brexit or COVID-19 policies at the workplace – is such that employees could become vocal, indeed very heated, about their political beliefs, and bullying, intimidation and harassment may take place. Were this to occur it should be monitored and action taken as a result. In that instance employers should encourage employees to be broad minded, tolerant towards each other and respectful towards the beliefs of their colleagues at work. A zero-tolerance policy on offensive language, conduct and behaviour should be adopted in the workplace. Clear guidelines should be put in place as to what is and what is not acceptable to be said, whether political or otherwise, at the workplace or other places, such as canteens, common rooms and other places connected with the employer. What is unfortunate is that the law – the former 2003 Regulations consolidated into the Equality Act 2010 – makes no express reference to political discrimination. The law certainly prohibits religious and philosophical beliefs but does not state that the word "philosophical" includes "political." Indeed. It will be recalled[174] that it was expressly stated that political beliefs are excluded from philosophical beliefs. In spite of that statement, Scottish independence was held to constitute a philosophical belief in the *McEleny* case,[175] as was left-wing democratic socialism in *Henderson*,[176] democratic socialism in *Oliver*[177] and democratic

174 See pp. 113–114 above and Hansard dated 11 July 2005 at col. 1109.

175 See discussion at pp. 127–128 above.

176 See discussion at pp. 141–142 above.

177 See discussion at pp. 128–129 above.

republicanism in *Gibbins*.[178] It is thus abundantly clear that each case brought before the tribunal is decided upon its own specific or particular facts. This fact-specific issue, of course, is of little assistance to the employer in understanding their legal obligations when political problems arise at the workplace. The best advice which can be given to the employer is the one mentioned above, while at the same time the employer should take into consideration the five *Nicholson* criteria in respect of the employee's prospects of fulfilling successfully each of those five criteria. In other words the employer needs to put themselves into the shoes of the employment judge, and if the judge believes – a difficult decision indeed – that there is a strong case that the five criteria would be met and therefore the employee's belief could qualify as a philosophical belief, then it would be advisable for the employer to adopt an alternative method other than castigating the employee. Employers thus need to pause, ponder and consider the potential legal consequences before taking any action against an employee on political issues, for this may constitute discrimination on grounds of philosophical belief contrary to the 2010 legislation.

Effective communication with the workforce is of utmost importance. Employees should be made aware of all policies and particularly those which relate to them directly. They should also be informed on what the consequences would be if they were in breach of those policies. These policies should be updated to account for societal evolution and applied in a consistent manner and communicated to employees on a regular basis as well as on social media. The Dr Mackereth case[179] is an example of where the right of persons to manifest their religion or belief would be restricted to protect the dignity of others. Furthermore, employers should ensure that they implement equal opportunities policies and training to reduce the risk of discriminatory behaviour in the workplace.

Training is of particular importance. Managers of every department in a firm should receive training on the equal opportunities policy; how to recognise bullying, intimidation and harassment tactics; and how to deal with these situations. Staff training should also include religious beliefs and other widely held beliefs.

Effective grievance and disciplinary procedures should be set up to deal with breaches of workplace rules or breaches of discrimination (and other) laws. Where a complaint has been lodged it should be carefully examined, and disciplinary actions should be taken where a breach is substantiated. In such cases employers should be careful of employees holding strong beliefs, whether they be political or otherwise. Employers should bear in mind the apparent trend by tribunals and courts alike towards an expansion of philosophical beliefs. Where the employee brings an action against the employer and the tribunal finds that the

178 See discussion at pp. 125–127 above.

179 See discussion at p. 118 above. See also discussion in the *McClintock* case (at pp. 9–10 above), where a magistrate declined to place children in foster homes with same-sex couples as a result of a recently changed law to prevent discrimination placed on same-sex couples and that the sex of the parents would not be the sole justifiable reason for declining placement.

claimant's belief qualifies as a protected philosophical belief, the employer could be in breach of the Equity Act 2010. It is therefore advisable for the disciplinary committee to record carefully and appropriately the disciplinary process and the reasoning for the decision taken. Such recording could be a useful tool by the employer to refute the claim. Employers should therefore take care as to how to treat employees who hold strong beliefs, whatever their nature be.

Guidance should be given by the employer as to what extent employees may express their views to colleagues and others. Because of the nature of the business, the employer may wish to maintain a neutrality policy on political, religious or philosophical issues.

Employers should be made aware that claims on discrimination may arise in circumstances where the employer is sure that dismissal of the employee is justified. Is dismissal really justified in such cases as membership of the British National Party?

Employers should review company procedures and policies where updating is necessary and ensure when doing so that no offence is created to individuals and/or groups and that they are not disadvantaged as a result of such review.

In the light of the high-profile case of *Casamitjana Costa*, it would be necessary, when organising events at the workplace where catering and drinks are offered, to take into consideration those who hold certain protected philosophical beliefs and thus provide a vegan option for ethical vegans. This, it is submitted, constitutes a legal requirement. It should also be borne in mind that not every vegan will be able to demonstrate the same level of fundamental belief as shown in the *Casamitjana Costa* case, but for protected ethical vegans employers are advised to encourage and welcome vegan beliefs and thus create a culture of respect and understanding in the workforce. This could mean that the employer would need to review the firm's policies and make the necessary changes to emphasise the support offered to ethical vegans.

As the British law stands at the time of writing, there is no legal obligation on employers to provide a vegan option for vegans or to cater for any other diet based on religion and belief. Nevertheless even though ethical vegans are not employed by a firm, given the great and steadily increasing number of vegans recorded by the Vegan Society,[180] it is both desirable and courteous that where catering is provided in the workplace that vegan options be offered to those employees who have vegan diets or beliefs.

The implications of the *Casamitjana Costa* case are considerable, not least because the legal protection would apply beyond the employment sphere in areas

180 According to Finder.com in November 2020, 2% of UK citizens are currently vegan. By the end of 2020 the number is set to double increasing the population to 2.2 million. While the number of vegetarians and pescatarians has remained very similar to 2019, the research estimates that the biggest change statistically is veganism. The number of vegans in the United Kingdom increased by 49,000 – 62 per cent since 2019. www.vegansociety.com/news/media/statistics.

such as the supply of goods and services,[181] transport, the workplace and in the education, hospital, prison, hospitality and other public spheres. Vegan catering is already taking place on a voluntary basis in numerous British restaurants and cafés and this research shows that some hospitals,[182] universities,[183] prisons[184] and schools also cater for vegans. The Ministry of Defence has announced that all dietary requirements are catered for including vegan meals in all three military services, namely the Royal Navy, the army and the Royal Air Force and their reserve forces.

Although there is no legal obligation in the UK for employers and others to provide a vegan option for vegans or cater for their diet, Scotland is taking an active lead in this field. The Convenor of the Public Petitions Committee, Johann Lamont MSP, said following the evidence session that the Committee agreed to write to the Scottish government, the Scottish health boards and the local authorities to find out what provisions are currently made for vegans and what the cost implications would be. Furthermore, the Scottish parliament has been petitioned[185] to have vegan food on all public sector menus from schools and hospitals to prisons and councils. Barbara Bolton, a solicitor who deals with vegan food, condemned the "systematic failure" to provide for vegans while giving evidence in support of the petition. She argued[186] that public organisations have an obligation to provide vegan options

> for vegans have legal protection under human rights and equality law because the vegan philosophy passes the test of non-religious belief that is serious, cogent and worthy of support. The protected status of veganism means that we have a right to live in a way that avoids using and killing animals or paying someone else to do that for us and not to be discriminated against on account of our veganism. Ultimately if nothing is done in terms of the human rights and equality issues there will be claims that will go to court.

181 See the statement of the legal head of the Vegan Society, Dr Jeanette Rowley: "It's a fantastic day for animals and it's a fantastic day for vegans who should get more institutional support in hospitals or in schools." (Viva, Dr Justine Butler, 6 October 2020).

182 For example, Croydon and Hammersmith Hospital, Birmingham Women's Hospital and Sussex Hospital at Bury St. Edmunds.

183 Examples include the universities of Hull, Manchester, Newcastle, Southampton, Aberdeen, Edinburgh and St. Andrews.

184 For example, HMP Bronsfield, HMP Isle of Wight, HMP Kennet and HMP Guys Marsh. It is estimated that 10% of the UK's prisoners are vegan.

185 The public sector organisations have been warned that they would be taken to court unless more is done to provide plant-based diet options to menus in schools, hospitals, prisons and council buildings. The Scottish Parliament Petition was submitted by Mark Bonahan. (*Scottish Sun*, 7 December 2018).

186 *Daily Record*, 6 December 2018.

Employment tribunal decisions are not binding on other tribunals and courts under the British doctrine of judicial precedent, it is however suggested that the *Casamitjana Costa* case is having, and will continue to have, important and far-reaching societal effects, these in turn could influence judicial thinking in future cases even though judicial precedent would not be applicable. Of course, ethical veganism is unlikely to have a direct or significant impact on the majority of employers in the day-to-day running of their firm because ethical vegans do not exist in abundance in companies; nevertheless, it is a useful reminder to employers that the Equality Act 2010 exists and provides protection to employees against discrimination, harassment, intimidation and other unfair treatment.

Similarly, when providing uniforms for vegans it would be advisable for employers to cater for their beliefs by providing uniforms which only contain manmade or natural fibres. It would also be indelicate to a vegan employee to make such employee visit a client who supplies, eats or cooks meat or fish products or processes them or again distributes them at a till in a supermarket.

Furthermore, the supply of leather seats, desks with a leather working surface, leather wastepaper baskets and other leather office equipment should be avoided. Also to be avoided are perfumes or eaux de toilette which have been tested on animals, as well as such vaccines as the coronavirus vaccine,[187] which has been tested on several animals.[188]

As for victimisation and harassment, each of these could be unlawful. Victimisation could be held to be unlawful in situations where vegans complain that they have been discriminated against or harassed because of their vegan beliefs and because of that complaint, they have been ill-treated. Such situation could entitle an individual to make a victimisation claim against the employer. Harassment could occur where unwanted and linked to a protected characteristic which violates someone's dignity or creates an offensive or degrading environment, such as jokes made against ethical vegans or where they are taunted, goaded or provoked in an offensive manner or reproached sarcastically or contemptuously or jibed in a wounding manner. Both could constitute indirect discrimination. Indirect discrimination is defined as a practice, policy or rule which applies to everyone equally, but which could put people with a protected characteristic such as ethical

187 Several animals have been used in the coronavirus vaccine research programme. They include mice, rhesus macaques, ferrets, pigs and hamsters, In the United Kingdom, research on the virus vaccine took place at the University of Oxford, at Imperial College, London and at the PHE laboratory at Porton Down. See too the European Animals Research Association based in London and Brussels, which talks of vaccines.

188 To be noted is the fact that Vegans avoid using animals "as far as is practicable and possible." This definition recognises that "it is not always possible to make a choice that avoids the use of animals. Sometimes you have no alternatives to taking prescribed medication. Looking after yourself and other people makes you to be an effective advocate for veganism" (The Vegan Society – Medication).

vegans or those following particular diets for religious reasons at a disadvantage. In both cases indirect discrimination is not unlawful if it can be justified and what is justifiable depends on the circumstances of each case. The small employer may be justified in not providing a vegan, kosher or halal diet because he does not have the resources to do so but the larger employer or a multinational will find it difficult not to provide a vegan or other specific diet.

It has even been suggested[189] that the *Casamitjana Costa* case could pave the way for ethical vegans to bring a judicial review against the Bank of England by reason that the five-pound bank notes contain animal products! So far that suggestion has not been challenged.

Employers should expect to see future legal protection to the employees extended to their beliefs, particularly as these become more established in society. It is suggested that the concept of philosophical belief is one of the most interesting areas for development in discrimination law. The cases mentioned in this chapter epitomise and reinforce the fact that the belief must be a strongly held and genuine one and must particularly show how much of a fundamental impact that belief has on all aspects of the life that the individual leads and the necessary degree of adherence to the particular belief in question. The acquisition of protection of a philosophical belief is extremely high thus making it less likely to apply to the vast majority of employees. Employers should note the possibility of strongly held beliefs attracting protection and be aware of the potential necessity of accommodating certain beliefs, but do not need to worry unduly about floodgates to philosophical beliefs being opened.[190] All that is advised is that employers should use their common sense and at the same time have a heightened consideration of their employees' needs.

Discrimination spells intolerance, bigotry, inequity, unfairness, narrow-mindedness, favouritism, partisanship, sexism, chauvinism, racialism, anti-Semitism, heterosexism, bias, agism, classism and one-sidedness. One readily sees signs that mankind is living in an evolving and progressive legal entourage in the discrimination field!

Did not a Rwandan author say, "Look at the sky and count the stars, look down and realise we are all from the same universe and stop discrimination."[191]

Note

This chapter attempts to state the law as at 5th September 2022.

189 www.thetimes.co.uk/article/court-ruling-gives-vegans-protection-under-equality-laws-37bbd.

190 It should be noted that establishing the belief of being capable of protection is only the first step in the equation. The second step is for the tribunal to ascertain whether the employer unlawfully discriminated in connection to that belief.

191 Bangambiki Habyarimana, "Book of Wisdom" Smashwords Edition (Kindle Edition).

Bibliography

Law Cases (Alphabetical)

Ahman v United Kingdom [1091] 114 – EHRR 126.
J. Anderson v Chesterfield High School UKEAT/2006/14/MC.
Arrowsmith v United Kingdom [1078] 3 EHRR 293.
Campbell and CosConisbee v Crossley Farms Ltd v United Kingdom 4 EHRR 293.
J. Casamitjana Costa v The League Against Cruel Sports ET/3331129/2018.
Chondol v Liverpool City Council [2009] UKEAT/0298/08.
Conisbee v Crossley Farms Ltd. et al. ET/3335357/2018.
Dr. A Dunn v University of Lincoln ET/2691819/17.
Dr. David Mackereth v Department of Work and Pensions ET/394602/2018.
Ellis v Parmagon Ltd. [2014] Eq.LR 343.
Eweida v British Airways plc. [2010] 2 All ER 253.
Farrell v South Yorkshire Police Authority ET/2083085/10.
Ghaidan v Godin-Mendoza [2004] 2 AC 557.
A. Gibbins v British Council ET/2200088/2017.
Grainger Plc & Others v Nicholson [2010] ICR 360 (EAT).
Gray v Mulberry Company (Design) Ltd. [2019] EWCA. Civ. 1720.
M. Harron v Chief Constable of Dorset Police UKEAT/0234/15/DA.
Hasham v Milton Park (Dorest) Limited t/a Orchard Park ET/3105555/2009.
Hawkins v Universal Utilities Ltd t/a/Unicorn ET/2051234/2012.
Islington London Borough Council v Ladele [2009] EWCA Civ. 534.
Kalac v Turkey [1997] 27 EHRR 552.
Kokkinasis v Greece (04307/88) [1993] EHRR 397.
K(SB) v Governors of Denbigh High School [2007]1 AC 100.
D. Maistry v British Broadcasting Corporation ET/1313142/2010.
C. McEleny v Ministry of Defence ET/4105347/2017.
McFarlane v Relate Avon Ltd. UKEAT/0106/09/DA and [2010] EWCA Civ. 771.
C. Oliver v Department of Work and Pensions ET/1701407/2011.
A. Power v Greater Manchester Police Authority EAT 8th October 2010 and [2011] EWCA Civ, 534.
Redfearn v The United Kingdom [2012] ECHR 1878.
Regina v Registrar General ex parte Segerdal [1970] 2 QB 697.
Sahin v Turkey [2005] 19 BHRC.
Streatfield v London Philharmonic Orchestra ET/2390772/2011.

Acts of Parliament (Alphabetical)

Disability Act 1995.
Enterprise and Regulatory Reform Act 2013 c.24.
Equality Act 2010 c.15.
Human Rights Act 1998.
Race Relations Act 1976.
Sex Discrimination Act 1998.

Council of Europe Convention

European Convention on Human Rights.

Statutory Instruments (In Alphabetical Order)

Employment Equality (Religion and Belief) Regulations, 2003 S.I. 2003 No. 1660.
Employment Tribunals (Constitution and Rules of Procedure Regulations, 2013 S.I.No. 2013 1237.

Code of Practice

Equality Act 2010 Code of Practice of the Equality and Human Rights Commission.

Journals

Hansard 13th July 2005 column 1109.
Leto Coriolu "*The Right to be Offended by Members of the British National Party; An Analysis of Serco Ltd. v Redfearn in the Light of the European Convention on Human Rights*." Industrial Law Journal Vol. 15, Issue No. 4. 4th December 2006, pp. 415–430.

Books

Deakin S. and G. Morris "Labour Law" (2012) Hart Publishing.
Habyarimana Bangambiki "Book of Wisdom" Smashwords Edition (Kindle Edition).
McGaughy Ewan "A Casebook on Labour Law" (2018) Hart Publishing.
Vickers Lucy "Religious Freedom, Religious Discrimination and the Workplace" (2008) Hart Publishing, Bloomsbury.

Report

Hellman, Anja Dr., Professor Yvonne Kelly, Professor Richard Wall "Equally protected? A Review of the Evidence on the Physical Punishment of Children."

Websites

https://metro.co.uk/2017/03/10/it-is-now-illegal-not-to-offer-vegan-food-at-prisons-hospitals-and-schools-in-Portugal6501872/
https://telegraph.co.uk/news/uknews15670/Magistrate-appeals-in-gay-adoption-row.html
www.equalityhumanrights.com
www.vegansociety.com/news/media/statistics

7 Employment Discrimination in Australia

The Challenges of Pursuing a Substantive Equality Approach

Therese MacDermott

1 Introduction

There has been anti-discrimination legislation in Australia prohibiting discrimination in employment with respect to a broad range of attributes for many decades. However, the way in which the regulatory system has evolved, with parallel and overlapping federal, state and territory legislative schemes, makes the system highly complex and difficult to navigate. In addition, the current legislative framework in Australia governing employment discrimination imposes very few positive rights or obligations. It is principally centred on the prohibition by statute of certain discriminatory conduct and the establishment of processes by which individuals can challenge the treatment they receive. Australian human rights and equal opportunity agencies ('equality agencies') are not engaged in the strategic enforcement of non-discrimination obligations. Their role in relation to alleged contraventions of anti-discrimination obligations is predominately limited to investigating the circumstances surrounding complaints and, where possible, resolving them by conciliation.

A common feature of the dispute resolution framework dealing with employment discrimination claims in Australia is the requirement to first seek to resolve a complaint through conciliation before having access to the courts or tribunal system. As a consequence, there are high settlement rates, and few employment discrimination complaints proceed to a full hearing before a court or tribunal. This means that trends and implications are not easy to draw and that the jurisprudence is underdeveloped, particularly regarding the underlying purpose of Australian anti-discrimination laws. The few anti-discrimination law cases determined by superior courts in Australia have been characterised as indicative of a lack of coherency and consistency as to the underlying rationale of Australian anti-discrimination laws.[1]

This chapter examines the various legislative schemes operating in Australia that regulate employment-based discrimination and highlights how fundamental

1 A. Taylor, The Conflicting Purposes of Australian Anti-Discrimination Law, 42 *UNSW Law Journal*, 1, p. 188 (2019).

DOI: 10.4324/9781003306962-9

problems with scope, burden of proof, exceptions and enforcement limit the reach of the existing legal protections. As the pre-eminent Australian anti-discrimination law scholar has suggested, Australian anti-discrimination laws run the risk of being 'officially statements of formal equality which have great symbolic significance' but with 'limited capacity to alleviate actual or substantive inequality'.[2] This chapter explores whether Australian anti-discrimination laws live up to the challenge of advancing substantive equality and is structured as follows. Section 2 provides an overview of the regulatory system governing employment discrimination in Australia. Section 3 outlines the manner in which Australian anti-discrimination laws prohibit discriminatory conduct at work. Section 4 deals specifically with the problem of establishing effective forms of regulation in response to the endemic nature of workplace sexual harassment. Section 5 looks at the institutional processes and mechanisms for seeking redress. Section 6 offers some concluding observations.

2 The Regulatory Landscape

Australia lacks a national framework providing constitutional guarantees of equality and non-discrimination. Nor does it have legislative protections in the form of a national Human Rights Act or a Charter of Rights. This leaves the equality and non-discrimination principles that Australia is committed to through its ratification of various international human rights treaties to be enacted principally by way of domestic anti-discrimination laws. In federated states like Australia, federal laws are not the only relevant source of equality and non-discrimination obligations, with each of the eight states and territories having their own anti-discrimination laws. Similarly, there are separate state, territory and federal equality agencies which all engage in complaints handling, education and policy development, and other human rights–related activities. Although the pursuit of multiple proceedings for the same conduct using different avenues of redress is generally precluded by statute,[3] the operation of these parallel jurisdictions adds to the complexity of the legislative arrangements governing employment discrimination. There is further fragmentation due to the existence of distinct non-discrimination obligations and avenues for redress in the national labour laws that sit alongside state, territory and federal anti-discrimination laws. This level of complexity detracts from achieving an accessible, fair and effective dispute resolution system, and from realising the goal of substantive equality.

Each legislative scheme sets different parameters in terms of the attributes which are covered, what the legislation designates as discriminatory conduct or treatment, and any exceptions or exemptions which apply. There are also procedural differences in how complaints are dealt with, how a claim is pursued in the

2 M. Thornton, *The Liberal Promise: Anti-Discrimination Legislation in Australia* (Oxford 1990), p. 12.

3 See for example the Fair Work Act 2009 (Cth) s 732.

event that it is not resolved by non-adversarial forms of dispute resolution at the initial stage, differences in what remedies are available, and the awarding of costs where a matter is resolved by court or tribunal proceedings. It can be difficult to determine the most appropriate pathway to pursue, particularly for employees trying to make informed choices without access to legal advice or other forms of support. This contrasts with the systems that operate in other countries, where there is a dedicated framework for dealing with *all* claims relating to employment by the one institution.

A further complication is that there is not a single Equality Act in the federal area covering all attributes. The standard model for federal anti-discrimination legislation is that the coverage of each Act is limited to a single attribute, or a constellation of characteristics related to that attribute. The principal pieces of federal legislation are the Racial Discrimination Act 1975 (Cth), the Sex Discrimination Act 1984 (Cth), the Disability Discrimination Act 1992 (Cth), the Age Discrimination Act (2004) (Cth) and the Australian Human Rights Commission Act 1986 (Cth). Attempts were made to introduce a consolidated federal Act as part of a plan for a new human rights framework, but this process stalled in 2013 and was subsequently abandoned. Consequently, complaints made in relation to alleged breaches of federal anti-discrimination legislation must be lodged under a particular Act, depending on the attribute(s) to which the alleged breach relates. As such, the pursuit of employment discrimination complaints in Australia is dominated by what has been termed the 'single axis' model[4] of distinct attributes giving rise to separate claims. Complaints that are framed in this way have been criticised as 'not allowing the complexity of identity, and its impact on the experience of discrimination, to be revealed'.[5] In theory, complaints of multiple discrimination relating to a range of attributes can be brought under this structure by making separate complaints relating to different attributes under the separate federal statutes. Hence, a claim of employment discrimination by an older woman could invoke the jurisdiction of both the Sex Discrimination Act and the Age Discrimination Act, as a way of capturing the intersectionality experience of discrimination in these circumstances.[6] However in practice, complaints of this kind are very uncommon.[7] In contrast, states and territory anti-discrimination

4 K. Crenshaw, Demarginalizing the Intersection between Race and Sex: A Black Feminist Critique of Anti-discrimination Doctrine, Feminist Theory and Anti-racist Politics, 139 *University of Chicago Legal Forum*, pp. 139–140 (1989).

5 H. Astor, A Question of Identity: The Intersection of Race and Other Grounds of Discrimination, in Race Discrimination Commissioner (ed.), *Racial Discrimination Act 1975: A Review* (Canberra: Australian Government Publishing Service, 1995), p. 269. See also A. Thackrah, From Neutral to Drive: Australian Anti-Discrimination Law and Identity 33 *Alternative Law Journal*, 31, pp. 32–33 (2008).

6 P. Alon-Shenker & T. MacDermott, Intersection Age and Gender in Workplace Discrimination Complaints, 41 *Comparative Labor Law and Policy Journal*, p. 522 (2020).

7 Ibid., p. 532.

legislation[8] generally takes the form of a single piece of legislation covering a range of attributes, including coverage of some of the same attributes dealt with by the federal anti-discrimination legislative schemes.

The Australian regulatory approach also lacks a general framework for employment equity or affirmative action. There is one designated piece of federal legislation, the Workplace Gender Equality Act 2012 (Cth), which imposes obligations on larger employers to report to a government agency on a range of gender equality indicators.[9] It is a soft compliance measure that seeks to encourage workplace improvements with respect to gender equality through awareness raising and by requiring employers to release their reports publicly. This system is not replicated with respect to other attributes covered by Australian anti-discrimination laws. However, measures implemented by employers to provide specific opportunities in employment for individuals from disadvantaged groups can be justified as positive actions or special measures under Australian anti-discrimination legislation.[10]

3 Prohibiting Discrimination

Australian anti-discrimination laws utilise a traditional model of proscribing direct and indirect discrimination covering a range of attributes, with the proscription applying to nominated areas of public life, including employment and its associated aspects, accompanied by specified exceptions and exemptions. The concepts of direct and indirect discrimination used in Australian anti-discrimination laws are modelled on a disparate treatment-disparate impact dichotomy. Australian anti-discrimination laws set out complex statutory definitions of direct and indirect discrimination, with Australian courts designating these as mutually exclusive categories.[11] The Racial Discrimination Act uses more encompassing language by prohibiting any

> distinction, exclusion, restriction or preference which has the purpose or effect of nullifying or impairing the recognition, enjoyment or exercise, on an equal footing, of any human right or fundamental freedom in the political, economic, social, cultural or any other field of public life.[12]

The requirement to make reasonable workplace adjustments under the Disability Discrimination Act is not expressed as a free-standing positive obligation. Instead,

8 Anti-Discrimination Act 1977 (NSW); Equal Opportunity Act 1984 (SA); Equal Opportunity Act 1984 (WA); Anti-Discrimination Act 1991 (Qld); Discrimination Act 1991 (ACT); Anti-Discrimination Act 1992 (NT); Anti-Discrimination Act 1998 (Tas); Equal Opportunity Act 2010 (Vic).

9 Workplace Gender Equality Act 2012 (Cth) ss 13 & 3.

10 See Racial Discrimination Act 1975 s 8; Sex Discrimination Act 1984 (Cth) s 7D; Disability Discrimination Act 1992 (Cth) s 45; Age Discrimination Act 2004 s 33.

11 Waters v Public Transport Corporation (1991) 173 CLR 349.

12 Section 9. This approach is also found in some state and territory legislation: See Anti-Discrimination Act 1992 (NT).

it is written into the Act's definitions of direct and indirect discrimination,[13] contributing to complicated interpretative questions regarding the operation of the reasonable adjustment obligation.[14]

Each piece of Australian anti-discrimination legislation sets out the type of conduct or circumstances where an exception or exemption applies. Many of these are tailored to cater for the circumstances surrounding a particular attribute. For example, the exception for the employment practices of religious educational authorities applies to some of the attributes covered by the Sex Discrimination Act[15] but is not found in the other attribute-specific federal Acts. An exception based on an inability to carry out the inherent requirements of the job only applies to employment-based age and disability discrimination.[16] There are other exceptions for acts done in direct compliance with laws or some forms of statutory authority, such as an award or enterprise agreement setting out the terms and conditions of employment or an order of the Fair Work Commission, the national workplace relations tribunal.

3.1 Coverage of Attributes

There is significant variation in the attributes covered by the various legislative schemes which regulate employment-based discrimination. In the case of the four principal pieces of federal anti-discrimination legislation, each Act has a defined coverage that generally pertains to a discrete attribute and certain related aspects. The terminology used in the Racial Discrimination Act 1975 (Cth) is that of race, colour, descent, or national or ethnic origin. In the case of the Sex Discrimination Act 1984 (Cth), it applies to discriminatory treatment based on a person's sex, marital or relationship status, pregnancy or potential pregnancy, breastfeeding or family responsibilities. In 2013, the coverage of the Sex Discrimination Act was extended to also include discrimination on the basis of sexual orientation, gender identity and intersex status, when attempts to add these attributes to a new consolidated Act did not eventuate. The general prohibitions on discrimination in the Sex Discrimination Act can be used to address pay equity claims, although these are more commonly dealt with under the equal remuneration provisions of the Fair Work Act.[17]

The Disability Discrimination Act 1992 (Cth) uses a very broad approach to the concept of disability which includes past, present and future disabilities and imputed disabilities.[18] The question of whether a distinction is drawn between a disability and its manifestations (such as disruptive behaviour) has been the

13 Disability Discrimination Act 1992 (Cth) ss 5 & 6.

14 See Sklavos v Australasian College of Dermatologists [2017] FCAFC 128.

15 Section 38.

16 Age Discrimination Act 2004 (Cth) s 18(4); Discrimination Act 1992 (Cth) s 21A.

17 Section 302.

18 Section 4.

subject of judicial consideration at the highest appellate level.[19] The definition of disability in the Disability Discrimination Act now includes a statement that 'to avoid doubt, a disability that is otherwise covered by this definition includes behaviour that is a symptom or manifestation of the disability'. However, difficulties can still arise with establishing that the alleged discriminatory treatment which may be triggered by the manifestations satisfy the statutory requirement of being 'because of' the disability.

The Age Discrimination Act (2004) (Cth) has a non-exclusive definition of age which simply states that it 'includes age group'.[20] The vagueness of this concept has meant there can be uncertainty when evaluating the treatment of a hypothetical comparator or group for the purposes of establishing direct or indirect discrimination. For example, is the comparator a year or two younger or older than the complainant, or someone in an entirely different age group (however that might be defined)? The limited case law on age discrimination has meant this has not been resolved in a decisive manner.

The Australian Human Rights Commission Act 1986 (Cth) provides the legislative basis for the operation of the national equality agency (the Australian Human Rights Commission), establishes the roles of the specialist Commissioners and sets out the requirements for lodging and dealing with complaints in the federal system. It also provides a further avenue for employment-related complaints with respect to a broad range of attributes, implementing the requirements of the International Labour Organization's employment discrimination convention.[21] A complaint made through this process can be investigated and conciliated by the Commission but does not provide an avenue for an enforceable outcome in the federal court system if it is not resolved by conciliation. While some complainants could have recourse to other statutory schemes, not all of the attributes covered by the ILO convention are consistently dealt with by other legislative schemes, particularly criminal records, trade union activity, political opinion and religion.

One noticeable omission in the federal system is coverage of discrimination on the basis of religious belief. While most state and territory legislative schemes provide some protections for this attribute, there has to date been no specific federal anti-discrimination laws covering religious belief. The issue received widespread media coverage following the termination of the employment of a high-profile rugby player in 2019 for serious breaches of the mandatory code of conduct in his contract when he publicised religiously motivated homophobic views on social media.[22] The previous federal government had released two versions of a draft Religious Discrimination Bill which prohibits religious discrimination, and a further version of the Bill was tabled in the

19 Purvis v New South Wales (Department of Education and Training (2003) 217 CLR 92.

20 Age Discrimination Act 2004 (Cth) s 5.

21 Discrimination (Employment and Occupation) Convention, 1958, No 111.

22 S. Clench, One Unresolved Legal Question at the Heart of Israel Folau's Case, available at www.news.com.au/sport/sports-life/one-unresolved-legal-question-at-the-heart-of-israel-folaus-case/news-story/387b057b25ab325d35ea494b9ed087b3 (accessed 15 September 2020).

federal parliament in December 2021.[23] However, due to uncertainty regarding support for the passage of the Bill through Parliament, the Bill was not pursued. While the prospect of a federal statute outlawing religious-based discrimination is not particularly controversial in itself, the drafting of this particular Bill has provoked considerable controversy and many submissions on the draft Bills from interested parties.[24] One particular concern with the framing of the Bill is the way in which it seeks to prevent employers disciplining employees for expressing religious beliefs which could be construed as homophobic or transphobia. Another concern is the way the proposed legislation seeks to override existing anti-discrimination laws and has the potential to encroach on other human rights protections, particularly those in the Sex Discrimination Act against discrimination on the basis of sexual orientation, gender identity and intersex status.[25]

The attributes protected by Australia's national labour laws (the Fair Work Act 2009 (Cth)) are race, colour, sex, sexual preference, age, physical and mental disability, marital status, family and carer's responsibilities, pregnancy, religion, political opinion, national extraction and social origin.[26] An example of the breadth of coverage provided by state and territory anti-discrimination laws is the Queensland Anti-Discrimination Act 1991 which prohibits discrimination on the basis of sex, relationship status, pregnancy, parental status, breastfeeding, age, race, impairment, religious belief or religious activity, political belief or activity, trade union activity, lawful sexual activity, gender identity, sexuality, family responsibilities and association with, or relation to, a person identified on the basis of any of the above attributes.[27]

3.2 Establishing That Discrimination Has Occurred

The standard approach under Australian anti-discrimination laws is that the burden falls to those who claim to have experienced discrimination to pursue a complaint against their employer, although the national workplace laws take a different approach (discussed below). Generally direct discrimination is established where a person is treated less favourably than a person without the protected attribute in the same or similar circumstance, and the treatment is causally related to the protected attribute. As such, it is a relative concept that requires an actual or hypothetical comparator with comparable skills, qualifications and experience,

23 Religious Discrimination Bill 2021 (Cth).

24 See www.ag.gov.au/rights-and-protections/consultations/religious-freedom-bills-first-exposure-drafts and www.ag.gov.au/rights-and-protections/consultations/religious-freedom-bills-second-exposure-drafts.

25 See for example Australian Human Rights Commission, Submission on the Draft Religious Discrimination Bill, 2019, available at https://humanrights.gov.au/about/news/submission-draft-religious-discrimination-bill (accessed 29 November 2020).

26 Section 351.

27 Section 7.

rather than relying on the unfavourable nature of the treatment itself. Proving the nexus between the relevant attribute and the alleged discriminatory treatment is often problematic, particularly in relation to hiring decisions where a prospective employee has no real way of knowing whether a particular aspect of their identity impacted on the outcome. This issue of proof has been identified as significantly limiting the ability of anti-discrimination laws to address systemic forms of racial discrimination in employment in Australia.[28] Australian anti-discrimination laws have not undergone the same reforms which have occurred in other jurisdictions that shift the onus in direct discrimination claims onto the employer to negate that an attribute protected by anti-discrimination laws was a factor in the alleged discriminatory treatment. This problem has been particularly apparent in relation to claims of racial discrimination, with a review of the reported case law from 2005 to January 2015 finding that there were only six successful litigated outcomes under the federal legislation over the fifteen-year period.[29] The 'failure to deal with the difficulty of proving the racial basis of treatment' was identified in the review as a major reason for the poor success rate of litigated claims.[30]

Under Australian law, indirect discrimination is established where an employment practice, requirement or condition has the effect of disadvantaging the complainant (and those who share the attribute that forms the basis for the claim), and that practice, requirement or condition is not reasonable when all the circumstances are taken into account. A landmark employment law case dating back to the 1980s saw the High Court of Australia find that redundancy practices applying a 'last in first out' approach was a form of indirect sex discrimination where a past history of discriminatory hiring practices regarding 'suitable' roles for women at that workplace meant that women were more vulnerable to being made redundant than men because they had waited longer for a 'suitable' job to become available, and the practice was found not to be reasonable.[31] Other leading cases have seen practices such as the requirement to work full-time[32] and the wage assessment tool used to determine payments to persons with intellectual disabilities employed in Australian Disability Enterprises[33] successfully challenged as forms of indirect discrimination. However, the burden of proving a complaint based on indirect discrimination is burdensome, particularly in terms of substantiating the disparate impact dimension. Some anti-discrimination legislation shifts the burden to the employer to refute the unreasonableness of its practices.[34]

28 See J. Hunyor, Skin-Deep: Proof and Inferences of Racial Discrimination in Employment, 25 *Sydney Law Review*, p. 535 (2003).

29 B. Gaze, The Racial Discrimination Act after 40 Years: Advancing Equality, or Sliding into Obsolescence? In *Perspectives on the Racial Discrimination Act* (Australian Human Rights Commission, 2015).

30 Ibid., p. 78.

31 Australian Iron & Steel Pty Ltd v Banovic (1989) 168 CLR 165.

32 Hickie v Hunt & Hunt (1998) EOC 92–910.

33 Nojin v Commonwealth (2012) 208 FCR 1.

34 See for example Sex Discrimination Act 1984 (Cth) 7B.

4 Sexual Harassment

While sexual harassment can be pleaded as a form of sex discrimination, the prevailing model in Australian anti-discrimination legislation is to have a dedicated statutory prohibition that specifically defines the conduct that constitutes workplace sexual harassment. This type of provision appears in the federal Sex Discrimination Act 1984 (Cth) and in each state and territory anti-discrimination statute. The reach of these laws has expanded over time to include coverage of workplace participants (rather than relying on the parties sharing the same workplace and the same employer) and by a recognition in the case law that a person's place of work can include environments away from the physical site of the workplace (e.g. social settings, entertainment venues, and through social media exchanges) where the contact the parties have stems from a work connection.[35] Some anti-discrimination laws also prohibits harassment on the basis of other attributes such as disability[36] and age.[37] The Fair Work Act was amended in September 2021 to explicitly provide an avenue for stopping sexual harassment, and it might be dealt with through the general protections provisions, as giving rise to an unfair dismissal, or within the Fair Work Commission's anti-bullying jurisdiction. There has also been renewed interest in reframing sexual harassment as within the scope of Australian workplace health and safety laws where the threat of enforcement weighs more heavily on employers.[38]

Sexual harassment is one area of Australian anti-discrimination laws where there is a measure of commonality in the legislative approach across different jurisdictions. Although the wording may differ, the three core elements of the legislative prohibitions are relatively clear in terms of the unwelcomeness of the conduct, the conduct being of a sexual nature and the application of a form of reasonable person test. The reasonable person test contained in the Sex Discrimination Act is highly contextual, taking the target of the conduct and their circumstances as the starting point. It is not determined by the views of the person engaging in the conduct and recognises that the power dynamics in workplaces may mean that the unwelcomeness of the conduct may not have been verbalised. Nor will the fact that a complainant may themselves have participated in inappropriate conduct at some other point in time preclude them for claiming that they were offended, humiliated or intimidated by the conduct in question, as the courts acknowledge that 'everyone [is] entitled to draw a line somewhere'.[39]

35 Vergara v Ewin [2014] FCAFC 100.

36 Disability Discrimination Act 1992 (Cth) s 35.

37 Anti-discrimination Act (NT) s 20(1)(b).

38 See T. MacDermott, The Duty to Provide a Harassment-Free Work Environment, 37 *Journal of Industrial Relations*, 4, pp. 495–523 (1995); B. Smith, M. Schleiger, & L. Elphick, Preventing Sexual Harassment in Work: Exploring the Promise of Work Health and Safety Laws, 32 *Australian Journal of Labour Laws*, 2, p. 219 (2019).

39 Horman v Distribution Group Ltd [2001] FMCA 52, [64].

Where a workplace sexual harassment claim is litigated in Australia, a respondent employer will often argue that it should not be held responsible for the actions of the perpetrator because it had no knowledge of the conduct and had policies and procedures in place that provide evidence of the steps it took to minimise the risk of such conduct occurring.[40] The Australian case law shows that very few employers succeed in meeting the bar of having taken 'all reasonable steps' to prevent and eliminate harassment so as to avoid a finding of liability for the conduct of their employees. One of the few case examples where an employer successfully made this argument was on the basis of evidence that the employer had engaged in *sustained efforts* to make employees aware of its policies and the consequences of breaching the policies and ensure that the culture of the organisation matches the message delivered in training, with breaches of the policy neither tolerated nor left unaddressed.[41]

The landmark Australian decision of *Richardson v Oracle Corporation Australia Pty Ltd* (*Oracle*)[42] confirmed the need for sustained effort and effective implementation strategies on the part of employers. It also overturned what had developed as the 'permissible range' of damages awarded in sexual harassment case, which had the effect of limiting awards of general damages in substantiated sexual harassment cases to between $12,000 and $20,000, except in cases of significant psychological trauma or ongoing incapacity to work.[43] From an original determination of an award of $18,000,[44] the appeal in *Oracle* found this level of damages to be inadequate and increased the general damages awarded to $100,000 and added an additional $30,000 for economic loss. The *Oracle* appeal empathically rejected the notion of a 'permissible range', and instead relied on the community's 'deeper appreciation of the experience of hurt and humiliation that victims of sexual harassment experience and the value of loss of enjoyment of life occasioned by mental illness or distress caused by such conduct' to find the initial award of $18,000 manifestly inadequate. The Court of Appeal found that, while that sum was in keeping with previous cases of this kind, it was 'out of step with the general standards prevailing in the community regarding the monetary value of the loss and damage of the kind Ms Richardson sustained'.[45] The decision was heralded as offering a new approach to quantifying the harm caused to individuals who experience sexual harassment. However, given that most claims are settled on a confidential basis, it is difficult to ascertain whether this has in fact eventuated. Moreover, lack of access to legal advice and representation, the expense of running court proceedings, and the

40 An employer can avoid being liable for the conduct of its employees if it can establish that it took all reasonable steps to prevent such conduct occurring: Sex Discrimination Act, s106.

41 For an example where the employer succeeded, see Saldana v John Danks and Son Pty Ltd [2009] VCAT 448.

42 Richardson v Oracle Corporation Australia Pty Ltd [2014] FCAC 82.

43 See for example Poniatowska v Hickinbotham [2009] FCA 680.

44 Richardson v Oracle Corporation Australia Pty Limited [2013] FCA 102.

45 Richardson v Oracle Corporation Australia Pty Ltd [2014] FCAC 82, at [118].

threat of an adverse costs order should the claim fail in the courts, means that significant barriers still remain for complainants in pursuing workplace harassment claims.

Despite the existence of legislation prohibiting sexual harassment for many decades, qualitative and quantitative research in this area has consistent found that sexual harassment is persistent, prevalent and underreported in Australian workplace.[46] The results of the fourth national survey conducted by the Commission in 2018 found that '71% of Australians have been sexually harassed at some point in their lifetimes', and that 'more than four in five (85%) Australian women and over half (56%) of Australian men over the age of 15 have been sexually harassed at some point in their lifetimes'.[47] The survey report also indicates that fewer than one in five people (17%) who experienced sexual harassment at work made a formal report or complaint.[48] This evidence shows that despite employees continuing to experience unwelcome and inappropriate conduct of a sexual nature in their workplaces, the majority of these employees do not use internal workplace grievance mechanisms or lodge formal complaints due to the perceived risk of negative consequences for their employment. At the same time, many employers continue to rely on the lack of sexual harassment complaints, either internally or to equality agencies, to maintain that a problem does not exist in their workplace, and that in the absence of anyone stepping forward, they are not in a position to take the issue further, beyond the standard compliance approach of policy induction and ongoing training programmes. The prominence of this issue in public debates in recent years led to the establishment of a national inquiry on sexual harassment, conducted by the Australian Human Rights Commission. The Report from this inquiry,[49] released in 2020, contains a raft of recommendations on ways to address the persistence and prevalence of workplace sexual harassment. Central to the report's findings is the need for a regulatory framework that 'encourages and supports employers to take proactive and preventive measures to address sexual harassment, rather than relying on individual complaints.'[50] The report recommends that the Sex Discrimination Act be amended to impose a positive duty on employers to prevent sexual harassment and to invest the Australian Human Rights Commission with the power to inquire into systemic sexual harassment. It also recommends amendments to the Fair Work Act to address the lack of an express prohibition on sexual harassment and a clear avenue for redress in the national labour laws. While the

46 See Australian Human Rights Commission (AHRC) Everyone's Business: Fourth National Survey on Sexual Harassment in Australian Workplaces (2018). Prior surveys were conducted by the AHRC in 2003, 2008 and 2012.

47 Ibid., p. 8.

48 Ibid., p. 11.

49 Australian Human Rights Commission Respect@Work: National Inquiry into Sexual Harassment in Australian Workplaces (2020).

50 Ibid., p. 517. The Report's key recommendations relating to the legal and regulatory framework are contained in Chapter 5.

previous federal government implemented a number of the recommendations[51] including giving the Fair Work Commission the power to make orders requiring sexual harassment to stop, akin to the 'stop bullying orders' that are currently within the Fair Work Commission's jurisdiction.[52] The current government has committed to implementing the recommendation of introducing a positive duty on all employers.

5 Institutional Process and Mechanisms

5.1 Conciliation

Because so few employment discrimination claims are resolved by court or tribunal proceedings, the way in which complaints are settled in the absence of a hearing and the support provided in reaching this outcome are significant factors. The reliance on forms of alternative dispute resolution to resolve employment claims is a long-standing feature of the Australian workplace relations system, which was founded in 1904 on a model of using conciliation to resolve the differences between the parties by consensus, with arbitration to be used to determine a matter as a last resort.[53] This preference for using forms of alternative dispute resolution was adopted by equality agencies when they were tasked with handling complaints regarding alleged breaches of anti-discrimination laws.

A consensus-based and informal dispute resolution mechanism like conciliation does offer a speedy and cost-effective resolution for some employment discrimination complaints, particularly where the confidentiality of the process offers complainants some protection from the negative career ramifications of making a complaint or the subject matter of the complaint is of a sensitive nature. But this does come at a cost in terms of raising public awareness of the nature and the extent of discriminatory treatment being experienced in Australian workplaces. Equality law scholars have noted that 'anti-discrimination agencies fiercely guard the confidentiality requirement, making it difficult to conduct research which would reveal important information about the [conciliation] process'.[54] The lack of transparency can also have consequences for marginalised groups in terms of empowerment.[55]

51 See the Sex Discrimination and Fair Work (Respect at Work) Amendment Act 2021.

52 Fair Work Act, Part 6–4B.

53 See J. Issacs & S. Macintyre (eds.), *The New Province for Law and Order: 100 Years of Australian Conciliation and Arbitration* (Cambridge 2004).

54 M. Thornton & T. Luker, The New Racism in Employment Discrimination: Tales from the Global Economy, 32 *Sydney Law Review*, 1, p. 5 (2010).

55 M. Thornton, Equivocations of Conciliation: The Resolution of Discrimination Complaints in Australia (1989) 733 *Modern Law Review*, p. 760 (1989).

Although the high rate of settlement of discrimination complaints in Australia is at one level laudable, it should be acknowledged that settlements can be a product of the obstacles that complainants face in pursuing a claim further. There are concerns that some complainants have limited support and resources for pursuing their claim, and hence may have little option but to settle for what is being offered through conciliation.[56] Hence while conciliation is appropriate in some situations, other institutional and structural arrangements, such as the ability of agencies to institute proceedings on behalf of complainants and to provide support and advice, need to supplement this system to bring about the type of structural change necessary to advance substantive equality.

5.2 Remedies

Where an employment discrimination complaint is not able to be resolved by conciliation, the complainant may choose to pursue the claim through court or tribunal proceedings. A range of statutory remedies are available in the event that the claim is upheld, such as an order requiring the payment of 'damages by way of compensation for any loss or damage suffered', injunctive relief, a variation of the employment contract, or an apology.[57] As these are inclusive rather than exclusive options, there is the scope for creative outcomes to tackle the systemic forms of discrimination, but these rarely feature in the orders made by courts and tribunals. In practice, the outcomes of successfully ligated claims usually involve awarding damages for breach of anti-discrimination obligations. However, these awards have consistently been low, with the consequence that they have limited deterrent effect. Although the process of assessing damages in discrimination cases has been characterised as analogous to tortious claims, Australian courts have made clear that the actual basis for any award is the relevant statute.[58] The cautious approach of Australian courts in assessing general damages claims echoes the approach of the English courts; that excessive awards 'do almost as much harm to the policy and the results which it seeks to achieve as do nominal awards' and that 'injury to feelings, which is likely to be of relatively short duration, is less serious than physical injury to the body or the mind which may persist for months, in many cases for life'.[59] Australian courts have also been reluctant to award aggravated damages, and uncertainty remains over whether exemplary damages can be awarded for substantiated discrimination claims.[60]

56 See M. Green, Tackling Employment Discrimination with ADR: Does Mediation Offer a Shield for the Haves or Real Opportunity for the Have-nots? 26 *Berkeley Journal of Employment & Labor Law*, p. 321 (2005).

57 For remedies available where claims are lodged under federal anti-discrimination legislation, see Australian Human Rights Commission Act 1986 (Cth) s 46PO.

58 Hall v Sheiban (1989) 20 FCR 217.

59 Alexander v Home Office [1988] 2 All ER 118,122.

60 Wotton v State of Queensland (No 5) [2016] FCA 1457.

5.3 Redress Through the Workplace Relations Jurisdiction

The regulation of workplace relations in Australia dates back to 1904, with a national tribunal invested since that time with the capacity to resolve disputes by conciliation and arbitration. The national tribunal has been reconfigured and renamed on a number of occasions, with the Fair Work Commission being the current iteration. Over time, the tribunal's original focus on dealing with collective workplace disputes has evolved to encompass a range of individual rights-based claims in response to the growing individualisation of employment claims.[61] The Fair Work Commission has a broad remit that extends to making, reviewing and varying modern awards; approving, varying and terminating enterprise agreements; making orders to stop or suspend industrial action; determining rights of entry; and dealing with disputes under the dispute resolution procedures of modern awards and enterprise agreements. However, the bulk of the Commission's work now involves individual applications in relation to unfair dismissal and general protections claims.[62] When the Fair Work Act was enacted in 2009, a new avenue of redress became available in the form of legislative protections, referred to as 'general protections'.[63] These provisions apply to adverse action taken against current and prospective employees, where the treatment is because any of the listed attributes.

The scope of these provisions is broad and does not depend on there being a termination of the employment relationship. It includes alleged discriminatory treatment while a person is still employed, such as injuring the employee in their employment, altering the employee's position to their prejudice, or discriminating between the employee and other employees.[64] Hence it can apply to discrimination which occurs in selections for promotion or training opportunities, or receiving less favourable terms of employment with respect to benefits or bonuses. Employers can counter a general protections claim by establishing that the impugned conduct was not unlawful under any anti-discrimination laws in the jurisdiction that the events took place, that the person is not able to satisfy the inherent requirements of the job, or the actions taken involving staff of a faith-based institution were taken in good faith and to avoid injury to the religious susceptibilities of adherents of that faith.[65] There is a procedural complexity to the resolution of these complaints where they are not resolved by conciliation, as

61 See T. MacDermott & J. Riley, Alternative Dispute Resolution and Individual Employment rights: The Evolving Role of Fair Work Australia, 53 *Journal of Industrial Relations*, p. 718 (2011).

62 Fair Work Commission, Annual Report 2019–2020. The composition of the Commission includes the President, Vice Presidents, Deputy Presidents and Commissioners who are appointed until the age of 65 and are full-time or part-time. On the changing nature of the dispute resolution functions of the Commission, see T. MacDermott & J. Riley, ADR and Industrial Tribunals: Innovations and Challenges in Resolving Individual Workplace Grievances, 38 *Monash University Law Review*, p. 82 (2012).

63 Fair Work Act Part 3–1.

64 Fair Work Act s 342.

65 Fair Work Act s 351 (2).

only some can be determined by the Fair Work Commission while others require judicial determination through the federal courts.[66]

When the general protections regime was first introduced, some of its features were seen as offering an answer to the type of problems that exist with seeking redress under the general anti-discrimination legislative schemes. One such feature is the reserve onus provision,[67] which means that where an employee alleges that adverse action was taken for a prohibited reason, the employer must negate that by showing some other motivation for the conduct or decision-making. However, over time, the case law has shown that this innovation has not lived up to expectations. A series of litigated claims dealt with by superior courts have attributed considerable weight to the decision maker's state of mind and where this is presented as without a connection to the discriminatory attribute, no breach is established.[68] For example, the courts accepted the characterisation of an employer's decision to make adverse changes to the rostered shifts of an employee as attributable to his attendance rather because he exercised his right to carer's leave.[69] This highlights the capacity for potentially discriminatory conduct to be reframed so as to avoid a breach of the general protections provisions being established. Along similar lines, the High Court of Australia found that an employer did not take impermissible adverse action when it dismissed an employee for holding up a sign condemning 'scabs', on the grounds that the decision to terminate his employment was as a consequence of his conduct being in flagrant breach of the employer's workplace civility policy rather than due to his trade union activities.[70] As the case law has developed, other features have given rise to concerns, such as the prospect of a narrow reading of the application of the provisions to direct discrimination only, and a requirement for evidence of an intention to discrimination for a breach to be substantiated – approaches that do not accord with the jurisprudence regarding the protections provided by general anti-discrimination laws.[71]

6 Conclusion

This chapter has conveyed both the promise and the limitations of the legislative framework dealing with employment discrimination in Australia. While many employment discrimination claims are resolved through non-adversarial dispute

66 There was an amendment to the Fair Work Act to allow some contested applications that would otherwise need to be dealt with the federal courts to be resolved at the Commission by consent arbitration.

67 Fair Work Act (Cth) s 361.

68 Board of Bendigo Regional Institute of Technical and Further Education v Barclay (2012) 290 ALR 647, 657. See B. Gaze & A. Chapman, The Human Right to Non-discrimination as a Legitimate Part of Workplace Law: Towards Substantive Equality at Work in Australia, 4 *International Journal of Comparative Labour Law and Industrial Relations*, pp. 355–374 (2013).

69 CFMEU v Endeavour Coal Pty Ltd (2015) 231 FCR 150.

70 CFMEU v BHP Coal Pty Ltd (2014) 253 CLR 243.

71 B. Gaze & B. Smith, *Equality and Discrimination Law in Australia: An Introduction* (Cambridge 2017), pp. 232–234.

resolution processes such as conciliation, the current regulatory framework does not drive the type of structural changes in employment practices which are necessary to advance the goal of substantive equality. The reliance on individual complainants to pursue their claims in accordance with the highly proscriptive nature of the legislative requirements makes the response to discriminatory treatment at work both piecemeal and reactive.

There is a clear need for the renewal and updating of the Australian legislative framework to shift the emphasis away from negative prohibitions on discriminatory conduct to a more positive, rights-based model. This could involve a reframing of the relevant statutory obligations to a form of positive duty to take action to prevent and eliminate discrimination and harassment, accompanied by greater guidance on steps to achieve compliance in order to empower employers to act in non-discriminatory ways. In addition, the system lacks the type of enforcement processes that can incentivise greater compliance, such as the threat of proceedings being instituted by equality agencies, the regular auditing of employment practices and monitoring of compliance, the issuing of infringement notices and the use of enforceable undertaking. A shift in enforcement away from an over-reliance on individual complaints also requires procedural reforms that extend the capacity for public interest litigation and representative proceedings, as well as measures that address the chilling effect that the risk of an adverse costs order can have on the pursuit of ligated outcomes. Finally, there is the need for better mechanisms for providing information, advice and assistance to empower individuals who experience discrimination at work in finding appropriate and effective pathways to resolve their claims. Publicly funded legal representation and advice for those seeking to pursue discrimination claims is largely absent, undermining access to justice for those seeking redress. Channelling complaints through internal workplace procedures or forms of alternative dispute resolution offered by equality agencies is only a partial solution. Overall, in the absence of substantive reforms, the legal framework governing employment discrimination in Australia has limited capacity to overcome entrenched inequality and discrimination.

Bibliography

Books

Astor H, A Question of Identity: The Intersection of Race and Other Grounds of Discrimination, in Race Discrimination Commissioner (ed) *Racial Discrimination Act 1975: A Review*, Canberra: Australian Government Publishing Service, 269 (1995).

Gaze B, The Racial Discrimination Act after 40 Years: Advancing Equality or Sliding into Obsolescence?' in *Perspectives on the Racial Discrimination Act* (Australian Human Rights Commission, 2015).

Gaze B & B Smith, *Equality and Discrimination Law in Australia: An Introduction*, 232–234 (Cambridge, 2017).

Thornton M, *The Liberal Promise: Anti-Discrimination Legislation in Australia*, 12 (Oxford, 1990).

Articles

Alon-Shenker P & T MacDermott, Intersection Age and Gender in Workplace Discrimination Complaints, 41 *Comparative Labor Law and Policy Journal* 522 (2020).

Crenshaw K, Demarginalizing the Intersection between Race and Sex: A Black Feminist Critique of Antidiscrimination Doctrine, Feminist Theory and Antiracist Politics, *University of Chicago Legal Forum* 139, 139–140 (1989).

Gaze B & A Chapman, The Human Right to Non-Discrimination as a Legitimate Part of Workplace Law: Towards Substantive Equality at Work in Australia, 4 *International Journal of Comparative Labour Law and Industrial Relations* 355–374 (2013).

Green M, Tackling Employment Discrimination with ADR: Does Mediation Offer a Shield for the Haves or Real Opportunity for the Have-Nots? 26 *Berkeley Journal of Employment & Labor Law* 321 (2005).

Hunyor J, Skin-Deep: Proof and Inferences of Racial Discrimination in Employment, 25 *Sydney Law Review* 535 (2003).

Issacs J & S Macintyre (eds), *The New Province for Law and Order: 100 Years of Australian Conciliation and Arbitration* (Cambridge, 2004).

MacDermott T, The Duty to Provide a Harassment-Free Work Environment, 37 *Journal of Industrial Relations* 4, 495–523 (1995).

MacDermott T & J Riley, Alternative Dispute Resolution and Individual Employment Rights: The Evolving Role of Fair Work Australia, 53 *Journal of Industrial Relations* 718 (2011).

MacDermott T & J Riley, ADR and Industrial Tribunals: Innovations and Challenges in Resolving Individual Workplace Grievances, 38 *Monash University Law Review* 82 (2012).

Smith B, M Schleiger & L Elphick, Preventing Sexual Harassment in Work: Exploring the Promise of Work Health and Safety Laws, 32 *Australian Journal of Labour Laws* 2, 219 (2019).

Taylor A, The conflicting Purposes of Australian Anti-Discrimination Law, 42 *UNSW Law Journal* 1, 188 (2019).

Thackrah A, From Neutral to Drive: Australian Anti-Discrimination Law and Identity, 33 *Alternative Law Journal* 31, 32–33 (2008).

Thornton M, Equivocations of Conciliation: The Resolution of Discrimination Complaints in Australia, *Modern Law Review* 733, 760 (1989).

Thornton M & T Luker, The New Racism in Employment Discrimination: Tales from the Global Economy, 32 *Sydney Law Review* 1, 5 (2010).

Statutes

Racial Discrimination Act 1975 (Cth)
Anti-Discrimination Act 1977 (NSW)
Sex Discrimination Act 1984 (Cth)
Equal Opportunity Act 1984 (SA)
Equal Opportunity Act 1984 (WA)
Australian Human Rights Commission Act 1986 (Cth)
Discrimination Act 1991 (ACT)
Anti-Discrimination Act 1991 (Qld)
Disability Discrimination Act 1992 (Cth)
Anti-Discrimination Act 1992 (NT)

Anti-Discrimination Act 1998 (Tas)
Age Discrimination Act 2004 (Cth)
Fair Work Act 2009 (Cth)
Equal Opportunity Act 2010 (Vic)
Workplace Gender Equality Act 2012 (Cth)

International Treaties

Discrimination (Employment and Occupation) Convention, 1958, No 111

Reports

Australian Government, *A Roadmap for Respect: Preventing and Addressing Sexual Harassment in Australian Workplaces* (2021).
Australian Human Rights Commission (AHRC), *Everyone's Business: Fourth National Survey on Sexual Harassment in Australian Workplaces* (2018).
Australian Human Rights Commission (AHRC), *Respect@Work: National Inquiry into Sexual Harassment in Australian Workplaces* (2020).
Fair Work Commission, *Annual Report* (2019–2020).

Cases

Alexander v Home Office [1988] 2 All ER 118.
Australian Iron & Steel Pty Ltd v Banovic (1989) 168 CLR 165.
Board of Bendigo Regional Institute of Technical and Further Education v Barclay (2012) 290 ALR 647.
CFMEU v BHP Coal Pty Ltd (2014) 253 CLR 243.
CFMEU v Endeavour Coal Pty Ltd (2015) 231 FCR 150.
Hall v Sheiban (1989) 20 FCR 217.
Hickie v Hunt & Hunt (1998) EOC 92–910.
Purvis v New South Wales (Department of Education and Training (2003) 217 CLR 92.
Horman v Distribution Group Ltd [2001] FMCA 52.
Nojin v Commonwealth (2012) 208 FCR 1.
Poniatowska v Hickinbotham [2009] FCA 680.
Richardson v Oracle Corporation Australia Pty Limited [2013] FCA 102.
Richardson v Oracle Corporation Australia Pty Ltd [2014] FCAC 82.
Saldana v John Danks and Son Pty Ltd [2009] VCAT 448.
Sklavos v Australasian College of Dermatologists [2017] FCAFC 128.
Vergara v Ewin [2014] FCAFC 100.
Waters v Public Transport Corporation (1991) 173 CLR 349.
Wotton v State of Queensland (No 5) [2016] FCA 1457.

Websites

https://humanrights.gov.au/about/news/submission-draft-religious-discrimination-bill.

www.ag.gov.au/rights-and-protections/consultations/religious-freedom-bills-first-exposure-drafts. www.ag.gov.au/rights-and-protections/consultations/religious-freedom-bills-second-exposure-drafts.

www.news.com.au/sport/sports-life/one-unresolved-legal-question-at-the-heart-of-israel-folaus-case/news-story/387b057b25ab325d35ea494b9ed087b3

8 The Changing Face of Discrimination in Aotearoa/New Zealand

Gordon Anderson and Dawn Duncan

1 Introduction

New Zealand's path to comprehensive antidiscrimination law was initiated within employment. The Government Services Equal Pay Act 1961 implemented the principle of equal pay for work of equal value within government employment. A decade later the Equal Pay Act 1972 extended this principle to the private sector. Broader developments to protect against discrimination were, however, sluggish and largely driven by the need to ensure domestic legislative compliance with New Zealand's international obligations rather than responding to domestic pressure.[1] Legislation tended to be enacted shortly before New Zealand's scheduled formal ratification of international human rights instruments.[2] Hence New Zealand's first broad antidiscrimination legislation, the Race Relations Act 1971, preceded its formal 1972 ratification of the 1965 Convention on the Elimination of All Forms of Racial Discrimination. Similarly the first comprehensive legislation on discrimination, the Human Rights Commission Act 1977, preceded New Zealand's 1978 ratification of the 1968 International Covenant on Civil and Political Rights and the International Covenant on Economic, Social and Cultural Rights. These two pieces of legislation were consolidated in the Human Rights Act 1993 and, so far as discrimination affects employment, partially embedded in employment legislation together with some additional forms of specific employment-related discrimination. While the administrative and judicial structures supporting human rights legislation have been modified from time to time, the core provisions have remained largely unchanged apart from some modifications to the definitions of the prohibited grounds; for example, the definition of marital status has been extended to cover civil unions.

While the concept of discrimination is now well recognised and identified in the law of Aotearoa/New Zealand, that is not to say that the legislation has been

1 New Zealand has ratified 11 of the 14 United Nations human rights instruments: for details see https://tbinternet.ohchr.org/_layouts/15/TreatyBodyExternal/Countries.aspx (accessed: 17 February 2021).

2 New Zealand government policy has long been that ratification of an instrument should not take place until the appropriate implementing legislation is in place.

DOI: 10.4324/9781003306962-10

particularly effective in achieving its longer-term objectives. Thus while equal pay legislation achieved its principal objective of the 1970s, that of eliminating separate male and female pay scales for the same work, it has done relatively little in subsequently advancing pay equity generally. Given that the legislation was predicated on the industrial relations structures of the 1970s, which included a system of "awards" that set the terms and conditions of employment for an industry or occupation,[3] that aspect of the Act became increasingly archaic with the neoliberal reforms of the 1990s. Similarly, while prohibiting discrimination in employment on grounds such as sex, race or ethnic or national origins opened many occupational doors for members of such groups, it would be naïve to think that such occupational discrimination no longer exists.

In this chapter we will first outline the current legal structure relating to discrimination in employment and discuss the weaknesses of that structure. We will then go on to discuss what reforms might be necessary to combat discrimination in employment more effectively and in particular the reforms that might be needed to meet the changing needs of contemporary Aotearoa/New Zealand.

2 The Current Legal Structure

The current legislative framework, consisting of three Acts, is essentially that enacted during the 1970s. While there has been some limited expansion of the original framework, the current law has changed little in the last 40 years. The following account briefly summarises the current structure of legal protection from discrimination in employment.[4]

2.1 The Human Rights Act 1993[5]

This Act is the primary legislation regulating discrimination and human rights matters. The Act establishes the Human Rights Commission, which is the principal government agency dealing with human rights issues.[6] The Commission's primary functions are those of advocating and promoting respect for and understanding of human rights; encouraging the maintenance and development of harmonious relations between individuals and among the diverse groups in New Zealand society; promoting racial equality and cultural diversity; promoting equal employment opportunities including pay equity; and promoting and protecting the

3 Gordon Anderson, *Reconstructing New Zealand's Labour Law: Consensus or Divergence?* (Wellington: Victoria University Press, 2011) at 30. While an award was agreed through a collective negotiation process, legally, the final document was a regulatory instrument issued under the authority of the relevant Act.

4 For a commentary on the law of discrimination in employment see Mazengarb's Employment Law (online ed., LexisNexis, Wellington).

5 The full text of all New Zealand legislation can be accessed at www.legislation.govt.nz/.

6 See www.hrc.co.nz/ (accessed: 1 February 2021) for detailed information on the Commission's activities.

full and equal enjoyment of human rights by persons with disabilities. In order to perform those primary functions the Commission is empowered to exercise an extensive range of subsidiary functions, including in relation to education, policy and international human rights instruments. The Commission's functions in relation to equal employment opportunities include evaluating the roles that legislation, guidelines and voluntary codes of practice play in facilitating and promoting equal employment opportunities; leading the development of guidelines and voluntary codes of practice to facilitate and promote best practice; and monitoring and analysing progress in improving equal employment opportunities and reporting to the minister on the results.

Second, the Act defines the "prohibited grounds" which may constitute unlawful discrimination. These are sex, marital status, religious belief, ethical belief, colour, race, ethnic or national origins, disability, age, political opinion, employment status, family status and sexual orientation. In addition to the prohibited grounds the Act proscribes a range of "other forms of discrimination" encompassing particular behaviours, including sexual and racial harassment and the adverse treatment of persons affected by family violence. It also sets out the circumstances in which discrimination on those grounds is unlawful. These include discrimination in employment matters; discrimination within partnerships; discrimination by industrial and professional associations or by qualifications bodies; discrimination in relation to access to public places or facilities; discrimination in the provision of goods and services or in the provision of land, housing and other accommodation; and discrimination in access to educational establishments.

Finally, the Act establishes the various institutions and processes empowered to resolve human rights complaints and the remedies available to a complainant. These are discussed further below.

2.2 The Employment Relations Act 2000

The discrimination provisions in Part 9 of this Act largely mirror the definitions in the Human Rights Act but extend the prohibited grounds to include union membership status or involvement in union activities. These provisions are embedded in the Act primarily to provide access to the personal grievance procedure, the primary mechanism through which employees can challenge an unjustified dismissal or other unjustified employer actions.[7] While the great majority of personal grievance claims concern allege unjustified dismissal or unjustified disadvantage during employment, a range of other claims may also be resolved through that procedure. These include claims that the employee has been discriminated against in their employment on the basis of one of the prohibited grounds or that they have been subjected to sexual or racial harassment. Employees are able to make an election as to whether they pursue a discrimination complaint under the

7 See Gordon Anderson and Dawn Duncan, *Employment Law in Aotearoa New Zealand* (3rd ed, Wellington, LexisNexis, 2022) at chap 9.

Employment Relations Act or the Human Rights Act. The respective processes are described below.

It should be noted that personal grievance claims can only be raised once a contract of employment is agreed. Claims relating to alleged discrimination occurring during the recruitment process must therefore be brought under the Human Rights Act complaints procedure.

2.3 The Equal Pay Act 1972

As the name suggests, this Act deals specifically with equal pay. When first enacted the Act was effective in eliminating separate sex-based pay scales for the same work, but it subsequently proved to be largely ineffective in dealing with pay equity generally. The Act had been assumed to be moribund. Political developments following the *Terranova*[8] decision saw the Act substantially amended in 2020. The *Terranova* decision was not a substantive decision on a pay equity claim, rather an interpretative decision that the Act allowed such a claim to be brought. The Court of Appeal decision referred the case back to the Employment Court, among other things, to determine the criteria by which such a claim might be resolved. Rather than leave this matter to the courts, the government intervened to legislate how such claims should be resolved. These amendments are the most significant legislative development in employment-related discrimination for several decades and are discussed further below.

3 Employment-Related Discrimination

The key provision relating to employment is s. 22 of the Human Rights Act. This provides that where an applicant for employment or an employee is qualified for work of any description, it shall be unlawful for an employer, or any person acting on behalf of an employer,

> (a) to refuse or omit to employ the applicant on work of that description which is available; or
> (b) to offer or afford the applicant or the employee less favourable terms of employment, conditions of work, superannuation or other fringe benefits, and opportunities for training, promotion, and transfer; or
> (c) to terminate the employment of the employee, or subject the employee to any detriment, in circumstances; or
> (d) to retire the employee, or to require or cause the employee to retire or resign, –

by reason of any of the prohibited grounds of discrimination.

8 Terranova Homes and Care Ltd v Service and Food Workers Union Nga Ringa Tota Inc [2014] NZCA 516.

It is also unlawful for a person procuring employment for another to treat a person seeking employment differently from other persons in the same or substantially similar circumstances by reason of any of the prohibited grounds.

This provision is supplemented by s. 23, which provides that

> It shall be unlawful for any person to use or circulate any form of application for employment or to make any inquiry of or about any applicant for employment which indicates, or could reasonably be understood as indicating, an intention to commit a breach of section 22.

These sections are supported by several other provisions intended to prevent indirect discrimination or discrimination through third parties. Thus the Act also makes it unlawful to publish advertisements that could reasonably be understood as indicating an intention to discriminate. This provision was particularly effective in the early years of the Act as it made newspapers, then the main source of job advertisements, responsible for ensuring job advertisements were not discriminatory. Section 65 provides that any "conduct, practice, requirement, or condition that is not apparently in contravention" of the Act will be unlawful if it has the effect of "treating a person or group of persons differently on one of the prohibited grounds of discrimination."

In principle, these provisions provide a comprehensive legal framework to prevent employment-related discrimination. The question is, of course, how effective are they in practice?

4 The Effectiveness of the Current Framework

Given the lack of robust data, it is difficult to evaluate the success of New Zealand's discrimination legislation. It is, however, probably accurate to suggest that discrimination within employment is, with some particular exceptions, relatively low. Discrimination, on the majority of the prohibited grounds, is more likely to occur at the point of recruitment rather than during employment. The (admittedly unsatisfactory) data on the number of formal complaints arguably supports this position. To the extent that significant discrimination continues to exist within employment, it is likely to take the form of either racial or sexual harassment.

4.1 The Complaints Process

Both the Human Rights Act and the Employment Relations Act provide processes for resolving discrimination complaints in employment. Employees have a choice of which procedure to access, but persons complaining of discrimination in obtaining employment must use the Human Rights Act process. As both are complainant driven, the number of complaints and how far they are taken will be affected by the nature of the process, the probability of success and the costs of pursuing a complaint.

The procedure is similar under both Acts. Both strongly encourage an agreed resolution to complaints through informal processes or through mediation. Attempted mediation is generally a prerequisite to accessing the adjudicative stage of the process. If mediation is unsuccessful, a complainant may take their complaint to either the Human Rights Review Tribunal or the Employment Relations Authority. While both bodies determine complaints through an adjudicative process, their respective Acts do provide somewhat greater flexibility than a normal court. While the principles of natural justice must be observed, in the sense that the parties must receive a fair hearing and be able to answer and respond to the case against them, the tribunals may make their determination "according to equity and good conscience" and "according to the substantial merits of the case, without regard to technicalities". In both cases there may be an appeal to the High Court or the Employment Court as appropriate, with a further appeal on points of law only and with the leave, to the Court of Appeal.

Mediation favours compromise and negotiated settlements, an outcome that is unlikely to fully satisfy a complainant and which, because mediated resolutions are subject to a confidentiality agreement, does little to discourage discrimination more broadly. Moreover, mediation does not involve any formal admission that discrimination occurred. Mediation is "successful" in the sense that the great majority of complaints are resolved by mediation.[9] Mediation does have the advantage that it is free and does not attract awards for costs.

The high level of mediated resolutions also reflects the disincentives to invoking the adjudicative stages of the complaints process. In particular, the fact that a complainant bears the burden of proof at the adjudicative stage except when the employee alleges that the discrimination was by reason of the employee's union membership status or involvement in union activities. If employee was engaged in such activity in the 18 months before the discriminatory action occurred, there is a rebuttable presumption that the discrimination was by reason of that status or activities. Placing the onus of proof on the complainant, combined with the adversarial character of the adjudicative process, operate as strong disincentives in taking a complaint beyond the mediation stage[10] especially as an unsuccessful complainant will be liable for the defendant's costs in addition to their own costs. Most complainants are unlikely to meet New Zealand's criteria for accessing legal aid. While the Office of Human Rights Proceedings is able to accept complaints for free legal representation, the number of successful applications is low. In the 2019–2020 year, the Office granted only 19 employment-related complaints for free legal representation, and of those only ten were for representation in the Human Rights Review Tribunal. These factors also explain the relative dearth of reported cases.

9 There are no accurate figures for the number of cases resolved in mediation, let alone particular classes of case, but the overall settlement rate appears to be approximately 90 per cent.

10 Post Office Union (Inc) v Telecom (Wellington) Ltd (1989) 3 NZILR 527 LC) and Managh v Wallington [1998] 2 ERNZ 337; [1998] 3 NZLR 546 (CA).

Cases concerning discrimination or sexual harassment constitute only 2% of the total, and a review of the 2019–2020 decisions of the Human Rights Review Tribunal disclosed only six employment-related decisions, none of which was a substantive determination. While the Authority issued 13 decisions relating to discrimination, only five of these were stand-alone claims. In the remainder discrimination was one of several grounds alleged to support a claim that a dismissal was unjustified. The five successful claims involved either age or union activities.

On a more optimistic note, it may be that discrimination on grounds such as ethnicity, colour, national origin and sex have diminished over recent decades as the composition of the workforce has become increasingly diverse, as discussed below. This effect is likely to be particularly apparent where discrimination occurs during employment. Over the past decade, many sectors of the workforce have become dependent on skilled or semi-skilled migrant labour, both short-term and long-term. This is particularly true of dairy farming, horticulture and construction.

It should be stressed that some forms of discrimination, including sexual and racial harassment, remain a significant problem. Harassment, however, is more likely to originate from co-workers or others in the workplace rather than formal or informal employer policy. Such forms of harassment have received considerable publicity over the last five years as a result of the #MeToo movement and sensitivity following the 2019 Christchurch mosque shootings. Employers are under increasing social and legal pressure to take effective measures to minimise such behaviours and while management responses may vary, factors such as the ubiquity of smartphones and social media increasingly promote zero-tolerance policies.

4.2 Pre-employment Discrimination

Discrimination on traditional grounds such as ethnicity and sex is more likely to occur during the recruitment phase of employment. While discrimination at this level is unlawful, and third parties such as recruiters and human resource consultants are liable should they discriminate on behalf of a client, discrimination is exceptionally difficult to prove. While some such discrimination may be inadvertent, as in the case of badly trained algorithms, more worryingly is when discrimination occurs by recruiters deliberately filtering out some categories of applicant. Similarly, interview panels looking for "team fit" and the like can have the effect of discriminating against some groups. Such strategies as rejecting applications from applicants with non-European names are clearly unlawful, but the lack of effective deterrence makes it likely that such conduct is far from unusual.[11] Even if such discrimination were able to be demonstrated, an individual applicant is extremely unlikely to be able to establish that their application would have been successful in obtaining the position but for the discrimination. It also seems likely,

11 Astrid Podsiadlowski & Colleen Ward, Global Mobility and Bias in the Workplace, in Stuart Carr (ed.), *The Psychology of Global Mobility* (New York: Springer, 2010), § 282.

given the diversity of employment in major sectors of the labour market, that this form of discrimination may be more prevalent in professional, semi-professional and administrative employment in the private sector than elsewhere.

5 Issues in Contemporary Aotearoa/New Zealand

Aotearoa/New Zealand's discrimination law has changed little since the late 1970s and, as such, it still reflects the social and demographic characteristics of the 1970s. Since that time, however, New Zealand society has undergone significant changes both demographically and economically. The legislative architecture of the 1970s was primarily targeted at providing a remedy for conscious discrimination against individuals in their economic life, including employment. A combination of increasing demographic diversity and the discriminatory side effects of labour market deregulation has resulted in the focus of discrimination policies moving away from individual cases to a greater focus on the macro-level problems.

Three of the most important influences in this shift are the growing influence of *tikanga Māori* in the law, the increased multicultural character of Aotearoa/New Zealand and the discrimination that is embedded in many aspects of social inequality. In this short section we summarise the shape and direction of this new approach to discrimination as it applies to employment.

5.1 Increased Ethnic Diversity

Probably the most important development in the New Zealand labour market over recent decades is demographic.[12] In the 1976 census, carried out the year before the current legal framework was put in place, 86% of New Zealanders identified as European, 9% as Māori and 2% as Pacific, with all other ethnicities constituting just 1% of the population. In the 2018 census, the proportion identifying as European has declined to 70%, while 17% of New Zealanders identified as Māori, 8% as Pacific, 15% as Asian and 3% as either Middle Eastern/Latin American/African or other. Over the same period, the proportion of the population born in New Zealand has dropped from 83% to 73%. A significant internal migration of Māori people also took place, with only 26% of Māori living in urban areas in 1945, growing to 62% in 1966 and nearly 80% by 1986.

The consequence of these changes is that the New Zealand workforce is now considerably more diverse than at any time in the country's history. This obviously does not mean that discrimination against individuals has disappeared, but it does mean that the changed character of the workforce is increasingly accepted in employment generally. For this reason, one might be optimistic that in-employment discrimination on the traditional prohibited grounds is likely to become more marginalised in future years.

12 Figures used in this chapter were obtained though StatsNZ: www.stats.govt.nz/.

5.2 In-Work Poverty

As a result of the deregulation of the New Zealand labour market in 1991, many workers suffered significant cuts in income and job security, the loss of collective bargaining power and an increasing degree of precariousness in the labour market. The extent of in-work poverty has been revealed in a report commissioned by a number of government agencies.[13] The authors estimate that 7% of working households fall within the threshold of in-work poverty, but that figure increases significantly when ethnic grouping is taken into account. The in-work poverty rate for Māori is 8.6% and for each of Pacific peoples, Asian and the "other ethnicities" grouping, 9.5%. The report notes that these figures have remained stable for at least a decade. While in-work poverty is partly attributable to wage levels, the problem is of course somewhat more complex. Typically households suffering in-work poverty also have relatively low educational achievements and tend to have more members. Nevertheless, the fact that many such workers are in sectors of the labour market characterised by low wages, a high degree of precariousness and unstable incomes is a significant contributor to household poverty.[14]

5.3 New Developments in Pay Equity

The Equal Pay Amendment Act 2020 created a new process to "facilitate resolution of pay equity claims" and to allow the law to respond better to these "macro-level" inequality issues.[15] While the 1972 Equal Pay Act had included a pay equity provision (requiring equal pay for work of equal value), it remained "largely mute"[16] until the *Terranova* decision, which accepted a claim that in principle the Act applied to a situation where both male and female aged care workers were being paid a lower rate of pay "than would have been the case if care giving were not work predominantly performed by women". Following this decision, the Government set up the Joint Working Group on Pay Equity Principles to make recommendations on how it should respond. The Government then negotiated with the unions representing the caregivers for a significant wage settlement. Similar settlements were also reached with unions representing other workers in female-dominated industries with low pay due to historic undervaluation.

The Amendment Act was passed to create a process for future claims, including those in the private sector, where the Government would not be involved in the settlement. The new process allows groups of workers to bring claims where they are performing work predominantly performed by female employees and it

13 Alexander Plum, Gail Pacheco and Rod Hick *In-Work Poverty in New Zealand* (New Zealand Work Research Institute, 2019).

14 Human Rights Responses to Poverty in Working Households He Urupare Tika Tangata mō te Pōharatanga ō ngā Whānau Whaimahi (New Zealand Human Rights Commission, 2020).

15 See Jane Parker & Noelle Donnelly, The Revival and Refreshing of Gender Pay Equity in New Zealand, 62 *Journal of industrial Relations*, p. 560 (2020).

16 Terranova, supra n. 8, at p. 1.

is arguable that the work is currently undervalued or has been historically undervalued. Once a claim has been made the parties enter in to "pay equity bargaining" with a view to reaching a negotiated settlement. The Amendment Act provides for mediation to assist the parties, and then facilitation by the Employment Relations Authority, with some limited ability for the Authority to determine the matter as a last resort.

While the pay equity amendments go some way to addressing the original failings of the 1972 Equal Pay Act, they have significant limitations, with calls for further reform. For example, the amendments do not create an obligation on employers to monitor, disclose or report on pay rates or on any actions taken by them to address issues identified. The lack of a pay transparency requirement makes bringing claims more difficult and costly for workers. Attempts to introduce such obligations in 2017 were unsuccessful, but there is currently a campaign, led by the Human Rights Commission, unions, and other groups, calling for pay transparency legislation similar to that in Australia, parts of Europe and South Africa to accompany the reforms.[17] The South African approach of requiring businesses to report on pay rates by gender and ethnicity, and vertical and horizontal wage inequality potentially offers New Zealand a model better suited to addressing contemporary economic inequalities.[18] In addition to the lack of pay transparency obligations, New Zealand's pay equity amendments did not create a specialist pay equity agency to report on trends; provide specialist advice to parties; assist in the preparation, evaluation or resolution of pay equity claims; or monitor compliance, as exist in other jurisdictions. For example, in Australia compliance with reporting obligations is a condition of obtaining a Government contract with its Workplace Gender Equality Agency publicly displaying a "non-compliant list".[19]

Finally, the amendments only relate to the undervaluing of the work traditionally performed by women. There is no process for addressing pay equity issues related to historical racism in employment practices or labour market policies, the ongoing impacts of colonisation or the disproportionate negative impacts of economic policies on Māori and Pacific workers. Recent reports, such as *Talanoa: Human Rights Issues for Pacific Peoples in Aotearoa New Zealand*,[20] *Māori in the Labour Market*[21] and the previous Treasury report on the impacts of

17 See further www.demandpaytransparency.org.nz.

18 South Africa's recent amendments to their Employment Equity Regulations came into force 1 January 2021 and create a pay transparency measure for federally regulated private sector employers with 100 or more employees. These reporting obligations extend beyond the gender pay gap to other areas. See www.gov.za/documents/employment-equity-act-regulations#.

19 For information about Australia's Workplace Gender Equality Agency WGEA, and state-based agencies, such as the Victoria Gender Equity Commissioner, see www.wgea.gov.au and www.genvic.org.au.

20 Human Rights Commission Talanoa: Human Rights issues for Pacific peoples in Aotearoa New Zealand (December 2020).

21 Ministry of Business, Innovation and Employment Māori in the Labour Market (June 2020).

ethnic wage gaps[22] highlight the significant gaps between the pay and employment conditions of Pākehā (European New Zealanders) and Māori and Pacific workers. Some academics have called for the taking of an intersectional approach to antidiscrimination law in New Zealand, highlighting the interplay of factors involved in the lower pay rates of Māori women.[23] In relation to the Māori workers' pay gap, the Government is required to take action to address historical injustices and structural inequalities under Te Tiriti o Waitangi/The Treaty of Waitangi, with equality guaranteed under Art. 3.[24] It may be possible to bring a claim relating to historical discrimination resulting in pay inequity or economic disadvantage to the Waitangi Tribunal (e.g. claims relating to a historical Crown action or ongoing inaction, or legislation or policy decisions that breach the Treaty). Such claims are just beginning to be made. The first inquiry, relating to economic disadvantages affecting Māori women, commenced nationwide hearings in 2021 and these are still continuing. The Tribunal has also commissioned a number of supporting research reports.[25] While addressing complex and intersecting economic inequalities and the legacy of colonisation require reforms that go well beyond the employment sphere or the proposed amendments to the antidiscrimination legislation, examining the legal structures creating and regulating the contemporary relationships of work are an important part of addressing economic inequality.[26]

In mid-2020, the Human Rights Commission released research on opinions and experiences of pay equity,[27] and in late 2020, the Equal Opportunity Commissioner launched an inquiry into the Pacific workers' pay gap, which seeks to understand the nature and extent of discrimination experienced by Pacific workers, focusing on pay equity, working conditions and recruitment and retention issues.[28] Pacific workers are some of the lowest paid, with Pacific women being the lowest paid

22 The New Zealand Treasury Statistical Analysis of Ethnic Wage Gaps (September 2018) www.treasury.govt.nz/sites/default/files/2018-08/ap18-03.pdf.

23 Amanda Reilly, Maori Women, Discrimination and Paid Work: The Need for an Intersectional Approach, 50 *VUWLR*, p. 321 (2019).

24 Te Tiriti o Waitangi/The Treaty of Waitangi 1840 was signed by the British Crown and a number of Māori chiefs and is generally regarded as New Zealand's founding constitutional document. The effect of the Treaty was that Māori ceded their sovereignty to the British Crown and obtained the rights of British subjects. It should be noted that the exact terms and meaning of the Treaty are strongly contested and that the Māori and English versions are not consistent. See Matthew Palmer, *The Treaty of Waitangi in New Zealand's Law and Constitution* (Wellington: Victoria University Press, 2008).

25 The Wai 2700 Mana Wāhine Inquiry examines economic disadvantage to Māori women. More information can be found on the Waitangi Tribunal website: https://waitangitribunal.govt.nz/inquiries/kaupapa-inquiries/mana-wahine-kaupapa-inquiry/.

26 See Matthew Scobie & Anna Sturman, Economies of Mana and Mahi Beyond the Crises, 45 *New Zealand Journal of Employment Relations*, p. 77 (2020).

27 Human Rights Commission Opinions and Experiences of Unequal Pay and Pay Transparency (June 2020).

28 Human Rights Commission press release on the Inquiry "Human Rights Commission launches inquiry into "discriminatory" Pacific pay gap" (7 December 2020): www.hrc.co.nz/news/human-rights-commission-launches-inquiry-discriminatory-pacific-pay-gap/.

group in New Zealand. For example, the latest labour force data shows the pay gap between Pākehā men and Pacific women working in the public sector is 27%. This inquiry is an important start to widening our legal responses to pay inequality.

5.4 Specific Reforms to Antidiscrimination Law – Gender Minorities

In addition to the current focus on pay equity, a number of specific reforms are underway to bring the antidiscrimination law into alignment with contemporary society and changing values. One such area is the protection of gender minorities. "Sex" and "sexual orientation" are included in the prohibited grounds of discrimination. Absent from the drafting, however, are explicit protections for people with diverse gender identities; for example intersex people and people who identify as trans, agender or gender non-confirming, or the wide range of gender identities found in Māori and Pacific communities.[29] In 2019, the United Nations Human Rights Council made a number of recommendations to New Zealand as part of its Universal Periodic Review, including improvements to the protections available for LGBTQI people.[30] Chile, Australia and Iceland also specifically highlighted the need to introduce protections for intersex people and those with minority gender identities.[31] In 2020, the Human Rights Commission issued *Prism: Human Rights Issues Relating to Sexual Orientation, Gender Identity and Expression and Sex Characteristics (SOGIESC) in Aotearoa New Zealand.*[32] The report made six sets of recommendations. These included: amending section 21 to explicitly include gender identity, gender expression and sex characteristics as prohibited grounds of discrimination; updating the New Zealand Standard *Rainbow Inclusive Workplaces: A Standard for Gender and Sexual Diversity in Employment* (NZS8200:2015); providing comprehensive educational resources, including for employers and providing ongoing workplace training.[33] The New Zealand Labour Party (currently in Government) had as its 2020 election policy that it would review this area, although no indication of when this will be done has been given.[34]

The protection of people with minority gender identities in New Zealand has a complicated history. In 2004, a private members bill had been introduced by New Zealand's first trans Member of Parliament, Georgina Beyer, to add "gender

29 See Elizabeth Kerekere, Part of the Whānau: The Emergence of Takatāpui Identity – He Whāriki Takatāpui (PhD Thesis, Victoria University of Wellington, 2017); Niko Besnier & Kalissa Alexeyeff (eds.), *Gender on the Edge: Transgender, Gay and Other Pacific Islanders* (e-book, University of Hawaii, 2014).

30 United Nations Human Rights Council Universal Periodic Review New Zealand (Third cycle, 2019), available at www.ohchr.org/EN/HRBodies/UPR/Pages/NZIndex.aspx.

31 Universal Periodic Review Matrix of Recommendations, 122.102 (Chile), 122.52 (Australia), 122.51 (Iceland).

32 Human Rights Commission, June 2020.

33 Prism, at pp. 3–5.

34 New Zealand Labour Party "Rainbow Policies" available at www.labour.org.nz/rainbow.

identity" to the prohibited grounds of discrimination.[35] This Bill was withdrawn following an opinion by Crown lawyers that the amendment was unnecessary, as the word "sex" had been interpreted to include both "gender" and "gender identity" within it. Following this opinion, the Human Rights Commission has accepted complaints of discrimination relating to gender identity, with other organisations treating gender identity as falling within the protections of the Human Rights Act and making policy changes.[36] In 2006, the Human Rights Commission undertook a world first Inquiry into Discrimination Experienced by Transgender People, releasing *To Be Who I Am/Kia noho au ki tōku anō ao* in 2008, which highlighted the prevalence of employment-related discrimination.[37] The protections available under the Employment Relations Act also developed to prohibit discrimination against gender minorities, with the official advice to employers stating that employers must support their employees who choose to transition, and providing specific guidelines on the required support.[38] The Employment Relations Authority has found that the dismissal of an employee who disclosed her intention to transition was unjustifiable as not meeting the statutory standard of a "fair and reasonable employer" and was a breach of the employer's statutory obligations of good faith.[39] While discrimination against gender minorities is arguably already prohibited by law in New Zealand, the form of that prohibition is less explicit, visible or effective. The pressure on the Government to improve the legal response in this area is perhaps a reflection of increasing expectations on the usability and practical effectiveness of antidiscrimination law.

5.5 Specific Reforms to Antidiscrimination Law – Workers With Disabilities

Another key area where reforms to antidiscrimination law are currently being sought is in relation to disability. As in other countries, Aotearoa/New Zealand has a long and difficult history when it comes to recognising the rights of people with disabilities,[40] with employment discrimination still a significant issue. The unemployment rate for disabled people is more than twice that for non-disabled people, with the unemployment rates for Māori and Pacific people with disabilities higher still.[41] New Zealand ratified the United Nations Convention on the Rights

35 Human Rights (Gender Identity) Amendment Bill.

36 For example, the Department of Internal Affairs introduced an additional gender option to passports, and the New Zealand Transport Agency changing drivers license options the following year.

37 Human Rights Commission To be who I am/Kia noho au ki tōku anō ao (Human Rights Commission, 2008) at 39.

38 www.employment.govt.nz/#gref.

39 Hemmingson v Swan t/a Barkers Groom Room [2016] NZERA Auck 212.

40 Martin Sullivan and Hilary Stace "A brief history of disability in Aotearoa New Zealand" (October 2020), available on the Office for Disability Issues website at www.odi.govt.nz/guidance-and-resources/a-brief-history-of-disability-in-aotearoa-new-zealand/.

41 June 2019 rates for disable people 8.6% and non-disabled 3.8%.

of Persons with Disabilities (Convention), in 2008, and the Optional Protocol to the Disability Convention (the Optional Protocol) in 2016. The Human Rights Act includes and broadly defines "disability" within the prohibited grounds in section 21 but allows for a range of exceptions which are currently being called in to question. The 2020 report of the *Independent Monitoring Mechanism of the Convention on the Rights of Persons with Disabilities*[42] highlighted New Zealand's "mixed record" and the need for reforms. In relation to Art. 5 of the Convention on equality and non-discrimination, the IMM recommended amending the Human Rights Act to strengthen disabled people's right to non-discrimination. This included removing or reducing the disability-related exemptions, introducing an explicit definition of reasonable accommodation (consistent with Art. 2 of the Convention) and creating an explicit duty of reasonable accommodation.[43] At present, the law relating to reasonable accommodation in employment is underdeveloped and unclear, with little case law and only general-level information and guidance available for employers on what is required.[44] The IMM also recommended urgently conducting an audit of existing legislation for conformity with the Convention, specifically the right to non-discrimination and equality before the law. The IMM reiterated previous recommendations to amend the Minimum Wage Act 1983 to eliminate minimum wage exemption permits.[45] Presently, the law allows employers to apply for a permit to pay workers with disabilities less than the minimum wage.

The position of Māori and Pacific disabled people was particularly highlighted, with the IMM recommending the Government address the poorer socioeconomic outcomes for Māori and Pacific peoples, and specifically identify and address the disproportionate impacts of these inequities on *tāngata whaikaha* (Māori disabled people) and Pacific disabled peoples.[46] In relation to the existing actions taken by the Government, the IMM concluded that "current initiatives are yet to yield significant or reliably durable shifts in employment outcomes", with greater focus and resources required and recommending "serious consideration to instituting temporary special measures or affirmative actions".[47] Again in this area, there is a shift beyond just having the provisions in the legislation, to their usability and practical economic effect.

42 Independent Monitoring Mechanism of the Convention on the Rights of Persons with Disabilities Aotearoa/New Zealand 2014–2019 Making Disability Rights Real Whakatūturu Ngā Tika Hauātanga (June 2020).

43 Recommendation 10, at 21 of IMM Report.

44 See McClelland v Schindler Lifts NZ Ltd [2015] NZHRRT 45, and Reasonable accommodation of persons with disabilities in New Zealand (2015), available on the Human Rights Commission website for the currently available guidance: www.hrc.co.nz/news/reasonable-accommodation-guide-focussing-persons-disabilities-released/. The only specific regulations relate to the accessibility of buildings.

45 Recommendation 97, at 33.

46 Recommendations 3 and 4, at 20.

47 At 17 of IMM report.

6 Conclusion

New Zealand's antidiscrimination law remains largely as it was 40 years ago, reflecting international expectations of that time. In the case of discrimination within employment, the law has achieved acceptable, but not spectacular, success in providing remedies for individual complainants alleging discrimination on the grounds set out in the legislation. The combination of legislative reform, changing labour market needs and social changes has led to significant changes in the composition of the workforce and in the range of occupations accessible to many of the protected groups. However, the law has done little to deal with the considerably more complex areas of discrimination identified by modern analysis and intersectional analysis. The recent pay equity legislation may well signal the beginning of attempts to deal with these more complex issues. Certainly there is a change in the expectations of people in Aotearoa/New Zealand that antidiscrimination law ought to move beyond the goals of 1970s drafters and "pull more weight" in addressing economic and social inequalities.

Bibliography

Books

Anderson Gordon, *Reconstructing New Zealand's Labour Law: Consensus or Divergence?* (Victoria University Press, 2011).

Anderson Gordon and Dawn Duncan, *Employment Law in Aotearoa New Zealand* (3rd ed, Wellington, LexisNexis, 2022).

Besnier Niko and Kalissa Alexeyeff (eds), *Gender on the Edge: Transgender, Gay and Other Pacific Islanders* (e-book, University of Hawaii, 2014).

Mazengarb's Employment Law (online ed, LexisNexis).

Palmer Matthew, *The Treaty of Waitangi in New Zealand's Law and Constitution* (Victoria University Press, 2008).

Chapters

Podsiadlowski Astrid and Colleen Ward, "Global Mobility and Bias in the Workplace" in Stuart Carr (ed) *The Psychology of Global Mobility* § 282 (Springer, 2010).

Articles

Parker Jane and Noelle Donnelly, *The Revival and Refreshing of Gender Pay Equity in New Zealand*, 62 Journal of Industrial Relations 560 (2020).

Reilly Amanda, *Maori Women, Discrimination and Paid Work: The Need for an Intersectional Approach*, 50 VUWLR 321 (2019).

Scobie Matthew and Anna Sturman, *Economies of Mana and Mahi Beyond the Crises*, 45 New Zealand Journal of Employment Relations 77 (2020).

Theses

Kerekere Elizabeth, "Part of the Whānau: The Emergence of Takatāpui Identity – He Whāriki Takatāpui" (PhD Thesis, Victoria University of Wellington, 2017).

Reports

Human Rights Responses to Poverty in Working Households He Urupare Tika Tangata mō te Pōharatanga ō ngā Whānau Whaimahi (2020).

Independent Monitoring Mechanism of the Convention on the Rights of Persons with Disabilities Aotearoa/New Zealand 2014–2019, *Making Disability Rights Real Whakatūturu Ngā Tika Hauātanga* (June, 2020).

Ministry of Business, Innovation and Employment, *Māori in the Labour Market* (June, 2020).

New Zealand Human Rights Commission, *To be who I am/Kia noho au ki töku anö ao (Human Rights Commission* (2008).

New Zealand Treasury, *Statistical Analysis of Ethnic Wage Gaps* (September, 2018) www.treasury.govt.nz/sites/default/files/2018-08/ap18-03.pdf.

Opinions and Experiences of Unequal Pay and Pay Transparency (June, 2020).

Reasonable accommodation of persons with disabilities in New Zealand (2015).

Talanoa: Human Rights issues for Pacific peoples in Aotearoa New Zealand (December, 2020).

Cases

Hemmingson v Swan t/a Barkers Groom Room [2016] NZERA Auck 212.

Managh v Wallington [1998] 3 NZLR 546 (CA).

McClelland v Schindler Lifts NZ Ltd [2015] NZHRRT 45.

Post Office Union (Inc) v Telecom (Wellington) Ltd (1989) 3 NZILR 527 (LC).

Terranova Homes and Care Ltd v Service and Food Workers Union Nga Ringa Tota Inc [2014] NZCA 516.

Acts and Regulations

Employment Equity Act: Regulations (South Africa) www.gov.za/documents/employment-equity-act-regulations#.

Employment Relations Act 2000.

Equal Pay Act 1972.

Human Rights Act 1993.

Human Rights (Gender Identity) Amendment Bill.

New Zealand Legislation: www.legislation.govt.nz/.

Web Links

Human Rights Commission: www.hrc.co.nz/

StatsNZ: www.stats.govt.nz/

UN Treaty Body Database: https://tbinternet.ohchr.org/_layouts/15/TreatyBodyExternal/Countries.aspx

Victoria Gender Equity Commissioner: www.wgea.gov.au and www.genvic.org.au

Miscellaneous

Martin Sullivan and Hilary Stace, "A brief history of disability in Aotearoa New Zealand" (October, 2020), available on the Office for Disability Issues website here: www.odi.govt.nz/guidance-and-resources/a-brief-history-of-disability-in-aotearoa-new-zealand/

New Zealand Labour Party, "Rainbow Policies" available at: www.labour.org.nz/rainbow

United Nations Human Rights Council Universal Periodic Review New Zealand (Third cycle, 2019), available at: www.ohchr.org/EN/HRBodies/UPR/Pages/NZIndex.aspx

Universal Periodic Review Matrix of Recommendations, 122.102 (Chile), 122.52 (Australia), 122.51 (Iceland)

Part III

Facets of Employment Discrimination in Other Parts of the World

9 The Erasure of Sexual Harassment

Recourse for Sexual Harassment Under Labour Law Frameworks in Québec

Rachel Cox

1 Introduction

Historically, legal recourse in case of sexual harassment at work has been intrinsically linked to social recognition of the harms caused by sexual harassment, as well as the role it plays in terms of maintaining women's social and economic oppression.[1] As Patricia Hughes explains:

> Prohibitions against sexual harassment acknowledge that unacceptable sexual treatment of women by men in the workplace is not personal conduct between two individuals largely immunized from sanction by being considered "private", but is rather a reflection of systemic power relations experienced in the public realm and therefore worthy of public treatment (that is, within the law's purview). It further underscores that what is considered "unacceptable" must be significantly redelineated.[2]

In Québec, sexual harassment at work has been illegal for almost half a century. However, due to case law developments, institutional practises and legislative modifications, over the past few decades the legal framework for recourse in case of sexual harassment at work has evolved into a remarkably complex and fragmented one.[3] The human rights framework for sexual harassment at work now interacts with or has been replaced by labour law frameworks for psychological

1 See Anna-Maria Marshall, *Confronting Sexual Harassment: The Law and Politics of Everyday Life* (Ashgate: Aldershot, 2005); Constance Backhouse, Sexual Harassment: A Feminist Phrase That Transformed the Workplace, 24 *Canadian Journal of Women and the Law*, 2, p. 27 (2012); Catharine A. MacKinnon, *The Sexual Harassment of Working Women: A Case of Sex Discrimination* (New Haven, CT: Yale University Press, 1979).

2 Patricia Hughes, The Evolving Conceptual Framework of Sexual Harassment, 3 *Canadian Labour & Employment Law Journal*, 1, p. 3 (1994–1995).

3 In 2020, the Report of Québec's Expert Committee on Support for Victims of Sexual Assault and Domestic Violence concluded that the multiple recourses for targets of sexual assault and harassment at work sow confusion, increase the risk of secondary victimisation and can compromise access to justice: Rapport du Comité d'experts sur l'accompagnement des victimes d'agressions

DOI: 10.4324/9781003306962-12

harassment, grievance arbitration and workers' compensation. This raises the question as to whether today sexually harassed workers' interests are better served through recourse via mainstream labour law institutions, through traditional human rights institutions or through some combination of both. More broadly, to what extent is "mainstreaming" recourse for sexual harassment through labour law institutions a promising path for effectively establishing the widespread unacceptability of sexual harassment at work? Or is it a dangerous trend of individualising sexual harassment cases and minimising the connections between sexual harassment and other forms of violence and discrimination against women that is to be avoided?[4]

Québec's legal framework is not the only one to raise these questions. Over the past 25 years in North America and Europe, as well as other industrialised countries, much debate has arisen on the implications of the legal conceptualisation of injustices at work as gender-neutral violations of dignity rather than gender-specific violations of equality.[5] The process leading up to the adoption of the International Labour Organization (ILO) Violence and Harassment Convention (C-190) also touched on the question of mainstreaming of women's equality rights at work. In 2016, the Gender, Equality and Diversity Branch of the ILO commissioned a working paper to provide an overview of various regulatory approaches to workplace violence around the world.[6] The working paper inventoried categories of violence that disproportionately affect women, such as sexual harassment and domestic violence. However, the paper also underlined that in certain occupational sectors where women are disproportionately present, such as health care, education and domestic work, violence in all its forms is often more pervasive than in other sectors.

---

sexuelles et de violence conjugale (2020), Québec, Canada, pages 157–160 <www.justice.gouv.qc.ca/en/victims/consultation>.

4 See Colleen Sheppard, Systemic Inequality and Workplace Culture: Challenging the Institutionalization of Sexual Harassment, 3 *Canadian Labour and Employment Law Journal*, pp. 249–286 (1995); Kathrin Zippel, Practices of Implementation of Sexual Harassment Policies: Individual Versus Collective Strategies, 20 *Review of Policy Research*, 1, pp. 175–197 (2003); Catharine A. MacKinnon & Rebecca B. Siegel (eds.), *Directions in Sexual Harassment Law* (New Haven, CT: Yale University Press, 2004) [MacKinnon and Siegel].

5 See for example Anita Bernstein, Law, Culture, and Harassment, 142 *University of Pennsylvania Law Review*, pp. 1227–1331 (1994); Kathrin Zippel, *The Politics of Sexual Harassment: A Comparative Study of the United States, the European Union, and Germany* (Cambridge: Cambridge University Press, 2006); Gabrielle S. Friedman & James Q. Whitlan, The European Transformation of Harassment Law: Discrimination Versus Dignity, *Columbia Journal of European Law*, p. 241 (2003); Susanne Baer, Dignity or Equality? Responses to Workplace Harassment in European, German, and U.S. Law, in MacKinnon & Siegel, supra n. 4, pages 582–601; Noya Rimalt, Stereotyping Women, Individualizing Harassment: The Dignitary Paradigm of Sexual Harassment Law Between the Limits of Law and the Limits of Feminism, 19 *Yale Journal of Law & Feminism*, pp. 391–447 (2007–2008).

6 Katherine Lippel, *Addressing Occupational Violence: An Overview of Policy Considerations Viewed Through a Gender Lens* (Geneva: ILO, 2016), available at www.ilo.org/gender/Informationresources/Publications/WCMS_535656/lang--en/index.htm.

In light of these findings, the Violence and Harassment Convention (C-190) adopted in June 2019 refers to "violence and harassment at work" rather than gender-based violence and harassment at work. However, Article 1 of the Convention explicitly defines "violence and harassment" as comprising "gender-based violence and harassment", including sexual harassment,[7] and then specifies that "definitions in national laws and regulations may provide for a single concept or separate concepts". The Convention acknowledges the importance of an "inclusive, integrated and gender-responsive approach" to ending violence and harassment in the world of work.[8] Indeed, its companion Recommendation (R-206) states as a core principle that Members should address violence and harassment in the world of work in labour and employment law, as well as in equality and non-discrimination law.[9] Thus, not only is the Convention itself an example of mainstreaming, but it also implicitly recognises locating recourse for sexual harassment within labour and employment law as a valid approach for ILO members, albeit subject to attaining the standards set out for enforcement and remedies in the Convention and using a gender-responsive approach in order to do so.

In Québec, one concrete consequence of the trend toward recourse for sexual harassment at work based on labour law frameworks rather than human rights frameworks is that the number of Québec Human Rights Tribunal decisions where sexual harassment at work is framed as a violation of fundamental Charter rights has dropped off dramatically. We have thus studied the *Tribunal administratif du travail*, or Labour Administrative Tribunal (hereinafter Labour Tribunal) decisions from 2004 until 2020 in order to understand how psychological harassment or workers' compensation legislation is applied when the complainant or claimant alleges facts amounting to sexual harassment. Our analysis reveals how these frameworks sometimes work to erase sexual harassment, not only as a legal concept but also as a factual situation within the purview of the law. It raises the delicate issue of whether decision-makers selected for their expertise in labour relations or workers' compensation who sit on the Labour Tribunal have sufficient expertise and sensitivity regarding sexual harassment. It also begs the question as to whether legislative reform is necessary to guarantee a remedy in case of violation of the right to a work environment free from sexual harassment, and if so, what this legislative reform might look like.

In this chapter, we will first provide a broad description of the legal framework for sexual harassment at work in Québec law (section 2). Next, we will delve into the ramifications of framing the consequences of sexual harassment as an employment injury under workers' compensation law (section 3). We will then

7 International Labour Organization (ILO), Violence and Harassment Convention, 2019 (No. 190), available at www.ilo.org/dyn/normlex/en/f?p=1000:12100:0::NO::P12100_INSTRUMENT_ID,P12100_LANG_CODE:3999810,en:NO.

8 Ibid., Article 4, paragraph 2.

9 International Labour Organization (ILO), Violence and Harassment Recommendation, 2019 (No. 206), available at www.ilo.org/dyn/normlex/en/f?p=NORMLEXPUB:12100:0::NO:12100:P12100_ILO_CODE:R206:NO.

examine the consequences of framing sexual harassment as psychological harassment (section 4). Finally, we will draw some tentative conclusions about pragmatic considerations that should be taken into account when it comes to weighing up the advantages and disadvantages of different avenues of recourse for a worker experiencing sexual harassment (section 5).

We recognise that non-binary people and men – in particular gay men – can be victims of sexual harassment. Nonetheless, in keeping with the literature indicating overrepresentation of women amongst victims and a marked overrepresentation of men amongst perpetrators, we use the pronouns "she" and "her" in this chapter to describe workers who are victims of sexual harassment.[10]

2 The Legal Framework for Sexual Harassment at Work

In Québec, in 1976, the coming into effect of the Québec Charter of Rights and Freedoms laid down a human rights framework for sexual harassment at work. The Québec Charter is a quasi-constitutional law which has precedence over other statutes (s. 52, Charter). The Charter applies to matters that come under the legislative authority of Québec, which is the case for the employment conditions of approximately 90% of the Québec workforce. Section 10 of the Charter affirms that "[e]very person has a right to full and equal recognition and exercise of his human rights and freedoms, without distinction, exclusion or preference" based on prohibited grounds. Section 10.1 of the Charter was added in 1982 and specifies that "[n]o one may harass a person on the basis of any ground mentioned in section 10." Prohibited grounds include "race, colour, sex, gender identity or expression, pregnancy, sexual orientation, civil status, age except as provided by law, religion, political convictions, language, ethnic or national origin, social condition, a handicap or the use of any means to palliate a handicap". Furthermore, section 16 of the Charter states that "[n]o one may practise discrimination in respect of the . . . conditions of employment of a person". Sexual harassment thus falls under the general category of "Charter-based harassment" in the realm of work. In the absence of repetition of the harassing behaviour, discrimination under sections 10 and 16 of the Charter can still be found.

For the purposes of this chapter, the term "sexual harassment" includes both harassment of a sexual nature and harassment because of a worker's gender that, while involving a misogynist animus or sexist overtones, is not necessarily of a sexual nature. The first type of sexual harassment is defined as "quid pro quo harassment", while the second is referred to as "poisoned work environment" or gender-based harassment.[11] Quid pro quo harassment is "unwelcome conduct of a

10 Paula McDonald, Sara Charlesworth, & Tina Graham, Workplace Sexual Harassment 30 Years on: A Review of the Literature, 53 *Asia Pacific Journal of Human Resources*, 1, pp. 41–58 (2015).

11 Rachel Cox & Geneviève Richard, Harcèlement psychologique et harcèlement discriminatoire, in JurisClasseur Québec (ed.), *Collection Rapports individuels et collectifs du travail, Fascicule 23.1* (Montréal: Lexis Nexis Canada, 2020) [JCQ Fas. 23.1].

sexual nature that detrimentally affects the work environment or leads to adverse job-related consequences for the victims of the harassment".[12] Gender-based or "poisoned work environment" harassment is

> more subtle, more insidious than harassment of a sexual nature. Typically no part of this type of situation suggests seduction. To the contrary, the comments, actions and gestures come together to demonstrate the inadequacy of the person in her work environment, generally male-dominated, but not exclusively either, simply because she is characterised by one of the grounds enumerated by section 10 of the Charter, in this case, because she is a woman. [author's translation][13]

Historically, a non-unionised victim of sexual harassment could bring a civil suit based on the Charter, as well as the general provisions of the Québec Civil Code on the employment contract. Today, however, the Labour Tribunal would appear to have exclusive jurisdiction over litigation resulting from psychological harassment at work,[14] although the Superior Court has left the door open to argument that this is not the case when the psychological harassment also constitutes a violation of the Charter.[15] In any case, the vast majority of non-unionised workers will turn to some form of administrative recourse to enforce their rights rather than the courts, given the prohibitive cost of bringing a civil suit.

To illustrate, the *Commission des droits de la personne et des droits de la jeunesse du Québec* (CDPDJQ), or Québec Human Rights and Youth Rights Commission (hereinafter Human Rights Commission), is responsible for processing complaints of violations of section 10, 10.1 or 16 of the Charter. If a complaint is admissible, the Human Rights Commission conducts an investigation. If it considers that the complaint has merit, it attempts to foster the negotiation of a settlement between the parties. In the absence of a settlement, the Human Rights Commission may bring the complaint forward to the *Tribunal des droits de la personne du Québec*, or Québec Human Rights Tribunal, a judicial court created in 1990 with broad-based remedial powers to ensure implementation of the right to equality guaranteed by the Québec Charter. If the Human Rights Commission refers a complaint to the Tribunal, it then assumes carriage of the complaint and offers free legal representation to the complainant. However, we will see that in recent years, various legislative and case law developments have considerably reduced the Human Rights Tribunal's jurisdiction with respect to sexual harassment at work.

12 Janzen c. Platy Enterprises Ltd., 1989 CanLII 97 (CSC), [1989] 1 RCS 1252, page 1284, https://canlii.ca/t/1ft75.

13 Commission des droits de la personne et des droits de la jeunesse (Lippé) c. Québec (Procureur général), 1998 CanLII 30 (QC TDP), https://canlii.ca/t/1fvm8, paragraph 167 [CDPDJQ (Lippé)].

14 See section 5, paragraph d and Annex I of the Act to establish the Administrative Labour Tribunal, RLRQ, ch. T-15.1.

15 Hardy c. Financière Banque Nationale inc., 2009 QCCS 5789 (CanLII), https://canlii.ca/t/273kt.

For example, in 1996, the Supreme Court of Canada ruled that if harassment at work causes physical or psychological incapacity, exclusive recourse for damages incurred during the period of incapacity lies with a claim for employment injury under workers' compensation legislation.[16] The claim is filed with the *Commission des normes, de l'équité, de la santé et de la sécurité du travail* (CNESST), or Labour Standards, Pay Equity and Work Health and Safety Commission (hereinafter the *CNESST*), which renders a decision on the claim in the context of an administrative process. This decision can then be appealed to the Labour Tribunal. As we shall see later, the no-fault and medico-legal nature of the regime, as well as its lack of adaptation to mental health claims in general, has led to difficulties for claimants who have suffered sexual harassment at work.[17]

Furthermore, when sexual harassment occurs in relation to work in a unionised workplace, since 2003, recourse in case of Charter-based harassment lies with grievance arbitration under the collective agreement.[18] In Québec, grievance arbitrators specialised in labour relations, rather than human rights adjudicators, now hear sexual harassment cases brought by unionised workers.[19]

Finally, in 2004, the Québec legislature recognised employees' right to a work environment free from psychological harassment under the Labour Standards Act[20] (hereinafter LSA), forbidding any vexatious behaviour that affects an employee's dignity and results in a harmful work environment (s. 81.19, LSA). Sexual harassment as well as other types of Charter-based harassment are included in the definition of psychological harassment. In 2018, Québec codified in part this interpretation of the definition of psychological harassment to specifically include harassment "of a sexual nature" (s. 81.18, LSA).

The provisions on psychological harassment are deemed to be an integral part of every collective agreement. Unionised employees must therefore exercise the recourse provided for in their collective agreement, which is to say a grievance. For non-unionised workers, recourse in case of psychological harassment lies with a complaint at the CNESST. The CNESST conducts an investigation

16 Béliveau St-Jacques c. Fédération des employées et employés, 1996 CanLII 208 (CSC), [1996] 2 RCS 345, https://canlii.ca/t/1fr86 [Béliveau St. Jacques].

17 Louise Langevin, Le harcèlement sexuel au travail: l'impact de l'affaire Béliveau Saint-Jacques, 9 *Revue Femmes et Droit*, pp. 17–45 (1997); Rachel Cox, From Sexual to Psychological Harassment: One Step Forward, Twenty-Five Years Back for Women's Equality at Work? in S. Day, L. Lamarche, & K. Norman (eds.), *Arguments in Favour of Human Rights Institutions* (Toronto: Irwin Law, 2014), Vol. 14, pp 237–278 [Cox 2014].

18 Denis Nadeau, La perméabilité du droit au sein des rapports collectifs du travail et la compétence arbitrale: nouveau regard sur la valse-hésitation de la Cour suprême du Canada, 69 *Revue du Barreau*, pp. 219–252 (2010).

19 In practise, however, most sexual harassment grievances are settled by the parties rather than the subject of grievance arbitration. In this chapter, we do not examine the small number of grievance arbitration awards that involve sexual harassment. For a rare arbitration award on sexual harassment, see 9008–4062 Québec inc (Frutta'si) c Travailleurs et travailleuses unis de l'alimentation et du commerce, local 500, (2010) AZ-50702654 (Azimut) (QCTA).

20 Act respecting Labour Standards, RLRQ, Ch. N-1.1.

into the complaint. It attempts to foster the negotiation of a settlement between the parties. In the absence of a settlement, if it considers that the complaint has merit, the CNESST refers the complaint to the Labour Tribunal and offers free legal representation to the complainant. Whereas a workers' compensation claim is actually decided by the Health and Safety Division of the CNESST, in the context of Labour Standards, the Labour Relations Division of the CNESST is simply responsible for intake and, if applicable, carriage of the complaint before the Labour Tribunal.

Since the coming into effect of Québec's legislation on psychological harassment in 2004, multiple cases where facts amount to sexual harassment (defined largely as above) have been framed as complaints of psychological harassment. In theory, non-unionised workers still have the choice to file a complaint of sexual harassment under the Québec Charter rather than filing a psychological harassment complaint under the LSA, but they rarely choose to do so.[21] Indeed, the practise of the Human Rights Commission is to encourage workers who have been sexually harassed at work to file a complaint of psychological harassment at the CNESST.[22] Only if the harasser is a third party to the employment relationship does the Human Rights Commission proceed with the complaint.[23] A Belgian study suggests that women find it less stigmatising to complain of psychological harassment at work than of sexual harassment.[24] Further research is necessary to determine if, beyond institutional practises of directing sexually harassed workers to the CNESST rather than the Human Rights Commission, other factors are also at play in the trend towards recourse for psychological rather than sexual harassment in Québec.

3 Sexual Harassment as an Industrial Accident

In 1996, the Supreme Court of Canada decided that the provisions of the Act Respecting Industrial Accidents and Occupational Diseases,[25] granting employers civil immunity in case of employment injury, prevail over the remedial provisions of the Québec Charter.[26] Thus, if harassment at work causes physical or psychological incapacity, exclusive recourse for damages incurred during the period of incapacity lies with a claim for employment injury under workers' compensation legislation.[27] What's more, in 1998, the Québec Court of Appeal ruled that even

21 Cox, supra n. 17.

22 JCQ Fas. 23.1, supra n. 11.

23 See for example Commission des droits de la personne et des droits de la jeunesse (C.P.) c. Busrel inc., 2021 QCTDP 5 (CanLII), https://canlii.ca/t/jdk68 [CDPDJQ v Busrel inc.].

24 Ada Garcia, Bernard Hacourt, & Virginie Bara. Harcèlement moral et sexuel: Stratégies d'adaptation et conséquences sur la santé des travailleurs et des travailleuses, 7 *Perspectives interdisciplinaires sur le travail et la santé (PISTES)*, 3, p. 8 (2005), available at https://journals.openedition.org/pistes/.

25 RLRQ, ch. A-3.001.

26 Béliveau St. Jacques, supra n. 16.

27 JCQ Fas. 23.1, supra n. 11.

if a sexually harassed worker has not actually filed a claim for workers' compensation, once their health has been compromised, the bar on any civil or Charter-based recourse stands.[28]

Under the workers' compensation legislation, sexual harassment is considered as a work-related or "industrial accident", defined as "a sudden and unforeseen event, attributable to any cause, which happens to a person" (AIAOD, s. 2). The consequences of the harassment are medicalised, as in order to file a claim at the CNESST, a doctor must make a diagnosis of the harassed worker's "illness":

> While the harasser remains at work, the harassed woman must undergo psychiatric evaluation by her own doctor or psychiatrist, and more often than not, by a psychiatrist hired by the employer. This further draws the legal debate to her mental health, the inadequacies of her personal and family life, her personality flaws, and weaknesses . . . rather than those of the harasser. The existence of these psychiatric expert reports may then find their way into the evidence in . . . hearings on psychological harassment, discrediting the target of harassment. [references omitted][29]

As Finn Makela points out, "the workplace accident compensation regime posits the victim as the site of regulation" and the consequences of sexual harassment "are transformed into symptoms of mental illness for the purposes of indemnification".[30] In this context, workers who have experienced violence or other trauma in the past may find it more difficult to obtain compensation than workers who have not experienced violence in the past.[31]

Specifically, in one Labour Tribunal decision, after an apprentice roofer refused sexual advances by a co-worker and then was not called back to work, a doctor she consulted for "uncontrolled crying" and "extreme stress" indicated "harassment" and then "harassment and job loss" on her medical certificate. Citing the absence of a prescription for medication or referral for psychological treatment, the Labour Tribunal ultimately refused the worker's claim, finding that she had not proved that she was afflicted by an "incapacitating pathology".[32]

Furthermore, the worker must prove that there is a relationship between her diagnosis and the harassment suffered at work. Psychological injury caused by dismissal itself falls outside the ambit of workers' compensation law. In another case, a newly hired factory worker was fired after reporting several instances of

28 Commission des droits de la personne et des droits de la jeunesse (Beaudet) c. Genest, 1997 CanLII 66 (QC TDP), https://canlii.ca/t/1fvd7, inf. [2001] AZ-50082198 (Azimut) (QC CA), leave to appeal to Supreme Court of Canada refused, 28436 (September 20, 2001). This is so whether it be a claim against their employer or the co-worker who harassed them.

29 Cox 2014, supra n. 17, pages 270–271.

30 Finn Makela, "Tell Me Where It Hurts": Workplace Sexual Harassment Compensation and the Regulation of Hysterical Victims, 51 *McGill Law Review*, pp. 27–46, page 37 (2006).

31 Cox 2014, supra n. 17.

32 Guay et Couvreur Roland Boudreault, 2019 QCTAT 5510 (CanLII), https://canlii.ca/t/j3x7c.

unwanted sexual touching and harassment by her foreman.[33] The Tribunal ruled that the causal relationship between the sexual harassment established by the evidence and the woman's psychological injury had not been established, as the judge considered that her injury was more related to distress subsequent to being dismissed after reporting the harassment than the harassment itself.[34]

Likewise, in another decision,[35] an accusation of criminal assault was laid against a corner store employee who, after harassing a cashier for months, ultimately sexually assaulted her. (Eventually, the harasser was absolved of the charge of common assault after he agreed to pay 400$ in fees.) After considering the treating doctor's diagnosis of "post-traumatic stress", the Tribunal nonetheless rejected the woman's claim, finding that the behaviour in question had clearly made the woman angry but did not cause her intense fear, helplessness or horror as required by the DSM-5's definition of post-traumatic stress syndrome.[36]

In contrast, the case law of the Human Rights Tribunal reflects a more informed approach to reprisals endured by women who report sexual harassment, especially in male-dominated work environments:

> In a traditionally masculine environment where integration of women is only just beginning, any form of expression of refusal or rejection of behaviour of a sexual nature is likely to have the opposite effect and provoke a reaction of intensification of the behaviour in question.[37]

While the "sudden and unforeseen event" required by the definition of an industrial accident can be proven through a series of micro-traumatisms, the sum of the events must nevertheless "go beyond the ordinary course of work activities" and be of an "objectively traumatic nature".[38] In one decision, the Tribunal rejected the claim of an indigenous officer working on an indigenous police force who had been subject to gender harassment culminating in a sudden physical assault – supposedly to enable her to hone her reflexes – by an openly hostile male colleague. In addition to the assault, and in spite of evidence of "undesirable and disrespectful" behaviour by several male colleagues, the Tribunal nonetheless rejected the woman officer's claim. The judge found that "objectively speaking", the events did not go beyond what was to be expected in the ordinary and foreseeable course of events in the tension-fraught work environment that prevailed in the police force at the time.

33 Compagnie A et D.V., 2018 QCTAT 1139 (CanLII), https://canlii.ca/t/hqt43.

34 See also E.G. et Compagnie A, [2005] AZ-50336721 (CLP), conf. [2006] AZ-50367337 (Azimut) (CLP).

35 M.V. et Compagnie A, 2014 QCCLP 1981 (CanLII), https://canlii.ca/t/g6d13.

36 American Psychiatric Association, *DSM-5: Diagnostic and Statistical Manual of Mental Disorders* (5th ed., Arlington, VA: American Psychiatric Association, 2013).

37 CDPDJQ (Lippé), supra n. 13.

38 Katherine Lippel & Rachel Cox, Droit de la santé au travail régissant les problèmes de santé mentale: prévention, indemnisation et réadaptation, in JurisClasseur Québec (ed.), *Collection Santé et Sécurité du Travail, Fascicule 27* (LexisNexis Canada, 2020) [JCQ Fas. 27].

On the one hand, framing sexual harassment as an industrial accident within a no-fault regime medicalises the victim and may have the effect of removing sexual harassment from the purview of the law. On the other, if the claim is accepted by the CNESST, the workers' compensation regime provides immediate access to income replacement benefits based on 90% of net annual income, as well as priority access to paid health care including psychotherapy. Benefits continue until the worker's injury is considered to be consolidated, and even for a longer period of time if the worker cannot return to her job and professional rehabilitation is necessary for her to obtain other, suitable employment. Thus, in spite of the egregious lack of fit between the concept of sexual harassment (the foreseeable consequence of unequal relationships between women and men) and the definition of an industrial accident ("a sudden and unforeseen event"), the workers' compensation regime has the potential to offer timely income support to sexually harassed workers who are temporarily unable to work. Receipt of income replacement benefits may help to avoid financial stress or even ruin, while access to paid psychotherapy may offer much-needed support. We note that over a four-year period (2016–2019), approximately one out of every two claims for "sexual harassment" (as defined by the CNESST coding system) was accepted (86 claims out of 166), either initially or on appeal.[39]

In terms of which recourse is available to the target of sexual harassment at work, much rests on whether health has been affected. Once the worker's health has been compromised, the remedies available to her under the Charter through a complaint to the Human Rights Commission (or a civil suit) or under the provisions of the LSA on psychological harassment are severely restricted. Specifically, under the LSA, once it finds psychological harassment, the Labour Tribunal can order reinstatement, lost wages, reasonable action to put a stop to the harassment, punitive and moral damages, an indemnity for loss of employment, payment of psychological support and modification of the disciplinary record of the employee. However, the Tribunal cannot make an order regarding lost wages, punitive and moral damages or payment for psychological support for "a period during which the employee is suffering from an employment injury" (s. 123.16, LSA). To make matters worse, the case law has established that the "period during which the employee is suffering from an employment injury" may in fact precede the period of work stoppage and persist after return to work,[40] thus adding a whole new dimension of uncertainty as to which remedies are available and when.

4 Sexual Harassment as Psychological Harassment

In Québec, the LSA recognised the right to a work environment free from psychological harassment in 2004. Following the rise of the #MeToo movement

39 CNESST, Statistiques sur la violence, le stress et le harcèlement en milieu de travail 2016–2019, CNESST, 2020, page 27, www.cnesst.gouv.qc.ca/sites/default/files/documents/statistiques-2016-2019-violence-stress-harcelement.pdf.

40 JCQ Fas. 23.1, supra n. 11.

in Québec and in an attempt to improve public confidence in the legal system, in 2018 the definition of psychological harassment was amended to explicitly include behaviour of a sexual nature:

> "psychological harassment" means any vexatious behaviour in the form of repeated and hostile or unwanted conduct, verbal comments, actions or gestures, that affects an employee's dignity or psychological or physical integrity and that results in a harmful work environment for the employee. For greater certainty, psychological harassment includes such behaviour in the form of such verbal comments, actions or gestures of a sexual nature.
>
> (s. 81.18, LSA)

The 2018 modifications to the LSA also extended employers' obligations with respect to prevention to include behaviour "of a sexual nature"[41] as well as with respect to psychological harassment in general:

> 81.19 Every employee has a right to a work environment free from psychological harassment.
>
> Employers must take reasonable action to prevent psychological harassment and, whenever they become aware of such behaviour, to put a stop to it. They must, in particular, adopt and make available to their employees a psychological harassment prevention and complaint processing policy that includes, in particular, a section on behaviour that manifests itself in the form of verbal comments, actions or gestures of a sexual nature.

At the same time, the remedial provision of the LSA was amended to allow the tribunal to take into account "the discriminatory nature of the behaviour", which would include Charter-based harassment such as sexual harassment.

The modifications to the definition of psychological harassment and to requirements for prevention policies raise two issues. First, the choice to name harassing behaviour of a sexual nature rather than all types of sexual harassment, as in the human rights definition, can be questioned. Margaret Thornton remarks that in general, singling out harassment of a sexual nature perpetuates "the conventional gendering of [the workplace]":[42]

> the more the harassing conduct is like heterosexed activity (conceptualised in terms of an active male harasser and a passive female "victim") the more likely it is to be accepted as sexual harassment. The less *sexualised*, albeit sexed, the harassing conduct is, the more likely it is to be normalised within

41 Interaction, or rather the lack of interaction, between this provision and the general prevention regime under Québec's Act respecting occupational health and safety, RLRQ, Ch. S-2.1, is an interesting subject but one that goes beyond the scope of this chapter.

42 Margaret Thornton, Sexual Harassment Losing Sight of Sex Discrimination, 26 *Melbourne University Law Review*, 2, 422, p. 425 (2002).

> the workplace and the more difficult it is for the complainant to obtain a remedy.[43]

Second, the choice to locate recourse for sexual harassment within the paradigm of dignity at work associated with the right to a work environment free from psychological harassment, rather than within the paradigm of equality associated with recourse under the Charter, has also drawn criticism. Amongst other things, framing sexual harassment as psychological harassment minimises the fact that sexual harassment is a form of violence against women and an integral part of systemic discrimination against women in the world of work.

At the time of the 2018 reform of the LSA, a provision was adopted in order to facilitate "cooperative arrangements" between the CNESST and the Human Rights Commission with respect to "any complaint that concerns discriminatory behaviour" (s. 123.6, LSA). However, by all accounts, so far little has come of the agreement eventually entered into by the two institutions.[44]

The lack of cooperation between the CNESST and the Human Rights Commission is particularly concerning given the fact that even when confronted with clear evidence of sexual harassment as defined by the Charter, the Labour Tribunal may nonetheless reject a complaint for psychological harassment "of a sexual nature". The reasons for this include the weighty burden of proof associated with the definition of psychological harassment and the de facto obligation to report psychological harassment, as well as the possibility that the complaint will be rejected if the employer demonstrates that he or she has taken all reasonable means to prevent or stop the harassment.

To illustrate, for a psychological harassment complaint to be accepted, several elements must be proven: vexatious behaviour, the repetitive and unwanted nature of the behaviour, that the employee's dignity was affected by the behaviour, and that the behaviour resulted in a harmful work environment for the employee.[45] A single serious incidence of vexatious behaviour may also constitute psychological harassment as long it has a lasting harmful effect on the employee.

In one psychological harassment case, the Tribunal focused on a single event where the complainant's supervisor climbed into bed with her and touched her breast during a company retreat. However, the judge chose to minimise the vexatious nature of the harasser's behaviour at other times. Although it concluded that the complainant had been the victim of sexual assault, the Tribunal looked at the event through the lens of a single serious incidence of vexatious behaviour. Given that it did not find that the sexual assault had had the required "lasting harmful effect" on the worker, the complaint was rejected.[46] Although the worker's complaint for wrongful dismissal in the wake of the events was successful, both the

43 Ibid.

44 JCQ Fas. 23.1, paragraphs 103–104, supra n. 11.

45 See section 81.18, Act respecting labour standards, RLRQ, ch. N-1.1.

46 Lizotte c. Alimentation Coop La Pocatière, 2008 QCCRT 240 (CanLII), https://canlii.ca/t/1xbc6, conf. 2008 QCCRT 521 (CanLII), https://canlii.ca/t/22170.

harasser and the employer were effectively absolved of any responsibility for the sexually harassing behaviour inflicted on the complainant. The sexual harassment per se was erased from the portrait of wrongdoing.

In another case, the Labour Tribunal found that there had been repeated, unwanted vexatious behaviour of a sexual nature on the part of the complainant's colleague: mimicking sexual intercourse by rubbing his genitals against the complainant from behind, placing his hands on her hips and so forth. The judge described the behaviour as "appalling and deplorable". The complainant testified that she had not reported the sexual harassment out of fear that she would lose her job. The judge nonetheless concluded that the behaviour had not resulted in a harmful work environment for the complainant, amongst other things because of humoristic email exchanges and certain socialising between the complainant and the harasser a year later. Shortly after a further incident with the harasser that the Tribunal qualified as the culmination of a "personality conflict" between the complainant and the harasser, the complainant left work and was diagnosed with depression and anxiety with elements of post-traumatic stress. Her psychological harassment complaint was rejected for lack of evidence of a harmful work environment, and her workers' compensation claim was refused for lack of overriding evidence that her medical condition was related to events at work.[47] Again, both the harasser and the employer were effectively absolved of any responsibility for the sexual harassment inflicted on the complainant.

A second way in which facts of sexual harassment may be disqualified when framed as psychological harassment has to do with the de facto obligation to report psychological harassment. Employers must "take reasonable action to prevent psychological harassment and, whenever they become aware of such behaviour, to put a stop to it." According to the case law, if an employer has a complaint processing policy, and the employee being harassed does not report the harassment in a timely fashion, the employer is considered to have taken reasonable precautions to prevent the harassment. In more than one instance where sexual harassment was framed as psychological harassment, the obligation to report has led to the rejection of the complaint.[48]

In contrast, in a human rights framework, the presence of a harassment policy cannot serve to attack the complainant's credibility if she delays in reporting the harassment, let alone lead to refusal of her complaint.[49] As one decision of the Human Rights Tribunal points out that

> the gestures, comments, attitudes and harassing behaviours are rarely if ever publicized. The victim endures them, and experiences them in a

47 Bonneau et Reitmans Canada ltée, 2018 QCTAT 2823 (CanLII), https://canlii.ca/t/hsh7b.

48 Beaulieu et 9015–6308 Québec inc. (Pizzeria Stratos Ste-Jeanne-d'Arc), 2017 QCTAT 5777 (CanLII), https://canlii.ca/t/hpjkk. See also Lachapelle-Welman et 3233430 Canada inc. (Portes et fenêtres ADG), 2016 QCTAT 3557 (CanLII), https://canlii.ca/t/gs3t3.

49 Commission des droits de la personne et des droits de la jeunesse (Pavilus) c Québec (Procureur général), 2008 QCTDP 8 (CanLII), https://canlii.ca/t/1w4qm.

> one-on-one context in which it inevitably it is up to her to report her colleague or supervisor in order to have a work environment free from harassment. Reporting does not happen smoothly or without fear. [author's translation][50]

A third illustration of how sexual harassment can be negated when it is framed as psychological harassment is if the employer demonstrates having taken reasonable means to prevent the harassment. For example, in one case the employer was a business offering cleaning services to hotels.[51] A cleaning woman was sexually assaulted by a hotel client in a hotel room. The Tribunal decided that the employer – the cleaning service – had taken all reasonable means to stop the harassment, amongst other things by assigning the cleaner to another floor and reporting the incident to the hotel. The complaint for psychological harassment was rejected.[52]

In contrast to the reasonable means obligation with respect to psychological harassment, the Charter imposes a performance obligation on employers to prevent Charter-based harassment.[53] Indeed, the Supreme Court of Canada has cautioned against an overly narrow approach to Charter-based or discriminatory harassment based solely on discrimination or wrongdoing by employers:

> Consider an employee who endures years of discriminatory harassment at the hands of a co-worker who commits that harassment covertly, such that the employer is unaware of it despite exercising diligent supervision. Under the narrow approach, this may not be discrimination "regarding employment" as the employer is unaware of the discrimination and thus may not be faulted for not intervening. A perverse consequence flows from this: as long the employer acted with reasonable diligence, the Tribunal may find that the complainant never suffered discrimination "regarding employment" for the period leading up to the moment when he or she finally musters the courage to report the years of abuse by their co-worker.[54]

Unfortunately, this is precisely the "perverse consequence" that occurs when sexual harassment that has not been reported in a timely manner is framed as psychological harassment. No matter how egregious the harasser's behaviour was, a complaint will be rejected if the employer was not made aware of it.

50 CDPDJQ (Lippé), supra n. 13.

51 Rodriguez Vergara c. 9169–1022 Québec inc., 2009 QCCRT 224 (CanLII), https://canlii.ca/t/23svg.

52 See also Maafi c. Aro inc., 2009 QCCRT 515 (CanLII), https://canlii.ca/t/26wpd.

53 See Robichaud c Canada (Conseil du trésor), [1987] 2 RCS 84, p. 90.

54 British Columbia Human Rights Tribunal v Schrenk, 2017 SCC 62 (CanLII), [2017] 2 SCR 795, paragraph 57, https://canlii.ca/t/hpb2k.

5 Pragmatic Considerations in Comparing Avenues of Recourse

One study of decisions on complaints for psychological harassment in the form of gender-based harassment and harassment of a sexual nature found that all but one of the 48 complainants – all non-unionised – had lost their jobs.[55] Not surprisingly, then, over a third of them (18 of the 48 complainants) had also filed complaints for wrongful dismissal (under s. 124, LSA) or prohibited reprisals after the exercise of a right under the Labour Standards Act (under s. 122, LSA). In certain circumstances, the LSA reverses the burden of proof through a rebuttable presumption of, respectively, dismissal without just and sufficient cause, or prohibited action because the employee has exercised a right under the Act. The Québec Charter contains no such presumption. Together with the possibility of filing all possible complaints – prohibited reprisal action, wrongful dismissal, psychological harassment – with the same institution (specifically the CNESST), the presumption means that in certain circumstances, the labour law framework could be more appropriate than the human rights framework for a sexually harassed worker who has lost her job.

In terms of delay, the labour law framework is considerably more rapid than the human rights framework. It takes an average of 22 months for the Labour Tribunal to render a decision on a complaint of psychological harassment. In contrast, many human rights complaints take over four years to reach the Human Rights Tribunal, given the gatekeeping role of the understaffed and notoriously bureaucratic Human Rights Commission.[56]

In terms of remedies, we note that workers' compensation is a no-fault regime. Although the worker may file a successful claim without proving the responsibility of the harasser or the employer, no remedies are available beyond compensation of the injured worker.

As previously stated, to the extent that harassment does not compromise their health, non-unionised workers who are victims of sexual harassment can file a complaint for psychological harassment at the CNESST. In spite of the fact that the psychological harassment provisions were intended to come into play *before* the worker's health is affected,[57] sexually harassed workers generally only file a complaint when they can no longer function at work or they no longer have any prospect of keeping their job.[58] However, even when a complaint of

55 Rachel Cox & Caroline Brodeur, La réforme des dispositions sur le harcèlement psychologique dans la Loi sur les normes du travail: l'appel à une plus grande sensibilité au genre sera-t-il entendu? 51 *Revue de droit d'Ottawa*, 1, pp. 51–97 (2020) [Cox and Brodeur 2020]. Eight of 48 complainants were men.

56 Ibid.

57 Cox 2014, supra n. 17.

58 Amy Blackstone, Christopher Uggen, & Heather McLaughlin, Legal Consciousness and Responses to Sexual Harassment, 43 *Law & Society Review*, 3, pp. 631–668 (2009); Laura K. Brunner & Maryanne Dever, Work, Bodies and Boundaries: Talking Sexual Harassment in the New Economy, 21 *Gender, Work and Organisation*, 5, pp. 459–471 (2014).

harassment under the LSA is successful, in reality, complainants are not reinstated. The Labour Tribunal awards monetary damages or, more often, reserves jurisdiction to allow the parties to negotiate damages.[59] Theoretically, the remedial powers of the Labour Tribunal allow for specific performance remedies, such as posting of the decision in the workplace where the harassment occurred, but so far, no remedies other than damages have been awarded to victims of sexual harassment under psychological harassment law.

Under the Charter, the Human Rights Tribunal has broad remedial powers to order "any measure of redress it considers appropriate", including reinstatement, indemnity for loss of employment, training on sexual harassment, adoption of a policy against sexual harassment and formation of a committee on sexual harassment.[60] However, these powers have not been used with respect to individual complaints of sexual harassment. In a recent, rare decision on the complaint of sexual and racist harassment brought by a temporary employment agency worker against a client of the agency and its supervising employee who harassed her, the Human Rights Tribunal awarded 5,000$ in moral damages. The Tribunal took a "silo" or single-axis approach to Charter-based harassment, affirming that "each of the grounds protected by section 10 of the Charter invoked in support of the alleged discrimination is an autonomous part of the elements that generate or encourage the discrimination".[61] A classic, intersectional human rights approach to sexual harassment implies recognition that sexual harassment of racialised women is qualitatively different to sexual harassment of non-racialised women,[62] and that to consider each prohibited ground of discrimination in an atomised fashion is to make invisible "how race and gender operate together to make black women's experiences of discrimination . . . particular".[63] Given that the complainant was of Haitian origin and that the harasser made blatantly stereotyped and biased comments about Haitian men and women, the Tribunal's approach is even more surprising. In short, in spite of the broad remedial powers of the Human Rights Tribunal, it would seem that systemic remedies for individual complaints of sexual harassment are not found in Québec Human Rights Tribunal case law any more than they are in Labour Tribunal case law.

Finally, the modest amounts awarded as damages in harassment cases brought under the LSA have been the object of criticism.[64] The 2018 amendment

59 Cox & Brodeur 2020, supra n. 55.

60 See sections 49 and 80 as well as section 111 of the Québec Charter. See also Commission des droits de la personne et des droits de la jeunesse (Beaudoin et autres) c. Gaz métropolitain inc., 2008 QCTDP 24 (CanLII), https://canlii.ca/t/20pxl.

61 CDPDJQ v Busrel inc., supra n. 23, paragraph 51.

62 Baylis-Flannery v DeWilde (Tri Community Physiotherapy), 2003 HRTO 28, paragraph 145.

63 Jennifer Nash, Theorizing Race, Theorizing Racism: New Directions in Interdisciplinary Scholarship, in Margaret Davies & Vanessa E. Munro (eds.), *The Ashgate Research Companion to Feminist Legal Theory* (Farnham: Ashgate, 2013), pages 125–138 at page 128.

64 Cox & Brodeur 2020, supra n. 55. See also Audra Ranalli & Bruce Ryder, Undercompensating for Discrimination: An Empirical Study of General Damages Awards Issued by the Human Rights Tribunal of Ontario, 2000–15, 13 *Journal of Law & Equality*, p. 91 (2017).

allowing the Labour Tribunal to take into account the discriminatory nature of the impugned behaviour leaves some hope that this situation will improve over the coming years.

6 Conclusion

In Québec, a multi-pronged trend has emerged of conceptualisation of violation of the right to a work environment free from sexual harassment within labour law frameworks. First, any worker who becomes incapacitated as a result of sexual harassment is considered to have suffered an industrial accident. Second, since adoption of the legislation on psychological harassment, litigants often frame facts amounting to sexual harassment as psychological harassment rather than as sexual harassment per se. Third, unionised workers no longer have access to human rights adjudicators if they suffer sexual harassment at work. Fourth, although formally, non-unionised workers still have access to human rights adjudicators if they suffer sexual harassment at work, they rarely use this access, nor are they encouraged to do so by the Québec Human Rights Commission.

From a pragmatic point of view, labour law frameworks have certain advantages for complainants. They provide more timely resolution of complaints and claims than the more bureaucratic human rights regime. They offer a single portal to file complaints for sexual harassment and other violations of Labour Standards, as well as claims for workers' compensation. Moreover, if the claim is accepted, the workers' compensation regime provides income replacement benefits which have the potential to stem secondary victimisation of the harassed worker by offering income stability and other benefits while she recovers and, if necessary, searches for alternative employment.

However, both the provisions on psychological harassment and the definition of an employment injury – and more specifically an "industrial accident" – can literally make sexual harassment disappear. Not only is sexual harassment no longer named as such, but even when sexual harassment is proven, it may not fit all the criterion for psychological harassment or an industrial accident. In this sense, as we have seen, labour law frameworks may have the unfortunate effect of negating sexual harassment as a prohibited practise.

Following a 2018 reform, attempts to harmonise psychological harassment law with human rights principles by naming behaviour "of a sexual nature" in the definition of psychological harassment and requiring a prevention policy for such harassment have so far remained largely symbolic. Expanded remedial power mandating the Labour Tribunal to take into account "the discriminatory nature of the behaviour" in determining compensation for psychological harassment has perhaps increased the amount of damages awarded in certain cases,[65] but not led

65 See for example Prado Paredes et Entreprise de placement Les Progrès inc., 2019 QCTAT 4593 (CanLII), <https://canlii.ca/t/j2xgw>.

to remedies of a more systemic nature, although interpretation of this provision may yet evolve.

In short, given their undeniable advantages in terms of delay, the simplicity of a single portal, and in the case of workers' compensation, the possibility of obtaining income replacement benefits without litigation, recourse for victims of sexual harassment at work under labour law frameworks cannot be dismissed. Nonetheless, important questions remain in terms of how to improve the interaction between human rights frameworks and labour law frameworks so that all workers can enjoy their fundamental right to a work environment free from sexual harassment and have access to effective, timely recourse in case of violation of this right. Further steps must be taken in order for Québec's legal framework to embody the "inclusive, integrated and gender-responsive approach" to ending sexual harassment at work put forward in the ILO's Violence and Harassment Convention (C-190).

Acknowledgement

The author would like to thank the anonymous reviewers for their astute and helpful comments on this chapter.

Bibliography

Books

American Psychiatric Association. *DSM-5: Diagnostic and Statistical Manual of Mental Disorders*, 5th ed., Arlington, Virginia (USA), American Psychiatric Association, 2013.

MacKinnon, Catharine A. *The Sexual Harassment of Working Women: A Case of Sex Discrimination*, New Haven, Connecticut, Yale University Press, 1979.

MacKinnon, Catharine A. and Rebecca B. Siegel (eds). *Directions in Sexual Harassment Law*, New Haven, Connecticut (USA), Yale University Press, 2004.

Marshall, Anna-Maria. *Confronting Sexual Harassment: The Law and Politics of Everyday Life*, Aldershot, Ashgate, 2005.

Zippel, Kathrin. *The Politics of Sexual Harassment: A Comparative Study of the United States, the European Union, and Germany*, Cambridge, Cambridge University Press, 2006.

Articles and Book Chapters

Baer, Susanne. "Dignity or Equality? Responses to Workplace Harassment in European, German, and U.S. Law". In C. A. MacKinnon and R. B. Siegel (eds.), *Directions in Sexual Harassment Law*, New Haven: Yale University Press, 2004, pp. 582–601.

Bernstein, Anita. "Law, Culture, and Harassment" (1994) 142 *University of Pennsylvania Law Review* 1227–1331.

Blackstone, Amy, Christopher Uggen and Heather McLaughlin. "Legal Consciousness and Responses to Sexual Harassment" (2009) 43:3 *Law & Society Review* 631–668.

Brunner, Laura K. and Maryanne Dever. "Work, Bodies and Boundaries: Talking Sexual Harassment in the New Economy" (2014) 21:5 *Gender, Work and Organisation* 459–471.

Clarke, Linda. "Sexual Harassment Law in the United States, the United Kingdom and the European Union: Discriminatory Wrongs and Dignitary Harms" (2007) 36 *Common Law World Review* 79–105.

Cox, Rachel. "From Sexual to Psychological Harassment: One Step Forward, Twenty-Five Years Back for Women's Equality at Work?". In S. Day, L. Lamarche and K. Norman (eds.), *14 Arguments in Favour of Human Rights Institutions*, Toronto: Irwin Law, 2014, pp. 237–278.

Cox, Rachel and Caroline Brodeur. "La réforme des dispositions sur le harcèlement psychologique dans la Loi sur les normes du travail: l'appel à une plus grande sensibilité au genre sera-t-il entendu?" (2020) 51:1 *Revue de droit d'Ottawa* 51–97.

Cox, Rachel and Geneviève Richard, "Harcèlement psychologique et harcèlement discriminatoire". In *JurisClasseur Québec*, Collection Rapports individuels et collectifs du travail, Fascicule 23.1, Montréal: Lexis Nexis Canada, 2020.

Friedman, Gabrielle S. and James Q. Whitlan. "The European Transformation of Harassment Law: Discrimination versus Dignity" (2003) *Columbia Journal of European Law* 241–274.

Garcia, Ada, Bernard Hacourt and Viriginie Bara. "Harcèlement moral et sexuel: Stratégies d'adaptation et conséquences sur la santé des travailleurs et des travailleuses" (2005) 7:3 *Perspectives interdisciplinaires sur le travail et la santé* (PISTES) 8. https://journals.openedition.org/pistes/.

Hughes, Patricia. "The Evolving Conceptual Framework of Sexual Harassment" (1994–1995) 3 *Canadian Labour & Employment Law Journal* 1–32.

Langevin, Louise. "Le harcèlement sexuel au travail: l'impact de l'affaire *Béliveau Saint-Jacques*" (1997) 9 *Revue Femmes et Droit* 17–45.

Lippel, Katherine and Rachel Cox. "Droit de la santé au travail régissant les problèmes de santé mentale: prévention, indemnisation et réadaptation". In *JurisClasseur Québec*, Collection Santé et Sécurité du Travail, Fascicule 27, Lexis Nexis Canada, 2020.

Makela, Finn. " 'Tell Me Where It Hurts': Workplace Sexual Harassment Compensation and the Regulation of Hysterical Victims" (2006) 51 *McGill Law Review* 27–46.

McDonald, Paula, Sara Charlesworth and Tina Graham. "Workplace Sexual Harassment 30 Years on: A Review of the Literature" (2015) 53:1 *Asia Pacific Journal of Human Resources* 41–58.

Nadeau, Denis. "La perméabilité du droit au sein des rapports collectifs du travail et la compétence arbitrale: nouveau regard sur la valse-hésitation de la Cour suprême du Canada" (2010) 69 *Revue du Barreau* 219–252.

Nash, Jennifer. "Theorizing Race, Theorizing Racism: New Directions in Interdisciplinary Scholarship". In Margaret Davies and Vanessa E. Munro (eds.), *The Ashgate Research Companion to Feminist Legal Theory*, Farnham: Ashgate, 2013, pp. 125–138.

Ranalli, Audra and Bruce Ryder. "Undercompensating for Discrimination: An Empirical Study of General Damages Awards Issued by the Human Rights Tribunal of Ontario, 2000–15" (2017) 13 *Journal of Law & Equality* 91.

Rimalt, Noya. "Stereotyping Women, Individualizing Harassment: The Dignitary Paradigm of Sexual Harassment Law Between the Limits of Law and the Limits of Feminism" (2007–2008) 19 *Yale Journal of Law & Feminism* 391–447.

Sheppard, Colleen. "Systemic Inequality and Workplace Culture: Challenging the Institutionalization of Sexual Harassment" (1995) 3 *Canadian Labour and Employment Law Journal* 249–286.

Thornton, Margaret. "Sexual Harassment Losing Sight of Sex Discrimination" (2002) 26:2 *Melbourne University Law Review* 422–444.

Zippel, Kathrin. "Practices of Implementation of Sexual Harassment Policies: Individual Versus Collective Strategies" (2003) 20:1 *Review of Policy Research* 175–197.

Case Law

9008–4062 Québec inc (Frutta'si) c Travailleurs et travailleuses unis de l'alimentation et du commerce, local 500, (2010) AZ-50702654 (Azimut) (QCTA).

Baylis-Flannery v DeWilde (Tri Community Physiotherapy), 2003 HRTO 28 (CanLII), <https://canlii.ca/t/1r5w0>.

Beaulieu et 9015–6308 Québec inc. (Pizzeria Stratos Ste-Jeanne-d'Arc), 2017 QCTAT 5777 (CanLII), <https://canlii.ca/t/hpjkk>.

Béliveau St-Jacques c. Fédération des employées et employés, 1996 CanLII 208 (CSC), [1996] 2 RCS 345, <https://canlii.ca/t/1fr86>.

Bonneau et Reitmans Canada ltée, 2018 QCTAT 2823 (CanLII), <https://canlii.ca/t/hsh7b>.

British Columbia Human Rights Tribunal c. Schrenk, 2017 CSC 62 (CanLII), [2017] 2 RCS 795, <https://canlii.ca/t/hpb2l>.

Commission des droits de la personne et des droits de la jeunesse (Beaudet) c. Genest, 1997 CanLII 66 (QC TDP), <https://canlii.ca/t/1fvd7>, inf. [2001] AZ-50082198 (Azimut) (C.A.), leave to appeal to Supreme Court of Canada refused, [2001] 2 S.C.R. vii.

Commission des droits de la personne et des droits de la jeunesse (Lippé) c. Québec (Procureur général), 1998 CanLII 30 (QC TDP), <https://canlii.ca/t/1fvm8>.

Commission des droits de la personne et des droits de la jeunesse (Beaudoin et autres) c. Gaz métropolitain inc., 2008 QCTDP 24 (CanLII), <https://canlii.ca/t/20pxl>.

Commission des droits de la personne et des droits de la jeunesse (Pavilus) c. Québec (Procureur général), 2008 QCTDP 8 (CanLII), <https://canlii.ca/t/1w4qm>.

Commission des droits de la personne et des droits de la jeunesse (C.P.) c. Busrel inc., 2021 QCTDP 5 (CanLII), <https://canlii.ca/t/jdk68>.

Compagnie A et D.V., 2018 QCTAT 1139 (CanLII), <https://canlii.ca/t/hqt43>.

E.G. et Compagnie A, [2005] AZ-50336721 (CLP), conf. [2006] AZ-50367337 (Azimut) (CLP).

Guay et Couvreur Roland Boudreault, 2019 QCTAT 5510 (CanLII), <https://canlii.ca/t/j3x7c>.

Hardy c. Financière Banque Nationale inc., 2009 QCCS 5789 (CanLII), <https://canlii.ca/t/273kt>.

Janzen c. Platy Enterprises Ltd., 1989 CanLII 97 (CSC), [1989] 1 RCS 1252, <https://canlii.ca/t/1ft75>.

Lachapelle-Welman et 3233430 Canada inc. (Portes et fenêtres ADG), 2016 QCTAT 3557 (CanLII), <https://canlii.ca/t/gs3t3>.

Lizotte c. Alimentation Coop La Pocatière, 2008 QCCRT 240 (CanLII), <https://canlii.ca/t/1xbc6>, conf. 2008 QCCRT 521 (CanLII), <https://canlii.ca/t/22170>.

Maafi c. Aro inc., 2009 QCCRT 515 (CanLII), <https://canlii.ca/t/26wpd>.

M.V. et Compagnie A, 2014 QCCLP 1981 (CanLII), <https://canlii.ca/t/g6d13>.

Prado Paredes et Entreprise de placement Les Progrès inc., 2019 QCTAT 4593 (CanLII), <https://canlii.ca/t/j2xgw>.

Robichaud c Canada (Conseil du trésor), [1987] 2 RCS 84.

Rodriguez Vergara c. 9169–1022 Québec inc., 2009 QCCRT 224 (CanLII), <https://canlii.ca/t/23svg>.

Laws

National

Act respecting industrial accidents and occupational diseases, RSQ 1985, ch. A-3.001.

Act respecting labour standards, RLRQ, ch. N-1.1.

Act respecting occupational health and safety, RLRQ, ch. S-2.1.

Act to establish the Administrative Labour Tribunal, RLRQ, ch. T-15.1.

Charter of Human Rights and Freedoms, RLRQ, ch.-12.

International Conventions

International Labour Organization (ILO), Violence and Harassment Convention, 2019 (No. 190), <www.ilo.org/dyn/normlex/en/f?p=1000:12100:0::NO::P12100_INSTRUMENT_ID,P12100_LANG_CODE:3999810,en:NO>.

International Labour Organization (ILO), Violence and Harassment Recommendation, 2019 (No. 206), <www.ilo.org/dyn/normlex/en/f?p=NORMLEXPUB:12100:0::NO:12100:P12100_ILO_CODE:R206:NO>.

Reports

CNESST. *Statistiques sur la violence, le stress et le harcèlement en milieu de travail 2016–2019*, CNESST (2020). <www.cnesst.gouv.qc.ca/sites/default/files/documents/statistiques-2016-2019-violence-stress-harcelement.pdf>.

Lippel, Katherine. *Addressing occupational violence: An overview of policy considerations viewed through a gender lens*, ILO, Geneva (2016). <www.ilo.org/gender/Information resources/Publications/WCMS_535656/lang – en/index.htm>.

Québec. *Rapport du Comité d'experts sur l'accompagnement des victimes d'agressions sexuelles et de violence conjugale* (2020), Québec, Canada. <www.justice.gouv.qc.ca/en/victims/consultation>.

10 Legal Instruments Against Discrimination in Employment in Switzerland

Kurt Pärli

1 Introduction

Discrimination in working life, as in other parts of the world, is also a social reality in Switzerland. Wages between women and men are still unequal despite legal measures, and senior roles are predominantly held by men. People from a migrant background have greater difficulty in gaining access to the labour market and enjoying career advancement. The same applies to people with disabilities. Other than in the area of gender equality, there are few legal instruments in Switzerland that can be used effectively against discrimination.

This chapter discusses in the first instance a few studies on the reality of discrimination in Switzerland. Second, the legal situation is explained. It will be shown, in particular, how international obligations and EU law affect Swiss law. The chapter concludes in the third instance with suggestions on how protection against discrimination could be supplemented by strengthening existing civil law instruments.

2 The Prevalence of Discrimination in Working Life

Discrimination occurs throughout the entire life cycle of an employment relationship. To mention but a few are discriminatory job advertisements and the refusal of job applications on discriminatory grounds. However, discriminatory contractual provisions or dismissals based on discriminatory grounds also happen in practice.

There is little reliable data available in Switzerland on the extent of discrimination in employment. Research into the reality of discrimination is still in its infancy. Nevertheless, a few relevant studies need to be mentioned.

In 2010, Switzerland took part in a Europe-wide survey of employees on various aspects of working conditions which was conducted by the European Foundation for Better Living and Working Conditions (Eurofound). Seven percent of the respondents claimed to have been discriminated against in the twelve months prior to the survey on the grounds of their sex, race, religion, age, nationality, disability or sexual orientation. Age discrimination was the most commonly cited by those interviewed (3%), followed by sex (reported by

DOI: 10.4324/9781003306962-13

more women [3%] than men [1%]). Discriminatory experiences based on racial, ethnic background, colour and nationality were experienced by 2% of the workers (for each form of discrimination), and 1% of those interviewed stated they had been discriminated against for reasons related to their religion, disability or sexual orientation.[1]

Beyond this empirical study, there is relatively little reliable information available in Switzerland about the nature and extent of discrimination in the world of work. The legal situation regarding discrimination on gender is the most researched. Study results regularly emerge providing evidence of wage discrepancies between women and men[2] or the negative effects of motherhood.[3] Likewise, the phenomena of the glass ceiling[4] is also well researched.[5] Some recent studies have dealt with racial discrimination in employment.[6] A heightened sensitivity to age discrimination is also evident.[7] A study confirmed that older workers who lose their job are at greater risk of experiencing long-term unemployment. The results of this study further pointed out that unemployed workers aged fifty-five and over are much less likely to be considered for hiring than those aged thirty-five with the same qualifications.[8] There is a need for sufficiently reliable empirical results on

1 Eurofound, Sixth European Working Conditions Survey: 2015, 70 (2015), available at https://www.eurofound.europa.eu/surveys/european-working-conditions-surveys/sixth-european-working-conditions-survey-2015 (accessed 30 August 2022).

2 Yves Tillé & Mihaela Catalina Anastasiades, Gender Wage Inequalities in Switzerland: The Public Versus the Private Sector, available at https://link.springer.com/article/10.1007/s10260-016-0368-5 (accessed 15 July 2020).

3 Daniel Oesch, Oliver Lips, & Patrick McDonald, The Wage Penalty for Motherhood: Evidence on Discrimination from Panel Data and a Survey Experiment for Switzerland, 37 *Demographic Research*, pp. 1793–1824 (2017), available at www.demographic-research.org/volumes/vol37/56/37-56.pdf (accessed 15 July 2020).

4 An intangible barrier within a hierarchy which prevents women and minorities obtaining upper level positions, Definition per Merriam-Webster, available at www.merriam-webster.com/dictionary/glass%20ceiling (accessed 18 February 2021).

5 Nanina Studer, Women Sell Mascara, Men Sell Machines? A Content Analysis of Gender Portrayals in Swiss Prime-Time TV Advertisements (Master Thesis, Stockholm University, Department of Media Studies, 2019, available at: https://www.diva-portal.org/smash/get/diva2:1331663/FULLTEXT01.pdf).

6 Eva Zschirnt & Rosita Fibbi, *Do Swiss Citizens of Immigrant Origin Face Hiring Discrimination in the Labour Market?*, Working Paper, NCCR Working Papers, 20 (2019), available at https://cadmus.eui.eu/handle/1814/65726; Christian Imdorf, Understanding Discrimination in Hiring Apprentices: How Training Companies Use Ethnicity to Avoid Organizational Trouble 69 *Journal of Vocational Education & Training*, 3 (2017): VET, Race and Ethnicity, available at www.tandfonline.com/doi/pdf/10.1080/13636820.2016.1278397 (accessed 15 July 2020).

7 Denis G. Humbert, Die Alterskündigung, AJP 6/2015 und Daniel Oesch Discrimination in The Hiring of Older Jobseekers: Evidence from two Survey Experiments in Switzerland (2019), OECD Bericht: Alterung und Beschäftigungspolitik Schweiz: Bessere Arbeit im Alter 123 (2014).

8 Daniel Oesch, Discrimination in The Hiring of Older Jobseekers: Evidence from Two Survey Experiments in Switzerland (2019). Hangartner D, Kopp D, Siegenthaler M: Monitoring hiring discrimination through online recruitment platforms. *Nature*, 20 January 2021. doi: 10.1038/s41586-020-03136-0.

disadvantages for employees with disabilities and those with chronic illnesses.[9] There is only limited data available on discrimination in working life on the basis of sexual orientation.[10] According to a survey by the Survey Institute (GFS), Muslims in Switzerland very often experience discrimination. For example, almost half of the Muslims interviewed stated that they had been discriminated against at least once on the grounds of their religion when looking for a job. A good third feel humiliated in their everyday working life, and eight percent of those questioned said that they had been dismissed because of their faith. The survey is not confirmed by further research. There are no sound findings on the nature and extent of discrimination on the basis of religion in employment and in particular on the basis of the Muslim faith.

The lack of data is problematic. Measuring discrimination is not meant to just serve the self-satisfaction of social science. Effective action against discrimination in all phases of an employment relationship (hiring, employment, dismissal) requires first of all, that solid empirical facts are available on this issue. Knowledge of structural discrimination is just as important. There is still much to be done in this respect. This is a job not only for the academic community but also for politicians who are called on to provide the necessary funds to finance such research.[11]

3 The Framework for Equality and Protection Against Discrimination in Employment Under International and Swiss Constitutional Law

Since the end of Second World War, protection against discrimination has been an integral part of international human rights protection.[12] Numerous international treaties contain prohibitions of discrimination, which impose on the ratifying states the obligation to provide effective protection against unequal treatment based on personal characteristics such as sex, origin, skin colour and so forth. The treaties restrict the contracting states in their scope for assessing

9 Inclusion Handicap, Schattenbericht: Bericht der Zivilgesellschaft anlässlich des ersten Staatenberichtsverfahrens vor dem UN-Ausschuss für die Rechte von Menschen mit Behinderungen 118 f. (2017), available at https://www.inclusion-handicap.ch/admin/data/files/asset/file_de/424/dok_schattenbericht_unobrk_inclusion_handicap_barrierefrei.pdf?lm=1528210534 (accessed 30 August 2022).

10 Islam IQ, Pilotstudie – Jeder zweite Muslim wird diskriminiert, available at www.islamiq.de/2018/01/03/pilotstudie-jeder-zweite-muslim-wird-diskriminiert/ (accessed 7 August 2020).

11 Kurt Pärli & Camill Oberhausser, Diskriminierungsfreie Messung der Lohngleichheit: Diskriminierungspotenzial einzelner Erklärungsfaktoren zur Messung der Lohngleichheit zwischen Frau und Mann auf gesamtwirtschaftlicher Ebene, N 51–56 (2019), available at https://jusletter.weblaw.ch/juslissues/2019/1002/diskriminierungsfrei_79fb444066.html__ONCE (accessed 16 October 2020).

12 Jörg Künzli & Walter Kälin, *The Law of International Human Rights Protection* (New York, NY: Oxford University Press, 2019), p. 335.

the reasons for which they wish to permit unequal treatment within their countries. The primary addressee of the obligations under international law is the state, one of whose duties is to ensure effective protection against discrimination among private individuals.[13] Thus, the prohibitions of discrimination relevant under international labour law have (at least) an indirect third-party effect.[14]

The following international agreements are binding on Switzerland, all of which require effective protection against discrimination, including the area of employment relationships:

- Universal Declaration of Human Rights[15]
- UN Human Rights Covenants of 1966 (UN Covenant I, ESC rights, UN Covenant II, civil and political rights)[16]
- UN Women's Rights Convention[17]
- UN Convention against Racism[18]
- UN Convention on the Rights of the Child[19]
- UN Disability Convention[20]
- Conventions No. 100 and 11 of the International Labour Organization[21]
- European Convention on Human Rights.[22]

13 Bernhard Waldmann, Das Diskriminierungsverbot von Art. 8 Abs. 2 BV als besonderer Gleichheitssatz: Unter besonderer Berücksichtigung der völkerrechtlichen Diskriminierungsverbote einerseits und der Rechtslage in den USA, in Deutschland, Frankreich sowie im europäischen Gemeinschaftsrecht anderseits 126 (2003).

14 Kurt Pärli, Freedom of contract, equal treatment and discrimination in private law employment relationships: international and constitutional law framework and significance of European Community law 221 f. (2009).

15 UN General Assembly, Universal Declaration of Human Rights (1948), U.N. GOAR, 3rd sess., Vol. I, A/RES/217(III)A, not legally binding stricto sensu but is to be considered as binding as part of customary law.

16 UN General Assembly, International Covenant on Economic, Social and Cultural Rights, International Covenant on Civil and Political Rights and Optional Protocol to the International Covenant on Civil and Political Rights (1966), U.N. GOAR, 21st sess., Supp. No. 16, A/RES/2200(XXI)A. Switzerland has signed the ESC but not yet ratified due to lack of political will.

17 UN General Assembly, Convention on the Political Rights of Women (1953), 7th sess., Supp. No. 20, A/RES/640(VII).

18 UN General Assembly, International Convention on the Elimination of all Forms of Racial Discrimination (1965), U.N. GOAR, 20th sess., Supp. No. 14, A/RES/2106(XX)A.

19 UN Commission on Human Rights, Convention on the Rights of the Child (1990), ESCOR, 46th sess., Supp. No. 2, E/CN.4/RES/1990/74.

20 UN General Assembly, Convention on the Rights of Persons with Disabilities (2006), U.N. GOAR, 61st sess., Supp. No. 49, A/RES/61/106.

21 General Conference of the International Labour Organization, Equal Remuneration Convention (1951), No. 100; General Conference of the International Labour Organization, Right of Association (Agriculture) Convention (1921), No. 11.

22 Council of Europe, European Convention for the Protection of Human Rights and Fundamental Freedoms (1952), ETS 9.

The Agreement on the Free Movement of Persons between Switzerland and the EU and its Member States (FMPA)[23] and the parallel agreement with EFTA[24] must be mentioned. At the heart of these agreements is a general ban on discrimination on the grounds of nationality, which applies within the scope of the agreement and is directly applicable.

Switzerland has ratified neither the European Social Charter (which also contains prohibitions of discrimination) nor the twelfth additional Protocol to the European Convention of Human Rights (ECHR).

Switzerland has entered a reservation regarding Article 26 of the UN Covenant on Civil Rights, which also contains an independent ban on discrimination.

When analysing the characteristics on the basis on which discrimination is prohibited, the prevailing importance of the characteristics of gender and race becomes apparent. The characteristics mentioned in the catalogues of the two UN Covenants and in the Convention against Racism – colour, national origin, national minority and ethnicity, and national origin – are closely related to (so-called) race; in EU law these grounds are summarised under the term "ethnic origin". Prohibitions of discrimination on the grounds of religion and belief/political opinion have also been part of global human rights protection since 1966 (UN Covenant I and II). The situation is different for discrimination on the ground of disability, which was only acknowledged by the UN Convention on Disability in 2006.[25] Age discrimination is not explicitly included in the lists of discriminatory grounds in human rights treaties. However, the European Court of Human Rights (ECtHR) and UN Human Rights Committees have recognised age as a ground of discrimination in various cases.[26] The basis for this was the term "other status" in Art. 14 ECHR. The ECtHR has subsumed "age" under "other status".[27] Sexual orientation is not explicitly anchored as a prohibited discrimination criterion under international law.

In addition to the prohibitions of discrimination under international law – which at least historically are primarily motivated by human rights – more economically oriented international law agreements contain prohibitions of discrimination on the basis of nationality. In Switzerland, the ban on discrimination by reason of

23 Agreement between the Swiss Confederation and the European Community and its Member States on the free movement of persons, 21 June 1999, CC 0.142.112.681, entry into force for Switzerland on 1 June 2002.

24 Convention on the Establishment of the European Free Trade Association (EFTA), 21 June 1999, CC, 0.142.112.681, entry into force for Switzerland on 1 June 2002.

25 See among other: Arlene S. Kanter, *The Development of Disability Rights Under International Law: From Charity to Human Rights* (Oxford, England: Routledge, 2015).

26 See UN Human Rights Committee, Seventy-seventh sessions. Date of Decision: 25 March 2003, John K. Love et al. v Australia, Communication No. 983/2001, U.N. Doc. CCPR/C/77/D/983/2001 (2003).

27 The Court has recognised that age constituted "other status" for the purposes of Article 14 of the Convention, see among others Schwizgebel v Switzerland, 2 Application no. 25762/07, 2010, § 85.

nationality of a contracting party to the aforementioned Agreement on the Free Movement of Persons is particularly important.

The antagonism – bans on discrimination based on human rights or economic grounds – is now being softened, particularly in EU law. For example, in the European Economic Community it was originally economic reasons which made it necessary to prohibit wage discrimination on the basis of sex. Today's EU anti-discrimination law has both a human rights and an economic background. For example, the adoption of the 2000 framework directives on discrimination (2000/78/EC and 2000/43/EC) was influenced by the Lisbon Strategy, with which the Union sought to increase the employment rate. In addition, the prohibition of discrimination on grounds of nationality has been enshrined in a separate article in the Charter of Fundamental Rights of the Union since the Lisbon Treaty became legally binding (Article 21(2) TFEU).[28]

However, an important difference cannot be ignored: in contrast to the human rights–based prohibitions of discrimination in agreements with global or regional validity, the prohibitions of discrimination on grounds of nationality only protect the nationals of the respective contracting parties. The application of these prohibitions of discrimination leads on the one hand to the well-known problem of discrimination against nationals (which must be solved in accordance with national constitutional law) and on the other hand to the problem of discrimination against third-country nationals: Only EU foreigners and Swiss nationals enjoy the protection of the ban on discrimination under the FMPA; nationals of other states do not, unless it is through a family relationship with an entitled person.

Protection against discrimination in working life is also required under constitutional law. With the revision of the Federal Constitution (Cst) in 1999, the previous case law on equality of rights and the prohibition of arbitrariness on the one hand and the prohibitions of discrimination applicable to Switzerland under international law on the other were incorporated into constitutional law.[29] Art. 8 para. 2 Cst lists nine discriminatory criteria that determine or at least characterise the identity of a person (sex, race, language, religion, ideology/political attitude, social position, way of life, age, disability) in a non-exhaustive list.

The prohibition of discrimination is a fundamental right and is primarily directed at the state and at institutions that perform state functions. According to Art. 35 para. 3 Cst, the authorities have to ensure that fundamental rights, as far as they are suitable for this purpose, are also effective among private persons. For the discrimination criteria of gender and disability, the constitutional legislature has enshrined specific legislative mandates in Art. 8 para. 3 and Art. 8 para. 4 of the Federal Constitution. According to Art. 8 para. 3 sentence 1, men and women

28 European Union, Consolidated version of the Treaty on the Functioning of the European Union, 13 December 2007, 2008/C 115/01.

29 Kurt Pärli, *Völker- und verfassungsrechtliche Grundlagen, in Diskriminierungsrecht: Handbuch für Jurist_innen, Berater_innen und Diversity-Expert_innen*, N 138, eds. Tarek Naguib et al. (Stämpfli Verlag, 2014).

have equal rights, and sentence 2 states that the law provides for their legal and factual equality, especially in the family, education and work. The legislature has implemented this mandate with the Gender Equality Act (GEA).[30] The mandate in Article 8(4) Cst is much less clear. It merely states that the law must provide for measures to eliminate discrimination against the disabled. The Federal Act on the Elimination of Discrimination against People with Disabilities (DDA)[31] implements the legislative mandate. The following diagram illustrates the preceding remarks:

Overview of constitutional obligations:

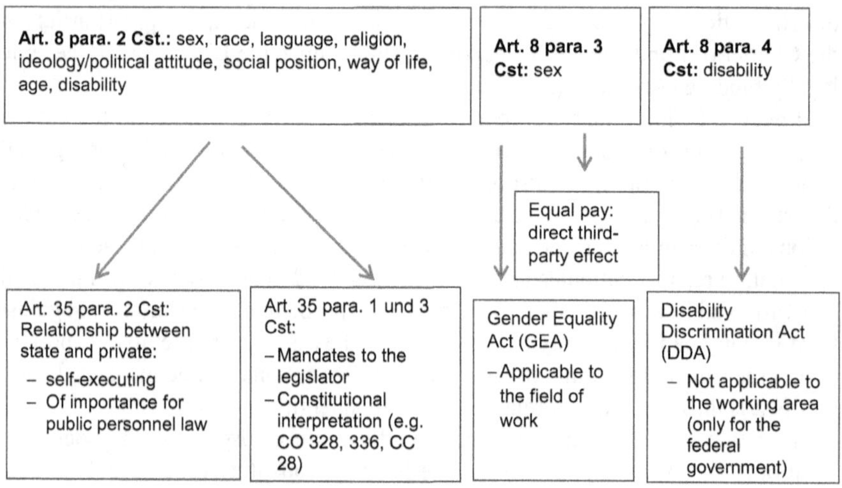

4 Contractual Freedom – A Free Pass for Discrimination?

The starting point for protection against discrimination in Swiss labour law is freedom of contract. In its landmark decision on the principle of equal treatment under labour law, the Federal Supreme Court stated that, insofar as a contractual provision existed, the principle of contractual freedom as one of the supporting pillars of the fundamental freedoms under private law was to be assumed.[32] It is also argued in the doctrine that, for example, any differentiation between individual employees would be permitted with regard to the agreed contractual content. If an employee negotiates worse conditions than their colleagues, they must in principle accept the resulting poorer working conditions.[33] The freedom

30 The Federal Assembly of the Swiss Confederation, Federal Act on Gender Equality of 24 March 1995, CC 151.1.

31 The Federal Assembly of the Swiss Confederation, Federal Act on the Elimination of Discrimination against People with Disabilities of 13 December 2002, CC 151.3.

32 BGE 129 III 276, C. 3.1.

33 Evidence in Pärli, supra n. 29, at marginals 13, 621 et seq. and 1475 et seq.

of contract takes precedence over protection against discrimination.[34] Freedom of contract is thus very important in Switzerland. This is also shown by the fact that freedom of contract is recognised as a fundamental right protected by the Constitution. As will be shown, this priority of contractual freedom over protection against discrimination is not absolute.

The freedom of contract under the employment contract includes the freedom to conclude contracts, as well as the freedom of content and termination (freedom of dismissal). The limitations of this freedom are found in the following:

- Art. 2 Swiss Civil Code (CC), duty to act in good faith;
- Art. 27–28 CC, protection of personality as a barrier to arbitrariness under private law;
- Art. 19–20 Swiss Code of Obligations (CO), morality, public order and the right of personality;
- Art. 328 CO, duty of the employer to protect employees' personal rights;
- Numerous public law barriers, labour law, aliens law and so forth;
- Prohibitions of discrimination according to the Equal Opportunities Act[35] and the Agreement on the Free Movement of Persons.[36]

The employer's duty to respect and protect the personal rights of the employee is particularly relevant for protection against discrimination during the employment relationship (Art. 328 CO). This protection under private law is flanked under public law by Art. 6 of the Employment Act (EmpA). The employer must protect the health and personal integrity of employees. According to Ordinance 3 of the Labour Code, the employer must take all measures that are "necessary to ensure the physical and mental health of employees". According to the relevant State Secretariat for Economic Affairs (SECO) guidelines, this includes protecting employees against discrimination on the basis of gender, race or religion. In the sense of an interpretation in line with fundamental rights, disabled persons must also be taken into account under Art. 8 para. 2 Cst.[37]

The so-called principle of equal treatment under labour law has only a very limited scope. According to doctrine and practice, it is only applicable in the case of voluntary benefits from the employer and within the scope of the right to

34 Thomas Geiser, Gibt es ein Gleichbehandlungsgebot im schweizerischen Arbeitsrecht? in *Recht im Wandel seines sozialen und technologischen Umfeldes: Festschrift für Manfred Rehbinder*, 38 ff., eds. Jürgen Becker et al. (Stämpfli Verlag, 2002).

35 The Federal Assembly of the Swiss Confederation, Federal Act on Gender Equality of 24 March 1995, CC 151.1.

36 Agreement between the Swiss Confederation and the European Community and its Member States on the free movement of persons, 21 June 1999, CC 0.142.112.681, entry into force for Switzerland on 1 June 2002.

37 Markus Schefer & Caroline Hess-Klein, *Behindertengleichstellungsrecht* (2014), p. 447.

issue instructions.[38] Furthermore, only the arbitrary discrimination of individual employees in relation to the majority is prohibited.[39]

Protection against discriminatory dismissal is not explicit but is provided for in Art. 336 para. 1 lit. a CO. A dismissal is abusive if it is carried out on the basis of a characteristic that a person is entitled to by virtue of their personal rights. Discriminatory characteristics prohibited under international and constitutional law are undoubtedly such characteristics.[40] However, a discriminatory dismissal is not null and void, but merely gives rise to a claim for compensation to the amount of a maximum of six months' wages (cf. Art. 336a para. 1 and 2 CO).

The freedom to choose a partner as part of the freedom of contract results in the freedom of the employer to determine their own criteria and evaluations for the employment decision. Job applicants enjoy minimal protection against discriminatory non-employment through Art. 28 CC (prohibition of unlawful violation of personality rights) and Art. 2 CC (duty to act in good faith). It is controversial whether Art. 328 CO (protection of the employee's personal rights) has any prior effect.[41] This protection against discrimination is flanked by the limitation of the employer's permissible data processing to the suitability of the employee and to data necessary for the performance of the employment relationship, as stipulated in Art. 328b CO.[42] Searching job applicants for personality traits without an objective reason (aptitude test) constitutes a violation of Art. 328b CO.

The protection against discrimination under Articles 2 and 28 of the Swiss Civil Code and Article 328b of the Swiss Code of Obligations is incomplete. According to Art. 28 of the Swiss Civil Code, anyone whose personality is unlawfully infringed may appeal to the courts for their protection and assert the remedies provided for in Art. 28a of the Swiss Civil Code (prohibition, elimination or determination of the infringement). In addition, damages and satisfaction may be claimed (Art. 28a para. 3 CC). A violation of personality rights is not unlawful if a justification can be given. In the case of discriminatory non-employment, the justification regularly consists of the justification grounds "overriding private interest". Anyone who does not get a job for discriminatory reasons (e.g. because of skin colour, age, disability) has to prove first that the non-employment was due to this reason. Art. 28 of the Civil Code does not foresee a lighter burden of proof, nor does it require the employer to give reasons for the refusal.

38 Adrian von Kaenel, Rudolph Roger, & Ullin Streiff, Arbeitsvertrag: Praxiskommentar zu Art. 319–362 OR (2012), Art. 322 OR N 20 and Art. 328 OR N 9; BGE 129 III 276, C 3.1.

39 Geiser, supra n. 34, at p. 45.

40 Catherine Reiter, Die Reformbedürftigkeit des Rechts der missbräuchlichen Kündigung im Lichte des Menschenrechtsschutzes, 09/2006 PJA, 1089 (2006).

41 Von Kaenel, Roger, & Streiff, supra n. 38, at N 21 with numerous references.

42 Art. 328b OR is, according to the legislative will, already applicable in the application procedure, see Pärli, supra n. 29, at margin no. 1275.

On the other hand, Article 6 of the Gender Equality Act does provide for a lighter burden of proof.[43] It stipulates that if discrimination is presumed, it only has to be established prima facie. However, its application is limited to the allocation of tasks, the organisation of working conditions, remuneration, training, promotion and dismissal. This means e contrario that a person affected by discrimination on the grounds of sex does not benefit from any alleviation of the burden of proof during the recruitment period.[44] The person concerned must provide full proof that they have not been employed on the grounds of discrimination. If the provision of evidence is successful, it is up to the employer to prove that the refusal of employment was based on a personality trait, but that it is objectively justified. If the employer does not succeed in justifying the refusal, the question remains as to the legal consequences of the violation of personality rights. Actions for removal, injunction and declaratory judgment are usually not very effective, since, in particular, an action for removal cannot be used to obtain employment. This leaves only the actions for damages or satisfaction. As a rule, there will be no relevant damages (only the application costs could be claimed). A claim for compensation presupposes that the damage is a serious violation of personality rights.

5 Evaluation of Swiss Tools Against Discrimination in Employment

5.1 Deficits in the Implementation of International Legal Obligations

As has been shown, Swiss labour law on protection against discrimination on the grounds of personal characteristics only contains general clauses on the protection of personality. From the perspective of international labour law, these provisions are insufficient. The implementation deficits have not gone unnoticed by the relevant supervisory bodies. Switzerland has repeatedly been criticised for its lack of willingness to implement them. In 2010, for example, the UN Committee on Economic, Social and Cultural Rights demanded that Switzerland not only enforce better existing anti-discrimination laws but also adopt comprehensive anti-discrimination legislation and implement it uniformly throughout the country.

The lack of protection against discrimination on grounds of disability and racial discrimination is particularly marked. Both the UN Disability Convention and the UN Anti-racism Convention prescribe relatively precisely to the ratifying states how protection against discrimination in the world of work must be structured. These requirements are further specified by the rulings of the monitoring bodies.

43 Art. 6 of the Gender Equality Act says: "In relation to the allocation of duties, setting of working conditions, pay, basic and continuing education and training, promotion and dismissal, discrimination is presumed if the person concerned can substantiate the same by prima facie evidence."

44 Nor does a person affected by sexual harassment benefit from the alleviation of the burden of proof, as it is not covered by Art. 6 GEA either.

The continuing criticism of inadequate protection against discrimination in general, and in the world of work in particular, has also led to numerous political advances.[45] In a comprehensive study, the Swiss Competence Centre for Human Rights also confirmed numerous gaps in discrimination protection law.[46] The authors of the study propose various measures to remedy the situation, in particular strengthening the protection of personality rights under civil law.[47] However, the Federal Council has shown little willingness to take up the impulses from the academic world.[48] Only with regard to protection against dismissal is it willing to examine certain adjustments.[49]

5.2 Influence of EU Labour Law on Swiss Court Practice With Regard to Selected Grounds of Discrimination

5.2.1 Ground of Discrimination: Age

Fifteen years after the Directive 2000/78/EC came into force, the prohibition of age discrimination in employment law still continues to intensively occupy the national courts, the European Court of Justice (ECJ) and also the scientific literature/academic world.[50] The problems are manifold, ranging from the question of the admissibility of taking years of service into account, privileging or discriminating against certain age groups of employees and age limits for hiring to statutory or contractual retirement dates.

Although there is no explicit legal provision prohibiting age discrimination, similar problems are to some extent also encountered in Swiss labour law practice. In the following, a brief comparative analysis of one of these problems (Swiss labour law and regulation according to Directive 2000/78/EC) will be made. It is of interest how dismissals in connection with retirement are dealt with both here and there.

45 After years of Parliament having rejected all attempts to improve protection against discrimination, the National Council agreed in December 2012 to a postulate that required the Federal Council to submit a report on the state of protection against discrimination (Martin Naef, Postulate 12.3543, 14 June.2012).

46 Study in which the Center for Human Rights prepared a total of eleven partial studies and a synthesis report, see Kälin Walter & Reto Locher, Access to Justice in Discrimination Cases – a Synthesis Report (2015), available at www.skmr.ch/cms/upload/pdf/160526_studie_diskrimination_Synthesebericht.pdf (accessed 15 July 2020).

47 See Synthesis Report, Walter & Locher, supra n. 46, at 102 ff.

48 Right to protection against discrimination, Report of the Federal Council in fulfilment of the postulate Naef 12.3543 of 14 June 2012, 25 May 2016, 25, see www.ejpd.admin.ch/dam/data/bj/aktuell/news/2016/2016-05-25/ber-br-d.pdf (accessed 7 September 2020).

49 Report Federal Council Discrimination, supra n. 48, at 17.

50 The extent to which the prohibition of age discrimination collides with the freedom of the social partners to conclude collective agreements is also the subject of controversial discussion; see e.g. the work of Monika Schlachter, *Das Verbot der Altersdiskriminierung und der Gestaltungsspielraum der Tarifvertragsparteien* (Frankfurt am Main: Bund-Verlag, 2014).

Directive 2000/78/EC prohibits any discrimination on grounds of age. Statutory and (collectively agreed) contractual provisions according to which working age automatically ends upon reaching retirement age have been declared by the ECJ to be compatible with the principle of equal treatment based on age. In the first decision, *Palacios de Villa*, the ECJ accepted a provision of Spanish labour law whereby collective agreements may provide for the retirement age of sixty-five. For the ECJ, it was important that employees who have not yet completed the required years of contributions to the social security system can continue to work until the waiting period is completed.[51] In the *Age Concern England* case, the ECJ confirmed that legal provisions on the possibility of dismissal upon reaching the statutory retirement age fall within the scope of the anti-discrimination directives. However, national legislation may provide for the dismissal of employees on grounds of retirement, provided that this is intended to implement legitimate social policy objectives. According[52] to the *Rosenbladt* judgment, parties to collective agreements may set a general "age limit 65", upon which the employment relationship automatically ends. It is also permissible for such a collective agreement to be declared generally binding by the state.[53] The ECJ recognised Germany's argument that the automatic termination of the retirement age is an expression of a general political and social consensus on the division of labour between the generations.[54]

In the *Georgiev* case, the ECJ examined the admissibility of a Bulgarian rule which provides that, from the age of sixty-five, university professors may continue their employment relationship only on the basis of a contract limited to one year and renewable twice at most. University professors are compulsorily retired at the age of sixty-eight at the latest.[55] For the ECJ, promoting the recruitment of younger workers is a legitimate objective of social and employment policy, which justifies a shift from the principle of equal treatment on grounds of age.[56] It further states that the intergenerational mixing that comes with the forced retirement of older professors favours cooperation between teachers and researchers of different generations, the exchange of experience, innovation and thus the quality of teaching and research at universities.[57] The ECJ concludes that reasons such as the creation of high-quality teaching and the optimal distribution of professorial posts between the generations are legitimate grounds for compulsory retirement.

According to the prevailing doctrine in Swiss labour law, dismissal on retirement does not constitute an abusive dismissal.[58] The Federal Supreme Court

51 ECJ, Judgment of 16 October 2007, Case C-411/05, ECLI:EU:C:2007:604 (Palacios de la Villa).

52 ECJ, Judgment of 5 March 2009, Case C-388/07, ECLI:EU:C:2009:128 (Age Concern England).

53 ECJ, Judgment of 12 October 2010, Case C-45/09, ECLI:EU:C:2010:601 (Rosenbladt).

54 ECJ, Judgment of 12 October 2010, Case C-45/09, ECLI:EU:C:2010:601 (Rosenbladt), para. 43–45.

55 ECJ, Judgment of 18 November 2010, Case C-250/09, ECLI:EU:C:2010:699 (Georgiev).

56 Ibid., para. 45.

57 Ibid., para. 46.

58 Sylvie Pétremand, La fixation de l'âge de la retraite en droit international, européen et suisse de la sécurité sociale 297 (2013); Olivier Subilia & Jean-Luc Duc, Droit du travail: elements de droit

followed this line of argument and rejected an appeal by a dismissed seventy-year-old driving instructor whose dismissal was expressly on age grounds.[59] In its reasoning, the Federal Court referred explicitly to the case law of the ECJ on Directive 2000/78/EC.[60] According to the ECJ, age limits correspond to a "legitimate socio-political objective" as provided for in the Directive, create a balanced age structure and promote the occupational integration of younger employees in the interest of a distribution of employment between the generations.

For the sake of completeness, the famous *Prigge* decision is to be mentioned. In this case the ECJ held that a provision in a collective agreement which provided for the end of the employment contract of commercial pilots at the age of sixty infringed the prohibition of discrimination on grounds of age.[61] A justification failed because the unequal treatment did not pursue any of the objectives recognised in Directive 2000/78/EC. Under Swiss labour law, the parties to a collective bargaining agreement are free to set an age limit, even one that is below the statutory retirement age.[62] An alignment with the legal situation in the EU through court decisions has not yet been observed.

5.2.2 Ground of Discrimination: Disability

The ECJ has had to deal with issues of discrimination against disabled workers on several occasions. Since the status "disability" results in a higher level of protection under labour law, it is obvious that the definition of disability under labour law is of particular importance. The ECJ has ruled that even a chronic illness can be classified as a disability within the meaning of Directive 2000/78/EC. A person[63] may also be *disabled* within the meaning of Directive 2000/78/EC if they are not themselves disabled but have a close relationship with a disabled person.[64]

Suisse 556 (2010); Kurt Pärli, Altersdiskriminierung: Von der Anstellung bis zur Kündigung, 1 *ARV*, pp. 1–12 (2018), available at https://avenir50plus.ch/avplus50/wp-content/uploads/2018/08/Swisslex_ARV-2018-S.-1.pdf (accessed 7 September 2020).

59 BGer, 17.02.2014, 4A_399/2013.

60 Specifically in C. 3.4 of the decision, the Federal Court refers to the ECJ Judgments of 5 July 2012, Case C-141/11, ECLI:EU:C:2012:421 (Hörnfeldt), para. 47; Judgment of 21 July 2011, Case C-141/11, ECLI:EU:C:2012:421 (Hörnfeldt), para. C-159/10 and C-160/10, ECLI:EU:C:2011:508 (Fuchs und Köhler), recitals 50 and 64, with reference to the earlier Judgments of 16 October 2007, Case C-411/05, ECLI:EU:C:2007:604 (Palacios de la Villa) and of 12 October 2010, Case C-45/09, ECLI:EU:C:2010:601 (Rosenbladt).

61 ECJ, Judgment of 13 September 2011, Case C-447/09, ECLI:EU:C:2011:573 (Prigge and others).

62 Denis G. Humbert, Die Alterskündigung, 6 *AJP*, 868, p. 877 (2015).

63 ECJ, Judgment of 18 December 2014, Case C-354/13, ECLI:EU:C:2014:2463 (FOA): "Obesity can be a disability"; ECJ, Judgment of 11 April 2013, Case C-354/13, ECLI:EU:C:2014:2463 (FOA): "Obesity can be a disability"; C-335/11 and C-337/11, ECLI:EU:C:2013:222 (Ring and Skouboe Werge): "Disease can be equated with disability"; ECJ, Judgment of 11 July 2006, Case C-13/05, ECLI:EU:C:2006:456 (Chacon Navas): "distinction between disease and disability".

64 ECJ, Judgment of 17 July 2008, Case C-303/06, ECLI:EU:C:2008:415 (Coleman): "Association discrimination".

The Disability Equality Act (DDA) is not applicable to employment relationships under private law.[65] Consequently, the problem of the demarcation between illness and disability, as required by Directive 2000/78/EC, does not arise in Swiss labour law. The provisions on the protection of personality under labour law are open in this respect; they allow protection against discrimination on the grounds of illness, as well as disability or a chronic illness.

5.2.3 Ground of Discrimination: Religion/Belief

In 2016 a local court handed down an important ruling in connection with discrimination on the grounds of religion. A female employee of an industrial laundry was dismissed for wearing a headscarf at her workplace for religious reasons. The employer could not convincingly explain why a headscarf ban is necessary for the smooth running of the work, nor was it possible to prove that the headscarf posed a safety risk and why it had a negative impact on hygiene. The dismissal was therefore abusive within the meaning of Art. 336 lit. a CO. Therefore, a compensation of three months' salary had to be paid to the woman by the company. Freedom of religion, which is to be respected in private employment relationships as well, was decisive in the decision of the court.[66]

If customers are annoyed about the fact that employees wear religious symbols or display their religion otherwise to the outside world, freedom of religion and the interests of the employer are affected. It is difficult to weigh these interests against one another. Is the employer allowed to prohibit the display of religious symbols on the grounds of customer needs? On grounds of a free social and market order, it goes without saying that a company focuses on the needs of its customers. If, however, customer needs collide with religious needs, which must be respected in employment relationships under fundamental rights, the legal system must not accept any invocation of customer needs. If this is consistently enforced, the employer who fails to meet discriminatory customer needs will not suffer any disadvantage, as the same rules apply to all market participants. A "customer needs constellation" was the basis for one of the two "headscarf cases" decided by the ECJ in 2017. Ms Bougnaoui was employed as a software designer and (also) wore the Muslim headscarf during a customer visit, which had offended a customer.[67] The ECJ had to assess the legality of the dismissal in the light of the prohibition of discrimination on grounds of religion. It concluded that it was inadmissible for the employer to take into account the wishes of the customer. Discriminatory unequal treatment based on religion was only lawful if there were objective reasons for it. The Zurich Labour Court has ruled in the same way in a case of employment discrimination. The employer had argued that she did not want to employ a Swiss woman of Macedonian origin because the clients

65 On the problem of this legislative solution, see Schefer & Hess-Klein, supra n. 35, at 76 ff.

66 Regionalgericht Bern-Mittelland, Judgment of 8 September 2016, CIV 16 1317 P57/BLM.

67 ECJ, Judgment of 14 March 2017, Case C-188/15, ECLI:EU:C:2017:204 (Bougnaoui), para. 2.

would not want "such people".[68] The Zurich Labour Court judged the employer's behaviour as a violation of personality rights.[69] The court of canton Thurgau had already issued a similar ruling in 1993. A company prohibited an employee from wearing the Islamic headscarf, arguing among other reasons that it was in the interest of the workforce to appear in a minimal uniform, Swiss, and non-Islamic image. The interest of a Swiss company in this external appearance was evident. The dismissal was abusive within the meaning of Art. 336 para. 1 lit. b CO. The claimed operational interest in a Swiss image of the company was not recognised as a justification.[70]

6 Further Findings and Overall Conclusion

Despite the lack of a relevant legal norm for protection against discrimination in employment relationships, it can be stated in individual cases that Swiss courts grant protection against discrimination comparable to the content of Directive 2000/78/EC by applying the provisions on the protection of personality under employment law and data protection. This is exemplified by the decision of the Zurich Higher Court of 4 April 2013[71] concerning the dismissal of an HIV-positive football professional for not disclosing his HIV status during the employment procedure. The court concluded, among other things, with references to Art. 328b of the Swiss Code of Obligations that the HIV infection need not be disclosed, and that there was no risk of transmission in professional football.[72] The dismissal due to the HIV infection could have been reviewed by the Labour Court also in the light of Art. 14 ECHR in conjunction with Art. 8 ECHR.[73] Likewise, the ECHR condemned Greece because the Greek courts had upheld the dismissal of an HIV-positive employee.[74] It is noteworthy that the Greek case would have led to the same result also in the light of Directive 2000/78/EC, because an HIV infection is to be qualified as a "disability" within the meaning of the Directive in the context of the previous case law of the ECJ on the concept of disability.[75] Accordingly, HIV-positive employees in the EU states are protected against discrimination.[76]

Directive 2000/78/EC provides, *inter alia*, that disabled workers are entitled to so-called reasonable accommodation to compensate for their disability in terms of job opportunities. According to Directive 2000/78/EC, employers should also be

68 For a look at the EU courts on this issue, see ECJ, Judgment of 10 Juli 2018, Case C-54/07, ECLI:EU:C:2008:397 (Feryn).

69 Arbeitsgericht ZH, Judgment of 13 January 2016, AN050401/U1.

70 Bezirksgericht TG, Judgment of 17 December 1990, published in 87/1991 RSJ 176 ff., 177; confirmed by High Court TG, Judgment of 27 May 1991, RBOG 1991, 80.

71 Zurich High Court, ruling of 08.04.2013, LA110040–0/U.

72 Ibid., C. 4.2.3–4.2.5.

73 See Kurt Pärli, Different Ways to fight against unfair dismissal on the grounds of HIV/AIDS Status, 6 *ELLJ*, p. 373 (2015).

74 ECHR, 03 October 2013, App. No. 552/10, (I. B. v Greece).

75 See Pärli, supra n. 73, at 383.

76 Federal Labour Court, 6th Senate, Judgment of 19 December 2013, AZR 190/12.

made responsible. The EU member states must include corresponding provisions in their anti-discrimination laws.

At first glance, there are no comparable provisions in Swiss labour law. However, an in-depth analysis shows that an obligation comparable to the objectives of Directive 2000/78/EC can be derived from Art. 328 CO (duty to protect personality). An illustration of this is the Federal Supreme Court decision 4A_102/2008 of 27 May 2008, in which the employer dismissed an employee because the employee was no longer able to work 100% but only 50% as a result of an accident. The Federal Supreme Court concluded that the dismissal was abusive within the meaning of Art. 336 para. 1 lit. d CO. Based on the employer's obligation to protect the personality (Art. 328 CO), the employee would have rightly claimed a reduction of his salary. The subsequent dismissal was thus a revenge termination which was inadmissible under Art. 336 para. 1 lit. d CO (protection against dismissal after the assertion of a claim justifiable in good faith). A dismissal due to health impairments is therefore only justified if the employer has done everything necessary and reasonable within the meaning of Art. 328 CO to ensure the integration of the employee with health impairments, or if such measures would not have been reasonable from the outset. It is precisely this requirement to protect disabled employees that Directive 2000/78/EC imposes.

In summary, Swiss labour law does not explicitly prohibit discrimination on the grounds of disability. However, the provisions on the protection of personality in Art. 328 of the Swiss Code of Obligations (and also the data protection norm in Art. 328b of the Swiss Code of Obligations) allow the courts to grant protection in cases of discrimination. The courts implicitly refer to concepts in the Equal Treatment Framework Directive 2000/78/EC. However, there are no explicit references to the ECJ practice regarding Directive 2000/78/EC in Swiss labour court practice. This probably has to do with the fact that the ECJ has had to decide far fewer cases on the discrimination criterion "disability" compared to "age".

It should be added that in Swiss labour law, the protection of disabled employees is also granted by Art. 27 of the UN Convention on the Rights of Persons with Disabilities and Art. 8 in conjunction with Art. 14 of the ECHR. For its part, the EU has already ratified the UN Disability Rights Convention and will also ratify the ECHR. This will lead to a harmonisation of the protection against discrimination at the level of international labour law and EU law. The Swiss protection against discrimination of disabled employees will continue to develop in this context, even without the formal adoption of the Equal Treatment Framework Directive 2000/78/EC.

Swiss labour law contains (apart from the characteristic of gender and the FMPA) only general clauses on personality protection. The EU, on the other hand, obliges the Member States to adopt comprehensive anti-discrimination legislation for the characteristics of age, disability, race/ethnic origin, religion/belief and sexual orientation.

An obligation for the legal anchoring of effective protection against discrimination arises from the numerous conventions under international labour law, which are (also) binding on Switzerland. Particularly noteworthy are the obligations regarding disability and race/ethnic origin. Deficits are apparent in the implementation of these obligations under international law. The government and legislators are very reluctant to remedy this situation. The majority of the parliament and the government follow the myth of freedom of contract and are therefore very hesitant about new prohibitions of discrimination. This ignores the fact that discrimination bans are entirely compatible with a free market economy and competition. Discrimination bans enable people to participate in working life. Discrimination bans thus realise freedom of contract for all, not just for the privileged.

However, there is also potential for implementation by the courts. They can (and should) use legislative concepts from EU anti-discrimination law, relevant ECJ decisions and the rulings of the human rights treaty monitoring bodies to interpret the CO provisions on the protection of personality (under labour law) in order to find fair solutions in cases of discrimination. It goes without saying that the limits of interpretation and judicial further development of the law must be respected here. Ultimately, the legislature is (also) required to fully implement the obligations under international labour law for effective protection against discrimination. The legislature can certainly orientate itself towards EU anti-discrimination law, but a "copy-paste" method is not obligatory. A possible solution for Switzerland could also be to supplement the existing civil law instruments instead of enacting new legal regulation.

Bibliography

Eurofound, Sixth European Working Conditions Survey: 2015, 70 (2015), https://www.eurofound.europa.eu/surveys/european-working-conditions-surveys/sixth-european-working-conditions-survey-2015 (accessed 30 August 2022).

Hangartner D, Kopp D, & Siegenthaler M, Monitoring Hiring Discrimination through Online Recruitment Platforms, *Nature* (20 January 2021). doi: 10.1038/s41586-020-03136-0.

Humbert Denis G., Die Alterskündigung, AJP 6/2015 und Daniel Oesch, Discrimination in The Hiring of Older Jobseekers: Evidence from two Survey Experiments in Switzerland (2019), OECD Bericht: Alterung und Beschäftigungspolitik Schweiz: Bessere Arbeit im Alter 123 (2014).

Imdorf Christian, Understanding Discrimination in Hiring Apprentices: How Training Companies Use Ethnicity to Avoid Organizational Trouble (2017), www.tandfonline.com/doi/pdf/10.1080/13636820.2016.1278397 (accessed 15 July 2020).

Künzli Jörg & Walter Kälin, *The Law of International Human Rights Protection* 335 (Oxford: Oxford University Press, 2019).

Oesch Daniel, Discrimination in The Hiring of Older Jobseekers: Evidence from two Survey Experiments in Switzerland (2019), https://serval.unil.ch/resource/serval:BIB_A7D7A65F25AC.P001/REF.pdf (accessed 15 July 2020).

Oesch Daniel, Oliver Lips & Patrick McDonald, The Wage Penalty for Motherhood: Evidence on Discrimination from Panel Data and a Survey Experiment for Switzerland, 37 *Demographic Research*, 1793–1824 (2017), www.demographic-research.org/volumes/vol37/56/37-56.pdf (accessed 15 July 2020).

Pärli Kurt, Freedom of Contract, Equal Treatment and Discrimination in Private Law Employment Relationships: International and Constitutional Law Framework and Significance of European Community Law 221 f. (2009).

Pärli Kurt, Völker- und verfassungsrechtliche Grundlagen, in *Diskriminierungsrecht: Handbuch für Jurist_innen, Berater_innen und Diversity-Expert_innen*, N 138 (Tarek Naguib et al. ed., Stämpfli Verlag, 2014).

Pärli Kurt, Altersdiskriminierung: Von der Anstellung bis zur Kündigung, 1 *ARV*, 1–12 (2018), https://avenir50plus.ch/avplus50/wp-content/uploads/2018/08/Swisslex_ARV-2018-S.-1.pdf (accessed on 7 September 2020).

Pärli Kurt & Camill Oberhausser, Diskriminierungsfreie Messung der Lohngleichheit: Diskriminierungspotenzial einzelner Erklärungsfaktoren zur Messung der Lohngleichheit zwischen Frau und Mann auf gesamtwirtschaftlicher Ebene, N 51–56 (2019), https://jusletter.weblaw.ch/juslissues/2019/1002/diskriminierungsfrei_79fb444066.html__ONCE (accessed on 16 October 2020).

Pétremand Sylvie, La fixation de l'âge de la retraite en droit international, *européen et therw de la sécurité sociale* 297 (2013).

Reiter Catherine, Die Reformbedürftigkeit des Rechts der missbräuchlichen Kündigung im Lichte des Menschenrechtsschutzes, *PJA*, 1089 (September 2006).

Schefer Markus & Caroline Hess-Klein, Behindertengleichstellungsrecht 447 (2014).

Studer Nanina, Women sell Mascara, Men Sell Machines?: A Content Analysis of Gender Portrayals in Swiss Prime-Time TV Advertisements (2019).

Subilia Olivier & Jean-Luc Duc, Droit du travail: elements de droit, *Suisse* 556 (2010).

Tillé Yves & Mihaela Catalina Anastasiades, Gender Wage Inequalities in Switzerland: the Public versus the Private Sector, https://link.springer.com/article/10.1007/s10260-016-0368-5 (accessed 15 July 2020).

von Kaenel Adrian, Rudolph Roger & Ullin Streiff, Arbeitsvertrag: Praxiskommentar zu Art. 319–362 OR (2012), Art. 322 OR N 20 and Art. 328 OR N 9; BGE 129 III 276, C 3.1.

Waldmann Bernhard, Das Diskriminierungsverbot von Art. 8 Abs. 2 BV als besonderer Gleichheitssatz: Unter besonderer Berücksichtigung der völkerrechtlichen Diskriminierungsverbote einerseits und der Rechtslage in den USA, in Deutschland, Frankreich sowie im europäischen Gemeinschaftsrecht anderseits 126 (2003).

Zschirnt Eva & Rosita Fibbi, *Do Swiss Citizens of Immigrant Origin Face Hiring Discrimination in the Labour Market?* Swiss National Science Foundation, National Center of Competence in Research, Working Paper #20 (2019).

11 Transformative Equality and Disability-Based Discrimination in Employment

A Case Study From India

Nimushakavi Vasanthi

> [I]t is the opinion of this Court that in a country where 26,810,557 individuals suffer from different disabilities, a one size fit all model might not be the most efficient. That 40% on the IDEA scale makes individuals more or less employable cannot be held ideal.
>
> (*Jadhav*, para. 27)[1]

1 Introduction

The United Nations Convention on the Rights of Persons with Disabilities (UNCRPD) envisages a transformative regime of rights which will move the understanding of disability from welfare and medical model towards a rights-based model.[2] The rights-based model draws attention to the stereotypes surrounding the abilities and capacities of persons with disabilities. It draws attention to the structural and attitudinal barriers that persons with disabilities face. Structural and systemic discrimination are forms of indirect discrimination, where discrimination is not obvious but hidden, need not be intentional but results in inequality, and is often evident only by examining patterns of exclusion, cultures and institutional practices.

The UNCRPD allows for a diverse experience of disability to be covered within its fold and does not confine itself to strict categories of scientifically identifiable groups. It requires that we move away from exclusionary definitions of disability. The UNCRPD which is premised upon placing rights at the centre of the law, rather than the disability itself, could lead to a change in exclusionary practices.

The Constitution of India, 1950 has a rights charter guaranteeing the right to equality and non-discrimination, as well as fundamental freedoms and liberty. The Constitution is considered the supreme law of the land, and all laws made by the

1 Jadhav Vishwas Haridas v Union Public Service Commission & Ors., 2016 SCC OnLine Del 5759.

2 Amita Dhanda, Constructing a New Human Rights Lexicon: Convention on the Rights of Persons with Disabilities, 8 *SUR – International Journal on Human Rights*, Page 43 (2008).

DOI: 10.4324/9781003306962-14

State conform to it. In the absence of a constitutional framework, international human rights such as the UNCRPD need to be read into the Constitution.

India ratified the UNCRPD in 2007 and has enacted two statutes: one before the convention in 1995 and the second to bring the legislation in conformity with the UNCRPD in 2016.[3] These statutes approach the question of employment discrimination through the provisioning of a quota in public employment. Quotas are a much-debated mechanism to address discrimination and are seen as a mechanism to address class/group-based discrimination. The Indian Constitution has explicit provisions on quotas for all those underrepresented in public employment, including women and persons with disabilities. These provisions become more significant given that labour law in India has no such provisions. Equal opportunity is a constitutional goal rather than a goal of labour law. While the proponents of group-based accommodations advocate that it addresses group identity and structural discrimination, its opponents claim that it causes social division, violates individual dignity,[4] and is undemocratic and discriminatory per se.

Disability jurisprudence addresses both individual- and group-based discrimination. It addresses individual needs by the flexible concept of reasonable accommodation while defining disability in terms of the social, physical barriers that persons with disabilities encounter. Both these aspects are equally important, and one cannot be ignored for the other. In the context of employment law, both these dimensions acquire an added dimension. Labour law has always focused on the class, while employment law has looked at individual contracts of employment. The need to integrate the ideas of group identity with individual needs is the challenge for labour law, and it is here that Noah Datz's idea of the two areas of law learning from each other becomes relevant.

Tristin Green[5] has called the narrow individual claims-based discrimination law "discrimination laundering". She argues that if the structural and cultural aspects of organisations are not taken into account, a transformative workplace would not be possible. She argues that the present law on discrimination in employment by focusing on the individual allows employers to make small changes in the workplace without really addressing systemic discrimination. In the context of disability, including individuals in the workplace without making any modification in the physical and social environments could empower them individually, but it does not bring about a transformation in the way our workplaces are structured. Giving effect to a rights-based approach requires organisational environments to change along with individuals.

3 The Persons with Disabilities (Equal Opportunities, Protection of Rights and Full Participation) Act 1995 (hereinafter PwD Act 1995) and the Rights of Persons with Disabilities Act 2016 (hereinafter RPwD Act 2016).

4 See for a detailed discussion, Julie C. Suk, Quotas and Consequences: A Transnational Re-evaluation (Ch.), in Deborah Hellman & Sophia Moreau (eds.), *Philosophical Foundation of Discrimination Law* (Oxford University Press, 2013), pp. 228–249 at p. 234.

5 Tristin Green, *Discrimination Laundering: The Rise of Organizational Innocence and the Crisis of Equal Opportunity Law* (Cambridge University Press 2017).

Despite the quota system used in employment since 1995, participation in employment for persons with disabilities in India continues to remain very low.[6] A statistical profile of persons with disabilities in India shows that only one-third of persons with disabilities were employed, and a majority of them were employed as agricultural labour; a bare 2% were employed in the public sector or any other employment. This is despite 10% of posts being identified as posts suitable for persons with disabilities[7] in public sector companies.

The inadequacies of a quota system to address systemic discrimination are evident in a recent decision from the Indian Supreme Court[8] which held that it was "reasonable, just and fair" to restrict eligibility to the position of a civil judge to a candidate with a specified degree of disability only. The case is startling not only for its decision on eligibility but also because the eligibility for the post was fixed in consultation with the judiciary, as the higher judiciary in India is the guardian of the subordinate judiciary and has a say in the eligibility of persons appointed. The ruling is surprising also because the Indian Constitution is an example of an otherwise modern constitution written at the time the world was drafting the Conventions on Human Rights, containing explicit and wide-ranging provisions against discrimination. This decision was overruled[9] using a constitutional analysis of the anti-discriminatory law and inclusive citizenship.

Judicial interpretation is a key tool to integrate international human rights into constitutional and legislative enactments. The chapter contrasts the approach in two cases of the Indian Supreme Court and highlights how interpretation can play a key role in bringing about a nuanced understanding of disability-based discrimination in employment. The two cases involved a quantification-based definition of disability in equal opportunities claims. The claims were rejected on the ground that they did not meet the requirements of being disabled. India has a dual system of dealing with discrimination: through a special statute on disability and through a constitutional framework. The chapter looks at how the two branches could be read together. The chapter will conclude by examining recent legislative proposals to address disability-based discrimination.

2 Equality, Non-discrimination and Equal Opportunity

Surendra Mohan was an assistant prosecuting officer who aspired to be a civil judge. The State had advertised positions for persons with disabilities but stated that the post of a civil judge in the State services could be held only by a person

6 SWADHIKAAR-AWARE-DRPI, Employment Rights of Persons with disabilities in India (2017), available at http://drpi.research.yorku.ca/wp-content/uploads/2018/08/Hyderabad-Report-English.pdf (accessed: 26 May 2021).

7 See N. Vasanthi, Right to Work for Persons with Disabilities in India: A Critical Disability Theory Perspective (Ch.), in Nilika Mehrotra (ed.), *Disability Studies in India: Interdisciplinary Perspectives* (Springer, 2020), pp. 243–259.

8 Surendra Mohan v State of Tamilnadu and Others (2019) 4 SCC 237.

9 Vikash Kumar v UPSC, 2020 SCC Online 84.

with partial blindness of 40%–50%. Mohan, who had a 70% disability, cleared the written exam but he was not called for the second stage (i.e. for the oral test). He filed a petition in the constitutional court and an interim order was issued stating that he may be allowed to take the oral exam, but the result must not be declared and must be kept in a sealed cover until further orders by the Court. While finally disposing of the case, the constitutional court held that Mohan was not eligible for the post. No mention was made about his performance in the oral test. The Supreme Court on appeal held that the reasons given by the Tamil Nadu Public Service Commission justified the requirement of disability up to 50% which was reasonable, just and fair.

The arguments made in the case by the petitioner before the Supreme Court of India were that (1) the post had been identified as suitable for a person with disability, and further quantification of 40%–50% could not be imposed under the PwD Act 1995; (2) there was no determination by an expert committee that only persons with 40%–50% disability could perform the job of a civil judge, and the High Court could not put itself in the position of an expert body to determine the degree of disability; and (3) that the imposition of a 40%–50% disability quantification would frustrate the provisions, as well as the objects of the PwD Act 1995.

Rejecting these arguments, the Supreme Court held that (1) the imposition of a restriction of 40%–50% disability even though the provisions of the Act did not prescribe such a restriction was fair, logical and reasonable[10] given the strenuous duties of a civil judge; (2) although the PwD Act 1995 did not define the term "partial blindness", it was legitimate for the constitutional court to bring about this change as it was a valid classification with a nexus to the object sought to be achieved;[11] and (3) that restricting the post to only those who had a disability of between 40% and 50% did not violate the spirit of the Act, as the requirement of reservation (quota) as mandated by the Act was being fulfilled.[12]

The Court essentially answered a claim on non-discrimination in terms of the doctrine of formal equality and legislative intent behind the quota in employment in the statute (i.e. the PwD Act 1995) rather than invoke any of the relevant constitutional principles of autonomy, stereotyping, dignity and equal opportunity or participation while determining whether the State action was discriminatory towards persons with disabilities.

2.1 Failure of Classification Doctrine

The case represents the failure of the established doctrines in constitutional law, such as the Doctrine of Arbitrariness and Reasonable Classification, to address discrimination. The Supreme Court used a narrow constitutional doctrine of

10 Surendra Mohan v State of Tamilnadu and Others, supra n. 9, para. 40.
11 Ibid., paras. 24 and 25.
12 Ibid.

Reasonable Classification to read in a restrictive interpretation of discrimination in the legislation. The Doctrine of Reasonable Classification is the most used doctrine to adjudicate on questions of equality in the Indian Constitution. Any law made by the State is subject to challenge on the ground that it violates Article 14 of the Constitution of India,[13] which reflects the Equal Protection Clause of the US Constitution and the rule of law principle. The two prongs of the doctrine are that the State law must have a rational basis and an intelligible differentia, and this differentia must have a nexus to the object sought to be achieved.[14]

This must, in cases of hostile or systemic discrimination, be supplemented with other considerations, such as the effect of the law on vulnerable groups and the rights that stand violated by the law. The notion of systematic discrimination is found both in the text of the Indian Constitution, which has explicit provisions for group-based representation in public employment, and the interpretations of equality. However, the Doctrine of Classification was used without the added elements of the effects doctrine particularly in cases of gender-based discrimination, which has been criticised.[15]

The limitations of this doctrine have been noticed by the Supreme Court, and a new Doctrine of Arbitrariness was introduced. The new doctrine enunciated that equality was "the antithesis of arbitrariness"[16] and that it militated against unreasonableness and any action that was capricious and whimsical.

Tarunabh Khaitan argues that while arbitrariness is understood as a lack of reason, many legislative actions, such as fixing the age of majority, are always arbitrary but have reasons. While it is difficult to establish the difference between, say, a person who is aged 17 years and 10 months from one who is aged 18 years, these distinctions are not completely baseless. Another example of a number-based distinction is the number of persons employed in an establishment to distinguish between a small and a large enterprise.[17] Thus arbitrariness, he argues, is not an adequate concept to challenge legislative distinctions and hostile discrimination.

This criticism is valid in the context of our case, where the court did not find sufficient weight in the arbitrariness claim. Khaitan has argued for an enhanced Doctrine of Classification which could include the object of the law and the impact

13 Article 14 of the Constitution of India, 1950. A.14: The State shall not deny to any person equality. before the law or the equal protection of the laws within the territory of India.

14 J. Das in State of West Bengal v Anwar Ali Sarkar AIR 1952 SC 75 para. 55.

15 See Air India v Nergesh Meerza (1981) 4 SCC 335 and its criticism in Shreya Atrey, Through the Looking Glass of Intersectionality: Making Sense of Indian Discrimination Jurisprudence under Article 15, *The Equal Rights Review*, 16, pp. 160–185 (2016); Kannabiran Kalpana, *Tools of Justice: Non-Discrimination and the Indian Constitution* (Routledge India 2012), p. 337; Deepti Shenoy, Courting Substantive Equality: Employment Discrimination Law in India, 34 *University of Pennsylvania Journal of International Law*, pp. 611–640, p. 612 (2013).

16 EP Royappa v State of Tamil Nadu (1974) 4 SCC 3.

17 Tarunabh Khaitan, Equality: Legislative Review under Article 14, (Ch.), in Sujit Choudhry et al. (eds.), *The Oxford Handbook of the Indian Constitution* (Oxford University Press, 2016), pp. 699–719.

on rights, and ask more questions than are currently asked in an equality-based review.[18] This could be a step in the right direction.

In contrast to the decision in *Surendra Mohan*, in *Vikash Kumar*[19] the Supreme Court invoked the concepts of inclusive citizenship, dignity and autonomy to extend facilities even when the required degree of disability was not established.

2.2 Newer Understanding of Equality

The Indian Supreme Court has moved away from the Doctrines of Arbitrariness and Classification.[20] It has invoked a wider understanding of discrimination by using the concept of stereotypical generalisations, which have a resonance in disability discrimination.

Starting from *Anuj Garg*,[21] the Court began to use concepts of anti-stereotyping and invidious discrimination.[22] The Court was dealing with the prohibition of employment of women and men under the age of 25 years in an establishment that served alcoholic beverages. The Court held that the prohibition was gender-based discrimination, holding that it was a "combination of social and biological determinants" which requires deeper scrutiny. This is an approach that has been used in disability discrimination, as disability also involves both social and biological (physical) factors. The fact of disability as a physical factor is also the cause of social and physical barriers.

Anuj Garg was followed by a subsequent case[23] dealing with the decriminalisation of homosexuality, wherein the Supreme Court introduced an expansive understanding of the right against discrimination to include systemic discrimination. The provisions for group discrimination in the Constitution of India go beyond the individual discrimination that is suffered and places the problem at the structure of society. The Constitution of India refers to social, economic backwardness as a result of systemic exclusion of certain groups from education and employment, which in turn prevents them from accessing social and economic equality. The Indian Constitution is understood as an inclusive constitution that directs the State not to be a passive institution but to take active steps for the elimination of discrimination.[24] The Court looks at the stigma that is cast on an already oppressed and discriminated class of people[25] and stressed

18 Tarunabh Khaitan, Beyond Reasonableness – A Rigorous Standard of Review for Article 15 Infringement, 50 *Journal of Indian Law Institute*, 2, pp. 177–208 (2008).

19 Vikash Kumar v UPSC, supra n. 10.

20 See Anuj Garg v Hotel Assn. of India (2008) 3 SCC 1, National Legal Services Authority v Union of India (2014) 5 SCC 438 at para. 66, Navtej Singh Johar v Union of India (2018) 1 SCC 791. Ministry of Defence v Babita Puniya (2020) 7 SCC 469.

21 Anuj Garg v Hotel Assn. of India supra n. 21, para. 44.

22 Ibid., para. 52.

23 Navtej Singh Johar v Union of India, supra n. 21, para. 123.

24 Ibid., para. 249.

25 Ibid.

the need to eradicate stigma, oppression and prejudice. The Court rejected the legal formalism that bound the provisions on equality and non-discrimination in Articles 14 and 15[26] of the Constitution of India by saying that it "buries the life-giving forces of the Constitution under a mere mantra".[27] The Court reiterated the position that Article 14 and non-discrimination have a substantive content which when read with liberty and dignity[28] result in a transformative[29] constitution.

In particular, the earlier ruling[30] setting out a narrow interpretation of equality was held to be patently incorrect.[31] The Court ruled that a discriminatory act will be tested against constitutional values and that discrimination will not survive constitutional scrutiny when it is grounded in and perpetuates stereotypes about a class constituted by the grounds prohibited in Article 15(1).

Reiterating the earlier rulings[32] about facially neutral legislature the court held that "[j]urisprudence across national frontiers supports the principle that facially neutral action by the State may have a disproportionate impact upon a particular class".[33] Prohibition of sex discrimination is meant to change traditional practices which legally, and often socially and economically, disadvantage persons based on gender.[34] The Court noted that hostility and exclusion resulted in creating systematic and deliberate barriers violating substantive equality.[35] The test of systematic

26 Article 15. (1) The State shall not discriminate against any citizen on grounds only of religion, race, caste, sex, place of birth or any of them.
(2) No citizen shall, on grounds only of religion, race, caste, sex, place of birth or any of them, be subject to any disability, liability, restriction or condition with regard to –
(a) access to shops, public restaurants, hotels and places of public entertainment; or
(b) the use of wells, tanks, bathing ghats, roads and places of public resort maintained wholly or partly out of State funds or dedicated to the use of the general public.
(3) Nothing in this article shall prevent the State from making any special provision for women and children.
(4) Nothing in this article or in clause (2) of article 29 shall prevent the State from making any special provision for the advancement of any socially and educationally backward classes of citizens or for the Scheduled Castes and the Scheduled Tribes.
(5) Nothing in this article or in sub-clause (g) of clause (1) of article 19 shall prevent the State from making any special provision, by law, for the advancement of any socially and educationally backward classes of citizens or for the Scheduled Castes or the Scheduled Tribes in so far as such special provisions relate to their admission to educational institutions including private educational institutions, whether aided or unaided by the State, other than the minority educational institutions referred to in clause (1) of article 30.
27 Ibid., para. 36 of J. Chandrachud's opinion.
28 Ibid., para. 53.
29 Ibid., paras. 85, 95 and 24.
30 Nergesh Meerza v Air India, supra n. 16.
31 Navtej Singh Johar v Union of India, supra n. 21, para 41.
32 West Bengal v Anwar Ali Sarkar supra n. 15.
33 Navtej Singh Johar v Union of India, supra n. 21, para. 43.
34 Ibid., para. 46.
35 Ibid., para. 47.

stigmatisation[36] was used to understand the link between discrimination and liberty. The Court held that

> The overarching ideals of individual autonomy and liberty, equality for all sans discrimination of any kind, recognition of identity with dignity and privacy of human beings constitute the cardinal four corners of our monumental Constitution forming the concrete substratum of our fundamental rights that has eluded certain sections of our society who are still living in the bondage of dogmatic social norms, prejudiced notions, rigid stereotypes, parochial mindset and bigoted perceptions.[37]

The Court used the concepts of sex stereotypes[38] and dignity[39] rather than rely on the Doctrines of Classification or Arbitrariness. The Court relied on the solemn constitutional values which every institution in the nation is bound to uphold and facilitate.[40]

The decision in *Vikash Kumar* builds on these cases and identifies the core issue, not as one involving a literal interpretation of statute but the actual realisation of equal opportunity. The case dealt with a claim to provide for a scribe for a person with disability. The State refused the claim on the ground that the facility of a scribe could only be provided to a person with benchmark disability.

Instead of getting caught up in the maze of statutes, rules and regulations, the court invokes constitutional ideals and international human rights law. Instead of taking a strict interpretation of the Statute, the court uses a more liberal and rights-based approach to the question of disability-based discrimination. The Court held that a discretionary and case-by-case approach was more in tune with the reasonable accommodation principle in the statute as well as the UNCRPD.

Examining the definition[41] of a person with disability as one that combines the nature of the disability with various barriers and its impact on full and effective participation in all aspects, the court observes that the legislation has created two sets of definitions. It distinguishes between benchmark disabilities and persons with disabilities. While special provisions such as quota may be limited to those with benchmark disabilities, a non-discriminatory approach (i.e. removal of barriers to participation) needs to be recognised distinctly from special provisions. To conflate special provisions with the right against non-discrimination was to ignore the imperatives of international human rights law.

36 Ibid., para. 53.

37 Ibid., para. 3 Justice Dipak Mishra.

38 Ibid., para. 54.

39 Ibid., para. 56.

40 Ibid.

41 "Person with disability" means a person with long-term physical, mental, intellectual or sensory impairment which, in interaction with barriers, hinders his full and effective participation in society equally with others.

The Court observed the need for a paradigm shift and held that the RPwD Act 2016 was a statutory manifestation of a constitutional commitment. While disability was not explicitly provided in the constitution, the constitutional commitment to full and equal citizenship meant that the full spectrum of rights in the constitution was to be extended to persons with disabilities.

The most interesting part of the decision is the recognition of the right to be different. The Court observes that

> The RPwD Act 2016 is fundamentally premised on the recognition that there are many ways to be, none more "normal" or "better" than the other. It seeks to provide the disabled a sense of comfort and empowerment in their difference.
>
> (para. 39)

The Court took on board both the individual rights claims of personal autonomy, evolving capacities of persons and the group stigma, prejudice and societal indifference that persons with disabilities face. It clearly articulated that there was a need to move beyond the class and accommodate specific individual needs to facilitate inclusion. The group need was met with providing for a quota; the individual need for accommodation needed to be met with providing the necessary support and facilities that individuals needed, such as the provision of a scribe.

3 Special Legislation to Address the Disability Discrimination Question

Given the conspicuous silences in the Constitution on the question of disability-based discrimination, the legislative framework seeks to fill this gap. The PwD Act of 1995 was drafted to provide for a conceptual understanding of disability and the measures required to engage meaningfully with it. It was quite clear from the litigation in the pre-legislative period that the disability question was largely addressed as a question of welfare.[42] The PwD Act 1995 became the first statute to provide for socioeconomic rights in terms of a limited right to employment, education and social security. It lacked the explicit articulation of a general right against discrimination and a right to equality.[43] It also entrenched the idea of linking disability with named impairments, and those seeking any benefits from the Act had to provide certification regarding the extent of their impairment.[44] The chapter on non-discrimination in the statute provides for access to public spaces dependent on the limits of the economic capacity of the appropriate government

42 See Vasanthi, supra n. 8, page 249 for a detailed discussion of the cases.

43 See Amita Dhanda, Establishing a Disability Studies Centre in a Law University: Recounting the CDS NALSAR Experience (Ch.), in Nilika Mehrotra (ed.), *Disability Studies in India: Interdisciplinary Perspectives* (Springer, 2020), pages 147–166.

44 Ibid., page 159.

and local authorities. This language of rights couched in discretionary terms is a feature of the Directive Principles of State Policy in Part IV of the Indian Constitution which confer limited socioeconomic rights.

The stated objective of the Act was promoting equal opportunity, protecting rights and ensuring participation. The Chapter on non-discrimination in employment is tagged to two provisions: the provision for a quota in public employment for a limited set of disabilities, and prohibiting the removal from employment of a person who acquired a disability again only in government employment excluding private employment from these provisions. The provision of quota in employment was further conditioned by a provision for identification of posts. There were other provisions for affirmative action which promoted self-employment.

These provisions made the Act a combination of constitutional provisions and statutory provisions.[45] The provision for quotas was similar to those in the Constitution of India, which provides quotas to socially and educationally backward classes and those who are not adequately represented in public employment. Since such a quota did not exist for persons with disabilities, the statute made the express provision. The other employment-related right was the right against being removed from employment on acquiring a disability. The difference between other labour laws and this Act was that it applied only to government service, whereas labour law applied to all establishments in the public and private sectors.

There was no general rule against discrimination in employment on the ground of disability in the Act or what would constitute direct or indirect discrimination. The conceptualising of discrimination was left unresolved.

The gaps in the PwD Act 1995 were observed in the *Jadhav* case, when the court held that the quantification of disability had a discriminatory effect and a discriminatory result.

> This court, therefore, concludes that there is some deficiency in the existing law, i.e. the PwD Act 1995, both with respect to providing reservations as well as the classification of all persons with disabilities as one having at least 40% of any specified or enumerated condition, which can well be the reason for ultimate discrimination. . . . This clearly has a discriminatory result, and an indirect discriminatory effect.[46]

The PwD Act 1995 provided for reservation for both individuals who are blind and those with low vision but did not provide for partial blindness. A person with low vision was defined under the Act as a person who could use vision for performing a particular task with an appropriate assistive device.

45 Indian law, like that of many countries with a written constitution, distinguishes between constitutional and statutory laws. Constitutional law is considered a supreme law and all statutes must conform to the Constitution. Article 13 of the Constitution of India provides that any law not in conformity with Fundamental Rights can be struck down by the Judiciary.

46 Jadhav Vishwas Haridas v Union Public Service Commission & Ors., supra n. 2, at para. 28.

In *Surendra Mohan*, the Court held that

> In view of the foregoing discussions, we, thus, came to the conclusion that prescription of disability to the extent of 40%–50% for recruitment for the post of Civil Judge (Junior Division) was valid and does not contravene any of the provisions of the Act, 1995 or any other statutory provision.[47]

The Court, while concluding that the eligibility condition was reasonable, just and fair, did not think it necessary to answer the question in terms of non-discrimination or substantive equality or denial of reasonable accommodation. The title of the Act itself contains a long description about it being legislation to ensure full participation, to end inequality of opportunities and protect rights, but that was not invoked by the Court and neither was the UNCRPD.

The Court in *Surendra Mohan* further observed that

> Moreover, given the need to prepare judgments based on the case papers and other material records in a confidential manner, the assistance of a scribe or the like completely takes away the secrecy and discreetness that come with the demands of the post.[48]

This is an assumption of capabilities that has an impact on not just employment and livelihood but dignity and an opportunity to participate in society. There is no discussion on the question of equal opportunity which is the basis of the legislation as well as the first articulation of rights for persons with disabilities in employment.

The understanding of equal opportunities for persons with disabilities under the Indian Constitution predates the legislation on disability. The express articulation of this by the Indian Supreme Court was in a seminal decision[49] on reservations (quota), wherein the Court held that reservation (quota) for the physically handicapped (this was a decision before the PwD Act 1995 and uses the older, pejorative term), if the state should so please, would be within the promise of equality of opportunity for all citizens in matters relating to employment or appointment to any office under the State. Persons with disabilities do not constitute a single class of persons in terms of their social and educational status. They constitute a class in terms of their underrepresentation in public services.

The right to equal opportunity was considered an important aspect of freedom and equality.[50] This right extends beyond equal starting points incorporating a

47 Surendra Mohan v State of Tamilnadu and Others, supra n. 9, at para. 41.

48 Ibid., at para. 40.

49 Indra Sawhney v. UOI, 1992 Suppl. (3) SCC 217 at para. 95.

50 In Lyndon B. Johnson's words, "freedom is not enough. . . . We seek not just freedom but opportunity"; www.americanyawp.com/reader/27-the-sixties/lyndon-johnson-howard-university-commencement-address-1965/ (accessed: 11 December 2020), quoted in the Report on the Equal Opportunity Commission, infra n.61.

formal understanding to equality of results and a more substantive understanding. Particularly in the context of disability, equal measures do not adequately meet the challenges that persons with disabilities face and equality of results, in terms of enjoying rights of education, employment, health, housing and other public resources must be the aim.

India has had a long history of equalising opportunities through the tool of reservations (quotas). The Indian Constitution has a framework that includes the fundamental rights and the directive principles of state policy in Parts III and IV of the Constitution of India. These provide for creating conditions and the use of state policies to ensure an equality of outcome. The basic framework of the constitution is understood as committed to social justice.[51] The Court observed that non-discrimination and affirmative action are both conceptions of equal opportunity although conceptually distinct.

Despite this available jurisprudence, the Court in *Surendra Mohan*[52] does not consider the question of equal opportunity as long as the formal requirement of the law of a quota is fulfilled.

3.1 Disability as a Complex Category

The most important characteristic of disability is the wide variance in both capacities and barriers that disabled persons face. The most important divisions within the disability movement have been between those with psychosocial ailments and those with physical disabilities. But this division is only the beginning of differences. The RPwD 2016 has three definitions of persons with disabilities: (1) a person with a disability; (2) a person with a benchmark disability; and (3) a person with high support needs. The three definitions determine the rights that they are entitled to. It is only persons with benchmark disabilities who can avail of quotas in employment.

When disability is experienced so differently, the legislation attempts to address these differences by enforcing uniformity. This is done by inserting a quantitative measure such as a 40% disability. Meeting this measure is a challenge both for physical disability, as well as for mental illness and intellectual disability. The further attempt at quantifying disability occurs when a specific quantity such as 40% is imposed, which is under inclusive and overinclusive at the same time. It is underinclusive when it fails to recognise that persons with less than 40% disability might suffer the same barriers and stigma that a person with 40% may suffer. At the same time, it also includes persons who have high support needs who may be unable to perform adequately the duties of employment. Due to this under- and overinclusiveness, *Surendra Mohan*[53] introduces a further quantification of between 40% and 50%.

51 M. Nagaraj v UOI (2006) 8 SCC 212.

52 Surendra Mohan v State of Tamilnadu and Others, supra n. 9.

53 Ibid.

The High Court in *Jadhav* observed that

> It is the opinion of this Court that a blanket 40% disability test to provide reservations in employment may be impracticable. A particular disability suffered by an individual might require specific aid and comes with specific restrictions. An individual suffering from a visual disability could avail specific benefits in terms of reservations in employment, as his mental condition is normal. Such an individual might be suffering from a disability of over 40% on the IDEA scale but his employability may not be affected.[54]

3.2 Does the New Law Bring About a Paradigm Shift?

The RPwD Act 2016 was intended to address long-standing problems in addressing disability based discrimination. It talks about stigmatisation and has a definition of reasonable accommodation as well as direct and indirect discrimination. The translation of this into a better understanding is hampered by older paradigms of stigma and stereotyping which persist.

A narrow approach to the question of defining disability continues despite the UNCRPD and domestic law. In an instance of appointment to a judicial post,[55] the reasoning in the decision remained within the express language of the statute and exhibits a predominance of the medical model of understanding disability. The decision records that the petitioner specifically argued that the RPwD Act 2016 is beneficial/welfare legislation and did not argue that the new Act was meant to usher in a new era of rights and non-discrimination. The State[56] argued that the disability the petitioner suffered from was not permanent, and hence the person did not qualify for consideration under the quota.

Despite legislative changes with a more fluid definition of disability, additional requirements, such as permanency of the disability, were read into the Statute when it was clear that the statute did not prescribe any such additional requirements. The real issue was that the State did not consider a person with disability as suitable for a judicial position. The counter-affidavit filed by the State argued that the position was a post with "great and multiple responsibilities" and involved "a severely stressful work-life and environment". The State argued that appointing a person with disability would not only create "a risk not only for the service rendered but also towards the overall mental health and wellbeing of the Petitioner".

The RPwD Act 2016 seems inadequate to address the questions of attitudinal barriers, exclusion from employment despite clear provisions. One explanation for this shortfall is the lack of a comprehensive employment discrimination

54 Jadhav Vishwas Haridas v Union Public Service Commission & Ors., supra n. 2, para. 27.

55 Bhavya Nain v High Court of Delhi, judgment dt. 8 May 2020, para. 38 available at Indian Kanoon – http://indiankanoon.org/doc/33826851/ (accessed 29 May 2021).

56 Ibid.

framework.[57] The other explanation is the limitation of a black-letter law approach, which seeks to confine the application of law only to those matters explicitly provided for and to take a strict, narrow interpretation of the law.

The next section will examine if dedicated legislation on discrimination holds the key to better enforcement of the right against discrimination in employment.

4 Other Legislative Proposals

India lacks dedicated legislation on employment discrimination. This means that the only forum to litigate employment discrimination is the higher judiciary (i.e. the High Courts and the Supreme Court). In the case of other forms of discrimination such as gender or caste, since Article 15 of the Constitution of India explicitly prohibits discrimination on these grounds, a petition is maintainable under this provision. Disability is not explicitly included here, and hence Article 15 does not get invoked in cases of disability discrimination. Petitions are brought under provisions of equal opportunity or equality and the right to life.[58] The access is restricted to certain groups and against state institutions only.

The Centre for Law and Policy Research (CLPR) has proposed an Equality Bill to remedy this situation by including 25 grounds on which discrimination is prohibited, including disability.[59] The Bill has a definition of discrimination which includes direct and indirect discrimination, multiple and intersectional discrimination, and systemic or structural discrimination. The proposed bill also seeks to set up Equality Courts in addition to internal mechanisms within institutions. The Bill is based on a broad and ambitious definition of protected groups that leaves little space for newer groups unless such a group is notified. It includes workplace harassment as well as newer forms of hate crime such as lynching and hate speech. It specifically meets the demand for a framework to include the private sector, which is usually outside the ambit of the constitutional protection against discrimination. Legislations like the RPwD Act 2016 also do not include the private sector for the purpose of quota in employment. The CLPR Bill builds on the framework of the RPwD Act 2016 and contains similar provisions on reasonable accommodation that will operate in the private sector along with the public sector.

57 Deepti Shenoy, supra n. 16, page 613.

58 Article 14, supra n. 16, Article 16. (1) There shall be equality of opportunity for all citizens in matters relating to employment or appointment to any office under the State, Article 21. No person shall be deprived of his life or personal liberty except according to procedure established by law.

59 The bill lists the following grounds as prohibited grounds: caste, race, ethnicity, descent, colour, sex, sexual orientation, gender identity, gender expression, tribe, nationality, disability, marital status, pregnancy, health (including HIV/AIDS status), occupation, political opinion and belief, linguistic identity, place of birth, age, migration, religion, refugee status, socioeconomic disadvantage, food preference or any combination of these characteristics (Section 2(oo)) 2020. See the Equality Bill 2019, available at https://clpr.org.in/wp-content/uploads/2019/06/Equality-Bill-2019.pdf (accessed 29 May 2021).

In contrast, the Report on the Equal Opportunity Commission underscores the provisions in the Indian Constitution that enshrine a substantive approach to equality and more importantly a distinct and perhaps radical approach to equality that is suited to the Indian scenario.[60] The Indian Constitution has specific provisions on representation in education, public employment and political representation at several levels for marginalised communities. The commitment in the Constitution extends to more than quotas and formal non-discrimination but encompasses a radical vision of social and economic rights perhaps unrivalled in the world. The proposed Commission would work with not only the concept of discrimination but also deprivation. The Report observes that deprivation which could include the non-availability of minimum threshold conditions would be useful to measure inequality of opportunity. The report recommended that a mechanism such as an Equal Opportunity Commission (EOC) be set up that could take measures on a range of rights and entitlements including employment.[61] In particular, the Report indicated that access to the Commission must not be restricted to predefined groups. This openness would be useful to newer claims that could be made instead of freezing protected groups.[62] In this understanding of discrimination law, which moves beyond simple employer or individual specific acts to structural and systemic causes requiring organisations to look beyond individuals and to root causes of discrimination, the ideas of a transformative constitution and its resonance in the workplace have more relevance than another statute on equality.

While both proposals do not meet the need for dedicated employment discrimination legislation, the experience of litigation on the ground of discrimination suggests that the constitutional framework does envisage a broad and integrated understanding of equality and discrimination. The case of *Surendra Mohan*[63] is an example that the constitutional court's jurisdiction is invoked despite the legislative framework and legislative mechanism.

5 Conclusion

The case of *Surendra Mohan*[64] demonstrates the inadequacy of the approach of special legislation as against a conceptual approach to discrimination in general and employment discrimination in particular. It also exposes the inadequacies of

60 Report of the Expert Group set up to examine the structure and function of an equal opportunity commission (2008) submitted to the Ministry of Minority Affairs available at www.minorityaffairs.gov.in/sites/default/files/eoc_wwh.pdf (accessed 22 December 2020), pages 17 and 18.

61 Ibid., at page 20, the proposed Equal Opportunity Commission could be instituted with the following operational definitions: "Equal Opportunities" mean such measures through and by which a person or persons can achieve parity of conditions or shedding of disadvantages in accessing education, employment, livelihood, health care, housing, credit or such other rights and entitlements.

62 Ibid., at page 33.

63 Surendra Mohan v State of Tamilnadu and Others, supra n. 9.

64 Ibid.

a quota in employment to address the questions of discrimination in employment. The quota provisions in a special statute on disability remain locked in a narrow and literal interpretation when they are not read in a manner that gives effect to their non-discriminatory objective. The spirit and intention of the legislation can be given effect only when the relevant principles on non-discrimination law are read into it. The wider understanding of constitutional principles would allow for a more expansive understanding of disability--based discrimination. It will also allow for disability discourse to influence the understanding of other groups where similar questions could arise. The proposed EOC, which can use high-profile litigation as a strategy to develop a transformative vision, may have more benefits not only with respect to questions of discrimination but also deprivation of basic conditions, which has a great significance in India. The *Surendra Mohan*[65] decision is a good example of discrimination laundering, where the statute and its interpretation are a "ticking all the boxes" kind of discrimination but do not address discrimination in a wider sense. This form of discrimination laundering does more to entrench than remove discrimination. The decision was overruled by invoking the concepts of dignity, autonomy, participation, inclusion and accessibility, equality and non-discrimination, and respect for differences through the concept of anti-stereotyping developed by the constitutional court. This demonstrates that constitutional jurisprudence which has been built over many decades should guide discrimination law and that will result in a transformed interpretation of non-discrimination legislation, such as the RPwD Act 2016.

Bibliography

Books

Green Tristin, *Discrimination Laundering: The Rise of Organizational Innocence and the Crisis of Equal Opportunity Law* (Cambridge University Press 2017).

Kannabiran Kalpana, *Tools of Justice: Non-Discrimination and the Indian Constitution* (Routledge 2012).

Chapters

Dhanda Amita, Establishing a Disability Studies Centre in a Law University: Recounting the CDS NALSAR Experience (Ch.) in Nilika Mehrotra (Ed.) *Disability Studies in India: Interdisciplinary Perspectives* pp. 147–166 (Springer 2020).

Khaitan Tarunabh, Equality: Legislative Review under Article 14 (Ch.) in Sujit Choudhry et al. (Eds.) *The Oxford Handbook of the Indian Constitution* pp. 699–719 (OUP 2016).

Suk Julie C., Quotas and Consequences: A Transnational Re-evaluation (Ch.) in Deborah Hellman and Sophia Moreau (Eds.) *Philosophical Foundation of Discrimination Law* pp. 228–249 at p. 234 (OUP 2013).

65 Ibid.

Vasanthi N., Right to Work for Persons with Disabilities in India: A Critical Disability Theory Perspective (Ch.) in Nilika Mehrotra (Ed.) *Disability Studies in India: Interdisciplinary perspectives* pp. 243–259 (Springer 2020).

Zatz Noah D., Discrimination and Labour Law: Locating the Market in Maldistribution and Subordination (Ch.) in Hugh Collins et al. (Eds.) *Philosophical Foundations of Labour Law* pp. 156–174 (OUP 2019).

Articles

Atrey Shreya, *Through the Looking Glass of Intersectionality: Making Sense of Indian Discrimination Jurisprudence under Article 15*, 16 The Equal Rights Review 160–185 (2016).

Dhanda Amita, *Constructing a New Human Rights Lexicon: Convention on the Rights of Persons with Disabilities*, 8 SUR – Int'l J. on Hum Rts. 43 (2008).

Khaitan Tarunabh, *Beyond Reasonableness – A Rigorous Standard of Review for Article 15 Infringement*, 50(2) Journal of Indian Law Institute 177–208 (2008).

Shenoy Deepti, *Courting Substantive Equality: Employment Discrimination Law in India*, 34 U. Pa. J. Int'l L. 611–640 (2013).

International Conventions and Other Materials

The Equality Bill 2019 available at: https://clpr.org.in/wp-content/uploads/2019/06/Equality-Bill-2019.pdf last accessed on 29th May 2021.

United Nations Convention on the Rights of Persons with Disabilities 2008.

Indian Laws

Constitution of India 1950.

The Persons with Disabilities (Equal Opportunities, Protection of Rights and Full Participation) Act 1995.

The Rights of Persons with Disabilities Act 2016.

Indian Case Law

Air India v Nergesh Meerza (1981) 4 SCC 335.

Garg Anuj v Hotel Assn. Of India, (2008) 3 SCC 1.

Haridas Jadhav Vishwas v Union Public Service Commission & Ors., 2016 SCC OnLine Del 5759.

Haridas Jadhav Vishwas v Union Public Service Commission & Ors., supra n.1, para. 27.

Johar Navtej Singh v Union of India, (2018) 1 SCC 791.

Kumar Vikash v UPSC, 2020 SCC Online 84.

Ministry of Defence v Babita Puniya (2020) 7 SCC 469.

Mohan Surendra v State of Tamilnadu and Others (2019) 4 SCC 237.

Nagaraj M. v UOI (2006) 8 SCC 212.

Nain Bhavya v High Court of Delhi, judgment dt. 8th May 2020 available at: Indian Kanoon – http://indiankanoon.org/doc/33826851/ last accessed on 29th May 2021.

National Legal Services Authority v Union of India, (2014) 5 SCC 438.

Royappa EP v State of Tamil Nadu (1974) 4 SCC 3.
Sawhney Indra v UOI 1992 Suppl. (3) SCC 217.
State of West Bengal v Anwar Ali Sarkar AIR 1952 SC 75.

Reports

Report of the Expert Group set up to examine the structure and function of an equal opportunity commission, (2008), submitted to the Ministry of Minority Affairs available at: www.minorityaffairs.gov.in/sites/default/files/eoc_wwh.pdf.

SWADHIKAAR-AWARE-DRPI, Employment Rights of Persons with disabilities in India, (2017), available at: http://drpi.research.yorku.ca/wp-content/uploads/2018/08/Hyderabad-Report-English.pdf.

Websites

https://clpr.org.in/

12 Gender Discrimination in Israel

Raphael Cohen-Almagor and Uki Maroshek-Klarman

Liberty means responsibility. That is why most men dread it.

—George Bernard Shaw

1 Introduction

The founding fathers of Israel wished that country to be a democratic Jewish home.[1] Cohen-Almagor has explained the inherent tensions between Judaism and democracy elsewhere, thus we will not elaborate on the reasoning here.[2] This chapter builds and expands on an article that deals with the status of women in Jewish law.[3] For the purposes of this discussion, we note the underlying premises and concepts upon which this chapter is based:

- *Freedom versus coercion*: People would like to lead their private matters as free and autonomous human beings. Thus, coercion that infringes privacy and interferes in our intimate affairs is foreign to us, offensive to our sensibilities and leads to an increased sense of alienation and resentment.
- *Gender equality*: Men and women should enjoy equal human and civil rights. Men are not inferior to women. Women are not inferior to men.[4] While men and women are biologically different, biology should not lead to a differentiation of rights and liberties. Countries which perceive biology as the dictating factor are racist countries.

1 David Ben-Gurion, How the State Be Established? in D. Ben-Gurion (ed.), *As Israel Fights* (Tel Aviv: Mapai, 1951), pp. 207–212; David Ben-Gurion, *Uniqueness and Mission* (Tel Aviv: Maarachot, 1971); D. Ben-Gurion, Divrei Haknesset (Knesset Proceedings), 20 February 1950, 117 meeting, Vol. IV, p 817 (all in Hebrew).

2 R. Cohen-Almagor, Avoiding the Destruction of the Third Temple: Separating State and Religion, in Yossi Goldstein (ed.), *Religion Nationalism: The Struggle for Modern Jewish Identity, An Interdisciplinary Annual* (Ariel: Ariel University, 2014), pp. 170–189.

3 R. Cohen-Almagor, Discrimination against Jewish Women in Halacha (Jewish Law) and in Israel, 45 *British Journal of Middle Eastern Studies*, 2, pp. 290–310 (2018).

4 Susan Moller Okin, Feminism, Women's Human Rights, and Cultural Differences, 13 *Hypatia*, 2, pp. 32–52 (Spring 1998).

DOI: 10.4324/9781003306962-15

- *Religion* is a matter of personal choice, faith and belief. Because religion provides an all-encompassing framework for all issues, people should be free to take what is appealing to them and reject aspects that are less appealing.
- Consequently, *freedom of religion* and *freedom from religion* are equally important. Both are matters of personal choice. Citizens in a democracy should enjoy the ability to choose one or the other. Each and every person should be allowed to choose their conception of the good as they see fit and appropriate for themselves, as long as doing so does not harm others.
- *Public versus private*: A clear distinction has to be drawn between the communal character of the State and personal matters. Personal matters are, by definition, personal. The State should limit its involvement in such matters to an absolute minimum and intervene only when there are significant countervailing public interests.
- *Values*: As Jews, as human beings, we uphold Hillel's postulate: "What is hateful to you do not do unto your fellow people".[5] As liberals, we uphold John Stuart Mill's Harm Principle, which holds that the only purpose for which power can be rightfully exercised over any member of the community, against her will, is to prevent harm to others.[6] On this issue, Judaism and liberalism are in complete harmony.

It is argued that Israeli democracy should give precedence to liberty and equality over Judaism. Section 2 explains the *halachic* grounds for discrimination against women. It is argued that the establishment of patriarchy in Jewish law and its impact on Israeli society negates the premises of gender equality. Section 3 argues that the Israeli-Palestinian conflict advances a militaristic agenda that favours men. The ongoing state of war between Israel and the Palestinians, as well as between Israel and some of its bordering countries, gives centrality to the issue of state security. The military has an instrumental role in the ideological construction of masculine identities that justify and reinforce gender hierarchy where women are second to men. Predominantly male, especially in the upper echelons, this system rewards men not only during their military service but also when they enter the job market.

Section 4 analyses the neoliberal economic structure and the education system that both disadvantage women. Section 5 discusses manifestations of gender discrimination in Israel. These include the lack of women's representation in power positions, the pay gap between men and women, and violence against women. Men enjoy clear power over women. Patriarchal religion, Jewish law (*Halacha*) which excludes women from positions of power and influence, the Arab-Israeli conflict which dictates the necessity for having a strong military, the shift to neoliberal economy which weakened the welfare state, and old-fashioned chauvinism

5 Hillel (Babylonian Talmud. Sabbath 31a).

6 J. S. Mill, *Utilitarianism, Liberty, and Representative Government* (London: J. M. Dent, 1948), Everyman's edition, at 114, or *On Liberty*, available at www.utilitarianism.com/ol/three.html.

have all been instrumental in the creation of sustained discrimination against women and the continuation of gender inequality. Section 6 details milestones in legislation and Supreme Court rulings that aimed to promote women's rights and decrease gender discrimination. The chapter calls for substantive changes to promote gender equality. Israel is required to invest in and empower women. Empowerment of women is not only just: it is bound to lead to the improvement of the social conditions of the entire society.

2 Women in Jewish Law (Halacha)

Jewish law, Halacha, does not perceive men and women as equal. Many of the *Halachot* (dictates in Hebrew) stand in striking contradiction to present conceptions of basic human and civil rights. They negate liberal democracy. Some of these inegalitarian Halachot are still adhered to in Israel today.

In Jewish law, the hierarchy between men and women is clear. Jewish law specifies the ways in which the wife must accept man's rule, tend to matters of the home and fulfil all the duties of practical daily life. She is obligated to serve her husband, revere him like a king, honour and obey him. The woman is required to care for her husband's bed, food and hygiene.[7] The wife is required to soothe her man, comfort him, reassure him and prioritise his wishes above hers.[8] She is required to take care for their children and provide clothing.[9]

In the public sphere, women cannot serve in power positions. Women are excluded from the executive and judicial offices, as well as from the spiritual sphere. The Torah dictates: "be sure to appoint over you a king",[10] not a queen.[11] Women cannot serve as judges[12] or witnesses.[13] They cannot give evidence.[14] In the spiritual sphere, women are expected to defer to men in order to protect public honour.[15] In the private sphere, a woman is always under the authority of a man.

7 Babylonian Talmud: Tractate Kethuboth, Folio 61a, available at www.come-and-hear.com/kethuboth/kethuboth_61.html.

8 Rabbi Forsythe, Shalom Bayis (Peaceful Marriage). Torah and Family Issues When Considering Divorce, available at www.shemayisrael.com/rabbiforsythe/shalombayis/issues.htm.

9 Babylonian Talmud: Tractate Yebamoth, Folio 63a, available at www.come-and-hear.com/yebamoth/yebamoth_63.html; Bava Metzia 59, available at www.dafyomi.co.il/bmetzia/points/bm-ps-059.htm.

10 Deuteronomy 17.

11 Maimonides, Laws of Kings and Wars, available at http://halakhah.com/rst/kingsandwars.pdf.

12 Shulchan Aruch/Choshen Mishpat/7, available at http://en.wikisource.org/wiki/Shulchan_Aruch/Choshen_Mishpat/7. Although Deborah led Israel as a judge. The opening Judges 4:4–5 says: "At that time Deborah, a prophetess, wife of Lappidoth, was judging Israel. She used to sit under the palm of Deborah between Ramah and Bethel in the hill country of Ephraim; and the Israelites came up to her for judgment."

13 Deuteronomy 19:17.

14 Babylonian Talmud: Tractate Baba Kamma 88a, available at www.come-and-hear.com/babakamma/babakamma_88.html.

15 The sages said: "a woman should not read from the Torah mipnei kevod hatzibbur – out of respect for the congregation." See Natalie Bergner, Qeri'at ha-Torah: Public Torah Reading, *Women of the Wall*, available at http://womenofthewall.org.il/qeriat-ha-torah-public-torah-reading/.

First, she is under the authority of her father, and once she weds she is subjected to the authority of her husband.[16]

Halacha discriminates against women and imposes upon them offensive rituals, such as *halizah*, that reflects and illustrates the intricate question of religious coercion in a mostly secular society.[17] In this ceremony, a Jewish widow who has no children releases her brother-in-law from the obligation to marry her in accordance with the law of levirate (*yibum*) and obtains her own freedom to remarry.[18] Another halachic coercive imposition is the lot of women who are unable to live with their husbands for various reasons. Those women cannot remarry until they receive a divorce decree, namely a *get*,[19] from their husbands. Sometimes those women, who are called *agunot* (chained), are subjected to blackmail from the husband who exploits his position to extort financial and other gains as a precondition for granting the bill of divorce.[20]

Women are discouraged from pursuing higher education or religious pursuits. This is because women have "frivolous minds"[21] and also because they have important roles to fulfil at home as wives and mothers.[22] As these tasks are very demanding, women are incapable of splitting their time between the home and pursuits of high education or religion to which they are ill-equipped; thus, success in them would demand from them more effort at the expense of caring for the home. Women must never neglect their husbands and children. The priorities are clear.

The common defence for maintaining this state of affairs holds that the exemptions that women are given from religious and other obligations are meant to foster women's ability to carry out their own tasks.[23] The structured view of the world yields constructive allocation of time for each gender to perform its duties. Freedom of choice is limited. Contrary to the liberal tradition, where people are able to decide what they wish to do, in the halachic world people should abide by the Torah and other religious tracts that provide exact directives as to how people should guide and direct their lives, not as they see fit but rather as God commands. Tout court denial of choice undermines women's ability to lead what they may perceive as a meaningful way of life.

16 Babylonian Talmud: Tractate Kethuboth 48a, available at www.come-and-hear.com/kethuboth/kethuboth_48.html. For further discussion, see Rachel Biale, *Women and Jewish Law: The Essential Texts, Their History, and Their Relevance for Today* (New York: Schocken, 1995).

17 R. Cohen-Almagor, Israeli Democracy, Religion and the Practice of Halizah in Jewish Law, 11 *UCLA Women's Law Journal*, 1, pp. 45–65 (Fall/Winter 2000).

18 Ibid.

19 Spelled also *gett*.

20 Robert Gordis, Agunot: A Different Kind of Hostage, *My Jewish Learning* (2021), available at www.myjewishlearning.com/article/agunot-a-different-kind-of-hostage/.

21 Tirzah Meacham, Legal-Religious Status of the Jewish Female, *Jewish Women Encyclopedia*, available at http://jwa.org/encyclopedia/article/legal-religious-status-of-jewish-female.

22 The Role of Women, Judaism 101, available at www.jewfaq.org/women.htm.

23 Rabbi Mark Goldfeder, Defining Equality in Judaism, available at http://morethodoxy.org/2012/10/25/defining-equality-in-judaism-by-rabbi-mark-goldfeder/; R. Cohen-Almagor, *Discrimination against Jewish Women in Halacha (Jewish Law) and in Israel*, pp. 290–310.

Halacha explains that men and women have different qualities. Men are anatomically and spiritually external, and often view life from a more external viewpoint. Women, on the other hand, are anatomically and spiritually internal. They see the world from a more internal and holistic perspective.[24] Women should not try to be men. God has assigned men for particular tasks and women for others. Women are equal, but different. Jewish women have their own mission, their own identity, their own worth. The Torah commands that "[a] man shall not wear a woman's garment", so equally it commands "[a] man's garment shall not be on a woman".[25] Neither men nor women should imitate the other. "A woman has no reason to feel inferior to a man, and therefore she has no need to try to be as a man".[26] Claims made by critique of Judaism about women's inferiority and discrimination are false. God assigned women and men distinct identities that supplement each other. Women's honour is inward, taking care of the house, of the men, of the children, providing a safe haven for the men who go about doing their God-given tasks. Men recognise this and thus let them be in charge of household matters.[27] In Israel, this also means that women often go to work to support their families while their husbands spend their time studying, debating and rehearsing verses in the "tent of Torah".[28]

The tension between Israel's Jewish identity and the commitment of its founders to democratic principles greatly impacts gender equality. The legislature enacted some important laws to advance the status of women. Alongside this progressive legislation there are also impressive efforts of civil society organisations to promote gender equality. However, there are also societal processes that hinder the impact of advanced legislation. The security situation, the unresolved Israeli-Palestinian conflict and the gradual economic transition from a socialist structure to a social democratic one to neoliberalism, which is the current ethos guiding economic considerations, impact unfavourably the status of women.

3 The Israeli-Palestinian Conflict

Since the establishment of the State of Israel and for several years prior to its establishment, Israel has been in conflict with its neighbours and with the

24 Meir Goldberg, Moral problems in Halacha: Women, available at http://truetorah.blogspot.com/2013/07/moral-problems-in-halacha-women-with.html.

25 Equal Rights, Sichos in English, available at www.sichosinenglish.org/essays/70.htm.

26 Equal Rights, Sichos in English, available at www.sichosinenglish.org/essays/70.htm.

27 Rabbi Forsythe, Shalom Bayis (Peaceful Marriage). Torah and Family Issues When Considering Divorce, available at www.shemayisrael.com/rabbiforsythe/shalombayis/issues.htm; Bava Metzia 59a.

28 This phrase is used also against those who demand equality in the burdens of citizenship, with the implication that religious men should serve like secular men in the Israeli Defence Forces (IDF). See, for instance MK Parush: "Incitement Against Those Who Kill Themselves in the Tent of the Torah", *Kooker* (30 January 2014).

Palestinian people. Wars and life-threatening security incidents occur as a matter of routine.[29] This security situation impacts upon the country's citizens in myriad ways, and one of the primary ones is its effect on inequality between men and women.

The largest institution which deals with safeguarding the country's residents – or as some might put it, maintaining the Israeli occupation over the West Bank and Gaza – is the Israel Defense Forces (IDF). This institution is run predominantly by men. The High Command of the IDF and its middle ranks are vested almost exclusively by men. Already in 1996, the sociologist Eva Etzioni-Halevy argued that the military is among the primary factors resulting in women's exclusion from governmental power centres and positions in the upper echelons of the Israeli business sector.[30]

Israel is a nation in arms. The IDF is one of the only armies in the world that recruits women to its service by virtue of a Compulsory Recruitment Law. Women make up 25% of the officer corps.[31] Yet as one climbs the military ranks, the number of women decreases. One of the reasons is that while some women serve in combat units, they do not habitually do this. The number of women in combat units is small: in 2017, 7% of women in the IDF were serving in combat units.[32] Hegemonic masculinity reinforces practices of gendered identities and gender stereotypes are applied in the analysis of war policies and performances. These stereotypes prevent women's incorporation into combat roles, which hold the highest professional status in the military.[33] Thus women who are able to be admitted to combat units are facing a battle not only against the enemies of the State but also against the patriarchal nature of the military.[34]

Many high school graduates enlist in the IDF. The length of service is 30 months for men and 24 months for women.[35] As such, it is the first political apparatus that they embark on in the world. The first experience these young men and women have is an encounter with an essentially all-consuming, masculine institution in which women serve men at different levels. Young women serve as clerks,

29 Charles D. Freilich, *Israel National Security* (New York: Oxford University Press, 2018); Raphael Cohen-Almagor and Amos Guiora, Democracy and Security in Israel, in Leonard Weinberg, Elizabeth Francis et al. (eds.), *Routledge Handbook of Democracy and Security* (London and New York: Routledge, 2021), pp. 172–190.

30 Eva Etzioni-Halevy, Civil-Military Relations and Democracy: The Case of the Military Political Elites' Connection in Israel, 27 *Armed Forces and Society*, pp. 401–417 (1996). For further discussion, see Orna Sasson-Levy, Research on Gender and the Military in Israel. From a Gendered Organization to Inequality Regimes, 26 *Israel Studies Review*, 2, pp. 73–98 (2011).

31 Data from the Israel Defense Forces' spokesperson's office (12 July 2018).

32 Ayelet Harel-Shalev & Shir Daphna-Tekoah, *Breaking the Binaries in Security Studies: A Gendered Analysis of Women in Combat* (New York: Oxford University Press, 2020), p. 8.

33 Ibid., p. 75.

34 Ibid., p. 97.

35 R. Cohen-Almagor, *Just, Reasonable Multiculturalism* (New York and Cambridge: Cambridge University Press, 2021), chap. 10.

receptionists and other positions of that nature.[36] While in recent years there has been an increase in women serving in positions of a different nature and more women serve in combat units, there is only a negligible minority of women whose experience differs from the aforementioned service positions.[37]

These facts are of great importance because this is the realm in which consciousness on the matter of service and labour relations between Jewish women and men in Israel is shaped for the first time. Women soldiers enlist at age 18, while their commanders, who hold higher ranks, are in the main considerably older men who have garnered experience and expertise. In this framework there is very little gender equality. The consciousness created in these young women is that of women filling lower positions versus men with seemingly superior abilities. Furthermore, women who have military roles that are similar to those that men have still do not feel equal. One combatant woman described herself by saying "I am not a strong woman, but a kind of weak man".[38] That this woman described herself as a "weak man" and not as a "strong woman" or simply a "woman" is telling. The masculinity bias is especially vivid in the military.[39] For these 18-year-old Israeli women, the military experience normalises a worldview of inequality. Women subsequently enter the labour force having in their psyche a view of a structured reality where women serve men.

At times, women soldiers serve at a great distance from their homes, and this physical distance creates conditions in which commanders exploit the power at their disposal to impose pressure that sometimes borders on sexual harassment. In 2004, there were 358 reported sexual offences; 102 of these consisted of sexual assaults against female soldiers.[40] Another report indicated that one in five female soldiers was sexually harassed during 2003.[41] In 2017, an IDF report indicated that one in six female soldiers was sexually harassed.[42] About 110 soldiers are suspected of sexual harassment each year.[43] Some of these cases involve senior male officers who sexually harassed or attacked young female soldiers under their command, abusing their power and authority to inflict trauma on their victims. One can assume that there are many more cases that are neither exposed nor handled by the relevant military apparatus. Every once in a while, such cases are reported

36 Brigadier General Rachel Tevet-Wiesel and Lt. Col Ariel Wiener, Charging Forward Against All Odds, 456 *Maarachot*, pp. 38–41 (21 August 2014) (Hebrew).

37 Ibid.

38 Ayelet Harel-Shalev & Shir Daphna-Tekoah, *Breaking the Binaries in Security Studies: A Gendered Analysis of Women in Combat*, p. 78.

39 Sarah Bulmer & Maya Eichler, Unmaking Militarized Masculinity: Veterans and The Project of Military-to-Civilian Transition, 3 *Critical Military Studies*, 2, pp. 161–181 (2017).

40 "Statistics on Sexual Violence in the IDF", *Makom* (24 January 2005) (Hebrew), www.macom.org.il/definitions/stats-home/stats-army/.

41 Ibid.

42 Gili Cohen, Internal IDF Survey: One in Six Female Soldiers Was Sexually Harassed During Military Service, *Haaretz* (10 September 2017) (Hebrew).

43 Imry Levi Sadan, Military and Security News, *Walla* (20 November 2017) (Hebrew).

on the media. For instance, in November 2017 six female soldiers and officers filed a sexual harassment complaint against a lieutenant colonel in their unit.[44]

The sense of camaraderie and brotherhood fostered during military service continues to filter into general civic society after soldiers have been discharged from the military. They support and help their fellow soldiers professionally when they search to fill vacancies. With that sort of built-in pecking order, women are left behind. Women find it very difficult to penetrate this informal screening process that takes place in the workplace. The men who run it are not necessarily conscious of these inclinations and may even be among those who define themselves as supporting gender equality. One example of this proclivity can be found in the high-tech industry, which compensates its employees well and is often populated by this kind of selection that disadvantages women.[45]

It is not only the joint service of men and the brotherhood fostered by serving together that causes them to prefer their peers over women who are equally talented and equal in skill. This tendency is bolstered by economic considerations. The IDF provides valuable training of certain highly sought-after professions, such as computer science. Naturally, business people prefer to employ the most professionally trained candidate, who in this case was trained in the military, over others whom the employer must train at his own expense. It goes without saying that a discharged Air Force pilot would be hired as a pilot for a commercial airline, whereas a woman who could not serve in that position in the military would not be accepted. High-tech and the airline industry are but two examples of many.[46]

Prioritising Israel's security issues over other issues causes the country's citizens to prefer people with military experience to hold positions in other realms of power and influence. Thus, women in Israel who strive for competitive positions find themselves almost doomed to failure from the outset. Households that are led and sponsored by women are 15%–20% poorer compared to households that are sponsored mainly by men.[47] According to the 2013 Central Bureau of Statistics, women's salaries average 66% of men's.[48] On this issue, Israeli women do not progress to the same extent that women in many countries in the western world progress. In 2018, a woman's average monthly salary was 69% of a man's

44 Nir Dvori, Lt. Col. Suspected of Sexually Harassing Female Soldiers, *N12* (19 November 2017) (Hebrew), available at www.mako.co.il/news-military/security-q4_2017/Article-4dc9015ef03df51004.htm.

45 Imry Levi Sadan, Military and Security News, *Walla* (20 November 2017) (Hebrew).

46 Gavriela Davidovich-Weisberg, Want to Be a Pilot at El Al? Maybe Now You'll Have a Better Chance, *The Marker* (18 June 2018) (Hebrew).

47 Miri Endeweld & Daniel Gottlieb, *The Socio-Economic Status of Women in Israel 1997–2011* (Jerusalem: National Insurance Institute, October 2013), p. 2 (Hebrew), available at www.btl.gove.il.

48 Israel Central Bureau of Statistics (2013). See also Israel Ranked 55 in the World According to the Equality Index Between Men and Women, *Haaretz* (2 November 2011), available at www.haaretz.co.il/news/education/1.1553548; Linda Efroni, Men's Salary Is 1.9 Times Higher Than Women's Salary, *Noga* (1996, Hebrew), available at http://lib.cet.ac.il/pages/item.asp?item=3131.

salary.[49] A recent World Economic Forum (WEF) report found that women make 65%–68% of what the average man makes.[50]

In 2014, the State Comptroller surveyed 68 government companies. All general directors of these companies were men.[51] Another report, from 2017, surveyed the number of female CEOs in the country. The report found that out of 50,000 CEOs, 8,700 were women. In percentages, that means 17%, or one in six. The improvement may be the result of more female entrepreneurs founding and heading their own small companies, rather than changes in the general selection process.[52]

The United Nations Committee on the Elimination of Discrimination against Women (CEDAW) in its 2017 report on Israel stressed gender discrimination stemming from Israel's unholy alliance of religion and state, indicating the low number of women in the Knesset (Parliament), ministerial positions, senior academic and diplomatic positions, and the fact that women cannot serve as judges in rabbinical courts.[53] The majority of women tend to work in jobs that are seen as "feminine": teaching, nursing and clerical assistant positions, which are relatively low paid and offer limited benefits. This is despite the fact that women are more educated than men.[54]

The political arena in Israel has witnessed strong involvement of army generals. Former chiefs of staff, Yitzhak Rabin and Ehud Barak, served as prime ministers. Rabin filled this role twice. General Ariel Sharon also filled the most senior role in Israeli politics. Recently, a centrist political party led by former generals received popular support to fill key positions in running the country, despite lacking necessary civic experience. The trio comprised former chiefs of staff: Benjamin Gantz, Gabi Ashkenazi and Moshe (Bogie) Ya'alon. The longest-serving prime minister in the history of the country, Benjamin Netanyahu, served in one of the IDF elite combat units.[55]

49 Michal Margalit, Women Still Earn Less But the Income Gap Has Narrowed – The Lowest Since 1990, *Ynet* (17 December 2018, Hebrew), available at www.ynet.co.il/articles/0,7340,L-5427560,00.html.

50 Israel Plummets in Gender Equality Ranking, *Ynet* (22 December 2019), available at www.ynetnews.com/article/SJw11cXT0H.

51 Yael Fridson, State Comptroller: 68 General Directors of Government Companies – All Men, *NRG* (4 March 2014) (Hebrew), available at www.nrg.co.il/online/1/ART2/561/945.html?hp=1&cat=402&loc=1.

52 Shahar Ilan, Despite Progress, Only One in Six Israeli CEOs Is a Woman, New Report Says, *Calcalist* (29 January 2020), available at www.calcalistech.com/ctech/articles/0,7340,L-3784650,00.html.

53 Religion & Gender Discrimination in Israel, *Hiddush* (27 November 2017), available at http://hiddush.org/article-22155-0-Religion__gender_discrimination_in_Israel.aspx.

54 Shahar Ilan, Despite Progress, Only One in Six Israeli CEOs Is a Woman, New Report Says, *Calcalist* (29 January 2020), available at www.calcalistech.com/ctech/articles/0,7340,L-3784650,00.html. See also Israel Ministry of Foreign Affairs, Women in Israel Today (8 March 2016), available at https://mfa.gov.il/MFA/AboutIsrael/Spotlight/Pages/Women-in-Israel-today.aspx, and Directorship of Research and Economy, *20 Facts on Employment Gaps Between Women and Men* (Jerusalem, 2010), p. 3 (Hebrew).

55 It is noted that one woman, Golda Meir, served as prime minister.

Women who seek to attain key positions in Israeli society and particularly in politics will encounter substantial obstacles relating to their lack of military experience and valuable connections. In response, women's organisations have been trying to promote gender equality via educational means, as well as via involvement in the advancement of peace; this is in the hope of influencing societal values and power relations. In October 2020, the international community marked the twentieth anniversary of UN Security Council Resolution (UNSCR) 1325 and its two decades of efforts to integrate women and their perspectives in peace and security.[56] Resolution 1325, adopted by the Security Council at its 4213th meeting, on 31 October 2000, "urges Member States to ensure increased representation of women at all decision-making levels in national, regional and international institutions and mechanisms for the prevention, management, and resolution of conflict". The Resolution also

> [u]rges Member States to increase their voluntary financial, technical and logistical support for gender-sensitive training efforts, including those undertaken by relevant funds and programmes, inter alia, the United Nations Fund for Women and United Nations Children's Fund, and by the Office of the United Nations High Commissioner for Refugees and other relevant bodies.[57]

In this context, women are waging a struggle to redefine "security" in a fashion that incorporates their interests and concerns, for example, their personal security against male violence. The women's groups that support UN Resolution 1325, such as the Women Wage Peace movement comprising 40,000 members, promotes legislation that will prevent unnecessary wars. The group declares:

> We are a grassroots movement with tens of thousands of members from the right, center and left of the political spectrum, Jews and Arabs, religious and secular, united in the demand for a mutually binding non-violent agreement between Israelis and Palestinian, involving women in the process.[58]

In 2020, Women Wage Peace initiated a draft bill that calls for the creation of a legally binding decision-making process for the government that would require to maintain a systematic examination of non-military options before launching military campaigns.[59] The bill wishes to circumvent the militarisation of Israeli society and to promote peace and gender equality.

56 What is UNSCR 1325? US Institute of Peace, available at www.usip.org/gender_peacebuilding/about_UNSCR_1325.

57 UN Resolution 1325 (31 October 2000), available at www.un.org/en/ga/search/view_doc.asp?symbol=S/RES/1325 (2000).

58 Women Wage Peace, available at https://womenwagepeace.org.il/en/.

59 Patricia Golan, A Law to Prevent the Next War? *Jerusalem Post* (12 August 2020), available at www.jpost.com/jerusalem-report/a-law-to-prevent-the-next-war-637328.

4 The Neoliberal Economic Structure and Gender Equality

In the nascent years of the State of Israel, its economic infrastructure had social democratic foundations.[60] Israel inherited from the British Mandate the ideas of care for the poor and the foundations of the welfare state. The socialist leaders of the young country believed in building a broadly inclusive social infrastructure. This infrastructure had undergone a significant transformation since 1977, when the right-wing party Likud first came to power. The Likud-led coalitions have strong tendencies to neoliberal economy. Privatisation had become a part in the economic programmes of many countries, including Israel, at the beginning of the 1980s. This trend was exacerbated due to the collapse of the Soviet Union and the communist countries in Eastern Europe during that period. The economic difficulties faced by companies owned by the General Organization of Workers in Israel, the *Histadrut*, forced the government to sell companies to the private sector.[61] The shift from a socialist economy to a neoliberal economy grew in the 21st century. Currently, the Israeli economy supports minimal economic intervention and the privatisation of public institutions.[62] The government is basically limited to providing security, minimal education and basic health care. Most social needs are provided by the private market or by various NGOs.[63]

This shift from a socialist economy to a neoliberal economy has had a significant effect on the status of women in Israel. Women occupy low-paid public service positions more than men.[64] Increasing privatisation of the public service coupled with the abolition of parts of it affects the dismissal of women and concurrently their bargaining power in competing with men's salaries.[65] The lack of State-funded educational institutions for children up to the age of 3 and the lack of sufficient public budgets for preschool children daycare requires one parent to remain at home. This role is habitually assigned to women. Women either give up their job or opt for part-time work.[66] This leads to an economic dependence on men.

60 Ben-Zion Zilberfarb, From Socialism to Free Market – The Israeli Economy: 1948–2003, in R. Cohen-Almagor (ed.), *Israeli Democracy at the Crossroads* (London: Routledge, 2005), pp. 12–22.

61 Ibid.

62 Asaf Shapira, Privatization – a Theoretical and Historical Overview, 64 *Parliament* (23 March 2010) (Hebrew), available at www.idi.org.il/parliaments/11097/11145.

63 Ernie Lightman, On the Demise of the Welfare State, *Haaretz* (14 March 2008).

64 Dana Yarkazi and or Ravid, "Work as Teachers and Caregivers – Earn Less: Israeli Women in Numbers, *Walla* (6 March 2017, Hebrew), available at http://news.walla.co.il/item/3046163.

65 Yael Hasson, Privatization of Public Services in Israel, in *Women's Employment in the Days of Privatization* (Adva Center, 28 October 2007) (Hebrew). For general discussion, see Amir Paz-Fuchs, Ronen Mandelkern, & Itzhak Galnoor (eds.), *The Privatization of Israel: The Withdrawal of State Responsibility* (London: Palgrave Macmillan, 2019).

66 Hila Weisberg, I Gave Up a Career to Raise the Kids – What a Miss, *The Marker* (29 August 2013) (Hebrew); Shiri Grosbard, When We Start a Family We Are Basically Giving Up Our Place in the Race for a Career, *Mako* (18 September 2017) (Hebrew), available at www.mako.co.il/study-career-career/articles/Article-bbdb5d29c008e51006.htm.

Sylvie Fogiel-Bijaoui explains that three interrelated factors shape and contribute to gender inequality in Israel. The first is that Israel has a neoliberal economic policy that is fuelled by the "secondary work" ideology. Women more often than men are incorporated in the workplace in conditions of paid work for a limited period of time, have no control over their working conditions, lack protection in employment, and earn low incomes. Second, the Israeli-Palestinian conflict sustains a comprehensive social and cultural structure that benefits men far more than women. The military provides men with more personal, social and institutional capital, which helps them to establish themselves in civilian life, especially in politics. Third, religion is central to the codification of the social order to the detriment of women.[67]

Former Deputy Knesset Speaker Naomi Chazan adds a further explanation. Chazan argues that privatisation, the downsizing of state involvement in the economy, and the slashing of the social security network left many women in a precarious situation. While a greater number of women entered the workforce since the beginning of the 2000s, many women found themselves in less remunerative fields, in part-time jobs, and earning 30%–50% less than their male counterparts. Men continue to control power positions while women remain impoverished and underutilised. Gender inequality with all its negative ramifications is further solidified.[68]

5 Manifestations of Gender Discrimination

Israel's first prime minister, David Ben-Gurion, wished to maintain unity of the Zionist secular and religious elements of society. At the same time, he wished to demarcate cultural and religious disparities between the Arabs and the Jews.[69] Aiming to establish a monolithic Zionist-Israeli-Jewish identity, Ben-Gurion negotiated the identity of the newly established State with the religious Orthodox community. The Israeli government decided to grant the rabbinical courts jurisdiction over issues pertaining to personal status, which were most important for the Orthodoxy. Israeli leaders acknowledged that the survival of Israel and of

67 Sylvie Fogiel-Bijaoui, Navigating Gender Inequality in Israel: The Challenges of Feminism, in Eliezer Ben-Rafael, Julius Schoeps, Yitzhak Sternberg, & Olaf Gluckner (eds.), *Handbook of Israel: Major Debates* (Berlin: De Gruyter Oldenbourg, 2016), pp. 423–436, available at www.researchgate.net/publication/334721534_Navigating_Gender_Inequality_in_Israel_-The_Challenges_of_Feminism. See also Sylvie Fogiel-Bijaoui, *Democracy and Feminism: Gender, Citizenship and Human Rights* (Ra'anana: The Open University, 2011) (Hebrew); Momi Dahan, *Did the Economic Melting Pot Succeed?* Discussion Paper Series (Jerusalem: The Hebrew University of Jerusalem, The Feher Institute, 2013) (Hebrew).

68 Naomi Chazan, Israel at 70: A Gender Perspective, 23 *Israel Studies*, 3, pp. 141–151 (Fall 2018).

69 Efraim Karsh (ed.), *Israel: The First Hundred Years: Volume I: Israel's Transition from Community to State* (London: Routledge, 2014). See also Zaki Shalom, *David Ben-Gurion, the State of Israel and the Arab World, 1949–1956* (Brighton and Portland: Sussex Academic Press, 2002); Shabtai Teveth, *Ben-Gurion and the Palestinian Arabs: From Peace to War* (Oxford: Oxford University Press, 1985).

the Jewish people depends on their connection to Judaism.[70] Consequently, such matters are determined in accordance with religious laws by the religious courts.[71] The religious courts are granted exclusive jurisdiction over matters of marriage and divorce and concurrent jurisdiction with the civil courts regarding issues of maintenance and succession. In 1949, the Israeli government pledged in a letter to the ultra-religious party Agudat Yisrael that it would never introduce civil marriage and divorce, which could lead to de-homogenisation of the Israeli-Jewish identity and enable interfaith marriages.[72]

The majority of Israeli Jews feel a strong sense of belonging and affinity to the State of Israel and for Judaism. For most of them, it is important to live in Israel and to be part of Israeli society and the Jewish people.[73] While appreciating religion, for the majority of Israeli Jews this is a matter of personal choice. A 2019 survey of Israeli adult Jews asks them about self-definition. Ten percent defined themselves as ultra-orthodox, 11% as religious, 13% as traditional/religious, 18% as traditional/not very religious, and 48% defined themselves as not religious or as secular.[74] That means 67.8% of the Jewish population in Israel would most likely object to religious coercion. A 2015 Gallup poll shows that Israel is one of the world's least religious countries. Fifty-seven percent of Israelis described themselves as non-religious, while 8% said they were convinced atheists. Only 30% described themselves as religious.[75] A more recent poll ranked Israel 9 on a list of the 20 least religious countries in the world. In this poll too, 30% of Israelis "feel religious."[76]

While the rabbinical courts retain sole authority on issuance of divorce decrees and on determining who is married and who is not, the civil courts are granted parallel jurisdiction in issues related to divorce such as child custody, alimony and division of property. The civil courts are operating in accordance with the 1995 Family Courts Law. All matters involving family members, from probate to business disputes, are litigated in the Family Courts. Both the civil family courts and the rabbinical courts must apply Jewish law governing divorce unless an overriding norm is set in specific civil law provisions. In inheritance, the rabbinical court authority is contingent on the consent of all parties involved. If one party objects

70 Nissim Rejwan, *Israel in Search of Identity: Reading the Formative Years* (Gainesville: University Press of Florida, 1999), p. 106.

71 Frances Raday, Self-Determination and Minority Rights, 26 *Fordham International Law Journal*, 3, p. 492 (2002).

72 Yuksel Sezgin, The Israeli Millet System: Examining Legal Pluralism through Lenses of Nation-Building and Human Rights, 43 *Israel Law Review*, p. 641 (2010).

73 Asher Arian et al., *A Portrait of Israeli Jews* (Jerusalem: The Israel Democracy Institute, 2012), p. 12.

74 *Religion and State Index 2019* (Jerusalem: Hiddush, 2019) (Hebrew).

75 Poll: Israel Is One of the World's Least Religious Countries, *The Algemeiner* (21 April 2015), available at www.algemeiner.com/2015/04/21/poll-israel-is-one-of-the-worlds-least-religious-countries/#

76 Oliver Smith, Mapped: The World's Most (and Least) Religious Countries, *The Telegraph* (14 January 2018), available at www.telegraph.co.uk/travel/maps-and-graphics/most-religious-countries-in-the-world/.

to consideration of the case in the rabbinical courts, the case will be referred to the family courts or to the inheritance registrar.[77]

The Chief Rabbinate has a clear bias against women. The rabbinical courts tend to seek peace in the home even when the husband is a drug addict, has a history of violence against his wife and children, and even if the couple has not lived together for a number of years.[78] Because rabbinical courts have the monopoly on dealing with personal matters, women are unable to petition the civil courts for assistance. Only rabbinical courts can rule that a woman is *agunah*, and only rabbinical courts can assist in resolving this problematic situation. As mentioned earlier, in many cases, refusal to give a *get* is a form of spousal abuse designed to exert control over a wife. An abusive husband may refuse to grant his wife a *get* because he wants to leverage his power in civil court over his spouse so she would consent to less spousal support or grant him custody or visitation with the children. Many such women are waiting to receive their divorce bills from the Rabbinate.[79]

Consequently, women who wish to divorce their husbands are forced to agree to economic concessions. The gender inequality is staggering, as child support determined by the rabbinical courts is 30% lower than child support determined by the civil family courts, in the incidents when the woman in question rushed to open the alimony file in the civil court.[80] Furthermore, men who refuse divorce can start a new family without fearing that the children born as a result of the new bond will be considered bastards.[81] The UN Committee on Economic, Social and Cultural Rights in its 2003 concluding observations said that the Jewish religious courts' interpretation of personal status law with respect to divorce discriminates against women, especially the regulation that allows the husband to remarry even when the wife is opposed to the divorce, whilst the same rules do not apply to the wife.[82] The Committee recommended that Israel should take steps to modify the Jewish religious courts' interpretation of the law concerning divorce to ensure

77 Daphna Hacker, Religious Tribunals in Democratic States: Lessons from the Israeli Rabbinical Courts, 78 *Journal of Law and Religion* (2012).

78 Jewish Law Watch, *The Agunah Dilemma* (Jerusalem: The Schechter Institute of Jewish Studies, 2000), pp. 5–7.

79 See For Sarah's & Tami's Sake . . ., ICAR (International Coalition for Agunot) (without date or place of publication); Marriage and Divorce, in David Golinkin (ed.), *Selection of Answers and Halachic Judgments in Marriage* (Jerusalem: Masorti Movement Publications, 1993): 68–71 (Hebrew); Tal Carmon, The Situation of Agunot Women Proves: Women Are Still Discriminated Against in Israel 2018, *Davar* (25 February 2018) (Hebrew), available at www.davar1.co.il/112409/.

80 Yuval Merin, The Right to Family Life and (Civil) Marriage – International and Local Law, in Yoram Rabin & Yuval Shany (eds.), *Economic, Social and Cultural Rights in Israel* (Tel Aviv: Ramot, 2004), p. 713 (Hebrew).

81 Daphna Sharfman, *Living Without a Constitution* (Armonk, NY: M.E. Sharpe, 1993), p. 79.

82 Concluding Observations of the Committee on Economic, Social and Cultural Rights: Israel. 23/05/2003. E/C.12/1/Add.90, para. 23. See www.unhchr.ch/tbs/doc.nsf/(symbol)/e.c.12.1.add.90.en?opendocument.

equality between men and women, as provided for in Article 3 of the Covenant on Economic, Social and Cultural Rights.[83] Article 3 of the Covenant provides: "The States Parties to the present Covenant undertake to ensure the equal right of men and women to the enjoyment of all economic, social and cultural rights set forth in the present Covenant".[84] These incursions into women's personal rights are compounded by the fact that Jewish law discriminates against women also in the laws of evidence. As noted earlier, women are not permitted to serve as judges or witnesses.

The low status of women in Halacha has ramifications on the way men treat women at home and in the workforce. Between 2004 and 2018, 163 women have been murdered by their spouses.[85] The main variables that recur in murder cases by the spouse are separation, divorce and ongoing conflict after the divorce and difficulty in coming to terms with the separation. Property struggles, disagreements regarding custody and sight arrangements related to the common children might also spark violence against women.[86] In 2018 alone, 478 violent men and 6,488 women victims of violence were treated at the 113 Ministry of Welfare's Domestic Violence Prevention Centers.[87]

COVID-19 has had dire implications on women's situation at home. The lockdowns enforced by the government have exacerbated violence against women. The level of violence against women at home during 2020 was five times higher compared to the previous year's figures.[88] In 2020, 20 women were murdered, 18 of them during the COVID-19 crisis. There has been a 300% increase in inquiries to aid agencies and a 350% increase in the number of patients in centres for the prevention and treatment of domestic violence.[89] According to welfare officials, there are currently 200,000 battered women and 600,000 battered children in Israel who witness violence.[90] That means that about a million people – men, women and children, or one-ninth of the Israeli population – are within the cycle of domestic violence.

6 Constructive Steps to Promote Gender Equality

The picture is not all bleak. There have been serious attempts to promote gender equality. The legislation and policies as well as the Supreme Court judgments

83 Ibid., para. 39.

84 Covenant on Economic, Social and Cultural Rights, available at www.unhchr.ch/html/menu3/b/a_cescr.htm.

85 Ministry of Labor, Welfare and Social Services, Publication of annual data on the treatment of domestic violence (June 2020).

86 Ibid.

87 Ibid.

88 WIZO's Violence Index for 2019–2020, available at www.wizo.org.il/page_35805; Avishag Shacham Hadad and Chen White, WIZO's Violence Index for 2019–2020 (WIZO, 24 November 2020) (both in Hebrew).

89 Ibid.

90 Ibid.

have tried to address the serious challenges which women are facing in the field of societal representation both at the workplace and at home. In 1951, the Knesset enacted the Women's Equal Rights Law (1951).[91] The law instructs that men and women have equal status with regard to any legal proceeding; any provision of the law which discriminates with regard to any legal proceeding against women shall be invalidated, and that a married woman shall be fully competent to own and deal with property as if she were unmarried; her rights in property acquired to before marriage shall not be affected by her marriage.

In 1954, the Knesset enacted the Employment of Women Law, 5714–1954.[92] The law includes provisions on the prohibition of night work, absences from work, protection from dismissal during maternity leave, and the registration of female workers. In the following decades, there were some important attempts to promote gender equality. Thus, in 1973 the National Labour Court ruled for the first time in support of women's equality in the workplace.[93] And the Male and Female Workers (Equal Retirement Age) Law, 5747–1987 prohibits discrimination with regard to mandatory retirement on the basis of gender, which was common in collective agreements.[94] The law states that when a collective agreement prescribes for female worker a retirement age lower than that prescribed therein for a male worker, the female worker shall have the right to retire from employment at any age between her retirement age and the retirement age prescribed for a male worker.[95]

The more significant breakthrough in advancing the status of women took place in the 1990s. In 1990, the Supreme Court delivered for the first time a decisive, unambiguous ruling on the supremacy of the principle of equality under the Women's Equal Rights Law, this in the context of the issue of equal retirement age for women: "where there is no *expressly* contrary provision, the courts must prefer that statutory interpretation which is consistent with the principle of equality between the sexes".[96]

In 1992, the Knesset enacted the Basic Law: Human Dignity and Liberty. The law states that there should be no violation of the life, body or dignity of any person, and no violation of person's property.[97] This law has been interpreted by the courts as securing the principle of gender equality as a basic principle of the legal system. Basic Laws could not be violated except by a law that is in accordance

91 Women's Equal Rights Law (1951), available at www.knesset.gov.il/review/data/eng/law/kns1_women_eng.pdf.

92 Employment of Women Law, 5714–1954, available at www.ilo.org/dyn/natlex/docs/ELECTRONIC/3196/97925/F1643712133/ISR3196.pdf.

93 El-Al Airlines v Edna Chzin, National Labour Court (1973), Vol. 4: 365 (in Hebrew).

94 Male and Female Workers (Equal Retirement Age) Law 5747–1987, https://wcmstraining2.ilo.org/dyn/natlex/natlex4.detail?p_lang=en&p_isn=6028&p_count=179&p_classification=05&p_classcount=23.

95 Ibid.

96 HC 104/87, Nevo v the National Labor Court et al. (22 October 1990) (Hebrew).

97 Basic Law: Human Dignity and Liberty 5752–1992, available at www.ilo.org/dyn/natlex/docs/ELECTRONIC/39134/97918/F1548030279/ISR39134.pdf.

with the values of the State of Israel as a Jewish and democratic State, that is for a justified purpose, and that is not disproportionate for the achievement of that purpose. The law includes an instruction regarding its permanence and protection from changes by means of emergency regulations.

In 1994, the Knesset enacted Basic Law: Freedom of Occupation. The law stipulates the right of *every* citizen or inhabitant to engage in any occupation, profession or trade unless a law which corresponds with the values of the State of Israel, and which was designed for a worthy end, determines otherwise.[98] The law includes an instruction regarding its permanence and protection from changes by means of emergency regulations. Only a majority of the Knesset members can amend the law.

The Supreme Court has come to the aid of women in some important precedents that promote gender equality. Thus, for instance, the Court ruled that the rabbinical courts must apply certain civil laws, such as those guaranteeing equal property rights to women[99] and those protecting personal privacy.[100] In the 1994 *Bavli* case, the High Court of Justice imposed on the rabbinical courts the obligation to abide by the principle of equality in the division of matrimonial property. Justice Aharon Barak held that the Jewish law principle of separation of matrimonial property could not satisfy this requirement since it resulted in women receiving a negligible share of the property on divorce. The Court's decision was in conformity with the Women's Equal Rights Law (1951), which excluded only the matter of license or prohibition in marriage and divorce from the purview of the equality principle and not related matters, such as property, maintenance and custody.[101]

In 1991, the Prevention of Family Violence Law, 5751–1991 came into force.[102] The law stipulates that a court may, at the request of a family member, the attorney general or his or her representative, a police prosecutor or welfare officer, grant a protection order against a person who committed physical violence, a sexual offence or psychological abuse against a family member.[103]

In 1995, Alice Miller submitted a petition to the High Court of Justice protesting the army rejection of her application to be a candidate for the pilots' course because of her gender. In a majority of three to two decision, the High Court of

98 Basic Law: Freedom of Occupation 5754–1994, available at https://wipolex.wipo.int/ar/text/343841.

99 High Court of Justice 1000/92 Bavli v Great Rabbinical Court (1994). For further discussion, see Frances Raday, *Equality, Religion and Gender in Israel, the Encyclopedia of Jewish Women* (Jewish Women's Archive, 2009).

100 High Court of Justice 6650/04 Doe v District Rabbinical Court of Netanya (2006). See also Daphna Hacker, Religious Tribunals in Democratic States: Lessons from the Israeli Rabbinical Courts, 27 *Journal of Law and Religion*, 1, p. 63 (2012).

101 HC 1000/92 Bavli v Rabbinical Court of Appeals, 48[2] P.D. (1994) (Hebrew); Frances Raday, *Equality, Religion and Gender in Israel* (The Shalvi/Hyman Encyclopedia of Jewish Women, 2021), available at https://jwa.org/encyclopedia/article/equality-religion-and-gender-in-israel.

102 Prevention of Family Violence Law, 5751–1991.

103 Ibid.

Justice ruled that women had the right to equality in their military service – both formally and on the ground – and that the army's policy of barring them from service as pilots was unacceptable.[104] Consequently, in 2000 the Defense Service Law was amended to state that every woman, just as every man, had the right to serve in any position in the army unless the inherent nature of the position required otherwise. But, as mentioned earlier, only a small percentage of women are serving in combat units.[105]

Both the Government Companies Law, 1975 and the Civil Service (Appointments) Law were amended during the 1990s to allow and encourage affirmative action favouring women as a means of furthering equality at the workplace. The amendments require the civil service to take positive measures to insure fair representation at the workplace.[106] The Male and Female Workers Equal Pay Law, 5756–1996 establishes an obligation of gender equality with respect to wages and other work-related compensation.[107] Until recently, the law only imposed an obligation on certain employers to report gender data regarding employee wages (mainly those that are budgeted by state and public entities). However, in August 2020, the government published a significant amendment to the Law, imposing a duty on all employers with more than 518 employees to publish information about the average wage differentials between male and female employees.[108]

In 1998, the Knesset passed the Employment (Equal Opportunities) Law.[109] The law holds that an employer shall not discriminate among his employees or among persons seeking employment on account of their sex, sexual tendencies, personal status or because of their age, race, religion, nationality, country of origin, views, party or duration of reserve service, in any of the following: (1) acceptance for employment; (2) terms of employment; (3) advancement in employment; (4) vocational training or supplementary vocational training; or (5) dismissal or severance pay. The law provides that where, under the terms of employment applying at her place of employment, a female employee is entitled to absence from work by reason of illness of her child, such right shall also vest in a male employee employed at a place where the terms apply if his spouse is an employee and is not absent from work by virtue of entitlement as aforesaid or has sole custody of the

104 HC 4541/94 Miller v Minister of Defense 49(4) P.D. (1995) (Hebrew).

105 Harel-Shalev & Daphna-Tekoah, supra n. 38, at p. 8.

106 Stephen J. Adler, National Labour Law Profile: The State of Israel (2021), available at www.ilo.org/ifpdial/information-resources/national-labour-law-profiles/WCMS_158902/lang–en/index.htm.

107 The Male and Female Workers Equal Pay Law, 5756–1996, available at www.ilo.org/dyn/natlex/natlex4.detail?p_isn=49589. The law replaced the 1964 Male and Female Workers Equal Pay Law.

108 Orly Gerbi, Maayan Hammer-Tzeelon, Nir Gal, Keren Assaf, & Ohad Elkeslassy, The Employment Law Review: Israel (18 March 2021), available at https://thelawreviews.co.uk/title/the-employment-law-review/israel.

109 Employment (Equal Opportunities) Law 5748–1988, available at www.ilo.org/dyn/natlex/docs/ELECTRONIC/36155/97933/F1175607179/ISR36155.pdf.

child. Furthermore, the law also regulates sexual harassment, protection of complainant, jurisdiction, remedies and related matters.[110]

That same year, 1998, the Authority for the Advancement of the Status of Women was established, and the Knesset approved the Prevention of Sexual Harassment Law, 5758–1998.[111] The purpose of the law is to prohibit sexual harassment in order to defend human dignity, freedom and privacy and in order to promote equality between the sexes. Sexual harassment is any one of the following acts:

> (1) extortion by threat, within the meaning thereof in the Penal Law 5737–1977, when the act that the person is required to perform is of a sexual nature;
> (2) indecent acts, within their meaning in the Penal Law;
> (3) repeated propositions of a sexual nature, addressed to a person who has demonstrated to the harasser that he is not interested in the said propositions;
> (4) repeated references addressed to a person and focused on his sexuality, when that person has demonstrated to the harasser that he is not interested in the said references;
> (5) an insulting or debasing reference to a person in connection with his gender or sexuality, including his sexual preference;
> (6) propositions or references as referred to in paragraphs (3) or (4) even if the harassed person has not demonstrated to the harasser that he is not interested in the said propositions or references.[112]

During 2006–2007, a number of significant amendments were made to the Women's Employment Law, 5714–1954. *Inter alia*, the employment of women during their maternity leave was prohibited; the period of leave permitted after hospitalisation was prolonged and the period during which an employer is prohibited from dismissing an employee returning from maternity leave was extended to 60 days; maternity leave was extended from 12 to 14 weeks; after six weeks' maternity leave the father is permitted leave in her stead, for the duration of the maternity leave.[113]

In 2007, the Knesset enacted the Gender Implications of Legislation Law (Legislative Amendments), 5767–2007 which imposes a duty to systematically examine the gender implications of any primary and secondary legislation before it

110 Ibid.

111 Prevention of Sexual Harassment Law, 5758–1998, available at https://knesset.gov.il/review/data/eng/law/kns14_harassment_eng.pdf.

112 Ibid.

113 Israel Ministry of Foreign Affairs, Ensuring Equal Rights for Women in Israel (31 December 2013), available at https://mfa.gov.il/MFA/AboutIsrael/State/Law/Pages/Ensuring-equal-rights-for-women-in-Israel.aspx.

is enacted by the Knesset.[114] That same year, the Government decided to obligate ministers to appoint women to directorates of Government Corporations until they achieve a 50% representation of women within two years from the date of the Resolution. The decision had immediate effect. As a result, in 2009, 43% of all directors in Governmental Corporations were women, compared to 37% in February 2007 and 38.5% in February 2008.[115]

In 2008, the Knesset enacted the Encouragement of Incorporation and Advancement of Women at Work and of Adjustment of the Labour Environment to Women Law, 5768–2008. The law is designed to bring about a change in the business culture and enhance public awareness to encourage the incorporation and advancement of women in the labour force.[116]

In 2012, the Supreme Court ruled that according to the Equal Pay Law, 5756–1996, once a female employee proved that her salary was significantly lower than that of a male employee performing the same task, the burden of proof shifts to the employer to prove that the difference in salary could be justified. If the employer fails to justify such difference a prima facie case of gender discrimination would be established.[117] In 2014, the Supreme Court ruled that women are eligible to serve in senior administrative roles in the rabbinical courts. Deputy president of the Court, Justice Elyakim Rubinstein, wrote:

> At a (good) time when women occupy a place of honour in a variety of public service positions, it is inconceivable that their representation in the administration of rabbinical courts would not be adequately expressed. In opening the gates of the tribunal to women who will serve in managerial positions, there is great value . . . not only to the female public as a whole but also to strengthening the status of the tribunal, in which the public's trust is an essential condition.[118]

However, the World Economic Forum (WEF) Global Gender Gap Report of 2020 ranked Israel 64 of the 153 surveyed countries.[119] In 2018, Israel was ranked 46th. Israel has been doing particularly poorly when it comes to the WEF's measures for "economic participation and opportunity" and "political

114 Authority for the Advancement of the Status of Women, The Status of Women in Israel Beijing +20 (October 2014).

115 Israel Ministry of Foreign Affairs, supra n. 113. See also Committee on the Elimination of Discrimination against Women reviews the report of Israel (31 October 2017), available at www.ohchr.org/EN/NewsEvents/Pages/DisplayNews.aspx?NewsID=22337.

116 Israel: Encouragement of Incorporation and Advancement of Women in the Labor Force, Library of Congress (2 May 2008), available at www.loc.gov/item/global-legal-monitor/2008-05-02/israel-encouragement-of-incorporation-and-advancement-of-women-in-the-labor-force/.

117 Israel Ministry of Foreign Affairs, supra n. 113.

118 HC 8213/14 Kahana-Dror et al. v Minister of Religious Services and President of the Great Rabbinical Court (15 August 2017) (Hebrew). We are grateful to Justice Rubinstein for his advice.

119 World Economic Forum, *Global Gender Gap Report 2020* (Geneva: World Economic Forum, 2019).

empowerment." Only 27% of "legislators, senior officials and managers" in Israel were females, even though women make up 55.7% of the workforce.[120] In 2020, Deputy Attorney General Raz Nizri called on the government to increase women's representation on public committees and ministry policy teams, as few serve in senior government ministry positions. Nizri called on government ministry director generals and legal advisers to abide by the law and ensure proper representation of women on advisory committees, investigative panels and public committees.[121]

Israeli women are caught between two problems – ageism and sexism – in the context of a segregated work market, discrimination against women, and persistent wage gaps.[122] In 2007, the State Labor Court ruled that "freedom of contract" does not justify discrimination such as that evidenced by paying different salaries to men and women performing the same tasks. The court stated that in these circumstances, the principle of equality prevails over freedom of contract.[123]

7 Conclusion

Jewish law discriminates against women. Key positions in business, politics and the social service sector give priority to men, both out of allegiance to caring for each other after their discharge and because their military training offers employers a workforce trained for free. Women are not equally represented in this labour force and find themselves excluded from these arenas. They are disproportionately disadvantaged to access jobs in the labour force. Their ability to pursue positions of prestige is limited. The connections fostered between young men during their military service lay a robust foundation of kinship, intimacy and connection that women are at a loss to circumvent. Gender discrimination in the labour market undermines women's rights and their ability to secure an equal footing in the family dynamic. And so the vicious circle of sustained gender inequality continues.

Hillary Rodham Clinton said:

> There cannot be true democracy unless women's voices are heard. There cannot be true democracy unless women are given the opportunity to take responsibility for their own lives. There cannot be true democracy unless all citizens are able to participate fully in the lives of their country.[124]

120 Israel Plummets in Gender Equality Ranking, supra n. 50.

121 Lee Yaron, Israel Must Increase Women's Representation in Policy-making, Deputy Attorney General Says, *Haaretz* (25 August 2020).

122 Authority for the Advancement of the Status of Women, The Status of Women in Israel Beijing +20 (October 2014).

123 Israel Ministry of Foreign Affairs, supra n. 113.

124 Hillary Rodham Clinton, available at www.mtholyoke.edu/~carve22r/classweb/eightwomen/rodham-clinton.html.

The protection of basic human and civil rights should be applied equally to both genders and also to transgender individuals. One gender should not be held superior to another. Equality between humans should be an enshrined value in Israeli society which demands much commitments from all its citizens, notwithstanding gender. Women, already in the pre-state period, were partners to the state building enterprise. They contributed their fair share in making the desert bloom, and the borders secure. Religion should not undermine human solidarity and common decency.

Solidarity is of an utmost importance value in Israeli society which was built to provide a home for all Jews all over the world, for the residents who were in Israeli territory when the country was founded in 1948, and for their descendants. To be a fair, just, compassionate and caring society, gender equality and, indeed, equality for all, is an imperative. One of the country's principal documents, the 1948 Declaration of Independence, holds that Israel will foster the development of the country for the benefit of all its inhabitants; that it will be based on the foundations of liberty, justice and peace; that it will uphold complete equality of social and political rights to all of its citizens irrespective of religion, race or sex, and that it will guarantee freedom of religion, conscience, language, education and culture.[125]

In Israel, matters of personal status are determined in accordance with religious laws by the Orthodox religious courts. Orthodox Judaism retains the patriarchal norms in the division of matrimonial property, inheritance, divorce, the penalty for adultery and the eligibility of participation of women in any power position.[126] The monopoly that the Orthodoxy enjoys is to the detriment of women who have to fight against men's chauvinism and their religious entitlement. The dual way to fight against this endemic gender discrimination is to separate between state and religion, providing greater scope for personal matters to be resolved by civil courts, and also by empowering non–Orthodox Jewish denominations that are gender egalitarian. The Orthodoxy, however, would resist both propositions. Women have a high and rugged mountain to climb in order to secure their fair rights.

The former president of the Supreme Court, Meir Shamgar, argued for a comprehensive written constitution that would guarantee rights and duties for all citizens. Shamgar believed that the first component of egalitarian democracy is the transformation of abstract ideas of rights into written constitutional norms and their integration into the legal system. By having a comprehensive written constitution Israel could secure human rights and democratic principles. Shamgar advocated: "The most perfect way to safeguard in Israel rights and duties, obligations

125 Israel's Ministry of Foreign Affairs, available at http://mfa.gov.il/mfa/foreignpolicy/peace/guide/pages/declaration%20of%20establishment%20of%20state%20of%20israel.aspx.

126 Frances Raday, supra n. 71. See also Frances Raday, Religion, Multiculturalism and Equality – The Israeli Case, 25 *Israel Yearbook on Human Rights*, pp. 193–241 (1995); F. Raday, Culture, Religion and Gender, 1 *I.CON, International Constitutional Law Journal*, 4, pp. 663–715 (2003).

and limitations, prescriptions and norms is by defining them clearly in written form and in this context, in a written and comprehensive constitution".[127]

Furthermore, Shamgar wrote, "a constitution ensures the existence of clarity in the definition of powers, functions and rights and expresses their binding force, clearly and in unequivocal terms".[128] Such a comprehensive, written constitution would clarify and substantiate the character of constitutional rights and their legal force, as well as the formulation of sanctions. Very importantly, such a constitution would have an overarching importance, superseding Halacha. Shamgar spent many years in advocating and promoting the idea of having such a constitution but to no avail. Strong political powers, including the religious parties which object to human-made constitutions which would override the Godly constitution, stood on the way and prevented President Shamgar from seeing his dream materialise. But the need for a comprehensive, written, egalitarian constitution remains valid and strong.

While Israel as a country that respects the rule of law has strove to promote women's rights via legislation, the need for further reform in women's rights to offset discriminatory halachic dictates is evident. Women have to fight against the male-orientated Jewish Orthodox tradition and also against the male-orientated military norms; both are entrenched in Israeli society. The first is anchored in religion that for its followers is sacred. Women are chained to play second violin in a community that has made inequality part of life for thousands of years. The second, the IDF, is a sacred institution as it is entrusted with the most fundamental task of ensuring Israel's survival. It is not easy for Israeli women to break their chains and enjoy equal rights.

The challenge is great because many people in Israel are not aware of the many problems that women are facing. Hence, the first step is to increase awareness regarding women's inequality, explaining their strife and calling for change. The second step is education that must start in the kindergarten and continue on all levels of education. The message is and should be loud and simple: all people are equal. Some are not superior to others. Gender should not dictate one's limitations and successes. Gender should not pose the glass ceiling that might restrict women's achievement. The third step is legislation that would anchor gender equality in specific laws relating to all spheres of life. And the fourth step relates to government implementation of policies that are based on gender equality and on positive discrimination to ensure that women will have ample springboards to advance themselves in society, paving the way to a fair and just equilibrium between men and women. These vital steps will make gender equality a reality which hopefully one day we will take for granted, because any other reality is coercive, discriminatory, unjust and exploitative.

127 Meir Shamgar, On the Need for a Constitution, in Raphael Cohen-Almagor (ed.), *Israeli Institutions at the Crossroads* (London: Routledge, 2005), p. 84.

128 Ibid., p. 81.

Israel has a social responsibility to all its citizens notwithstanding gender, religion and ethnicity.[129] It must show true commitment to gender equality in the labour market, social services and welfare schemes. It should protect against poverty; ensure quality and equality in the job market; protect women against domestic violence; ensure adequate female representation upon a principle which is expressly committed to gender equality in decision-making processes, and promote the involvement of women in all public institutions. Just public policy must be supported concretely by the establishment of a supervisory and enforcement authority on the basis of respecting the dignity of the person qua person. The struggle for equality will continue until this just aim is achieved.

George Bernard Shaw said: "Liberty means responsibility. That is why most men dread it."[130] In Israel, many men find it convenient to deny certain rights to women as this inequality serves their partisan interests. Women should resist this chauvinistic inclination. They cannot rely on men to do this for them. It is the women's responsibility to fight for human rights for all. Surely some men will assist women who stand for themselves and who fight for equal rights; but it is women who need *to lead* the fight for a fair and just change. The sooner, the better.

Bibliography

Adler, Stephen J., *National Labour Law Profile: The State of Israel* (2021), https://www.ilo.org/ifpdial/information-resources/national-labour-law-profiles/WCMS_158902/lang-en/index.htm.

Arian, Asher, et al., *A Portrait of Israeli Jews* (Jerusalem: The Israel Democracy Institute, 2012).

Authority for the Advancement of the Status of Women, *The Status of Women in Israel Beijing +20* (October 2014).

Babylonian Talmud: Tractate Kethuboth, 48a, http://www.come-and-hear.com/kethuboth/kethuboth_48.html.

Babylonian Talmud: Tractate Kethuboth, Folio 61a, http://www.come-and-hear.com/kethuboth/kethuboth_61.html.

Babylonian Talmud: Tractate Yebamoth, Folio 63a, http://www.come-and-hear.com/yebamoth/yebamoth_63.html.

Bava Metzia 59, http://www.dafyomi.co.il/bmetzia/points/bm-ps-059.htm.

Ben-Gurion, David, *Divrei Haknesset* (Knesset Proceedings), 20 February 1950, 117 Meeting, Vol. IV, p. 817 (Hebrew).

Ben-Gurion, David, "How the State Be Established?", in D. Ben-Gurion (ed.), *As Israel Fights* (Tel Aviv: Mapai, 1951): 207–212 (Hebrew).

129 Raphael Cohen-Almagor, Ori Arbel-Ganz, & Asa Kasher (eds.), *Public Responsibility in Israel* (Tel Aviv and Jerusalem: Hakibbutz Hameuchad and Mishkanot Shaananim, 2012) (Hebrew). For further discussion, see Ronny Manos & Israel Drori, *Corporate Responsibility: Social Action, Institutions and Governance* (London: Palgrave Macmillan, 2016); Eliezer Ben-Rafael et al. (eds.), *Handbook of Israel: Major Debates* (2nd ed., Berlin: De Gruyter Oldenbourg, 2018).

130 https://governingprinciples.wordpress.com/2009/04/03/liberty-means-responsibility-that-is-why-most-men-dread-it-george-bernard-shaw/.

Ben-Gurion, David, *Uniqueness and Mission* (Tel-Aviv: Maarachot, 1971) (Hebrew).

Ben-Rafael, Eliezer, et al. (ed.), *Handbook of Israel: Major Debates* (Berlin: De Gruyter Oldenbourg; 2nd edition, 2018).

Biale, Rachel, *Women and Jewish Law: The Essential Texts, Their History, and Their Relevance for Today* (New York: Schocken, 1995).

Bulmer, Sarah, and Maya Eichler, "Unmaking Militarized Masculinity: Veterans and The Project of Military-to-Civilian Transition", *Critical Military Studies*, 3(2) (2017): 161–181.

Carmon, Tal, "The Situation of Agunot Women Proves: Women are Still Discriminated Against in Israel 2018", *Davar* (25 February 2018) (Hebrew), https://www.davar1.co.il/112409/.

Chazan, Naomi, "Israel at 70: A Gender Perspective", *Israel Studies*, 23(3) (Fall 2018): 141–151.

Cohen, Gili, "Internal IDF Survey: One in Six Female Soldiers was Sexually Harassed During Military Service", *Haaretz* (10 September 2017) (Hebrew).

Cohen-Almagor, Raphael, "Israeli Democracy, Religion and the Practice of *Halizah* in Jewish Law", *UCLA Women's Law Journal*, 11(1) (Fall/Winter 2000): 45–65.

Cohen-Almagor, Raphael, "Avoiding the Destruction of the Third Temple: Separating State and Religion", in Yossi Goldstein (ed.), *Religion Nationalism: The Struggle for Modern Jewish Identity, An Interdisciplinary Annual* (Ariel: Ariel University, 2014): 170–189.

Cohen-Almagor, Raphael, "Discrimination against Jewish Women in *Halacha* (Jewish Law) and in Israel", *British J. of Middle Eastern Studies*, 45(2) (2018): 290–310.

Cohen-Almagor, Raphael, *Just, Reasonable Multiculturalism* (New York and Cambridge: Cambridge University Press, 2021).

Cohen-Almagor, Raphael, Ori Arbel-Ganz, and Asa Kasher (eds.), *Public Responsibility in Israel* (Tel Aviv and Jerusalem: Hakibbutz Hameuchad and Mishkanot Shaananim, 2012) (Hebrew).

Cohen-Almagor, Raphael, and Amos Guiora, "Democracy and Security in Israel", in Leonard Weinberg, Elizabeth Francis et al. (eds.), *Routledge Handbook of Democracy and Security* (London and New York: Routledge, 2021): 172–190.

Committee on the Elimination of Discrimination against Women reviews the report of Israel (31 October 2017), https://www.ohchr.org/EN/NewsEvents/Pages/DisplayNews.aspx?NewsID=22337.

Covenant on Economic, Social and Cultural Rights, http://www.unhchr.ch/html/menu3/b/a_cescr.htm.

Dahan, Momi, "Did the Economic Melting Pot Succeed?", Discussion Paper Series (Jerusalem: The Hebrew University of Jerusalem, The Feher Institute, 2013) (Hebrew).

Davidovich-Weisberg, Gavriela, "Want to be a Pilot at El Al? Maybe Now You'll have a Better Chance", *The Marker* (18 June 2018) (Hebrew).

Directorship of Research and Economy, "20 Facts on Employment Gaps between Women and Men" (Jerusalem, 2010) (Hebrew).

Dvori, Nir, "Lt. Col. Suspected of Sexually Harassing Female Soldiers", *N12* (19 November 2017) (Hebrew), https://www.mako.co.il/news-military/security-q4_2017/Article-4dc9015ef03df51004.htm.

Efroni, Linda, "Men's Salary is 1.9 Times Higher Than Women's Salary", *Noga* (1996, Hebrew), http://lib.cet.ac.il/pages/item.asp?item=3131.

El-Al Airlines v Edna Chzin, National Labour Court (1973), Vol. 4: 365 (in Hebrew).

Endeweld, Miri, and Daniel Gottlieb, *The Socio-Economic Status of Women in Israel 1997-2011* (Jerusalem: National Insurance Institute, October 2013) (Hebrew), www.btl.gove.il.

Equal Rights, Sichos in English, http://www.sichosinenglish.org/essays/70.htm.

Etzioni-Halevy, Eva, "Civil-Military Relations and Democracy: The Case of the Military Political Elites' Connection in Israel", *Armed Forces and Society*, 27 (1996): 401–417.

Fogiel-Bijaoui, Sylvie, *Democracy and Feminism: Gender, Citizenship and Human Rights* (Ra'anana: The Open University, 2011) (Hebrew).

Fogiel-Bijaoui, Sylvie, "Navigating Gender Inequality in Israel: The Challenges of Feminism", in Eliezer Ben-Rafael, Julius Schoeps, Yitzhak Sternberg, and Olaf Gluckner (eds.), *Handbook of Israel: Major Debates* (Berlin: De Gruyter Oldenbourg, 2016): 423–436, https://www.researchgate.net/publication/334721534_Navigating_Gender_Inequality_in_Israel_-The_Challenges_of_Feminism.

"For Sarah's & Tami's Sake. . .", ICAR (International Coalition for *Agunot*) (without date or place of publication).

Freilich, Charles D., *Israel National Security* (New York: Oxford University Press, 2018).

Fridson, Yael, "State Comptroller: 68 General Directors of Government Companies – All Men", *NRG* (4 March 2014) (Hebrew), http://www.nrg.co.il/online/1/ART2/561/945.html?hp=1&cat=402&loc=1.

Gerbi, Orly, Maayan Hammer-Tzeelon, Nir Gal, Keren Assaf, and Ohad Elkeslassy, *The Employment Law Review: Israel* (18 March 2021), https://thelawreviews.co.uk/title/the-employment-law-review/israel.

Golan, Patricia, "A Law to Prevent the Next War?", *The Jerusalem Post* (12 August 2020), https://www.jpost.com/jerusalem-report/a-law-to-prevent-the-next-war-637328.

Goldberg, Meir, *Moral problems in Halacha: Women*, http://truetorah.blogspot.com/2013/07/moral-problems-in-halacha-women-with.html

Goldfeder, Mark, *Defining Equality in Judaism*, http://morethodoxy.org/2012/10/25/defining-equality-in-judaism-by-rabbi-mark-goldfeder/.

Gordis, Robert, "Agunot: A Different Kind of Hostage", *My Jewish Learning* (2021), https://www.myjewishlearning.com/article/agunot-a-different-kind-of-hostage/.

Grosbard, Shiri, "When We Start a Family We are Basically Giving Up Our Place in the Race for a Career", *Mako* (18 September 2017) (Hebrew), https://www.mako.co.il/study-career-career/articles/Article-bbdb5d29c008e51006.htm.

Hacker, Daphna, "Religious Tribunals in Democratic States: Lessons from the Israeli Rabbinical Courts", *Journal of Law and Religion*, 27(1) (2012): 59–81.

Harel-Shalev, Ayelet, and Shir Daphna-Tekoah, *Breaking the Binaries in Security Studies: A Gendered Analysis of Women in Combat* (New York: Oxford University Press, 2020).

Hasson, Yael, "Privatization of Public Services in Israel", in *Women's Employment in the Days of Privatization* (Adva Center, 28 October 2007) (Hebrew).

High Court of Justice 104/87, *Nevo v the National Labor Court et al., P.D.* 44(4) 749 (22 October 1990) (Hebrew).

High Court of Justice 1000/92, *Bavli v Rabbinical Court of Appeals*, P.D. 48(2) 221 (1994) (Hebrew).

High Court of Justice 4541/94, *Miller v Minister of Defense,* P.D. 49(4) 94 (1995) (Hebrew).

High Court of Justice 6650/04, *Doe v District Rabbinical Court of Netanya,* P.D. 61(1) 581 (2006).

High Court of Justice 8213/14, *Kahana-Dror et al. v Minister of Religious Services and President of the Great Rabbinical Court* (15 August 2017) (Hebrew). https://mar

riage-il.com/hcj-8213-14-batya-kahana-dror-et-al-v-minister-of-religious-services-et-al-02-07-2017/.

Hillel, Babylonian Talmud. Sabbath 31a.

Ilan, Shahar, "Despite Progress, Only One in Six Israeli CEOs Is a Woman, New Report Says", *Calcalist* (29 January 2020), https://www.calcalistech.com/ctech/articles/0,7340,L-3784650,00.html.

Israel Central Bureau of Statistics (2013).

"Israel: Encouragement of Incorporation and Advancement of Women in the Labor Force", Library of Congress (2 May 2008), https://www.loc.gov/item/global-legal-monitor/2008-05-02/israel-encouragement-of-incorporation-and-advancement-of-women-in-the-labor-force/.

Israel Ministry of Foreign Affairs, *Ensuring equal rights for women in Israel* (31 December 2013), https://mfa.gov.il/MFA/AboutIsrael/State/Law/Pages/Ensuring-equal-rights-for-women-in-Israel.aspx.

Israel Ministry of Foreign Affairs, *Women in Israel today* (8 March 2016), https://mfa.gov.il/MFA/AboutIsrael/Spotlight/Pages/Women-in-Israel-today.aspx.

"Israel Plummets in Gender Equality Ranking", *YNET* (22 December 2019), https://www.ynetnews.com/article/SJw11cXT0H.

Israel's Ministry Of Foreign Affairs, http://mfa.gov.il/mfa/foreignpolicy/peace/guide/pages/declaration%20of%20establishment%20of%20state%20of%20israel.aspx.

Jewish Law Watch, *The Agunah Dilemma* (Jerusalem: The Schechter Institute of Jewish Studies, 2000): 5–7.

Karsh, Efraim (ed.), *Israel: The First Hundred Years: Volume I: Israel's Transition from Community to State* (London: Routledge, 2014).

Levi Sadan, Imry, "Military and Security News", *Walla* (20 November 2017) (Hebrew).

Lightman, Ernie, "On the Demise of the Welfare State", *Haaretz* (14 March 2008).

Maimonides, *Laws of Kings and Wars*, http://halakhah.com/rst/kingsandwars.pdf.

Manos, Ronny, and Israel Drori, *Corporate Responsibility: Social Action, Institutions and Governance* (London: Palgrave Macmillan, 2016).

Margalit, Michal, "Women Still Earn Less but the Income Gap has Narrowed – The Lowest Since 1990", *Ynet* (17 December 2018, Hebrew), https://www.ynet.co.il/articles/0,7340,L-5427560,00.html.

"Marriage and Divorce", in David Golinkin (ed.), *Selection of Answers and Halachic Judgments in Marriage* (Jerusalem: Masorti Movement Publications, 1993): 68–71 (Hebrew).

Meacham, Tirzah, "Legal-Religious Status of the Jewish Female", *Jewish Women Encyclopedia*, http://jwa.org/encyclopedia/article/legal-religious-status-of-jewish-female.

Merin, Yuval, "The Right to Family Life and (Civil) Marriage – International and Local Law", in Yoram Rabin and Yuval Shany (eds.), *Economic, Social and Cultural Rights in Israel* (Tel Aviv: Ramot, 2004) (Hebrew).

Mill, John Stuart, *Utilitarianism, Liberty, and Representative Government* (London: J. M. Dent, 1948), Everyman's edition, at 114 or *On Liberty*, http://www.utilitarianism.com/ol/three.html.

Ministry of Labor, Welfare and Social Services, Publication of Annual Data on the Treatment of Domestic Violence (June 2020).

Okin, Susan Moller, "Feminism, Women's Human Rights, and Cultural Differences", *Hypatia*, 13(2) (Spring 1998): 32–52.

Paz-Fuchs, Amir, Ronen Mandelkern, and Itzhak Galnoor (eds.), *The Privatization of Israel: The Withdrawal of State Responsibility* (London: Palgrave Macmillan, 2019).

"Poll: Israel is One of the World's Least Religious Countries," *The Algemeiner* (21 April 2015), http://www.algemeiner.com/2015/04/21/poll-israel-is-one-of-the-worlds-least-religious-countries/#.

Raday, Frances, "Religion, Multiculturalism and Equality – The Israeli Case", *Israel Yearbook on Human Rights*, 25 (1995): 193–241.

Raday, Frances, "Self-Determination and Minority Rights", *Fordham International Law Journal,* 26(3) (2002): 453–499.

Raday, Frances, "Culture, Religion and Gender", *I.CON, International Constitutional Law Journal*, 1(4) (2003): 663–715.

Raday, Frances, "Equality, Religion and Gender in Israel", in *The Encyclopedia of Jewish Women* (Jewish Women's Archive, 2009).

Raday, Frances, "Equality, Religion and Gender in Israel", in *The Shalvi/Hyman Encyclopedia of Jewish Women* (2021), https://jwa.org/encyclopedia/article/equality-religion-and-gender-in-israel.

Rejwan, Nissim, *Israel in Search of Identity: Reading the Formative Years* (Gainesville: University Press of Florida, 1999).

Religion & gender discrimination in Israel, *Hiddush* (27 November 2017), http://hiddush.org/article-22155-0-Religion__gender_discrimination_in_Israel.aspx

Religion and State Index 2019 (Jerusalem: Hiddush, 2019) (Hebrew).

Sasson-Levy, Orna, "Research on Gender and the Military in Israel. From a Gendered Organization to Inequality Regimes", *Israel Studies Review*, 26(2) (2011): 73–98.

Sezgin, Yuksel, "The Israeli Millet System: Examining Legal Pluralism through Lenses of Nation-Building and Human Rights", *Israel Law Review*, 43(3) (2010): 631–654.

Shacham Hadad, Avishag, and Chen White, *WIZO's Violence Index for 2019-2020* (WIZO, 24 November 2020) (Hebrew).

Shalom, Zaki, *David Ben-Gurion, the State of Israel and the Arab World, 1949-1956* (Brighton and Portland: Sussex Academic Press, 2002).

Shamgar, Meir, "On the Need for A Constitution", in Raphael Cohen-Almagor (ed.), *Israeli Institutions at the Crossroads* (London: Routledge, 2005).

Shapira, Asaf, "Privatization – A Theoretical and Historical Overview", *Parliament*, 64 (23 March 2010) (Hebrew), https://www.idi.org.il/parliaments/11097/11145.

Sharfman, Daphna, *Living Without a Constitution* (Armonk, New York: M.E. Sharpe, 1993).

Smith, Oliver, "Mapped: The World's Most (and Least) Religious Countries," *The Telegraph* (14 January 2018), https://www.telegraph.co.uk/travel/maps-and-graphics/most-religious-countries-in-the-world/.

"Statistics on Sexual Violence in the IDF", *Makom* (24 January 2005) (Hebrew), ww.macom.org.il/definitions/stats-home/stats-army/.

Teveth, Shabtai, *Ben-Gurion and the Palestinian Arabs: From Peace to War* (Oxford: Oxford University Press, 1985).

Tevet-Wiesel, Rachel, and Lt. Col Ariel Wiener, "Charging forward against all odds," *Maarachot* 456 (21 August 2014): 38–41 (Hebrew).

UN Resolution 1325 (31 October 2000), https://www.un.org/en/ga/search/view_doc.asp?symbol=S/RES/1325(2000).

Weisberg, Hila, "I Gave Up A Career to Raise the Kids – What a Miss", *The Marker* (29 August 2013) (Hebrew).

What is UNSCR 1325? US Institute of Peace, https://www.usip.org/gender_peacebuilding/about_UNSCR_1325.

WIZO's Violence Index for 2019-2020, www.wizo.org.il/page_35805 (Hebrew).
"Women Wage Peace", https://womenwagepeace.org.il/en/.
World Economic Forum, *Global Gender Gap Report 2020* (Geneva, 2019).
Yarkazi, Dana, and or Ravid, "Work as Teachers and Caregivers – Earn Less: Israeli Women in Numbers", *Walla* (6 March 2017, Hebrew), http://news.walla.co.il/item/3046163.
Yaron, Lee, "Israel Must Increase Women's Representation in Policy-Making, Deputy Attorney General Says", *Haaretz* (25 August 2020).
Zilberfarb, Ben-Zion, "From Socialism to Free Market – The Israeli Economy: 1948 – 2003", in R. Cohen-Almagor (ed.), *Israeli Democracy at the Crossroads* (London: Routledge, 2005): 12–22.

13 Discrimination in Employment Law

Key Themes and Perspectives

Jo Carby-Hall, Zbigniew Góral and Aneta Tyc

The chapters included in the book are representative current contributions in the complex field of discrimination in employment law. They embrace the most recent research which attempts to solve the most important scientific problems in diverse countries. The principles of non-discrimination and equal treatment are tackled not only from the perspective of the countries which regulate them in their constitutions (e.g. Poland, Germany, the Netherlands, Switzerland), but also from the point of view of countries which do not have a written or codified constitution (e.g. Israel, New Zealand, the United Kingdom) or where the principles of equality and non-discrimination have no roots in the constitution (e.g. Australia). Discriminatory employment laws are also analysed from the standpoint of the European Union and its Member States, the common law countries and provinces/countries from other parts of the world, namely, Québec, Switzerland, India and Israel. The authors present the relevant legal instruments and analyse the case law in their respective countries in order to illustrate their findings, conclusions and postulates. This book is not intended to create a typical work of a comparative legal nature because the chapters do not mirror a specific, identical system of issues on an identical topic. The authors present their original, novel research on the latest, most important issues in their countries. Even if some authors refer to the same issue, we should bear in mind what Gillian Hadfield said:

> It may be true that there is an "untranslatable abyss" between the law of one place and the law of another – just as there is between one person's experience of a strawberry and another's – but this does not mean that we have no business seeking to understand why law here produces this effect and law there produces that effect.[1]

The aim of this concluding chapter is to highlight some of the core issues which the three editors found when reviewing the chapters. One of such issues

1 Gillian Hadfield, The Strategy of Methodology: The Virtues of Being Reductionist for Comparative Law, 59 *The University of Toronto Law Journal*, 2, p. 223 (2009), available at https://www.jstor.org/stable/40211256.

DOI: 10.4324/9781003306962-16

problematised in this book is related to the burden of proof in discrimination cases. At the European Union level, the burden of proof has been regulated in a way which favours the victim of discrimination. This will be found in the Council Directive 97/80/EC of 15 December 1997 on the burden of proof in cases of discrimination based on sex.[2] According to its Article 4, Member States shall take such measures as are necessary, in accordance with their national judicial systems, to ensure that, when persons who consider themselves wronged because the principle of equal treatment has not been applied to them establish, before a court or other competent authority, facts from which it may be presumed that there has been direct or indirect discrimination, it shall be for the respondent to prove that there has been no breach of the principle of equal treatment. Importantly, this directive shall not prevent Member States from introducing rules of evidence which are more favourable to plaintiffs. The same mechanism has been introduced in other directives, including Article 8 of the Council Directive 2000/43/EC of 29 June 2000 implementing the principle of equal treatment between persons irrespective of racial or ethnic origin,[3] Article 10 of the Council Directive 2000/78/EC of 27 November 2000 establishing a general framework for equal treatment in employment and occupation,[4] Article 9 of the Council Directive 2004/113/EC of 13 December 2004 implementing the principle of equal treatment between men and women in the access to and supply of goods and services,[5] and Article 19 of Directive 2006/54/EC of the European Parliament and the Council of 5 July 2006 on the implementation of the principle of equal opportunities and equal treatment of men and women in matters of employment and occupation (recast).[6]

However, as Szilvia Halmos rightly reminds us, the shared burden of proof has been used even earlier in the case law of the CJEU (e.g. in the *Danfoss* case dating back to 1989 and the *Enderby* case of 1993). In her chapter, the author highlights that both practical arguments and doctrinal reasons have always constituted a strong support for such a concept. The entry into force of non-discrimination directives and a stable and unchanged line of the CJEU case law have consolidated the idea of a shared burden of proof in anti-discrimination claims thus dovetailing with the European tradition.[7] Naturally, these directives have been implemented into the national laws of the Member States and have placed the burden of proof on the employer if a plaintiff establishes a prima facie discrimination case. This is mentioned by both Manfred Weiss in regard to Germany and Susanne Burri for the Netherlands, and of course exists in Poland and other EU countries as well.

2 Official Journal L 014, 20 January 1998, pp. 6–8.
3 Official Journal L 180, 19 July 2000, pp. 22–26.
4 Official Journal L 303, 2 December 2000, pp. 16–22.
5 Official Journal L 373, 21 December 2004, pp. 37–43.
6 Official Journal L 204, 26 July 2006, pp. 23–36.
7 For more historical background see Burden of proof in sex discrimination cases – Commission adopts a proposal for a council directive, available at https://ec.europa.eu/commission/presscorner/detail/en/IP_96_658.

A closer look at the question of *onus probandi* in other legal jurisdictions makes us aware that the above-presented approach is not necessarily the standard situation. Taking a broader perspective we may discern that, for example, according to Australian anti-discrimination laws the burden of proof rests with those who claim to have experienced discrimination to pursue a complaint against their employer. Therese MacDermott points out that faced with such a "construction" of applicable rules, it is difficult to – in particular – address systemic forms of racial discrimination in employment. The problem is mirrored by the scarce number of successful litigated outcomes under the federal legislation because proving the racial basis of treatments turns out to be a very daunting task. Nevertheless, the chapter on Australia also sheds light on some national workplace laws which take a different approach and shift the burden on the employer. Indirect discrimination under the Sex Discrimination Act of 1984[8] has been given as an example.

Until recently, the same sort of problem with the *onus probandi* lying on the complainant at the adjudicative stage was also noticeable in New Zealand. Gordon Anderson and Dawn Duncan draw attention to the fact that this legislation acted as a deterrent to taking a complaint beyond the mediation stage and contributed to the low number of reported cases. However, section 119 of the Employment Relations Act of 2000 and its subsequent amendments have established a rebuttable presumption that the employer or representative of the employer discriminated (if certain conditions are satisfied[9]) against the employee on any of the prohibited grounds of discrimination, or the employee's union membership status or involvement in union activities, and alleged by the employee.

When discussing the distribution of burden of proof, we should also like to return to the chapter on Israel by Raphael Cohen-Almagor and Uki Maroshek-Klarman. The authors demonstrate that although women's inequality is rooted in Jewish law, the Supreme Court and the National Labour Court have been struggling for years to improve the situation. In this regard, it is worth noting that according to the Supreme Court's ruling of 2012, the Equal Pay Law 5756-1996 must be interpreted as introducing a prima facie case of gender discrimination, meaning that the burden of proof is reversed to the employer if a female employee proves that her salary is significantly lower than that of a male employee carrying

8 (Cth) 7B.

9 An employee is discriminated against in that employee's employment if the employee's employer or a representative of that employer . . .:

(a) refuses or omits to offer or afford to that employee the same terms of employment, conditions of work, fringe benefits, or opportunities for training, promotion, and transfer as are made available for other employees of the same or substantially similar qualifications, experience, or skills employed in the same or substantially similar circumstances; or

(b) dismisses that employee or subjects that employee to any detriment, in circumstances in which other employees employed by that employer on work of that description are not or would not be dismissed or subjected to such detriment; or

(c) retires that employee, or requires or causes that employee to retire or resign (Section 104 Discrimination). https://www.legislation.govt.nz/act/public/2000/0024/latest/whole.html#DLM60329.

out the same task. If that is the case, then the employer will have to demonstrate that the difference in salary could be justified. It is a big step forward in Israel but, on the other hand, the relaxation of the burden of proof remains limited to the issue of pay discrimination only.

The findings for Switzerland presented by Kurt Pärli indicate that in the case of discriminatory refusal of employment, an infringement is unlawful unless it is justified by an overriding private interest (Article 28 of the Civil Code). However, if a person is refused employment for legally protected characteristics, they have to prove first that it was due to this reason. Moreover, Article 6 of Federal Act on Gender Equality establishes a reduced burden of proof providing that in relation to the allocation of duties, setting of working conditions, pay, basic and continuing education and training, and promotion and dismissal, discrimination is presumed if the person concerned can substantiate the same by prima facie evidence. Listing the aforementioned areas *expressis verbis* in this provision means e contrario that a victim of sex discrimination does not enjoy any relaxation of the burden of proof during the recruitment period. Pärli adds that, similarly, a heavy burden of proof is imposed on a person who suffered sexual harassment at work because there is no such alleviation envisaged in Article 6 of Federal Act on Gender Equality.

Since we are on the subject of sexual harassment, it is essential to recall the conclusions made by Rachel Cox in her chapter. As illustrated in the author's findings, treating sexual harassment as psychological harassment or an industrial accident may easily lead to its denial. In the case of the former, the Labour Tribunal may reject a complaint for psychological harassment of a "sexual nature" even if there is clear evidence of sexual harassment as defined by the Québec Charter of Rights and Freedoms. This is because of a hard burden of proof (associated with the definition of psychological harassment) for a plaintiff to meet and the de facto obligation to report psychological harassment. Added to this, there is always the possibility that the complaint would be rejected if the employer proves that they have taken all reasonable means to prevent or stop harassment. Rachel Cox lists matters that must be proved in order for the psychological harassment complaint to be accepted. These include vexatious behaviour of a repetitive and unwanted nature, that the behaviour affected the employee's dignity and that it resulted in a harmful work environment for the employee. Revealingly, a single serious incidence of vexatious behaviour may also be classified as psychological harassment provided that it has a lasting harmful effect on the employee.

In the case of treating sexual harassment as an industrial accident, the Labour Tribunal likewise is ready to reject the workers' claims. Cox gives an example of a newly hired factory worker who was dismissed after reporting several instances of unwanted sexual touching and harassment by her foreman. The Administrative Labour Tribunal held that no causal connection between the sexual harassment established by the evidence and the woman's psychological injury was proved. The judge thus inferred that the victim's injury was "more related to distress subsequent to being dismissed after reporting the harassment than the harassment itself".

Another example from Cox's chapter is that of an apprentice roofer who refused sexual advances by a co-worker and then was not called back to work. As a consequence, the woman had to consult a doctor for "uncontrolled crying" and "extreme stress", and finally her medical certificate used the words "harassment" and "harassment and job loss". Unfortunately, the Labour Tribunal dismissed her claims because of the absence of a prescription for medication or referral for psychological treatment, as well as a failure to prove that she was afflicted by an "incapacitating pathology". Moreover, in such a situation the worker is also required to prove a relationship between a diagnosis and the workplace harassment.

In this final chapter of this edited volume, it is pertinent to reflect on the issue of protected characteristics in discrimination law, which has been covered in some of the chapters. It is worth noting that both Article 21 of the Charter of Fundamental Rights of the European Union and the Article 14 of the European Convention on Human Rights provide for an open catalogue of discriminatory grounds. In different countries, there are often enumerative or open catalogues. In the latter case, the lists of criteria are expanding due to the exponentially increasing body of case law. If we deal with an enumerative list, it often turns out that the continuously growing corpus of case law exerts impact on the meaning of individual criteria.

One of the key texts in this regard is Jo Carby-Hall's chapter in this book. According to the Equality Act 2010, there exist the following protected characteristics: age, disability, gender reassignment, marriage and civil partnership, pregnancy and maternity, race, religion or belief, sex and sexual orientation. However, the author chose to present a thorough analysis of only one of these namely, religion or belief. The *Casamitjana Costa* case heard in 2020 by a United Kingdom Employment Tribunal provided the background for further considerations. This Tribunal ruled that ethical veganism could be treated as a "philosophical belief" and thus qualify as a "protected characteristic" within the meaning of the Equality Act 2010. Crucially, the latter Act does not define the term "philosophical belief", and case law has therefore played an important role in establishing criteria for the belief to be protected.

Carby-Hall comes to a very interesting conclusion: if the *Casamitjana Costa* case would have been heard at the time when the Equality Act 2010 was enacted, it would have been doubtful if ethical veganism would have qualified as a protected characteristic. This case created a great deal of attention in the media and interest from the public at large and from practicing lawyers as to its effect and significance for employers and employee rights. Ethical veganism has been declared to be a protected characteristic and thus does not differ from any other legally protected feature, such as age, disability, race or sex. The author makes it clear in his chapter that the *Casamitjana Costa* case, as well as other cases in which the existence of a philosophical belief has been recognised, reflect the evolution which is taking place in society. This includes, *inter alia*, a belief in Scottish independence, a view that the United Kingdom should not be ruled by a hereditary monarch and that it should be a democratic and secular republic, a belief in human-made climate change and the alleged resulting moral imperatives or a belief in humanism. Tellingly, Jo Carby-Hall concludes that it is essential for discrimination law to adapt to changes which are taking place in societal values.

The role of case law in qualifying certain features as legally protected is also discussed by Aneta Tyc. Its significance is particularly apparent when examining the Polish Labour Code, which includes the non-exhaustive statutory catalogue of the following discriminatory criteria: sex, age, disability, race, religion, nationality, political beliefs, trade union membership, ethnic origin, denomination, sexual orientation, employment for definite or an indefinite term, and employment on a full-time or part-time basis. However, the role of case law is more limited in relation to the second most important act in the field of discrimination law, the Act of 3 December 2010 on the implementation of some regulations of the European Union regarding equal treatment. The reason for this is the adoption in it of a closed catalogue of the following discriminatory grounds: gender, race, ethnicity, nationality, religion, belief, worldview, disability, age and sexual orientation.

For a long time, a non-exhaustive list of the criteria regulated in the Labour Code was treated as referring to personal characteristics and qualities not related to the work performed, and of such great social importance that the legislature recognised them as prohibited criteria of differentiation in the field of employment. Thus, an open catalogue of these causes allowed for its supplementation only with other personal features of social importance, such as worldview, HIV status, a trainee attorney-at-law status, motherhood, parenthood, citizenship and even appearance, if under certain circumstances it could be regarded as a cause of differentiation of employees which constituted discrimination. However, since 2019, the legislature has given the courts a green light to extend the catalogue so as to include criteria related to the work performed and not necessarily referring to personal characteristics and qualities. In spite of this fact, the chapter highlights problems arising under the formal opinion expressed by the Supreme Court on the 2019 amendment to the Labour Code. Given that this Court assessed the changes as "redundant" and not bringing "any new normative content", it is doubtful that in the future the courts will deviate from a well-established line of case-law in that regard.

In her chapter, Nimushakavi Vasanthi focuses her attention on another protected characteristic: disability. The Constitution of India does not mention disability-based discrimination, but the legislative framework embraces this concept. More specifically, it was the question of, first, the Persons with Disabilities (Equal Opportunities, Protection of Rights and Full Participation) Act 1995, and second, the Rights of Persons with Disabilities Act 2016. Despite clear provisions, the latter is criticised by the author with reference to the inadequacy to address the questions of attitudinal barriers and exclusion from employment. The reasons for this are twofold: "the lack of a comprehensive employment discrimination framework" and "the limitation of a black-letter law approach, which seeks to confine the application of law only to those matters explicitly provided for and to take a strict, narrow interpretation of the law". Thus, Nimushakavi Vasanthi conveys a very important idea that in order to give effect to "the spirit and intention of the legislation", the relevant principles on non-discrimination law should be read into it. She highlights that a broader understanding of constitutional principles would allow to go beyond the literal wording of the statute and to adopt a broader and more expansive understanding of disability-based discrimination. In this vein, she identifies the important role of the constitutional jurisprudence to guide discrimination law, which should result in a transformed interpretation of non-discrimination legislation, in particular, the Rights of Persons with Disabilities Act 2016. Indeed, concepts developed by the Indian Constitutional Court are taken over by the Indian Supreme Court, and both cases described by Vasanthi (the *Vikash Kumar* case and the overruled *Surendra Mohan* case) serve as perfect examples of how rights-based approach to the question of disability-based discrimination is used. In the former case, the Supreme Court ruled that the support of a scribe for a person with disability was to be extended even though the threshold level of disability was not present. In the latter, the Supreme Court first held that it was just, fair, reasonable and logical to restrict eligibility to the position of a civil judge to a person with a specified degree of disability only, taking into consideration the strenuous duties in such a post. As a consequence, the post of a civil judge could be held only by a person with partial blindness of 40%–50%, and not 70%, as in the case of the claimant. However, the judgment was overruled by evoking the concepts of autonomy, dignity, participation, inclusion and accessibility, equality and non-discrimination, and respect for differences through the concept of anti-stereotyping developed by the Indian Constitutional Court.

An amended judgment of the Indian Supreme Court, as well as that of the *Vikash Kumar* case, in many ways resemble the EU approach and judgments of the CJEU. The unifying elements involve, in particular, a framework of commonly accepted values: dignity, participation, inclusive work environment, accessibility, equality, non-discrimination and so forth. For example, all these values were included in the most recent judgment of the CJEU delivered on 10 February 2022 in Case C-485/20 (HR Rail SA),[10] which states:

> Article 5 of Council Directive 2000/78/EC of 27 November 2000 establishing a general framework for equal treatment in employment and occupation must be interpreted as meaning that the concept of "reasonable accommodation" for disabled persons, within the meaning of that article requires that a worker, including someone undertaking a traineeship following his or her recruitment, who, owing to his or her disability, has been declared incapable of performing the essential functions of the post that he or she occupies, be assigned to another position for which he or she has the necessary competence, capability and availability, unless that measure imposes a disproportionate burden on the employer.

10 https://curia.europa.eu/juris/document/document.jsf;jsessionid=0494082C4553A14B72FE27794 0FBC244?text=&docid=253723&pageIndex=0&doclang=EN&mode=lst&dir=&occ=first&part= 1&cid=1863414.

It is noteworthy that the applicant in the main proceedings was diagnosed with a heart condition that required the fitting of a pacemaker, a device which is sensitive to the electromagnetic fields present, *inter alia*, on railway tracks, which prevented him from being able to carry out the essential functions of the post for which he was recruited, a specialist maintenance technician for railway tracks. Initially he was assigned to a warehouseman's position within the same undertaking, and after bringing an action against this decision, he was dismissed from work with a ban on his recruitment for a period of five years to the grade at which he had been recruited.

Protected characteristics is the common theme that unites individual chapters. In his chapter, Manfred Weiss points out that the General Act on Equal Treatment (GAET) implementing all the European directives on discrimination into German law has simply copied grounds of discrimination from the directives and has embraced the following: race or ethnic origin, sex or sexual orientation, religion or belief, age or disability. The author comments more broadly on two protected characteristics: age and religion. By analysing the CJEU judgment in the Nils-Johannes Kratzer case of 28 July 2016 (C-423/15), followed by the FLC and the LCA of the State of Hesse ruling, he points out how difficult it is to make the assessment of indirect age discrimination. Another judgment of the CJEU of 12 January 2010 in the Colin Wolf case (C-229/08) indicates controversies surrounding the possibility to set a maximum age for recruitment in the respective job. Moreover, Weiss reflects on the question whether and in what way it is possible to facilitate recruitment for elderly persons, especially in the context of fixed term contracts. In this regard, he discusses the Act on Part-Time Work and Fixed-Term Contracts of 2000 implementing Directive 99/70/EC on Fixed-Term Contracts, as well as the CJEU judgment of 22 November 2005 in the Werner Mangold case (C-144/04) which influenced changes in German law. Finally, what is problematised is an automatic termination of the employment relationship at a certain age and termination by way of dismissal, which creates major uncertainties under German law on age discrimination.

Weiss has also tackled a pertinent topic related to the exceptions granted to the churches in reference to prohibition of discrimination because of religion. In this context, he discusses the most recent German case law, enriching his reflections with the CJEU's case law, such as the judgment of 17 April 2018 in the Vera Egenberger case (C-414/16).

Obviously, this selection of protected characteristics by Weiss is made by way of illustration of some major practical problems. No doubt problems occur in all EU Member States also against the background of other discrimination criteria, such as sex. The most recent judgment of the CJEU of 24 February 2022 in the Tesorería General de la Seguridad Social (TGSS) case (C-389/20)[11] is a good

11 https://curia.europa.eu/juris/liste.jsf?language=pl&jur=C%2CT%2CF&num=C-389/20&parties=&dates=error&docnodecision=docnodecision&allcommjo=allcommjo&affint=affint&affclose=affclose&alldocrec=alldocrec&docdecision=docdecision&docor=docor&docav=docav&docsom=

example. The CJEU ruled that Council Directive 79/7/EEC of 19 December 1978 on the progressive implementation of the principle of equal treatment for men and women in matters of social security[12] precludes a national provision excluding unemployment benefit from the social security benefits granted to domestic workers by a statutory social security scheme. This is due to the fact that such a provision places female workers at a particular disadvantage compared with male workers and is not justified by objective factors unrelated to any discrimination on grounds of sex. In Spain, more than 95% of all domestic workers are women. The CJEU explained that the national Spanish legislation places female workers at a particular disadvantage and is a source of indirect discrimination on grounds of sex which is contrary to the above-mentioned directive unless it mirrors a legitimate social policy objective and is suitable and necessary for achieving that objective.

This concluding chapter attempts to identify challenges for employment discrimination law, as well as possible future research directions and postulates regarding changes in this field.

When analysing the EU law, Szilvia Halmos raises a very important problem which is likely to be more and more visible in the future. She points out that the classic, comparator-based model is not always sufficient to establish discrimination so scrutiny of discrimination should apply a wider range of methodologies. The author illustrates her considerations with many examples, one of which is related to multiple discrimination, in which it may be particularly difficult to find the person or group in a comparable situation with the victims. A dignity-based approach of equality could solve the problem and it could also lead to a more flexible treatment of the list of protected characteristics. It would be desirable because the practice of the CJEU shows that extension of the list of discrimination criteria under EU secondary law is not possible.

Next, Susanne Burri pays attention to huge challenges in addressing diverse forms of discrimination in the Netherlands. According to the research cited by the author, about one in four persons living in that country reported having experienced discrimination. Racism, sexism, pregnancy discrimination in employment and disability discrimination in the labour market are present in everyday life. Ethnic minorities are vulnerable groups, in particular, as regards the access to the labour market. Besides, since nationality is used as one of the criteria to detect fraud which leads to ethnic profiling, institutional discrimination by state organs in data systems related to social security and benefits is a common pathology. Discrimination also often occurs due to the use of algorithms. These are only examples, and more effective anti-discrimination measures are needed to combat stereotyping, as well as institutional and systemic discrimination. Admittedly,

---

docsom&docinf=docinf&alldocnorec=alldocnorec&docnoor=docnoor&docppoag=docppoag&radtypeord=on&newform=newform&docj=docj&docop=docop&docnoj=docnoj&typeord=ALL&domaine=&mots=&resmax=100&Submit=Rechercher.

12 OJ 1979 L 6, p. 24.

the government has recently developed some important initiatives in order to overcome discrimination, but much is still to be done in this area. The author proposes to integrate Dutch equal treatment legislation into one act in order to ensure its better awareness, application and enforcement. This idea embraces the General Equal Treatment Act, the Disability Discrimination Act, the Age Discrimination Act, the Equal Treatment Act of men and women and Article 7:646 of the Civil Code.

Raphael Cohen-Almagor and Uki Maroshek-Klarman notice the urgent need for change in the situation of women in Israel, where gender inequality is very high. The authors highlight that there is not sufficient awareness of the many problems that women are suffering from. They try to explain how to meet this challenge and, to this end, they propose four important steps that should make gender equality a reality. The first step should consist of awareness-raising activities as regards women's inequality. The second should be based on education at all levels, including in kindergarten. The third step should be related to legislation on gender equality concerning all spheres of life. Finally, the fourth one should embrace fair, adequate, transparent and comprehensive implementation by the government of positive discrimination and gender equality policies in order to help women overcome the challenges they face and obtain equality between women and men. Moreover, the findings of the Israeli chapter challenge the male-orientated Jewish Orthodox tradition and the Halachic grounds for discrimination against women. The authors point out that patriarchy in Jewish law negates the premises of gender equality. Thus, a separation between state and religion would be a welcome step towards improving the situation of women. Besides, the empowerment of unorthodox Jewish denominations that are gender egalitarian would constitute such a desirable move as well. Last but not least, the authors put pressure on the urgent need for a comprehensive, written constitution that would ensure democratic principles and human rights in Israel.

In her chapter, Therese MacDermott voices many weighty postulates regarding the Australian legislative framework. Some of them have already been mentioned in our first introductory chapter, but we should also take note of her analysis regarding sexual harassment. Given that in 2018 it was found that "71% of Australians have been sexually harassed at some point in their lifetimes", and 85% of Australian women and 56% of Australian men over the age of 15 have been sexually harassed at some point in their lifetimes, a national inquiry on sexual harassment was established by the Australian Human Rights Commission. The author highlights that it resulted in a report with recommendations according to which there is a need for a regulatory framework that "encourages and supports employers to take proactive and preventive measures to address sexual harassment, rather than relying on individual complaints". There is thus an urgency to impose a positive duty on employers to stop sexual harassment, as well as a necessity to equip the Australian Human Rights Commission with the possibility of inquiring into systemic sexual harassment. To this end, the Sex Discrimination Act should be properly amended. Similarly, the Fair Work Act should be changed in order to establish a clear prohibition on sexual harassment and a transparent way to seek redress in the national labour laws.

Gordon Anderson and Dawn Duncan's chapter yields some evidence about challenges related to discrimination employment law in Aotearoa/New Zealand, which had adopted a comprehensive legislative framework for discrimination law by 1977. It was based on international human rights instruments and initially had led to an improvement in the situation related, in particular, to the removal of occupational barriers to women. However, due to the subsequent limited impact of the universalist approach of the 1970s on reaching anti-discrimination aims, a new approach to discrimination began to emerge. The authors identify three crucial driving forces behind this new and more wide-ranging approach. The first one concerns the question of how to respond to the failures of the initial legislation. The second lifeblood of the new perspective is the need to reflect new challenges and developments that have been diagnosed in employment discrimination law over recent decades. The third driving force refers to the need to mirror the values and demographics of contemporary Aotearoa/New Zealand in new discrimination law. Furthermore, Anderson and Duncan have concluded that the New Zealand society has revised its expectations about discrimination law, which is now expected to make more significant progress in addressing economic and social inequalities.

Kurt Pärli takes a look ahead to what actions might help address the current problems in Switzerland, which are in particular related to deficits in the implementation of some obligations under international law, especially these concerning disability and race or ethnic origin. The author's analysis shows that there is much potential for implementation of conventions under international labour law by the courts, which in certain cases have possibilities and should draw from the EU discrimination law concepts, CJEU rulings, as well as the rulings of the human rights treaty monitoring bodies. On the other hand, Pärli places certain requirements on the legislature. Trying to ensure the effectiveness of the principle of non-discrimination, the latter should implement fully the obligations under human rights treaties. The author points to two possibilities in this regard: the Swiss legislature could benefit from the EU discrimination law or – instead of adopting a new legal framework – it could supplement the already existing civil law tools.

The topic tackled in this edited book is characterised by the extraordinary importance, beginning with the fact that the ILO Discrimination (Employment and Occupation) Convention, 1958 (No. 111) and Equal Remuneration Convention, 1951 (No. 100) are set within the core human labour rights. However, we realise that even if the right to non-discrimination belongs to the international human rights regime, compliance with it often leaves a lot to be desired in various parts of the world.

However, we cannot ignore the fact that a great deal of progress has already been made in diverse countries. For example, as highlighted by Anderson and Duncan, in New Zealand employment discrimination law has achieved acceptable success in the area of "providing remedies for individual complainants alleging discrimination on the grounds set out in the legislation". Another beneficial example in that country is that "discrimination on grounds such as ethnicity, colour, national origin and sex have diminished over recent decades as the composition of the workforce has become increasingly diverse". In other countries some positive trends are also observed; for instance, more and more laws on discrimination of great importance are passed (e.g. Israel), case law protecting employees is being developed (e.g. the UK), and the courts refer frequently to fundamental values like dignity, equality, participation, an inclusive work environment and accessibility (e.g. the Indian Supreme Court or the CJEU).

Quite diverse and divergent approaches among individual countries emerge from the whole picture. Concentrating on the positive aspects, we should consider what we can learn from each other's experiences. By reasoning in this manner, it occurs to us that, for example, following the model of the UK, the rest of the world could try in a similar way to adapt to changes which are taking place in societal values. The *Casamitjana Costa* case relating to a philosophical belief as a protected characteristic under the British equality laws followed the rulings in previous cases on this topic. It is apparent from them that the legal right to manifest one's belief must not be discriminated against. As indicated by Carby-Hall, the *Casamitjana Costa* case contributes to the evolution in society not only in the UK, where veganism is becoming more and more popular, but it also could influence other countries. The need to adapt to changes which are transforming societal values is clearly emphasised not only by Carby-Hall but also by Anderson and Duncan.

A variety of legal traditions to which we refer in this book offers more ideas to draw from. Pärli discusses the influence of EU labour law (e.g. the directive 2000/78/EC) on Swiss court practice with regard to selected grounds of discrimination. But we can go a step further and ask whether some other countries could be interested in drawing from the EU concept on the burden of proof in discrimination cases. Indeed, the research shows that not all countries have adopted the allocation of the burden of proof which is favourable to the victim. By the same token, the EU could derive inspiration from India and its Equality Bill of 2019, which includes definitions of multiple and intersectional discrimination, as well as systemic or structural discrimination. It is worth noting that the Equality Bill also embraces newer forms of hate crimes, such as lynching and hate speech. This book provides a wealth of other examples of how we can learn from each other.

Discrimination has been shown to be a multi-faceted phenomenon. Cohen-Almagor and Maroshek-Klarman refer to gender discrimination; Cox deals with sexual harassment; Burri mentions discrimination due to the use of algorithms and pregnancy discrimination; Carby-Hall focuses on philosophical beliefs; Vasanthi discusses disability-based discrimination; and the other authors point to the other protected characteristics. Discrimination continues to be a widespread pathology and – as confirmed by the research undertaken by the authors of this book – there is still much to be done in this field. To quote Tarunabh Khaitan: "Like democracy, the rule of law, and human rights, a system of law regulating discrimination has become key to how some states define themselves. These features have become markets of what 'civilised' society is".[13] If our world really wants to boast that it is committed to the concept of human rights, the struggle for non-discrimination and equality should constitute an important part of the fight for a better world for all. Otherwise, bad patterns of behaviour will spread, and next time the discriminated could be one of us.

13 Tarunabh Khaitan, *A Theory of Discrimination Law* (Oxford: Oxford University Press, 2015), pp. 3–4.

Index

For Product Safety Concerns and Information please contact our EU representative GPSR@taylorandfrancis.com
Taylor & Francis Verlag GmbH, Kaufingerstraße 24, 80331 München, Germany

www.ingramcontent.com/pod-product-compliance
Lightning Source LLC
LaVergne TN
LVHW021120300926
849160LV00010B/789